The Life and Works

of

Friedrich Schiller

The
Life and Works
of
Friedrich Schiller

By

Calvin Thomas
Professor in Columbia University

New York
Henry Holt and Company
1906

ROBERT DRUMMOND, PRINTER, NEW YORK.

TO

Eleanor Allen Thomas

Herzeliebe frouwe min,
  Got gebe dir hiute und iemer guot!
Kunde ich baz gedenken din,
  Des hæte ich willeclichen muot.

PREFACE

I HAVE wished to give a trustworthy account of Schiller and his works on a scale large enough to permit the doing of something like justice to his great name, but not so large as in itself to kill all hope and chance of readableness. By a trustworthy account I mean one that is accurate in the matters of fact and sane in the matters of judgment. That there is room for an English book thus conceived will be readily granted, I imagine, by all those who know. At any rate Schiller is one of those writers of whom a new appreciation, from time to time, will always be in order.

I have thought it important that my work, while taking due note of recent German scholarship, should rest throughout on fresh and independent study. Accordingly, among all the many books that have aided me more or less, I have had in hand most often, next to the works of Schiller, the collection of his letters, as admirably edited by Jonas. Among the German biographers I owe the most to Minor, Weltrich and Brahm, for the period covered by their several works; for the later years, to Wychgram and Harnack. Earlier biographers, notably Hoffmeister and Palleske, have also been found helpful here and there.

Of course I have not flattered myself, in writing of
a man whose uneventful career has repeatedly been
explored in every nook and cranny, with any hope of
adding materially to the tale of mere fact.   One who
gleans after Minor and Weltrich and Wychgram will
find little but chaff, and I have tried to avoid the
garnering of chaff.   One of my chief perplexities,
accordingly, has been to decide what to omit.   If there
shall be those who look for what they do not find, or
find what they did not expect, I can only say that the
question of perspective, of the relative importance of
things, has all along received my careful attention.
Thoroughness is very alluring, but life is short and
some things must be taken for granted or treated as
negligible.   Otherwise one runs a risk, as German
experience proves, of beginning and never finishing.

My great concern has been with the works of Schiller
—to interpret them as the expression of an interesting
individuality and an interesting epoch.   It is now some
twenty years since I first came under the Weimarian
spell, and during that time my feeling for Schiller has
undergone vicissitudes not unlike those described by
Brahm in a passage quoted at the very end of this
volume.   At no time, indeed, could I truthfully have
called myself a 'Schiller-hater', but there was a time,
certainly, when it seemed to me that he was very
much overestimated by his countrymen; when my
mind was very hospitable to demonstrations of his
artistic shortcoming.   Time has brought a different
temper, and this book is the child of what I deem the
wiser disposition.

For the poet who wins the heart of a great people

and holds it for a century is right; there is nothing
more to be said, so far as concerns his title to renown.
The creative achievement is far more precious and important than any possible criticism of it. This does
not mean that in dealing with such a poet the critic is
in duty bound to abdicate his lower function and to let
his scruples melt away in the warm water of a friendly
partisanship; it means only that he will be best occupied, speaking generally, in a conscientious attempt to
see the man as he was, to "experience the savor of
him", and to understand the national temperament to
which he has endeared himself.

This, I hope, defines sufficiently the spirit in which
I have written. In discussing the plays I have endeavored to deal with them in a large way, laying hold
of each where it is most interesting, and not caring to
be either systematic or exhaustive. Questions of
minute and technical scholarship, such as have their
proper place in a learned monograph, or in the introduction and notes to an edition of the text, have been
avoided on principle. Everywhere—even in the difficult thirteenth chapter—my aim has been to disengage
and bring clearly into view the essential, distinctive
character of Schiller's work; and where I have had to
fear either that the professional scholar would frown at
my sins of omission, or that the mere lover of literature
would yawn at my sins of commission, I have boldly
accepted the first-named horn of the dilemma.

NEW YORK, Nov. 6, 1901.

CONTENTS

CHAPTER I

Parentage and Schooling

CHAPTER II

The Robbers

CHAPTER III

The Stuttgart Medicus

CHAPTER IV

The Conspiracy of Fiesco at Genoa

CHAPTER V

The Fugitive in Hiding

Contents

CHAPTER IX

Don Carlos

CHAPTER X

Anchored in Thuringia

Contents

CHAPTER VI

Cabal and Love

CHAPTER VII

Theater Poet in Mannheim

CHAPTER VIII

The Boon of Friendship

Contents

CHAPTER XI

Historical Writings

CHAPTER XII

Dark Days Within and Without

CHAPTER XIII

Aesthetic Writings

Contents

Contents

CHAPTER XVII

Mary Stuart

CHAPTER XVIII

The Maid of Orleans

CHAPTER XIX

The Bride of Messina

Contents

LIFE AND WORKS OF SCHILLER

CHAPTER I

Parentage and Schooling

Nur, Vater, mir Gesänge.

From the poem 'Evening', 1776.

WHEN the Austrian War of Succession came to an end, in the year 1748, a certain young Suabian who had been campaigning in the Lowlands as army doctor was left temporarily without employment. The man's name was Johann Kaspar Schiller; he was of good plebeian stock and had lately been a barber's apprentice, — a lot that he had accepted reluctantly when the poverty of a widowed mother compelled him to shift for himself at an early age. Having served his time and learned the trade of the barber-surgeon, he had joined a Bavarian regiment of hussars. Finding himself now suddenly at leisure, after the Peace of Aix-la-Chapelle, he mounted his horse and rode away to the land of his birth to visit his relations. Reaching Marbach—it was now the spring of 1749—he put up at the 'Golden Lion', an inn kept by a then prosperous baker named Kodweis. Here he fell in love with his landlord's daughter Dorothea, a girl of sixteen, and in the course of the summer married her. He was at

1

this time about twenty-six years old.　He now settled
down in Marbach to practice his crude art, but the
practice came to little and Kodweis soon lost his property in foolish speculation.　So the quondam soldier
fell out of humor with Marbach, went into the army
again, and when the Seven Years' War broke out, in
1756, he took the field with a Württemberg regiment
to fight the King of Prussia.　He soon reached the
grade of lieutenant, in time that of captain; fought and
ran with his countrymen at Leuthen, floundered at peril
of life in the swamps of Breslau and otherwise got his
full share of the war's rough-and-tumble.　From time
to time, as the chance came to him, he visited his
young wife in Marbach.

These were the parents of the poet Schiller, who was
born November 10, 1759,—ten years after Goethe, ten
years before Napoleon.　It is worth remembering that
he who was to be in his way another great protestant
came into the world on an anniversary of the birth
of Luther.　He was christened Johann Christoph
Friedrich.

The childhood of little Fritz unfolded amid conditions that must have given to life a rather somber
aspect.　After the close of the war Captain Schiller
moved his little family to Lorch, a village some
thirty miles east of Stuttgart, where he was employed
by the Duke of Württemberg in recruiting soldiers for
mercenary service abroad.　This hateful business,
which was in due time to form a mark for one of the
sharp darts of ' Cabal and Love ', seems to have been
managed by him with a degree of tact and humanity;
for he won the esteem of all with whom he had to do.

At home, being of a pious turn and setting great store by the formal exercises of religion, he presided over his household in the manner of an ancient patriarch. Between him and his son no very tender relation ever existed, though the poet of later years always revered his father's character. The child's affections clung rather to his mother, whom he grew up to resemble in form and feature and in traits of character. She was a woman of no intellectual pretensions, but worthy of honor for her qualities of heart.[1] Of education in the modern sense she had but little. Her few extant letters, written mostly in her later years, tell of a simple and lovable character, tenderly devoted to husband and children. Tradition credits her with a certain liking for feeble poets of the Uz and Gellert strain, but this probably did not amount to much. Her sphere of interest was the little world of family cares and affections. Her early married life had been darkened by manifold sorrows which she bore at first with pious resignation, becoming with the flight of time, however, more and more a borrower of trouble.[2] At Lorch her trials were great, for Captain Schiller received no pay and the family felt the pinch of poverty. Here, then, was little room for that merry comradeship, with its *Lust zum Fabulieren*, which existed between the boy Goethe and his playmate mother at Frankfurt-on-the-Main.

In after-time, nevertheless, Schiller was wont to look

[1] What is known of her has been put together by Ernst Müller, in "Schillers Mutter, ein Lebensbild", Leipzig, 1894.

[2] "Unsere Mutter nährt sich gleichsam von beständiger Sorge", wrote her son to his sister in 1784.

back upon the three years at Lorch as the happiest part of his childhood. The village is charmingly situated in the valley of the Rems, a tributary of the Neckar, and the region round about is historic ground. A short walk southward brings one to the Hohenstaufen, on whose summit once stood the ancestral seat of the famous Suabian dynasty, and close by Lorch is the Benedictine monastery in which a number of the Hohenstaufen monarchs are buried. Here was the romance of history right at hand, but we can hardly suppose that it meant much to the child. The Middle Ages were not yet in fashion even for adults, and little Fritz had other things to think of. With his sister Christophine, two years older than himself, he was sent to the village school, where he proved so apt a pupil that his parents became ambitious for him and sent him to the village pastor, a man named Moser, to be taught Latin. The child looked up to his august teacher and resolved to become himself some day a preacher of the word. Not much is known of Moser, but to judge from his namesake in 'The Robbers', where all passions and qualities are raised to the nth power, he must have been a man for whom the reproof of sinners was not only a professional duty but a personal pleasure. The plan of making their Fritz a man of God was eagerly embraced by the pious parents and became a settled family aspiration.

The boy himself was very susceptible at this time to religious impressions. Sister Christophine carried with her through life a vivid memory of his appearance at family worship, when the captain would solemnly intone the rimed prayers that he himself had composed for a private ritual. 'It was a touching sight', she says in her recollections[1] of this period, 'to see the reverent expression on the child's winsome face. The pious blue eyes lifted to heaven, the light yellow hair falling about his forehead, and the little hands folded in worship, suggested an angel's head in a picture.' From the same source we learn that Fritz was very fond of playing church, with himself in the rôle of preacher. Another reminiscence tells how he one day ran away from school and, having unexpectedly fallen under the paternal eye in his truancy, rushed home to his mother in tearful excitement, got the rod of correction and besought her to give him his punishment before his sterner parent should arrive on the scene. Still another, from a somewhat later period, relates how the mother was once walking with her children and told them a Bible story so touchingly that they all knelt down and prayed. This is about all that has come down concerning Schiller's early childhood. He may have seen the passion-play at Gmünd, but this is uncertain. In any case it only added one more to the religious impressions that already dominated his life.

Toward the end of the year 1766, having exhausted his private resources at Lorch, Captain Schiller applied

[1] As quoted by Schiller's sister-in-law, Karoline von Wolzogen, in her 'Life of Schiller', first published in 1830. The Baroness von Wolzogen quoted from a manuscript by Christophine, which was at that time in the family archives and has since been published in the *Archiv für Litteraturgeschichte*, I, 452. Christophine wrote down her recollections in order to counteract the false stories of Schiller's childhood which began to get into print soon after his death. Of this character, for example, is the oft-repeated tale of his climbing a tree during a thunder-storm in order to see where the lightning came from. This is an invention of Oemler, his earliest biographer, who invented much besides.

for relief and was transferred to duty at Ludwigsburg,
where the family remained under somewhat more
tolerable conditions for about nine years. At Ludwigsburg he began to interest himself in agriculture and
forestry. In 1769 he published certain 'Economic
Contributions', which exhibit him as a sensible, public-
spirited man, eagerly bent upon improving the condition of Suabian husbandry. In 1775, having become
known as an expert in arboriculture, he was placed in
charge of the ducal forests and nurseries at Castle
Solitude, and there he spent the remainder of his days
in peaceful and congenial activity. He died in 1796.

For the impressionable Fritz one can hardly imagine
a more momentous change of environment than this
which took him from a quiet rural village to the garish
Residenz of a licentious and extravagant prince. Karl
Eugen,[1] Duke of Württemberg, whom men have often
called the curse, but the gods haply regard as the good
genius, of Schiller's youth, came to power in 1744 at
the age of sixteen. The three preceding years he had
spent at the Prussian court, where Frederick the Second
(not yet the Great) had taken a deep interest in him
and tried to teach him serious views of a ruler's
responsibility. But the youth had no stomach for the
doctrine that he was in the world for the sake of
Württemberg. Having come to his ducal throne prematurely, through the influence of the King of Prussia,
he began well, but after a few years shook off the
restraints of good advice and entered upon a course of
autocratic folly that made Württemberg a far-shining

[1] An excellent account of him is to be found in Vol. 15 of "Allgemeine
Deutsche Biographie".

example of the evils of absolutism under the Old
Régime. Early in his reign he married a beautiful
and high-minded princess of Bayreuth, but his prof-
ligacy soon drove her back to the home of her parents.
Then a succession of mistresses ruled his affections,
while reckless adventurers in high place enjoyed his
confidence and fleeced the people at pleasure. To
gratify his passion for military display he began to raise
unnecessary troops and to hire them out as mercenaries.
In 1752 he agreed with the King of France, in consideration of a fixed annual subsidy, to supply six
thousand soldiers on demand. The money thus
obtained was mostly squandered upon his private vices
and extravagances. On the outbreak of the Seven
Years' War the French king demanded the promised
troops; and so it came about that the Suabian Protes-
tants were compelled, in defiance of public sentiment,
to make war against their co-religionists of Prussia.
In the inglorious campaigns which followed, the Duke
of Württemberg cut a rather sorry figure, but criticism
only exasperated him. He promised another large
body of troops to France, and the men were raised by
harsh measures of conscription. The Estates of the
duchy protested against this autocratic procedure, and,
as Stuttgart sided with the opposition, the duke determined to punish his unruly capital by removing his
court to Ludwigsburg, where an ancestor of his, early
in the century, had founded a city to match Versailles
and serve the express purpose of a ' Trutz-Stuttgart '.

The removal of the court to Ludwigsburg took place
in 1764, three years before the Schiller family found a
home there. From the first a purely artificial creation,

the little city had been going backwards, but it now leaped into short-lived glory as the residence of a prodigal prince who was bent on amusing himself magnificently. The existing ducal palace was enlarged to huge dimensions and lavishly decorated. Great parks and gardens were laid out, the market-place was surrounded with arcades, and an opera-house was built, with a stage that could be extended into the open air so as to permit the spectacular evolution of real troops. Everything about the place was new and pretentious. The roomy streets and the would-be gorgeous palaces, flaunting their fresh coats of yellow and white stucco, teemed with officers in uniform, with blazing little potentates of the court and with high-born ladies in the puffs and frills of the rococo age. Here Karl Eugen gave himself up to his dream of glory, which was to rival the splendors of Versailles. He maintained a costly opera, procuring for it the most famous singers and dancers in Europe, and squandered immense sums upon ' Venetian nights ' and other gorgeous spectacles. For all this barbaric ostentation the people of Württemberg were expected to foot the bills. 'Fatherland!' said his Highness, when a protest was raised on behalf of the country, ' Bah! I am the fatherland.'

Here it was, then, that the young Friedrich Schiller got his first childish impressions of the great world; of sovereignty exercised that a few might strut in gay plumage while the many toiled to keep them in funds; of state policies determined by wretched court intrigues; of natural rights trampled upon at the caprice of a prince or a prince's favorite. There is no record that the boy was troubled by these things at the time, or looked upon them as anything else than a part of the world's natural order. It is a long way yet to President von Walter.

The house occupied by Captain Schiller at Ludwigsburg was situated close by the theater, to which the duke's officers had free admission. As a reward of industry little Fritz was allowed an occasional evening in front of the ' boards that signify the world '. The performances, to be sure, were French and Italian operas, wherein the ballet-master, the machinist and the decorator vied with one another for the production of amazing spectacular effects. People went to stare and gasp—the language was of no importance. It was not exactly dramatic art, but from the boy's point of view it was no doubt magnificent. At any rate it made him at home in the dream-world of the imagination, filled his mind with grandiose pictures and gave him his first rudimentary notions of stage effect. We are not surprised to learn, therefore, that in his home amusements playing theater now took the place of playing church. Sister Christophine was a faithful helper. A stage could be made of big books, and actors out of paper. When the puppet-show was outgrown, the young dramatist took to framing plays for living performers of his own age,—with a row of chairs for an audience, and himself as manager and protagonist.

Christophine relates that her brother's fondness for this sort of diversion lasted until he was thirteen years old. In the mean time, however, his chosen career was kept steadily in view. He was sent to the Latin school, from which, if his marks should be good, he might hope to advance in about five years to one of the so-called convent schools of Württemberg. After this his theological education would proceed for about nine years more at the expense of the state. The Ludwigsburg school was a place in which the language of Cicero and the religion of Luther were thumped into the memory of boys by means of sticks applied to the skin. Fritz Schiller was a capable scholar, though none of his teachers ever called him, as in the case of the boy Lessing at Meissen, a horse that needed double fodder. The ordinary ration sufficed him, but he memorized his catechism and his hymns diligently, fussed faithfully over his Latin longs and shorts, and took his occasional thrashings with becoming fortitude. On one occasion we hear that he was flogged by mistake and disdained to report the incident at home. Religious instruction consisted of mechanical repetition insisted on with brutal severity,—a mode of presenting divine things that must have contrasted painfully, for the sensitive boy, with his mother's simple religion of the heart. When it is added that he was often nagged and punished by a too exacting father, we get a not very sunny picture of our poet's boyhood. It is told,[1] and it may well be true, that he was subject to fits of moodiness, in which he would complain of his lot and brood gloomily over his prospects. Nevertheless a schoolmate[2] has left it on record that Schiller as a lad was normally high-spirited, a leader in sports as well as in study, and very steadfast in his friendships.

[1] By Schiller's youthful friend Petersen, *Morgenblatt*, 1807; quoted by Weltrich, "Friedrich Schiller", I, 77, and by other biographers.
[2] Wilhelm von Hoven, quoted by Karoline von Wolzogen.

While at Ludwigsburg he read from the prescribed Latin authors, making the acquaintance of Ovid, Vergil and Horace, and in time won praise for his facility in writing Latin verses. Some of his school exercises have chanced to be preserved. The earliest, dated Jan. 1, 1769, is a Latin translation in prose of some verses which seem to have been supplied by his teacher for the purpose. The handwriting and the Latin tell of faithful juvenile toil and moderate success—nothing more. Nor can we extract much biographic interest from the later distichs and *carmina* which he turned out at school festivals. Such things have flowed easily from the pen of many a bright schoolboy whom the bees of Hymettus failed to visit.

According to Schiller's own testimony[1] his earliest attempt at German verse was made on the occasion of his confirmation, in April, 1772. On the day before the solemn ceremony he was playing about with his comrades in what seemed to his mother an all too worldly frame of mind. She rebuked him for his unseasonable levity, whereat the youngster went into himself, as the Germans say, and poured out his supposed feelings in a string of verses so tender and soulful as to draw from his amazed father the exclamation: 'Fritz, are you going crazy?'

After such a beginning we are not surprised to learn that German poetry made its first strong appeal to him through the pious muse of Klopstock. His earliest more ambitious note is heard in a 'Hymn to the Sun', written in his fourteenth year. It is the note of

[1] As reported by his friend Conz, *Morgenblatt*, 1807. Cf. Weltrich, p. 80, foot-note.

supernal religious pathos. In rimeless lines of unequal length he celebrates the glory of God in the firmament, soars into celestial space and winds up with a vision of the last great cataclysm. All this is sufficiently Klopstockian, as is also the boyish dream of an epic about Moses, and of a tragedy to be called 'The Christians'.

But the time came when our young psalmodist of Zion was to be pulled out of his predetermined course and made to sing another song. Were the overruling powers malign or benevolent? Who shall say, remembering the Greek proverb that a man is not educated save by flaying? Let us not pause to speculate, but proceed as quickly as may be across the interval that separates these innocent religious effusions from the opening of a great literary career with the cannon-shot of 'The Robbers'.

About the year 1770 Duke Karl began to undergo a change of heart. Wearying at last of life's vanities and frivolities, the middle-aged sinner took up virtue and philanthropy, as if to show mankind that he too could be a benevolent father to his people. The new departure was due in part to the political success of the Estates in curbing his extravagance, but rather more, no doubt, to the personal influence of his mistress, Franziska von Hohenheim. This lady, whose maiden name was Bernerdin, had been given in marriage as a girl of sixteen to a worthless Baron von Leutrum, who misused her. Escaping from him with thoughts of divorce in her mind, she went to visit friends in Ludwigsburg. Here the inflammable duke fell in love with her, and, after a not very tedious resistance, carried her away to his castle. This was in 1772. Her divorce followed soon after, and she remained at court as the duke's favorite mistress. He presently procured for her an imperial title, that of Countess Hohenheim, and after the death of his duchess, in 1780, he married her. She was not beautiful or talented, but she possessed amiable qualities that made and kept her the object of Karl's honest affection. She knew how to humor his whims without crossing his stubborn will, and she chose to exert her influence in promoting humane enterprises and leading her liege lord in the paths of virtuous frugality. On the whole, the people of Württemberg, who had suffered much from mistresses of a different ilk, had reason to bless their ruler's fondness for his amiable 'Franzele'. She was not unworthy to sit for the portrait of Lady Milford.

An educational project, the founding of a school which later came to be known as the Karlschule, marks the beginning of the duke's career in his new rôle. He began very modestly in the year 1770 by gathering a few boys, the sons of officers, at his castle called Solitude, and undertaking to provide for their instruction in gardening and forestry. This Castle Solitude was itself an outcome of the same lordly mood that had led to the removal of the court to Ludwigsburg. It was situated on a wooded height some six miles west of Stuttgart. Here, by means of forced labor and at enormous expense,—and this was only one of many similar building enterprises,—he had cleared a site in the forest and erected a huge palace which, according to the inscription over the door, was to be 'devoted to tranquillity'. But how was a prince to enjoy tranquillity

without the necessaries of life? In a short time a score
of other buildings, including an opera-house and a
barracks, had sprung up about the castle in the woods,
while an immense outlying tract had been converted
into a park with exotic attractions in the style of the
time. Here, then, was need of expert forestry—whence
the opening of the school as aforesaid. Once started,
it became the duke's special pet and pride. His immense energy had found a new fad—that of the school-
master. He was bent on having a model training-
school for the public service. In his own house, under
his own eye, he proposed to mould the future servants
of the state like potter's clay. In this way he would
have them as he wanted them. To provide the clay
for his experiment he began to look around for promising boys, and thus his eye fell on Friedrich Schiller.
Summoning the father and making some gracious inquiries, he offered to provide for the boy's education at
the new school. The anxious captain, knowing that
divinity was not to be on the program at Castle Solitude, sought to evade his sovereign's kindness by
pleading that Fritz had set his heart upon the service
of the church. The reply was that something else,
law for example, would no doubt do as well. Resistance to the earthly Providence was not to be thought
of by a man in Captain Schiller's position; and so the
step was taken which deprived some Suabian flock of
a shepherd and gave the world instead a great poet.

It was on the 17th of January, 1773, that schoolboy
Schiller, with disappointment in his heart, said farewell
to his tearful mother and took his cold way up the long
avenue which led from Ludwigsburg to Castle Soli-

tude. According to the official record he arrived there with a chillblain, an eruption of the scalp, fourteen Latin books, and forty-three kreutzers in money. Soon afterwards his father signed a document whereby he renounced all control of the boy and left him in the hands of his prince.

The school at Solitude had now come to be known as the Military Academy, and well it deserved its name. The duke himself was the supreme authority in large matters and in small. The nominal head, called the intendant, was a high military officer who had a sufficient detail of majors, captains and lower officers to assist him in maintaining discipline. Under the eye of these military potentates the *élèves*, as they were called,—for the official language of the school was French,—lived and moved in accordance with a rigid routine. They rose at six and marched to the breakfast-room, where an overseer gave them their orders to pray, to eat, to pray again, and then to march back. Then there were lessons until one o'clock, when they prepared for the solemn function of dinner. Dressed in the prescribed uniform,—a blue coat with white breeches and waistcoat, a leather stock and a three-cornered hat, with pendent queue and at each temple four little puffs,—they marched to the dining-room and countermarched to their places. When his Highness gave the command, *Dinez, messieurs*, they fell to and ate. From two to four there were lessons again, then exercise and study hours. At nine they were required to go to bed. There were no vacations and few holidays. Visits to and from parents were prohibited, and letters sent or received

had to be submitted to the intendant. Books of a
stirring character were proscribed, along with tobacco
and toothsome edibles, and quarters were often searched
for contraband articles. Whoso transgressed received
a 'billet', which he took to headquarters. Punish-
ments were numerous, if not very severe, and were
sometimes administered by his Highness in person.
The duke wished his protégés to regard him as their
father, but his system tended to the encouragement not
so much of honest gratitude as of rank sycophancy.
On occasion he could be very gracious and conde-
scending,—would take the youngsters into his carriage,
give them fatherly counsel, box their ears, suggest
subjects for essays, offer himself as opponent at their
disputations, and so forth. He was very proud of
showing off the school to visitors. His birthday and
Franziska's were festal occasions, at which he would
distribute the prizes in person and allow the winners,
if of gentle birth, to kiss his hand ; if commoners, to
kiss the hem of his garment.

A modern reader will be very ready with his criticism of these educational arrangements. The constant and petty surveillance, the deliberate alienation
of boys from all ties of home and kindred, the systematic training in duplicity and adulation, were certainly
not well calculated for a school of manhood. Schiller
himself, after his escape from the academy, was wont
to speak very bitterly of the education that he had
received there. Nevertheless the school had its good
points, especially after the removal to Stuttgart, in 1775.
Here it became a combination of university (minus the
theological faculty) with a school of art, a school of

technology and a military academy proper. Several of the professors were inspiring teachers who made friends of their students. The fame of the institution brought together promising young men from all parts of Germany and from foreign parts ; and several of them besides Schiller attained distinction in after-life.[1] There was thus intellectual comradeship of the very best kind. And there was much freedom in the choice of studies.

But the solid merits of the academy were the growth of time ; in the beginning it was, for Schiller at least, mere chaos and misery. The boy grew rapidly into a lank, awkward youngster for whom the military discipline was a great hardship; he never got entirely rid of the stiff gait and ungainly bearing which resulted from these early struggles with the unattainable. Frequent illness led to a bad record on the books of the faculty. In 'conduite' he made but a poor showing, and he was several times billeted for untidiness. In Latin and religion he got along fairly well, and in Greek he actually took a prize toward the end of the year 1773. But the Greek which procured him this distinction hardly went beyond the rudiments and was mostly brought with him from Ludwigsburg. For mathematics he had but little talent. His bitterest trial, however, came with the law studies which he was obliged to take up in his second year. A dry subject, a dull teacher and an immature, reluctant pupil made a hopeless combination. And so he got the name of a

[1] For example : Cuvier, Dannecker and the musician Zumsteeg. The pros and cons of the Karlschule are discussed very fully by Weltrich and also by Minor in their biographies of Schiller.

dullard. During the whole of the year 1775 it is recorded that he was at the foot of his class.

Two bits of writing have come down to give us a glimpse of the boy's mind during these two years of helpless floundering. A detestable practice of the school authorities required the pupils to criticise one another in moral disquisitions. On one occasion the duke gave out the theme : ' Who is the meanest among you ? ' Schiller did his task in Latin distichs which have been preserved. They show a healthy feeling for the odiousness of the business, but he cleverly shifts the responsibility to *Dux serenissimus*, who must of course know what is good for him. Then he proceeds to depict one Karl Kempff as the worst boy in school, —*defraudans socios, rudis ignarusque*,—but he hopes that the wretched sinner will yet mend his ways and become worthy of his gracious prince's favor.

In a much longer prose document he portrays the characters of some two score schoolmates and finally his own. He begins modestly with a deprecatory address to his most gracious sovereign, without whose wise order he would never think of setting himself up as a judge of his fellows. The portraits are amusingly ponderous in style, but their substance is very creditable to their author's head and heart. Toward the end he burns more incense to the duke : ' This prince who has enabled my parents to do well by me ; this prince through whom God will attain his ends with me ; this father who wishes to make me happy, is and must be much more estimable to me than parents who depend upon his favor.' He frankly confesses his own short- comings : ' You will find me ', he writes, ' often over-

hasty, often frivolous. You will hear that I am obstinate, passionate and impatient; but you will also
hear of my sincerity, my fidelity and my good heart.'
He owns that he has not thus far made the best use of
his gifts, but he pleads illness in excuse. His gracious
prince knows how eagerly he has taken up the study
of the law and how happy he will be some day to enter
the service of his country. But, he ventures to insinu-
ate, he would be very much happier still if he could
serve his country as a teacher of religion.

The divinity was out of the question, but relief was
at hand. Toward the end of 1775, having come to
terms with the Stuttgart people, Duke Karl transferred
his academy to more commodious quarters in the city.
A department of medicine was added and Schiller
gladly availed himself of the duke's permission to enroll
in the new faculty. His professional studies were now
more to his taste and he applied himself to them with
sufficient zeal to make henceforth a decent though
never a brilliant record. His heart was already elsewhere. For some time past he had been nourishing
his soul on forbidden fruit,—books that had to be
smuggled in and were of course all the more seductive
for that very reason. With a few intimates—Scharffenstein, the Von Hovens and Petersen—he formed a
sort of literary club which read and discussed things.
What they read spurred them to imitation and to
mutual criticism. Presently they commenced sending
their productions to the magazines. Schiller began to
indulge in pleasing dreams of literary fame; and with
this new-born confidence in himself there came, as his
health improved, a firmer step, a more erect bearing

and an increased energy of character. To be a poet by grace of God was better than the favor of princes.

For some time, however, the youth's effusions gave little evidence of a divine call. His first poem to get into print was the one entitled 'Evening', which appeared in Haug's *Suabian Magazine* in the autumn of 1776. In irregular rimed verses—the rimes often very Suabian—we hear of sunset glories producing in the bard a divine ecstasy that carries him away through space. Then he returns to earth and hears in the voices of evening a general symphony of praise. It is still the Klopstockian strain of magniloquent religiosity, tempered somewhat by the influence of Haller. In 'The Conqueror', a poem published in 1777, the Klopstockian note is still more audible. The form is a pseudo-antique strophe such as Klopstock often used ; the substance a rhetorical denunciation of military ambition. The most awful curses are imprecated upon the head of the ruthless 'conqueror', whose badness is portrayed in lurid images and wild syntax that fairly rack the German language.[1] No wonder that editor Haug cautioned the young poet against nonsense, obscurity and exaggerated metatheses.

Nor is there much more of promise in the few occasional poems that have come down from Schiller's salad days in the academy. One of them was inspired by a visit of the emperor Joseph, whom our poet glorifies

[1] For example :

> Und mit offenem Schlund, welcher Gebirge schluckt,
> Ihn das Weltmeer mir nach,—ihn mir der Orkus nach
> Durch die Hallen des Todes—
> Deinen Namen, Eroberer !

in strains almost too fervid for utterance.[1]   The other
two are birthday greetings to Franziska von Hohenheim—effusions of 'gratitude', as it is called.   The
gratitude purports to come, in one of the poems, from
the *école des demoiselles*, which Franziska had founded
as a feminine pendant to the academy.   Schiller's
verses, truth to tell, sound like rank fustian.   The
duke's mistress is glorified as a paragon of virtue.   'Her
sweet name flies high on the wings of glory, her very
glance promises immortality.   Her life is the loveliest
harmony, irradiated by a thousand virtuous deeds.'
And so on.   As poetic spokesman of the girls he
pours out those 'Elysian feelings' which he supposes
them to cherish toward their kind and virtuous
'mother'.

There are two or three extant school orations which
likewise exhibit him in the rôle of a fervid eulogist.
The rhetoric of them is very highfalutin, and the flattery
would be nauseating if one did not remember that it
was largely a matter of fashion.   Custom required
that a prince be addressed in the language of adulation, and nothing in that line was too extravagant for
the taste of the time.   As for Schiller, he had got the
reputation of an orator and he only did what was expected of him as the public representative of the school.
Nor should we think too harshly of the duke for en-
couraging the foolishness, since he too only conformed
to the custom of the Old Régime.   At the same time
it is a pleasure to learn from certain well authenticated
anecdotes that he and his *élèves* did not always live in

[1] Weltrich, p. 182, argues that the poem is spurious.   The question is
hard to decide.

a fool's paradise of sycophancy. There is a story, vouched for by Weltrich, to the effect that Schiller, who had acquired fame as a mimic, was one day asked by the duke, with Franziska on his arm, to give an impromptu specimen of his powers by imitating his sovereign. The youth hesitated, but after some urging borrowed the duke's cane and proceeded to examine him. As his Highness did not answer well, Schiller exclaimed: 'Oh, you are an ass!' Then he took Franziska's arm and began to walk away with her. Serenissimus looked on with mixed emotions, but only said: 'Come now, leave Franzele to me!'

The young Schiller was nothing if not intense. When an emotion took possession of him it set him on fire, and the expression of it was like the eruption of a volcano. Toward the end of his course at the academy he had a misunderstanding with his dear friend Scharffenstein, with whom he had sworn eternal brotherhood. The result was a long letter of wild expostulation in this vein:

What was the bond of our friendship? Was it selfishness? Was it frivolity? Was it folly? Was it an earthly, vulgar, or a higher, immortal, celestial bond? Speak! Speak! Oh, a friendship erected like ours might have endured through eternity. . . . If you or I had died ten times, death should not have filched from us a single hour! What a friendship that might have been! And now! Now! What has become of it? . . . Hear, Scharffenstein! God is there! God hears me and thee, and may God judge!

And so on for six mortal pages, octavo print. The modern cynic will smile at this ecstatic cultus of friendship, but let him at the same time recall the saying of

Goethe that what makes the poet is a heart completely filled with one emotion.[1]

It is now time to glance at the really important phase of Schiller's youthful development—his reading. While his native Suabia, just then rather backward in literary matters, was still chewing the cud of pious conventionality, a prodigious ferment had begun in the outside world. What is called the 'Storm and Stress' was under way. The spirit of revolt, which in France was preparing a political upheaval, was abroad in Germany, where it found expression in stormy or sentimental plays and novels,—works composed on the principle that everything is permissible except the tame and the conventional. The productions of these young innovators differed widely from one another, but they had a common note in their vehement would-be naturalism. There were over-wrought pictures of daring sin and terrible punishment; novels and plays laying bare the *misère* of the social conflict; tragedies of insurgent passion at war with conventional ideas; of true love crossed and done to death by the prejudice of caste. And so forth.

How much of this literature fell into the hands of Schiller at the academy can not be told with perfect certainty, but it would seem that very little of it escaped him. He read and was deeply touched by Gerstenberg's 'Ugolino', with its horrific picture of the agonies of starvation. He read the early writings of Goethe, of Leisewitz and of Klinger, and was touched by the woes of Miller's Siegwart. In 'Emilia Galotti', with its drastic comment upon the infamies of princely

[1] "Götz von Berlichingen", Act I.

lust, he saw the subject of court life in a light very different from that in which it habitually appeared to the carefully guarded pupils of the Stuttgart academy. He became acquainted with Ossian, and the shadowy forms of the Celtic bard, big with their indefinable woe, increased the turmoil of his soul. Probably he read Rousseau more or less, though direct evidence of the fact is lacking. At any rate the air was surcharged with Rousseauite feeling. Certainly he read Plutarch and Cervantes, and along with all these came Shakspere,[1] to whom he was introduced—in the Wieland translation—by his favorite teacher, Abel.

The effect of this reading upon the mind of Schiller was prodigious. It changed the native docility of his temper, weaned him completely from his seraphic proclivities and carried him with a rush into the midcurrent of the literary revolution. There came a time when the young medical student, faithfully pursuing his routine and on festal occasions spouting fervid panegyrics of the noble Karl and the divine Franziska, was not altogether what he seemed to be. There was another Schiller, burning with literary ambition and privately engaged in forging a thunderbolt.

[1] The acquaintance began, it would seem, in 1775 or 1776. At first Schiller was repelled by Shakspere's 'coldness',—his intermixture of humor and buffoonery with pathos. Of this first impression he wrote many years later, in his essay on 'Naïve and Sentimental Poetry', as follows : "Durch die Bekanntschaft mit neueren Poeten verleitet, in den Werken den *Dichter* zuerst aufzusuchen, *seinem Herzen* zu begegnen . . . war es mir unerträglich, dasz der Poet sich hier gar nirgends fassen liesz und mir nirgends Rede stehen wollte. Mehrere Jahre hatte er meine ganze Verehrung, und war mein Studium, ehe ich sein Individuum lieb gewinnen konnte. Ich war noch nicht fähig, die Natur aus erster Hand zu verstehen."

Two dramatic attempts preceded 'The Robbers'. The first had to do with Cosmo dei Medici; the second, called 'The Student of Nassau', was based upon a newspaper story of suicide. Both were destroyed by their disgusted author, in what stage of progress we do not know. Still he was not discouraged; the tragic drama was clearly his field and he might succeed better the next time. But where to find a subject? His perplexity became so great that, as he said later, he would have given his last shirt for a good theme. Finally, in the year 1777, his friend Hoven drew his attention to a story by Schubart that had lately been published in the *Suabian Magazine*,—a story of a father and his two dissimilar sons, one of them frank and noble-minded but wild, the other a plausible moralist but at heart a scoundrel. Schiller took the hint and began to write, his interest being no doubt increased by the miserable fate of Schubart, who was then languishing in the Hohenasperg as the helpless victim of Karl Eugen's pusillanimous tyranny.[1]

Just how much progress was made with 'The Robbers' in the year 1777 is not known; probably not much, for Schiller soon decided to drop his literary pursuits for the present and devote himself closely to

[1] Schubart's crime was the utterance of a mild poetic lampoon to the effect that 'when Dionysius of Syracuse was compelled to go out of the tyranny business he became a Schulmeisterlein.' He had also commented too frankly on the duke's relation to Franziska. Angered by these things Karl caused him to be tricked over the borders into Württemberg, seized, and without trial shut up in the dungeon of Hohenasperg, where he was kept for ten years (1777–1787). Schiller visited him in November, 1781, and was received with tears of joy as the author of 'The Robbers'.

his medical studies. Perhaps he may have hoped
by hard work to finish his course in four years instead of the expected five. At any rate he now bent
to his toil and allowed the play to lie dormant in his
mind. In 1779 he submitted a thesis on 'The Philosophy of Physiology', but it was judged unfit for print.
The professors condemned it variously as tedious,
florid, obscure, and, worst of all, disrespectful toward
recognized authorities such as Haller. In these judgments the duke concurred. He found that Elève
Schiller had said many fine things and in particular
had shown much 'fire'. But the fire was too strong;
it needed to be 'subdued' by another year of study.

It has usually been assumed by Schiller's biographers that in his intense longing for liberty he was
embittered by this disappointment, and that in his
mood of wrath he now took up his neglected play and
poured into it, hissing hot, the whole fury of his quarrel with the world. There is, however, no evidence
that he really hoped to win his release from the academy in the year 1779, or that the thesis just spoken
of was regarded as a graduation thesis.[1] Neither his
own letters nor those of his friends indicate that he
was angry at being kept in school another year.
Probably the critics have made too much out of this
factor of personal disgruntlement. Schiller was a
poetic artist, and his first play is much more than the
wild expression of a plucked student's resentment.
Nevertheless it is only natural to suppose that his
proud and ambitious spirit chafed more or less under
the requirements of an academic routine that his man-

---

[1] Cf. Weltrich, I, 278.

hood had outgrown. That he succeeded after all, at the end of the year 1779, in capturing a number of prizes and received them in the presence of Goethe and the Duke of Weimar, who happened just then to be visiting Stuttgart, could do but little to sweeten the bitter dose that had been prescribed for him.

He now set about the preparation of a new thesis, and in the intervals of his professional occupation he worked with feverish energy upon ' The Robbers '. To gain time for writing he would often feign illness, and when the duke or an inspector surprised him would hide his manuscript in a big medical treatise kept at hand for the purpose. A few comrades who were in the secret eagerly watched the progress of his work and vociferously applauded the scenes which he now and then read to them. One of these comrades has left it on record that in the excitement of composition Schiller would often stamp and snort and roar.——And thus it was, in the stolen hours of the night and driven by the demon that possessed him, that he bodied forth his titanic drama of revolt. It was virtually finished during the year 1780. In after-time Schiller reasoned himself into the conviction that art must be ' cheerful ',[1] but very little of cheerfulness went to the composition of ' The Robbers '. It was the disburthening of an oppressed soul that suffered horribly at times from morbid melancholy—the chicken-pox of youthful genius. A letter of June, 1780, shows how he had battled with the specters of despair. Writing to Captain von Hoven, whose son had lately died, he says :

[1] "Ernst ist das Leben, heiter ist die Kunst."—*Prologue to ' Wallenstein'.*

A thousand times I envied your son as he was wrestling with death, and would have given up my life as calmly as I go to bed. I am not yet twenty-one years old, but I can tell you frankly that the world has no further charm for me. I have no delight in thinking of the world, and the day of my departure from the academy, which a few years ago would have been a day of festal joy, will not be able to force one happy smile from me. With each step, as I grow older, I lose more and more of my content-edness; and the nearer I come to the age of maturity, the more I could wish that I had died in childhood.

This sounds gloomy enough, but the desperate mood did not last long. A number of medical reports written in the summer of 1780 indicate that Schiller was able to take the calm professional view of a case very similar to his own. A fellow-student named Grammont was afflicted with hypochondria, and Schiller was set to watch him. His analysis of the case is eminently sane. He finds it difficult to decide whether the young man's malady has its seat in the mind or in the bowels; whether too much brooding over hard problems has ruined his digestion and given him a headache, or whether a physical derangement has confused his ideas of duty and religion. He thinks there is a fair chance of curing the patient by means of medicine and good advice.—A youth who can talk thus of another's *Weltschmerz* is himself in no great danger from the malady.

In November, 1780, he submitted a new thesis upon 'The Connection between Man's Animal and Spiritual Nature'. In this essay he considers the question whether, for the purposes of moral perfection, the body is to be regarded as the enemy and gaoler of the soul, or as its friend and coadjutor. The drift of his argu-

ment is to show in detail the dependence of the spirit
upon the flesh. Finding that philosophers have been
unjust to the body, he comes to its rescue,—expounding good doctrine in an interesting though rather
florid and unprofessional style. In the course of his
philosophizing he perpetrates the sly joke of quoting
from his own manuscript play and ascribing the words
to an imaginary 'Life of Moor', by one Krake.—Further comment upon the essay may be dispensed with,[1]
seeing that Schiller as a medical man does not greatly
interest us at the present time. Enough that it was
accepted and procured him his release from bondage
toward the close of the year.

Afterwards, in the bitterness of his quarrel with the
Duke of Württemberg, Schiller took an altogether
gloomy view of the training he had received at the
Military Academy. He saw only the forcing process
to which he had been subjected, the narrow life that
had kept him from a knowledge of the world, and the
petty restrictions that had prevented his love of poetry
from developing in a sane and natural manner. However, it is always the poet's fate to grow strong through
his own gifts and his own trials; what schools of any
kind can do for him or against him is of comparatively
little moment. Had Schiller enjoyed in his youth the
freedom of a real university, his literary career would
no doubt have opened differently, and with another beginning the whole would have been different; but
whether it would then have interested the world after
a hundred years, as that of the real Schiller does, is a

[1] Weltrich, I, 298 ff., analyzes it and discusses its scientific value at
some length.

question for omniscience. Speaking humanly one can only say that the misguided paternalism of Karl Eugen in rousing the tiger proved a blessing in disguise. And the schooling itself was by no means so despicable. Schiller left the academy a good Latinist, though with but little Greek. He had learned to read French, if not English. He had dabbled in such philosophy as there was going and acquired an interest in the fundamental problems. He had read not widely but intensely—which is always better. He had made a number of good friends. And not least important for his future career, he had had an excellent opportunity to observe the forms and usages of high life.[1]

[1] Kuno Fischer, "Schiller-Schriften", I, 139, has some very interesting remarks on this subject. "Woher gewann er [says Fischer], der Sohn eines Dorfbarbiers, . . . eine solche sichere und eingelebte Anschauung, ich möchte sagen, Fühlung fürstlichen Wesens, wenn nicht Herzog Karl, ein Meister in der Kunst fürstlichen Repräsentierens, ihn zum Modell gedient hätte?"

CHAPTER II

The Robbers

O über mich Narren, der ich wähnete die Welt durch Greuel zu verschönern und die Gesetze durch Gesetzlosigkeit aufrecht zu erhalten.—' *The Robbers* '.

AFTER leaving the academy Schiller soon began to look about for a publisher of his precious manuscript. Not finding one he presently decided to borrow money and print the play at his own expense. It appeared in the spring of 1781, accompanied by a modest preface in which the anonymous author pronounced his work unsuited to the stage but hoped it would be acceptable as a moral contribution to literature. In less than a year it had been played with ever memorable success and ere long it was the talk of Germany.

In dealing with ' The Robbers ' it has always been much easier to point out faults than to do justice. Schiller himself set the fashion of a drastic criticism which had the effect of advertising ' The Robbers ' as a violent youthful explosion containing more to be apologized for than to be admired. And indeed it is not a masterpiece of good taste. Upon an adult mind possessing some knowledge of the world's dramatic literature at its best, and particularly if the piece be read and not seen, Schiller's first play is very apt to produce the impression of a boyish extravaganza. The sentimental bandit who nourishes his mighty soul on the blood of his fellow-men, and undertakes to right a private wrong by running amuck against society in another part of the world, is a figure upon which we decline to waste our sympathy. We have no place for him in our scheme of art unless it be in comic opera or in the penny dreadful. Emotionally we have lost touch with him as we have with Byron's Corsair. When he stalks across the serious stage and rages and fumes and wipes his bloody sword, we are inclined to smile or to yawn. As for the villain Franz, with his abysmal depravity, and Amalia, with her witless sentimentalism, we find it hard to take them seriously; they do not produce a good illusion. And then the whole style of the piece, the violent and ribald language, the savage action, the rant and swagger, the shooting and stabbing,—all this seems at first calculated for the entertainment of young savages, and moves one to approve the oft-quoted *mot* of the German prince who said to Goethe: 'If I had been God and about to create the world, and had I foreseen that Schiller would write 'The Robbers' in it, I should not have created it.'[1]

This is one side of the story. The other side is that 'The Robbers' made an epoch in German dramatic literature. Not only is it the strongest and completest expression of the eighteenth-century storm and stress, but it proved a highly effective stage-play. Nor was its success ephemeral. Its author quickly outgrew it, but it maintained itself during the entire period of Germany's leadership in matters of dramatic art, and even

[1] Eckermann's "Gespräche mit Goethe", under date of Jan. 17, 1827.

to-day it preserves much of its old vitality. It is true that when a modern audience assembles to see a performance of 'The Robbers', they are not impelled solely by the intrinsic merits of the piece. Loyalty to the great dramatic poet of the nation plays its part. People think: Thus our Schiller began,—and they expect to make allowances. But when all such allowances are made, it remains true that 'The Robbers' is a powerful stage-play which reveals in every scene the hand of the born dramatist. We may call it boyish if we will, but its boyishness is like that of 'Titus Andronicus'. Each is the work of a young giant who in learning the use of his hammer lays about him somewhat wildly and makes a tremendous hubbub. But Thor is Thor, and such boys are not born every day.

The starting-point of Schiller's invention was the conception of the two hostile brothers, and this he had from Schubart, although other writers, notably Klinger and Leisewitz, had already made use of it in dramatic productions. In the Schubart story[1] we hear of a nobleman with two sons, of whom the elder, Karl, is high-minded but dissolute, while the younger, Wilhelm, is a hypocritical zealot. Karl plays the rôle of the prodigal son and his excesses are duly reported at home by his brother. After a while the sinner repents and writes his father a remorseful letter, which is intercepted by Wilhelm. Then the older brother returns to the vicinity of his home and takes service with a poor farmer. Here it falls to his lot to rescue his

---

[1] The Schubart story is reprinted by Weltrich, I, p. 183 ff., who attempts to trace its provenience. It was not entirely fiction. Cf. Minor, I, 298, to whom this chapter is indebted in many places.

father from the hands of assassins. It turns out that the instigator of the murder was no other than Wilhelm. When the plot is discovered the magnanimous Karl entreats pardon for his vile brother. His prayer is granted, Wilhelm receives a share of the estate and all ends in happy tears.— In publishing the sketch Schubart recommended it to the geniuses of the day as an excellent foundation for a novel or a comedy. Here was a chance, he thought, to prove that the Germans, notwithstanding the servility of their pens, were not the spiritless race that foreigners saw in them; 'to show that we too, in spite of our oppressive forms of government, which permit only a condition of passivity, are men who have their passions and can act, no less than a Frenchman or a Briton.' He therefore cautioned any playwright who might try his hand upon the subject to lay the scene not in a foreign country but in contemporary Germany.

We see here the thought that struck fire in the mind of young Schiller, whose bent was all for tragedy. If there was to be a proof that strong passion and bold action were still possible, notwithstanding the degeneracy of the age, what better object could there be for the passion to wreak itself upon than the age itself? If life had become vapid, and the German character servile and pusillanimous, here was the very field for a mad Ajax who should make havoc among the cowards and the pigmies. In Schubart's tragi-comedy there are no heroic passions whatever. Nothing is conceived in a large and bold way. The characters live and move throughout in the little world of their own selfish interests. Such a piece, in which the penitent hero bends his back to the plow and weakly pardons an abominable crime, did not comport with Schiller's mood of fierce indignation. So he converted the story into a tragedy and turned Schubart's meek and forgiving prodigal into a terrible avenger of mankind.

In the contrasted brothers we see what Minor[1] well enough calls the hot and cold passions. Karl is a hot-spur whose emotions are always keyed up to the highest pitch; he is never calm and is incapable of sober reasoning. His boiling blood and his insensate ambition are his only oracles. We may say that his motives are lofty, but in trying to set the world right and make it conform to his perfervid dreams of justice and freedom, he becomes a madman and a criminal. Franz, on the other hand, represents the scheming intellect sundered from conscience and natural feeling. He is a monster of cool, calculating, hypocritical villainy. At the end he cowers in abject terror before the phantom conscience that he has reasoned out of existence in the first act. The portrait of the two brothers, as thus conceived, is crudely simple. There are no delicacies of shading, no subtleties of psychological analysis. In short, Robber Moor and his brother give the impression of having been made to a scheme rather than copied from nature. Nevertheless the scheme is conceived with superb audacity and executed with a dramatic power and insight that had never been surpassed in Germany.

To understand the furore created by ' The Robbers ' one should read two other storm-and-stress plays, by writers of no mean dramatic talent, which present the

[1] " Schiller, sein Leben und seine Werke," I, 299.

same fundamental situation,[1]—'The Twins', by Klinger, and 'Julius of Tarentum', by Leisewitz. Both these plays came out in the year 1776 and were evidently studied with care by Schiller. Both follow the timid example which had been set by Lessing of laying the scene in a foreign land. Klinger gives us two brothers, Guelfo and Ferdinando, of whom neither the mother nor her physician can tell which was born first. But Ferdinando has always been treated as the elder, has enjoyed the favor of his father, risen to power and distinction and won the prize in love. He is of a noble and forgiving temper and plays only a subordinate part. The hero is Guelfo, who, like Schiller's Karl Moor, has read Plutarch and would fain do something great, like Brutus or Cassius. But he remains after all only a poor knight. His hand is unnerved and his heroic spirit paralyzed by the suspicion that he has been the life-long victim of a conspiracy; that he and not Ferdinando is the elder brother. The whole interest of the play turns upon the portraiture of his morbid, insensate jealousy. In the fourth act he takes a morning ride with his brother and murders him. Then he defiantly reports the deed at home and is himself slain by his father.

---

[1] Bitter family feuds, and particularly the fiction of the hostile brothers,—with motives of rivalry, jealousy and hatred, with paternal curses and parricide and fratricide and filicide,—were just then a literary fashion. It is worth noting in this connection that J. M. R. Lenz published in 1776 a story entitled "Die beiden Alten", in which a son shuts up his father in a cellar and sends a man to kill him. But the man's heart fails him and the prisoner escapes,—to reappear like a ghost among his kin. That Schiller read this story is at any rate thinkable, though there is no direct evidence of the fact.

In 'Julius of Tarentum' the younger brother, Guido, is, again, the man of action; a *miles gloriosus* who boasts of his strong arm and dreams of glory. He looks with contempt and hatred upon his gentle, sentimental brother Julius, who, though heir to the throne, prepares to renounce his career because he is thwarted in love. The girl Blanca, upon whom he has fixed his affections, is not deemed a suitable bride for him by his father and has been shut up in a convent. He determines to abduct her by night and flee with her to some romantic spot in the far north. In the execution of this purpose he is killed by his jealous brother Guido, who is then made to suffer death at the hands of his own father.

In both these plays we have, as in 'The Robbers', an aged father whose dynastic hopes center in an excellent son; this son the object of mad jealousy on the part of a younger brother, and both brothers in love with the same girl. The plays exhibit talent of a high order, but talent that always falls short of genius. Psychical states are portrayed by means of talk, and the talk is big enough; but very little actually happens. The mighty passions have to be taken largely upon trust and the conversation often drags. Dramatic possibilities are not fully grasped, the situations are felt but not seen, and there is an obvious reluctance to make unusual demands upon the stage. Even Klinger, whose play of 'Storm and Stress' gave a name to the whole contemporary movement in German literature, reads tamely enough in comparison with 'The Robbers'. But what is most noteworthy of all, Klinger and Leisewitz give us simply dynastic tragedies. In both the outlook is limited to the fortunes of a single house. In both we miss the great dramatist who looks upon life with a roving eye and intertwines his tale of private woe with the larger tangle of human destiny.

This last is what the young Schiller did with masterly insight. He converted the dynastic tragedy of his predecessors into a tragedy of the social revolution; and his work has lived because we can hear in it the preliminary roar of the storm which was soon to burst in the streets of Paris.[1] He laid his scene not in far-off Italy nor in the remote past, but in Germany and in the middle of the century which boasted of its enlightened philosophy and its excellent police regulations. Of the two brothers he took the sentimentalist for his hero, but made him at the same time a man of action, a man of heroic mould and a self-helper. The logic of Rousseau finds in Karl Moor a practical interpreter. What the Frenchman had preached concerning the infamies of civilization, the badness of society and politics, the reign of injustice and unreason, the petty squabbles of the learned, the necessity of a return to nature,—all this seethes in the blood of Moor, but he does not content himself with indignant rhetoric or sentimental repining. He takes arms against the sea of troubles. Instead of an excellent youth pitifully done to death by a jealous brother, we get a towering

---

[1] Cf. Minor, I, 300 : "Die Räuber des jungen Schiller, welcher sich damals nicht einmal um den nordamerikanischen Freiheitskrieg, geschweige denn um das gewitterschwüle Frankreich bekümmerte, waren nur ein Symptom und eine Vorahnung ; eine Wirkung im Kleinen vor der groszen Katastrophe."

idealist who is the moulder of his own fate. With sub-
lime $\H{v}\beta\rho\iota\varsigma$ he takes it upon himself to wield the avenging bolts of Jove, but finds that Jove rejects his assist-
ance. He errs disastrously in his judgment, like any
short-sighted mortal, and his work goes all agley.
But when the end comes it is not depressing. We see
no longer a revolting fratricide and the painful sacrifice of virtue to the meanest of passions, but the verdict
of the gods upon human presumption.

In making his hero a defiant self-helper and sending
him with sword in hand against the minions of the
established order, Schiller was obviously influenced by
the example of ' Götz von Berlichingen '. Like Götz,
Karl Moor regards himself as the champion of freedom
against the law, which is its enemy. Both are friends
of the oppressed and haters of pedantry and pettifog-
gery. Both fight like lions against tremendous odds.
Both assume the leadership of a band of outlaws whom
they cannot control, and thus become responsible for
revolting crimes not foreseen or intended. But along
with these and other resemblances that might be
pointed out there is an important difference. In the
fourth act of the earlier play a Heilbronn Councillor
says to Götz: ' We owe no faith to a robber.' Whereat
Götz exclaims: ' If you did not wear the emperor's
emblem, which I honor in the vilest counterfeit, you
should take back that word or choke upon it. Mine is
an honorable feud.' That is, the knight of the sixteenth century repudiates the name in which Karl
Moor glories. Says Schiller's Pater in the second act:
' And you, pretty captain ! Duke of cutpurses ! King
of scoundrels ! Great Mogul of all rogues under the

sun !' To which Moor replies : 'Very true. Very true. Just proceed.' In comparison with such a daredevil Goethe's hero seems to roar like a sucking dove. In his own mind Götz never really burns the bridge behind him. He is at heart a loyalist who recognizes the emperor's claim to his allegiance. As a free imperial knight he feels himself within his right under the feudal system. In resisting his enemies he does not set himself in opposition to governmental authority *per se*, but only to the abuse of authority by subordinates who disgrace their master and his. And in assuming the leadership of the insurgent rabble he thinks to restrain their ferocity and thus earn the thanks of the supreme authority.—It remained for Schiller to convert this rude self-helper in the age of expiring feudalism into a savage anarchist in the boastful age of enlightenment.

It was a bold idea to be conceived by a youth in a school where every third word was of virtue and philanthropy. Not that there was anything particularly audacious in a strong presentation of the spirit of revolt. For some time past this spirit had been nourished by the writings of Rousseau and those who followed in his wake, until attacks upon the social order, in some phase of it, had come to be almost the staple of literature. But the attacks had not been very dangerous. Either they were veiled by a distant setting of the scene, or the indictment of the age was presented incidentally in connection with some lacrimose tragedy of the individual. People had learned to sigh and weep that things should be so, but there the matter ended. The German princeling could look on with equanimity, assured that the rhetoric and the tears did not mean him, or that if they did it did not matter. In real life those who felt themselves oppressed by the civilization of Europe could emigrate, and they did emigrate in large numbers. This was one form of the return to nature. In literature, however, the usual expedient was to let the hero chafe himself to death and go down, without striking a blow, before the irresistible tyranny of the established order. Schiller's hero is of another ilk. Romantic flight with his lady-love does not occur to him. Surrender to the wrong is out of the question. He finds another form for the return to nature and puts into practice the maxim, Here or nowhere is America. He stays and fights at the head of a troop of bandits. Thus the play which was originally to have been called 'The Lost Son' became 'The Robbers'.

In their way, then, Schiller's outlaws stand for the state of nature. They represent natural man rising in brute strength against the oppressions of a depraved society. Such at least is Karl Moor's construction of the matter when he says to the Pater : 'Tell them that my business is retribution, that my trade is vengeance.' Under our modern development of the social sentiment we can hardly imagine a really high-minded youth setting out in such a Quixotic and fanatical enterprise. This feature of Schiller's plot, which has for us something of the burlesque about it, has been taken more than any other to prove his inexperience of life. But the fact is that the thing was after all not so unthinkable. Outlawry on a large scale was by no means unknown, and the romance of outlawry was familiar in literature. The Thirty Years' War had familiarized Germany with marauding bands who recognized no authority save that of their leader. Even in the eighteenth century the brigandage which was common in the Mediterranean countries continued to flourish in Southern Germany. As late as 1781, the very year in which 'The Robbers' appeared, we hear of the capture in Bavaria of a band of outlaws numbering nearly a thousand men. The year 1771 witnessed the execution of the robber-chieftain Klostermayer, who, under the name of the Bavarian Hiesel, became the subject of an idealizing saga in which we recognize the essential features of Karl Moor.[1]

Schiller's main fiction was thus, in a sense, warranted by the facts; and it gains further in artistic plausibility when we consider that the idealized bandit was already a familiar type in literature. The author of 'The Robbers' was acquainted with Robin Hood, and he had probably read 'The Two Gentlemen of Verona', in which the banished Valentine becomes the captain of a band of outlaws on condition that they " do no outrages on silly women or poor passengers ", and the outlaws reply that they " detest such vile, base practices."[2] He had also read, in 'Don Quixote', of the high-toned robber, Roque Guinart, who had more of compassion in his nature than cruelty. Cervantes makes Roque comment thus upon his mode of life : " Injuries which I could not brook and thirst for revenge first led me into it contrary to my nature ; for the savage asperity of my present behavior is a dis-

---

[1] Cf. Minor, I, 313 ff.
[2] Act IV, scene 1.

grace to my heart, which is gentle and humane." At the end of the episode Roque sends his captives away "admiring his generosity, his gallantry, and his extraordinary conduct, and looking upon him rather as an Alexander the Great than as a notorious robber." [1] Here was a sufficient hint for a criminal in the grand style, who should imagine himself the spiritual congener of Plutarch's heroes.

'A singular Don Quixote whom we abominate and love, admire and pity',—such was Schiller's own formula for his first dramatic hero. From the standpoint of ordinary logic it must be admitted that Moor's motive for becoming a robber (the lying letter that he receives from Franz) is quite insufficient. He is duped too easily and should have known his brother better. He is too ready to give up everything dear to him, including the dear Amalia. 'I have no sweetheart any more', is a weak surrender for a man of his heroic stamp. In any case the wrong that has been done him is a private wrong that has nothing to do with the constitution of society. One does not see how it is to be righted or how the world is to be purged of such baseness by killing and plundering people in the Bohemian Forest.

The only reply which our drama makes to this objection is to be found in Moor's crazy ambition for distinction. He has the 'great-man-mania'. What attracts him in the career of crime is not the wickedness but the bigness of it ; the opportunity of lifting himself above the common herd and sending his name down to posterity as that of a very extraordinary person. 'I

[1] "Don Quixote," Chapter 89.

loathe this ink-spattering century', he says, 'when I read in my Plutarch of great men. . . . I am to squeeze my body into a corset and lace up my will in laws. . . . Law has never made a great man, but freedom hatches out colossi and extremes. O that the spirit of Hermann were still glowing in the ashes ! Place me at the head of an army of fellows like myself, and Germany shall become a republic in comparison with which Rome and Sparta were nunneries.' Such monstrous egotism needs no motive, but only an occasion, for breaking with the order of civilization. An occasion is furnished by the letter.

But that which marks Karl Moor as a genuine child of Schiller's imagination and of the sentimental age is his combination of virile energy with soft-heartedness and true nobility of feeling. In all his robbings and burnings he does not become vulgarized like his comrades. He imagines that he is engaged in a righteous work and has God on his side. For this reason he has a right to his melting moods, as, for example, in the famous and oft-praised scene on the Danube. This delicacy of feeling, which to an American or Englishman is apt to seem absurd in a bandit-chief who is engaged in wholesale crime, is an essential part of Moor's character. It is this which, on German soil, gave to ' The Robbers ' tragic interest and insured its immortality. One sees all along that Moor is a wanderer in the dark, and one can sympathize with his purposes and his dreams while detesting his conduct. This makes him a heroic figure. And when the clearing-up comes and he discovers that he has been the victim not of society but of an individual villain ; that his attempt to right wrongs by committing new wrongs, to enforce the laws by lawlessness, and to correct violence by violence, was nothing but presumptuous and criminal folly,—when all this becomes clear to him, we have a tragic situation of the most pathetic character. This element of high tragic pathos was first given to a German drama by Schiller. It had not been given by Goethe and Lessing, nor was it in them to give it. This is why German tragedy in the true sense may be said to have its beginning in 'The Robbers'.

That Schiller in a sense sympathized with his hero is undeniable. What gives vitality to the character is here as always the fact that the author looked into his own heart and then wrote. This, however, only means that the moods of Moor are veritable moods of Schiller, raised to a white heat and translated into action. The young student, dreaming the dreams of youth and pining for freedom and action, had more than once felt his gorge rise to the choking-point as he found himself forced to plod on among the dull, oppressive, unheroic facts of life ; and those acts of official villainy against which Moor draws the sword he had himself seen flourishing unavenged in his native Württemberg. But, on the other hand, he was never for a moment insensible to the moral hideousness and the tragic folly of Moor's conduct. It was to be sublime, but insane and calamitous nevertheless. One is justified in thinking, therefore, that Goedeke goes too far, or does not express the truth felicitously, when he says that the author of 'The Robbers' 'felt himself one' with his hero.[1] He felt himself one with certain phases of

[1] "Grundrisz zur Geschichte der deutschen Dichtung", V, 19.

Moor's thought and feeling ; for the rest, however, the robber-chieftain was to be abominated as well as admired. There has been too much of the tendency to see in 'The Robbers' only a personal document ; only a youth's incoherent cry for liberty. The piece is a work of art, duly calculated with reference to artistic effects.

Turning now from the figure of Karl to that of his brother, one is struck at once with the artificiality of the portrait. We seem to have before us in Franz Moor the result of a deliberate effort to conceive the vilest possible travesty of human nature. Nothing here that was copied from nature, nothing that Schiller found in his own heart. It is all a brain-spun creation, born of his dramatic reading and of his studies in medicine and philosophy. In the first place we can observe that Franz is studiously contrasted with his brother. Karl is an idealist and a man of sentiment ; Franz is a materialist to whom the natural emotions of the heart are objects of cynical derision. For Karl, who knows his Klopstock as well as his Plutarch, love is a transcendental dream foretelling a spiritual union in a world without end ; for Franz it is carnal appetite. Karl wears his heart upon his sleeve ; Franz is wily and hypocritical. The one is handsome and chivalrous, the other ill-favored and cruel.

The jealous cadet who plots criminally against his more fortunate brother is common to both Leisewitz and Klinger, but in neither is he an intriguing villain. In 'Julius of Tarentum' Guido is really the more masterful man of the two. He despises his brother as a weakling and asserts no other claim than that of the strongest. In Klinger's play, as we have seen, everything is made to turn upon Guido's cankering doubt of his brother's seniority. One gets the impression that if the doubt could be settled by indisputable evidence in favor of Ferdinando, there would be no *casus belli;* the younger son would bow to the law of primogeniture and that would end the matter. Schiller, however, felt the need of a bolder contrast to his hero. The 'sublime criminal' required a colossal foil; and as equality with the sword was out of the question, the most obvious recourse was to pit natural depravity against natural greatness; scheming intellect against hot blood.

In working out his conception Schiller took counsel freely of Shakspere, whose name had now become for young Germany the symbol of all things great in dramatic writing. The first soliloquy of Franz Moor reminds one at once of Edmund in 'Lear', though there is none of the kind of borrowing which makes easy prey for the philologist. Both villains covet the wealth and station of a preferred brother; both make use of a specious obstetrical argument and both operate with forged letters. In general, however, the portrait of Franz was more influenced by Richard the Third than by Edmund, or Iago, or any of the other Shaksperian villains. Franz is the British Richard divested of his Shaksperian lordliness, transferred to a humbler sphere of action and provided with the mental outfit of an eighteenth-century *philosophe*, as seen by hostile critics. Both descant on their own deformity and confide to the public their villainous designs. But while Richard speaks in a tone of genial cynicism, as if his principal concern were only to bring a little variety into the tameness of "these fair, well-spoken days", the German villain solemnly turns himself inside out and regales us *ad nauseam* with the metaphysics of iniquity. This is his mode of reasoning:

Why did nature put upon me this burden of ugliness—this Laplander's nose, this Moorish mouth, these Hottentot eyes? Death and destruction! Why was she such a partisan?—But no, I do her injustice. She gave us wit when she placed us naked and miserable on the shore of this great ocean-world. Swim who can, and whoso is too clumsy let him sink. The right is with him that prevails. Family honor? A valuable capital for him that knows how to profit by it.—Conscience? An excellent scarecrow with which to frighten sparrows from cherry-trees.—Filial love? Where is the obligation? Did my father beget me because he loved me? Did he think of me at all? Is there anything holy in his gratification of carnal appetite? Or shall I love him because he loves me? That is mere vanity, the usual predilection of the artist for his own work.

Such is the ethical attitude of Franz Moor, as we gather it from his first soliloquy. One sees that Schiller was concerned to portray a scoundrel who had read deeply and come to the conclusion that in a world like this there is no valid reason why a man should be virtuous. Evidently the author had himself breathed the mephitic air of eighteenth-century skepticism. His natural goodness of heart safeguarded him from corruption, but it pleased him as artist to dip his pen in the blackest ink and draw the picture of the devil with whom he had wrestled in moments of solitary musing.

In spite of his intellectual subtlety, however, Franz is a rather dull villain. His philosophical and physiolog-

ical pedantry—for Schiller endows him lavishly with the
special lore of the medical man—obfuscates his vision
for the ordinary facts of human nature. He has upon
the whole a more intelligible motive for his rascality
than Iago, but he is much less interesting, much less
picturesque, for simple lack of mother-wit. What a
woeful blunder, for example, is his attempt to win
Amalia by depicting her absent lover, at great length
and with all manner of revolting details, as the victim
of the most loathsome of diseases ! And why should
such a crafty schemer risk his neck and put himself in
the hands of a dangerous confederate for the purpose
of hastening by a few hours the demise of a childish
old man who is already in his power ? And in his
final agony of terror, when we should expect him to
hide himself or try to escape, how absurd that he
should summon Pastor Moser merely for the purpose
of arguing with him upon immortality and judgment !
We see that he is after all a wretched coward who has
merely cheated us into the belief that he has put away
the superstitions of orthodox belief, while in reality
they still linger in his blood. We miss in him the in-
vincible sang-froid of villainy which might have given
a touch of Shaksperian grandeur to his character. As
it is, he is not grand, but pitiable and revolting. When
he strangles himself with his hat-band, one is quite satisfied with the unheroic manner of his taking-off.

The subordinate characters of the piece are hardly
worth discussing at any length. The elder Moor is a
mere nonentity,—a dummy in a rocking-chair would
have done as well. Evidently Schiller was concerned
to make the way as easy as possible for the clumsy

villainy of Franz.   A more vigorous father, he may
have felt, would have necessitated a more subtle and
plausible intrigue, which would have diverted attention
from the main issue of the contrasted sons.   The
heroine Amalia has always been recognized, and was
immediately recognized by Schiller himself, as the
weakest character in the play.   But posterity's criticism
is hardly that formulated by him, namely, that we miss
in Amalia the 'gentle, suffering, pining thing—the
maiden.'[1]   Of gentle, suffering, pining things there is
no dearth in the German drama, and they were not in
Schiller's line.   Nearly all of his women are made of
heroic stuff, and we honor him not the less for that.
No one should blame Amalia for boxing the ears of
Franz or drawing the sword upon him ; it is unlady-
like conduct, but very good storm-and-stress realism.

What one must deplore, however, is the general mental inadequacy that is paired with this spasmodic energy
of scorn.   Common sense is not the highest of dramatic
qualities, but a modicum of it would have made Schiller's first heroine, to say the least, more interesting.
She has no power of initiative and seems made only to
be duped.   Her inability to recognize her lover in the
fourth act is a terrible strain upon one's patience.   Indeed the whole love-affair between her and Karl is
utterly un-human.   What can one think, for example
of a pair of ecstatically faithful lovers to whom it has
evidently never occurred to write to each other ?   Here,
if anywhere, one recalls Schiller's oft-quoted observa-

[1] Sämmtliche Schriften, II, 365.   Citations from Schiller refer, unless
otherwise expressly indicated, to Goedeke's historico-critical edition in
15 vols. Stuttgart, 1867–1876.

tion that he had attempted in ' The Robbers ' to depict human beings before he had seen any.[1] Aside from his acquaintance with Franziska von Hohenheim, and an occasional nearer view of the coy maidens of the *école des demoiselles*, the female sex and the grand passion were for him only bookish mysteries.

Of the subordinate outlaws there are several whose portraits are very well drawn. Here Schiller was able to profit by the psychological observations he had made upon his comrades in the academy. There were no cutthroats there, but there were traits and exploits, animosities and fidelities, which only needed to be heated in the poetic crucible in order to befit the rôle of robbers in the Bohemian Forest. In particular we may guess that the blatherskite Jew, Spiegelberg, with his swaggering self-conceit and his bestial vulgarity, was copied to some extent from life, though nothing definite is known of his original. Taken as a whole the robbers form a picturesque company, each with his own character. Shakspere would probably have been content to say ' first robber ', ' second robber ', etc. ; but for Schiller, accustomed to the pose of leadership among his fellows, to company drill and to the weighing of men according to their moral qualities, this was not enough. There had to be sheep and goats, classified according to their loyalty. On the one hand, closest to the leader stand the devoted Roller, the sturdy Schweizer and the romantic idealist, Kosinsky; on the other are the envious malcontent, Spiegelberg, and the wretched Schufterle. The others, less distinctly characterized, represent the mass.

[1] Sämmtliche Schriften, III, 520.

It will now be in order to look at ' The Robbers ' a moment from the point of view of dramatic art.[1] In a suppressed preface to the first edition Schiller expressed himself very contemptuously with regard to the stage, declaring that he had essayed a dramatized story and not a stage-play. He would not advise that his work be put upon the boards; for the rabble of the theater would not understand him, would take him for an apologist of vice, and so forth. There seems no good reason to doubt the essential sincerity of these expressions, though their author quickly changed his tune when the staging of ' The Robbers ' became a practical question. In the heat of authorship, however, he had aimed at a literary rather than a dramatic triumph. His chief models were literary dramas. ' Götz von Berlichingen ' had won its way into favor as a book for the reader. The dramatic works of Klinger, Lenz, Wagner and the like, were for the most part too extravagant and amorphous for representation, and Shakspere's day had not yet come.

This being so, it is a fact of interest that ' The Robbers ' first captured the public as a stage-play, and that too in a very much modified version, from which all references to contemporary society had been expunged, the action having been dated back into the fifteenth century. This indicates that the initial success of the work was not due mainly to the social ' tendency ' which we see in it, but to its dramatic power. And the dramatic power is there. With but slender knowledge

[1] Cf. Bulthaupt, "Dramaturgie des Schauspiels," I, 209, who has some excellent remarks upon the dramatic qualities of the play and the histrionic problems connected with it.

of the rules and the conventions, without ever having
seen a moderately good play in his life, with little help
save from the poet's eye in a fine frenzy rolling, the
young student had shown himself at a stroke the
coming dramatist of his nation.

Let us freely admit that he had not shown himself a
master of dramatic craftsmanship. Faulty the piece
no doubt is in several particulars. The soliloquies of
Franz are too long-winded, and the same may be said
of some of the robber-scenes. Spiegelberg's vulgar
tongue is allowed to wag too freely. Contempt of
quotidian probability is now and then carried so far as
to produce an unintended effect of burlesque: as when
the robbers, who are merely dissolute students from
Leipzig, fight with twenty times their number of soldiers,
lose one man and slay three hundred. Again, one does
not quite see the moral necessity of honest Schweizer's
killing himself, when he has the misfortune to find
Franz dead. He has indeed promised to capture him
or die in the attempt, but his promise was never meant
to cover the case of the villain's suicide. Under the
circumstances his shooting himself is mere exuberance
of dramatic bloodshed.

But how absurd it would be to dwell upon these
things as if they were serious defects! Young Schiller
undertook to Shaksperize. His parole was not to be
the natural and the probable, but the extraordinary, the
tremendous. Why then should he have been more
timid than the author of ' Lear ' and ' Macbeth ' ?
One who is borne along by a whirlwind may be pardoned for ignoring the rules and the proprieties. Of
course it is not intended to compare ' The Robbers '

with the riper works of Shakspere. That would be absurd, and yet no more absurd than to gird at Schiller for doing what we pardon or even admire in Shakspere. Like every great dramatist Schiller has an indefeasible right to demand that we take his point of view, make his assumptions and enter into the spirit of his creation. And when we do this, how magnificently he carries us along! What animation in the dialogue everywhere, and what fire in the robber-scenes! From first to last the play fairly throbs with passion, and always with passion made visible. It is all action, all meant to be done and seen. Extravagant it is, no doubt; but while there are always hundreds of critics in the world who can see that and say it more or less cleverly, there is but one man in a century who can write such scenes.

CHAPTER III

The Stuttgart Medicus

So gewisz ich sein Werk verstehe, so musz er starke Dosen in Emeticis ebenso lieben als in Æstheticis, und ich möchte ihm lieber zehen Pferde als meine Frau zur Kur übergeben.—Review of 'The Robbers', 1782.

THE career that opened before Schiller on his release from the academy, in December, 1780, turned out a wretched mockery of his hopes. He had, or supposed he had, the right to expect a decent position in the public service and a measure of liberty befitting a man who had served his time under tutelage. What his august master saw fit to mete out to him, however, was neither the one nor the other: he was stationed at Stuttgart as 'medicus' to an ill-famed regiment consisting largely of invalids. His pay was eighteen florins a month—say seven or eight dollars. His duties consisted of routine visits to the hospital and daily appearance at parade, with reports upon the condition of the luckless patients whom he doctored savagely with drastic medicines. Withal he was required to wear a stiff, ungainly uniform which did not carry with it the distinction of an 'officer' and exposed him to the derision of his friends. A humble petition of Captain Schiller that his son be permitted

to wear the dress of a civilian and extend his practice among the people of the city met with a curt
refusal.

Of Schiller's personal appearance at about this time
we have two or three descriptions by friends who knew
him well.[1] Putting them together we get a picture
something like the following: He was about five feet
and nine inches in height, erect of bearing and knock-
kneed. He had reddish hair, a broad forehead, and
bushy eyebrows which came close together over a
long, thin, arched nose. He was near-sighted. His
eyes, of a bluish-gray color, were usually inflamed, but
very expressive when he spoke with animation. One
friend credits him with an ' eagle's glance ', another
with an uncanny, demonic expression. He had a
strong chin, a prominent under-lip, and sunken,
freckled cheeks. Altogether his face and bearing told
of immense energy.—One can imagine how the creator
of Karl Moor must have felt in his new situation. The
young lion had escaped from one cage into another
that was even worse.

Nevertheless the new life did not altogether preclude
an occasional sip from the cup of earthly cheer. The
young medicus found himself within easy reach of a
number of jovial friends whom he had known at the
academy. With one of these, a youth named Kappf,
he hired a room of a certain Frau Vischer, a widow
who was to become the muse of his high-keyed songs
to Laura. The furniture consisted of a table and two
benches. In one corner were usually to be seen a pile

[1] The somewhat conflicting data are subjected to a critical scrutiny
by Weltrich, I, 323 ff.

of potatoes and some plates.   Here the friends feasted upon sausage and potato-salad of their own make, a bottle of wine being added if the host happened to be in funds.   Sometimes there were convivial card-parties at a local inn, where more than enough wine was drunk and bills were run up that still remain unpaid.   Tradition tells of a military banquet from which our medicus had to be assisted home.

A nobler pleasure incident to the new life was the opportunity of frequent visits to Castle Solitude.   For eight years Schiller had been cut off from intercourse with his parents and sisters, save through the medium of officially inspected letters.   Returning now at last he found his mother in frail health, but his father still vigorous and active.   Sister Christophine had grown into a strong and self-reliant young woman, the mainstay of the household.   She took an interest in literature, loved her brother devotedly, had a sister's boundless faith in his genius, and now became his confidante and amanuensis.   Another sister, Louise, had reached the age of fourteen, two others had died, and the youngest of all, Nanette, was now three years old.   It was a happy, sensible, affectionate family-circle, in which the long-lost son and brother found sweet relief from the *misère* of Stuttgart.   The only cloud in the sky was the mother's anxiety for the welfare of her son's soul, with the resulting necessity of replying somewhat disingenuously to her tender inquiries into his religious condition.   To his parents and sister the disgruntled medicus expressed freely his disappointment at the provision which the duke had made for him.   A hard fate, indeed, to have studied seven

years for the privilege of starving one's mind and body
as an insignificant army doctor!

It was partly the hope of earning money that led
him to seek a publisher for ' The Robbers '. Friend
Petersen was exhorted to find one, if possible, and
was promised whatever he could get for the piece over
and above fifty florins. But Petersen had no luck and
at last the ambitious author decided, as the author of
' Götz ' had done before him, to print his drama at his
own expense. The money that he borrowed for the
purpose, on the security of a friend, involved him in
debts that were to hang over him for years and cause
him endless trouble.

His plan once formed he began to take counsel with
friends and revise his manuscript in the light of their
criticisms. Even after the printing had begun, the
revision continued. Things looked differently in the
cold type of the proof-sheet, and he saw that he had
occasionally gone too far in the direction of coarseness
and extravagance. Thus the original draft had provided that Amalia should actually be sent to a convent,
and that the furious Karl should appear with his robbers
and threaten to convert the nunnery into a brothel
unless his sweetheart should be delivered to him.
This scene was condemned and the exploit given a
more appropriate place among the *res gestae* of
Spiegelberg. In many places extravagant diction was
toned down. The original preface, which was mainly
occupied with a labored defence of the literary drama
as against the stage-play, was rejected, and a new
preface written which was devoted chiefly to moral
considerations. The author here admitted that he had

portrayed characters who would offend the virtuous, but insisted that he could not do otherwise if he was to copy nature, because in the real world virtue shines only in contrast with vice.   He went on to say:

He who makes it his object to overthrow vice, and to avenge religion, morality and social law upon their enemies, must unveil vice in all its naked hideousness and bring it before the eyes of mankind in colossal size; he must himself wander temporarily through its nocturnal labyrinths and must be able to force himself into states of feeling that revolt his soul by their unnaturalness. I may properly claim for my work, in view of its remarkable catastrophe, a place among moral books. Vice meets the end that befits it. The wanderer returns to the track of law. Virtue triumphs. Whoever is fair enough to read me through and try to understand me, from him I may expect, not that he admire the poet, but that he respect the right-minded man.

This attempt to recommend 'The Robbers' as a text-book in morality has now a curious sound.   It is a safe guess that the young attorney for the defence wrote with his tongue in his cheek and an eye on the censor.

The first edition, which appeared in May, 1781, was styled a 'Schauspiel' and bore the Hippocratic motto: *Quae medicamenta non sanant, ferrum sanat; quae ferrum non sanat, ignis sanat.* The author's name was not given and the work purported (fallaciously) to have been published at Frankfurt and Leipzig. The anonymity was not taken seriously, however, and the Stuttgart medicus soon found himself a bit of a literary lion.   He was pointed out on the street as the man who had written 'The Robbers', and distinguished travellers began to call upon him.   The reviewers mingled praise and blame, and the most thoughtful of them, one Timme, declared in the Erfurt *Zeitung* that here if anywhere was the coming Shakspere,—which was a little wild from posterity's point of view, but not an unpleasant thing for a young author to read in a newspaper.

Luckily for Schiller his work was not long left to make its way as 'mere literature'. Among those to whom he had sent the sheets was a Mannheim bookseller, named Schwan, who had an eye for dramatic merit. Before Schwan had read many pages it came over him that here was a prize for the stage, and he hurried with it to Baron Dalberg, intendant of the Mannheim theater. Dalberg was easily convinced,— only the work would need to be radically revised. A complimentary letter was addressed to Schiller, proposing a stage version of 'The Robbers' and offering to bring out future plays that he might write. Schiller was quite willing, notwithstanding his preface, and about the middle of August he addressed himself to his task. Profiting by the suggestions of Dalberg and the reviewers, he devoted six weeks to adding, subtracting, re-writing, and re-arranging,—a new masterpiece, he averred, would have cost him less labor. But Dalberg was not yet satisfied; correspondence ensued about various points, Schiller showing himself very tractable, and it was not until the close of the year that the stage version was finally ready. It was played on the 12th of January, 1782,—its author having stolen away from Stuttgart to see the performance,—and scored an unheard-of success.[1]   Shortly afterwards the new ver-

[1] Bulthaupt, I, 210, quotes from Pichler's history of the Mannheim theater the following account by an eye-witness : ' The theater was like a

sion, in slightly modified form, was published by Schwan under the name of a ' Trauerspiel ' by Friedrich Schiller.

The changes made in the new version do not reflect the free play of Schiller's dramatic instinct so much as his deferential attitude towards Dalberg. Thus we know that the most important of them all, the shifting of the action back into the age of expiring feudalism, was made reluctantly. Schiller felt, and had reason to feel, that the modernity of his drama was its very life-blood;[1] for the squeamish Dalberg, however, the robbers in the age of Frederick the Great were a painful anachronism. So they were put back three centuries and costumed in the style of the ' Ritterstück '. Other less dubious changes were also made. Thus the long soliloquies of Franz and the ribald garrulities of Spiegelberg were reduced to more tolerable proportions. Robber Schwarz and Pastor Moser were omitted, and the bastard Hermann was vitalized into a person of some account by means of his counter-plot against Franz. The un-lyrical songs by which Schiller had

mad-house,—rolling eyes, clenched fists, stamping feet and hoarse shrieks from the spectators. Strangers fell sobbing into each other's arms, and women staggered to the door at the point of fainting. There was a general dissolution, as in chaos, from the mists of which a new creation bursts forth.' This description is perhaps the best possible antidote to Matthew Arnold's fastidious observation that ' The Robbers ' is violent and tiresome.

[1] In a letter of Dec. 12, 1781, to Dalberg, he admits the cogency of the objection to his horde of robbers ' in our enlightened century ' and virtually expresses regret that he had not himself, from the beginning, imagined an earlier date for the action. But he fears that to change the time, now that the piece is finished, will result in making it a monstrosity, a ' crow with peacock's feathers '.

set great store were dropped, and the catastrophe was so changed as to bring the two brothers finally face to face. The life of Schweizer was spared and Franz, instead of being torn limb from limb, was derisively pardoned by his great-souled brother and then, amid mocking laughter, thrust into the selfsame dungeon in which he had confined his father. Much against Schiller's will Amalia was made to kill herself with a dagger snatched from one of the outlaws, instead of receiving her death at the hands of her lover.

The prodigious success of ' The Robbers ' upon the Mannheim stage, and upon other stages where it was soon produced in more or less garbled form, made the work famous. Famous and at the same time notorious. New editions, most of them pirated, began to appear, and a mania similar to the Werther-mania of the previous decade spread over Germany. The newspapers told of conspiring schoolboys whose heads had been turned toward a career of crime. A well-born youth who had essayed the rôle of Robin Hood near Strassburg and was hanged there in October, 1783, confessed suspiciously that he had been brought to his fate by the reading of bad books. The sedate authorities of Leipzig forbade the further performance of the play in their city because they had observed a sudden increase of burglary and petit larceny. An edition of 1782, which the publisher, possibly without Schiller's knowledge, had adorned with a rampant lion and the motto *In Tirannos*, probably added to the vogue of the piece as a revolutionary document. A French translation appeared in 1785 and drew the attention of the turbulent Gauls to that ' Monsieur Gille ', who was in time to receive the diploma of a French citizen. The first English translation dates from 1792.

It is not difficult to imagine the emotions with which Schiller, now at the fervid age of twenty-two, returned to his post after that intoxicating visit to Mannheim, and, his ears still tingling with the thunderous plaudits of the theater and the complimentary babble of his new friends, resumed the dosing of his sick grenadiers in Stuttgart. For a while things went on very much as before. In order to better his position in a professional way, he formed the plan of taking his doctor's degree and then qualifying for a professorship in physiology. But from the first the poet in him prevailed more and more over the medical man. Soon after leaving the academy he had published a long elegy upon the death of a young friend named Weckerlin. It is a rebellious, declamatory poem, in which the pathos of untimely death is made the occasion for ventilating radical views as to the goodness of God and the consolations of religion. Passages like the following show the young Schiller at his best as a poet:

> Liebe wird Dein Auge nie vergolden,
> Nie umhalsen Deine Braut wirst Du,
> Nie, wenn unsere Thränen stromweis rollten,
> Ewig, ewig, ewig sinkt Dein Auge zu.[1]

For the rest, the death of Weckerlin is a ' discord on the great lute ', and a ' barbarous doom '. And yet,

---

[1] " Love gilds not for thee all the world with its glow,
Never Bride in the clasp of thine arms shall repose ;
Thou canst see not our tears, though in torrents they flow,
Those eyes in the calm of eternity close."—*Bulwer's Translation.*

the poem continues, the dead youth has drawn the better lot; he will sleep calmly in his narrow house, unmindful of the wretched tragi-comedy going on above his head. So his friends are bidden 'to clap their hands and shout a loud *plaudite*'. As for a reunion, there will be one, but it will not be in the 'paradise of the rabble'.—In another poem dating from this period, 'The Chariot of Venus,' the love-goddess is put on trial and castigated for her sins. Her havoc among the sons of men is described in half a hundred rhetorical stanzas which were evidently inspired by the genius of the clinic or the hospital, rather than by one of the sacred nine.

Besides these poems a large number of others were written by Schiller during the year 1781, prior to the time when Dalberg's invitation caused him to turn his attention to the stage. It was of course important to acquaint the public with his lucubrations, but poetry in large quantities was not an easily marketable commodity. The usual mode of publication was the poetic 'almanac' or 'calendar', in which a number of ambitious verse-makers would unite their wares in a single volume. Of such almanacs there were several in Germany and one at least in Suabia. It was edited by one Stäudlin, a rival whom Schiller thought it would be both feasible and pleasant to outshine. So he sent out letters to his friends inviting contributions, and in due time there appeared, after a fresh outlay of borrowed money, an 'Anthology for the Year 1782'. It consisted of some four-score poems, signed with all manner of intentionally misleading symbols and purporting to emanate from Tobolsko, in Siberia. The most of the verses were the work of Schiller.[1]

Among the poems of the 'Anthology' there are none that have become very popular, none that are capable of affording any very keen delight to the lover of poetry. One sees that their author's lyric gift was not of the highest order. What is heard is not so much the note of honest feeling as the effort of an active intellect, searching heaven and earth for clever and striking things to say. Instead of learning from the folk-song, Schiller had learned originally from Klopstock; and what he had learned was to pose and philosophize and invest fictitious sentiment with a maze of bewildering and far-fetched imagery. Then he had lost sympathy with Klopstock's religiosity, had acquired a better opinion of the things of sense, and had had his introduction to doubt and disgust and rebellion. When now these moods sought expression in verse, the verse took the form of impassioned rhetoric. He sang not as the bird sings, but as a fervid youth sings who is eager to assert as strongly as possible his emancipation from conventional modes of thought and feeling.

The poems of the 'Anthology' are too numerous and in the main too unimportant for an exhaustive review; it must suffice to glance at a few of the more noteworthy. Several had been written at the academy and were now published with more or less of retouch-

---

[1] As different poems undoubtedly Schiller's were variously signed, and as many of his youthful effusions were excluded by him from the collection of 1801, the sifting out of his share in the 'Anthology' and the ascription of the remaining poems to their proper authors are tasks of no small difficulty. The critical student should consult Weltrich, I, 501 ff.

ing.   To this number, it would seem, belongs the one
entitled ‘ The Glory of Creation ’, which is a perfectly
serious and devout poem on the grandeur and beauty
of the world.   Along with this, however, we find
another, entitled ‘ To God ’, which tells of moods like
those which had led Werther to characterize Nature
as ‘ an eternally ruminating monster ’.   It consists of
five unrimed stanzas, all but one ending with an em-
phatic ‘ Thou big thing ’.

> Thou who didst summon earth and sky,
>   And earth and sky came forth ;
> Who sayest the word and worlds arise,
>   Who art thou, mighty thing ?
>
> O big, amazingly big thing !
>   My head swims when I look ;
> I shudder and start back afraid
>   And fall — upon my knees.

These verses—the translation may hold up its head
quite unabashed beside the original—hardly rise above
the plane of doggerel ; they signify nothing except that
their author has had his little quarrel with this best of
all possible worlds and is not unwilling to shock
people.

Of far greater poetic interest are the verses entitled
‘ Rousseau ’, whose neglected grave (he died in 1778)
is made the point of departure for a vigorous denunciation of the bigotry that had driven him from place to
place and denied him peace among the living.   The
poem foresees a time when streams of blood shall flow
for the honor of calling him son.   There is no effort

at portraiture, and no suggestion of any repellent or
pitiable traits.[1] We get not Byron's "self-torturing
sophist", but a martyred sage who suffered and died
at the hands of Christians,—'he who makes out of
Christians human beings'. Toward the end he is
apostrophized as the 'Great Endurer', and bidden to
leap joyously into Charon's boat and go tell the spirits
about this 'dream of the war of frogs and mice, the
hand-organ doodle-doodle of this life'.[2]

In this poem there is certainly no lack of that 'fire'
which Duke Karl found in Schiller's dissertation.
Indeed fire abounds everywhere in his youthful versifying. He never contemplates, never dwells upon a
temperate emotion. The poetry of common things
and of the gentler feelings seems to have been non-
existent for him. His imagination likes to occupy
itself with the supernal, the stupendous, or else with
the awful and the revolting. This is seen in the two
poems 'Elysium' and 'A Group from Tartarus'; the
one aiming to portray a land of ineffable happiness,
where sorrow has no name and the only pain is a
gentle ecstasy, the other depicting the infinite misery
of the inferno. In both there is a free blending of

[1] Schiller seems to have got his idea of Rousseau chiefly from H. P.
Sturz's "Denkwürdigkeiten von Johann Jakob Rousseau" (1779). The
famous 'Confessions' did not begin to appear until 1781. Curiously
enough our poem refers to Rousseau as 'suckled on the banks of the
Seine', and as having 'stood like a meteor on the banks of the Garonne'.

[2] Geh, du Opfer dieses Trillingsdrachen,
   Hüpfe freudig in den Todesnachen,
      Grosser Dulder, frank und frei !
   Geh, erzähl' dort in der Geister Kreise
   Diesen Traum vom Krieg der Frösch' und Mäuse,
      Dieses Lebens Jahrmarktsdudelei.

Christian with pagan conceptions, 'Elysium' being put for heaven and 'Tartarus' for hell. A similar blending is noticeable in many of the other poems, ancient mythology being made to furnish forth the setting and the symbols of modern passion. So it is, for example, in the lyric operetta 'Semele', the longest and most pretentious of the 'Anthology' poems. It consists of two scenes in irregular verses, dealing with Jupiter's love for the mortal Semele and Juno's jealousy. Artistically it is much in need of the file, and its sustained note of passionate pathos hardly comports, perhaps, with the type of the operetta. Nevertheless it contains powerful passages and telling stage effects. One can see that the young student—'Semele' appears to have been written at the academy—had learned, through his occasional visits to the opera, how to manage a conventional theme and conventional machinery in such a way as to startle and thrill.

More noteworthy, for the characterization of the youthful Schiller, is the ode entitled 'Friendship', which purports to be taken 'from the letters of Julius to Raphael, an unpublished novel'. In this poem we have not so much the expression of a real human affection as a philosophy of friendship; just as in the Laura poems we have a philosophy of love. The verses remind one immediately of Rousseau's saying that he was 'intoxicated with love without an object'. Friendship is described as a mystic attraction of souls, identical with the attraction of gravitation. This it is which makes the beauty and the glory of the spiritual world. 'We are dead groups when we hate, gods when we love.'

> If in creation's All I stood alone,
> Souls would I dream into the senseless stone
> And kiss them in a fond embrace.

Then we hear of a hierarchy of spirits, ascending 'from the Mongol to the Greek seer, who precedes the last of the seraphs'; and in this harmonious ring-dance of souls Raphael and Julius 'sweep onward to where time and space are submerged in the sea of eternal glory'.

Other poems which rise above the general level are 'The Bad Monarchs', a poetic castigation (without mention of names) of the type of ruler perfectly exemplified by Duke Karl of Württemberg, up to about the year 1770; 'In a Battle', a powerful description of the rage of combat, with all its sickening and inspiring details; 'The Pestilence', a gruesome tribute to the power of God as manifested in the horrors of the plague, and 'Count Eberhard the Quarreler', a patriotic battle-ballad in honor of a locally renowned Suabian fighter. Better than any of these, however, from a poetic point of view, is the 'Funeral Fantasy', which was occasioned by the death of young Von Hoven in 1780. One may perhaps doubt the genuineness of the grief that could find expression in such a pomp of words, but there is no doubting the poetic power of pictures like this:

> Pale, at its ghastly noon,
> Pauses above the death-still wood the moon ;
>   The night-sprite sighing, through the dim air stirs ;
>   The clouds descend in rain ;
>   Mourning, the wan stars wane,
>   Flickering like dying lamps in sepulchres !

Haggard as spectres, vision-like and dumb,
　　Dark with the pomp of Death, and moving　slow,
Towards that sad lair the pale Procession come
　　Where the Grave closes on the Night below.[1]

But the most famous and on the whole the most interesting of the effusions in the ' Anthology ' are the erotic verses addressed to Laura.　Whether Schiller was humanly in love with his landlady, Frau Luise Vischer, is a rather futile question which German erudition has argued pro and con these many years without coming to an inexpugnable conclusion.　Probably he was not, though he may have thought that he was. If he had been we should have heard of it sooner or later in authentic prose.　But she interested him as the first of her sex who had come under his close observation.　There were on his part the small gallantries of daily life, and on hers the responsiveness of a not very prudish widow quite willing to be adored.　She played the piano.　It was enough: the needy Petrarch had found a sufficient Laura—and never was a poet's goddess worshiped in such singular strains.　We miss in them altogether that captivating simplicity which the young Goethe, and later the young Heine, caught from the songs of the people.　Schiller is always in pursuit of the intense, the extraordinary, the ecstatic, and sometimes fails to impress through sheer superabundance of the impressive.　His imagination wanders between a wild sensuality,—so lubricious in its suggestions, now and then, as to occasion gossip to the effect that he had become a libertine,—and a sublimated phi-

---

[1] Bulwer's translation, which is here particularly good.

losophy based on Platonic conceptions of a prenatal
existence, or upon Leibnitzian conceptions of a pre-
established harmony.   But while the Laura poems are
sufficiently sensual, they are not sensuous; or if they
try to be, the sensuous element is unreal and unimaginable.   Some of them, with their overstrained
vehemence of expression, their fervid and far-fetched
tropes, their involved and sometimes obscure diction,
are little more than intellectual puzzles: they so occupy
the mind in the mere effort of comprehension that little
room is left for any emotion whatever.   They leave
one altogether cold.

A 'Fantasie to Laura' identifies the rapturous
passion with the force of gravitation which holds
planets and systems in order.   'Blot it out from the
mechanism of nature and the All bursts asunder in
fragments; your worlds thunder into chaos; weep,
Newtons, for their giant fall!'   And then Laura's
kiss!

> Aus den Schranken schwellen alle Sehnen,
>   Seine Ufer überwallt das Blut ;
> Körper will in Körper überstürzen,
>   Lodern Seelen in vereinter Glut.[1]

When Laura plays the piano, her adorer stands
there, one moment an exanimate statue, the next a
disembodied spirit,—while the listening zephyrs murmur
more softly in reverence.   In a 'Reproach to Laura'

[1] " Out from their bounds swell nerve, and pulse, and sense,
    The veins in tumult would their shores o'erflow ;
  Body to body rapt—and, charmèd thence,
    Soul drawn to soul with intermingled glow."
                              —*Bulwer's Translation.*

she is taxed with being the ruin of her lover's ambition. Because of her the 'giant has shriveled to a dwarf'. She has 'blown away the mountains', that he had 'rolled up' to the sunny heights of glory. In another poem, 'Mystery of Reminiscence', we hear of a cosmic golden age in which Laura, one with her poet, was a part of the Godhead. One and yet two, they swept through space in unimaginable ecstasy. Somehow,—the point is not made very clear,—there came a great cataclysm and separated them. Now they are beautiful fragments of the God, evermore yearning to restore the lost unity:

> Darum Laura dieses Wutverlangen,
> Ewig starr an deinen Mund zu hangen,
> Und die Wollust deinen Hauch zu trinken,
> In dein Wesen, wenn sich Blicke winken,
> Sterbend zu versinken.[1]

Without lingering longer over the erotic poems of the 'Anthology', one may say that they are characterized, like 'The Robbers', by a fiery intensity of expression which, in the search after the sublime, occasionally passes the bounds of good taste. Their author already has at his command a gorgeous poetic diction that is all his own. One is often amazed at his mere command of words, the audacity of his tropes, the sweep of his imagination. But he does not convince. When at his best he only produces an impression of magnificent feigning. The reader soon sees

[1] " And therefore came to me the wish to woo thee—
Still, lip to lip, to cling for aye unto thee;
This made thy glances to my soul the link—
This made me burn thy very breath to drink—
My life in thine to sink." —*Bulwer's Translation.*

that, notwithstanding all the impassioned hyperboles, it is really intellectual poetry,—a youth philosophizing about his passion. And the philosophy is little more than a matter of fine-sounding but vacuous analogies that have no root in the facts of experience.[1] And so the poetry does not take hold of one. Nor does it charm with its music; there is vigor and sweep and swing, but the subtler elements of melodious verse are lacking.

These qualities of the youthful Schiller's poetry foretell that he will never be a great lyrist, but they promise well enough for the poetic tale. This promise is seen notably in the poem called ' The Infanticide '. It is a gruesome thing, with the pathos here and there overstrained, but what a power of vivid narration! What a gift for the portraiture of frenzied passion! For the rest, it should not go unrecorded that certain poems of the ' Anthology ' went altogether too far in the defiance of conventional morality. The study of medicine, combined with the ardor of youthful revolt and the seductions of a new bohemian life, had so sensualized the mind of Schiller that, for a brief period in his career, he found pleasure in exploiting the in-decent. It was but a passing phase, and not very bad at its worst. Still, if Heine, and the other emanci-pators of the flesh who came later, had felt the need of supporting their cause by an appeal to distinguished authority, they might have referred quite unabashed to the youthful sins of the idealist Schiller.

[1] Concerning the provenience and the philosophic connection of the youthful Schiller's ideas of love and friendship the reader will do well to consult Kuno Fischer, " Schiller-Schriften ", I, 41 ff.

Little notice was taken of the ' Anthology ' even in Suabia, and none at all, apparently, in the outside German world.   The investment brought no immediate returns in fame or in money, and other experiments of a different character turned out but little better.

As early as the spring of 1781 Schiller had assumed the editorial charge of a would-be popular magazine intended to contribute to the ' benefit and pleasure ' of the Suabians.   It was a weak provincial affair that soon died of inanition.   The hack-work that Schiller did for it is of no biographical interest, save that it brought him into connection with Suabian writers and suggested to him that with a freer hand he might produce a better journal.   In the following year, accordingly, we find him starting, in conjunction with his friends Abel and Petersen, the *Wirtemberg Repertory of Literature*.   It was to be a quarterly, and bore the ominous legend: ' at the expense of the editors '.   To this journal Schiller contributed various essays and reviews which show that as a critic he had been influenced by Lessing, but had not acquired the knack of Lessing's luminous and straightforward style.   In a rather badly written paper on ' The Present Condition of the German Theater ', he takes up a question which was destined to interest him later,—that of the relation of the drama to morality.   He has no difficulty in showing that people are not deterred from the vices or impelled to the virtues that they see represented on the stage.

But by far the most important of these contributions to the *Repertory* are two reviews (of course anonymous) of his own writings.   In a long notice of ' The Robbers ' he discusses the work with a coolness that is simply amazing. His own child has become a *corpus vile* that he has the nerve to dissect without the slightest tremor of parental sympathy. Nearly everything that a century's criticism has found to urge against the play,— the dubiousness of the entire invention, the impossibility of such a devil as Franz, the insipidity of Amalia and the old Count Moor, the faults of the diction and the barbarism of the action,—is here set forth with remorseless severity. The review closes with the facetious comment which appears at the head of this chapter. Not quite so caustic is the notice of the 'Anthology', but it contains a significant 'admonition to our young poets' to the effect that 'extravagance is not strength, that violation of the rules of taste and propriety is not boldness and originality, that fancy is not feeling, and high-flown rhetoric is not the talisman on which the arrows of criticism break and recoil'.

Verily it is not given every young author to see himself thus clearly in the glass of criticism. We may guess, however, that these critical mystifications were not altogether free from the element of calculating humbug. Schiller knew full well that to be castigated in public would not be a bad thing for his budding reputation; and so, as no one else came forward to do the slashing, he did it himself. It is amusing to read that a Frankfurt correspondent was so pained by the review of 'The Robbers' that he sent in a defence of the piece and was greatly surprised to learn that reviewer and author were one and the same person.

These contributions to the *Repertory* appeared in the first two numbers; before the third came out Schiller

had turned his back for good and all upon his native
Württemberg. Ever since that first visit to Mannheim
he had felt drawn to the ' Greek climate of the Palatinate'. On the 1st of April, 1782, we find him writing
to Dalberg that it ' would be untrue were he to deny
his growing inclination for the drama'. The letter
goes on to say that he was then expecting to be very
much occupied, for several months, with medical
studies; but he hoped to finish a new play, ' Fiesco ',
by the end of the year. Toward the end of May,
taking advantage of the absence of the duke, he visited
Mannheim again and saw a second representation of
' The Robbers '. Through the indiscreet gossip of the
friends who accompanied him, the duke got wind of
this unauthorized journey, ordered ' the deserter ' under
arrest for two weeks, and forbade him all further intercourse with foreign parts.

Schiller made use of his enforced leisure to work
upon ' Fiesco ', and to plan a third drama, ' Louise
Miller ', which promised a chance of revenge upon
the petty tyrant who sought to own him body and
soul. After serving his time in the guard-house he
wrote an urgent appeal to Dalberg, to rescue him
from his intolerable situation by giving him employment at Mannheim. But Dalberg, a fearsome and
politic creature, had no mind to compromise himself
by befriending a youth who had quarreled with the
powerful duke of Württemberg. Schiller now began
to think of running away, and his thoughts were soon
quickened into resolution by fresh exasperations.

In the second act of ' The Robbers ' he had made
Spiegelberg refer to the Swiss canton of the Grisons as

the 'Athens of modern scalawags.' Tradition has it that the passage was a thrust at an unpopular Swiss overseer in the academy. It is probable, however, that it was in no way malicious, but merely a thoughtless jest at the expense of a canton which had actually got a bad reputation for lax enforcement of the law. Be this as it may, the passage gave offence to a patriotic Swiss named Amstein, who aired his grievance in print and demanded a retraction. When Schiller paid no attention to this, Amstein appealed to one Walter, a fussy official living at Ludwigsburg. Walter took up the case of the traduced canton with great zeal, and brought it to the attention of the duke. The result was a summons to Schiller, a sharp reproof, and an order to write no more 'comedies'. He was to confine himself strictly to medicine or he would be cashiered.

Matters now came swiftly to a head. On September 1, 1782, Schiller addressed to his sovereign a very humble letter of remonstrance, setting forth that his authorship had added more than five hundred florins to his income,[1] and that this money was absolutely necessary for the prosecution of his studies; that he was winning reputation and thus bringing honor to the academy and to its illustrious founder, and so forth. The duke's reply was to threaten him with arrest in case he should write any more letters upon this subject. Schiller now resolved to take his fate in his own hands. Resistance and submission to the autocrat were alike out of the question; the only recourse was flight from Württemberg.

[1] Of course this roseate statement to his Highness took no account of his debts, which had not yet begun to be particularly pressing.

In the days of German absolutism, this was a dangerous step to take. Technically he would be a deserter. He had reason to fear that he would not be allowed to make his way in the world by his own merit, unharmed and unhelped, but would be dogged by the malice of a despot and perhaps brought back to undergo the fate of Schubart. Worse still was the possibility that his father might be made to suffer from the duke's anger. Nevertheless he resolved to take the risk. He made known his purpose to a very few friends, one of whom, Frau von Wolzogen, offered him her house in Bauerbach, in the event of his sometime needing a quiet refuge. Another friend, Andreas Streicher, nobly offered to share his fortunes. Streicher, to whom we owe a classical account of this episode in Schiller's life, was a young musician living with his mother in Stuttgart. It had been planned that he should visit Hamburg in the near future, but he now persuaded his mother to advance him the money that was to have been devoted to his journey, in order that he might accompany his beloved Schiller into exile. So the friends bided their time and meanwhile ' Fiesco ' made rapid progress.

The wished-for opportunity came on the 22nd of September. The court was in a flutter over the visit of a Russian prince for whose reception great preparations had been made. In the general excitement Schiller counted upon getting away unobserved. So he bade a tearful farewell to his mother and sisters, who knew of the secret that had been kept away from the father for reasons of policy, and in the evening he drove out of Stuttgart with his friend Streicher, giving to the guard the names of Dr. Ritter and Dr. Wolf. The friends set their faces northward towards Mannheim.   As they passed the brilliantly illuminated Castle Solitude, so Streicher relates, Schiller fell into a long revery.   At last the exclamation ' My Mother! ' told the tale of his thoughts.   But the mood of sadness did not last long.   Cheerful talk enlivened the journey, and when the two travellers crossed the boundary of the Palatinate Schiller was jubilant.   He felt that he had entered a land of freedom and enlightenment, where art was esteemed and talent honored.

He had with him, virtually complete, the manuscript of the new play upon which he had built illusory hopes. It will be in order to consider ' Fiesco ' before we follow its author into the vicissitudes of his exile.

CHAPTER IV

The Conspiracy of Fiesco at Genoa

Ein Diadem erkämpfen ist grosz ; es wegwerfen ist göttlich.
                                                        ' *Fiesco*'.

As we have seen, ' Fiesco ' was written during the
summer and fall of 1782. The following winter,
having been rejected by the Mannheim stage, it was
published as a literary drama. This first edition bore
the sub-title: ' A Republican Tragedy.'

There is a very general agreement that ' Fiesco ' is
upon the whole the weakest of Schiller's plays. As a
' republican tragedy ' it is a disappointment, since
its political import, though obvious enough to one
acquainted with Schiller from other sources, is not
brought out distinctly in the play itself. Neither the
friend nor the enemy of republicanism, in any historical
or human sense of the word, can derive the slightest
edification from ' Fiesco.' The political talk is vague
and unpractical, and we get no clear idea of the contending forces. When the curtain goes down upon the
chaos of intrigue, one is at a loss to know how one is
expected to feel. And yet the play is full of powerful
scenes, developed with masterly dramatic skill. As a
mere spectacle it rivals ' The Robbers ', to which as a
drama it is decidedly inferior. In general its defects

strike the reader more than the spectator. It is not the hand of the dramatist but the eye of the historian that is lacking. In other words the author, with all his seeming profundity of philosophic reflection, was simply not ripe for historical tragedy.

The bare facts of Fiesco's conspiracy, related with as little ascription of motive as possible, are these: In the year 1528 Andrea Doria, who had won great distinction as an admiral in the French service, but had now quarreled with the King of France and hoisted the colors of Emperor Charles the Fifth, landed an expedition in Genoa and captured the city from the French. Historians agree that he could easily have made himself sovereign, but instead of doing so he restored the old aristocratic republic, thus winning for himself the enduring title of 'father and liberator of his country.' Although Doria was simply an influential citizen of Genoa and enjoyed the general esteem of his countrymen, his prominence in the state gave rise to animosities among the noble families, and these were increased when he made his young and headstrong kinsman, Gianettino, his heir. In the year 1547 the malcontents found a leader in the person of Giovanni Ludovigi Fiesco, Count of Lavagna. Fiesco was young, handsome, rich and ambitious—a dashing and unscrupulous cavalier. His first thought was to restore the French domination and make himself only a viceroy of the French king; but a fellow conspirator, Verrina, persuaded him to seize for himself the sovereign power to which his rank and talents entitled him. The conspiracy was carefully matured, Fiesco meanwhile, to divert suspicion, acting the part of a giddy spendthrift and man of fashion. On the night of January 2, 1547, the conspirators made their attack upon the city. Gianettino Doria was killed, but the aged Andrea made his escape. The success of Fiesco appeared to be complete, but as he was going on board a galley the gang-plank turned, he fell into the sea and his heavy armor bore him down. Without a leader the conspiracy instantly collapsed. On the following day Andrea returned and the Genoese republic went on as before.

It was a hint from Rousseau that suggested to Schiller, during his last year in the academy, the idea of dramatizing this episode of Genoese history. In the German 'Memoirs of Rousseau' by H. P. Sturz, referred to in the preceding chapter, he found Rousseau quoted as follows:

The reason why Plutarch wrote such noble biographies is that he never selected half-great men, such as exist by the thousands in quiet states, but grand exemplars of virtue or sublime criminals. In modern history there is a man deserving of his brush, and that is Count Fiesco, whose training made him the very man to liberate his country from the rule of the Dorias. . . . There was no other thought in his soul than to dethrone the usurper.[1]

Here was a tempting theme for a young dramatist who had fed his own soul upon Plutarch, was enamored of 'greatness' in whatever form, and had already tried his hand upon a 'sublime criminal.' What could be better for his purpose than a daring conspiracy, led by

[1] Schiller refers to the quoted passage in his review of 'The Robbers', Schriften, II, 357. It has not been found in Rousseau's writings. Sturz drew from unpublished sources.

a Plutarchian hero who was at the same time a single-minded patriot ?   In his earliest musings it is probable that Schiller accepted Rousseau's view of Fiesco at its face value, and when he began to consult the historians he found at first some support for his preconception. Among his sources was the 'Conjuration du Comte de Fiesque', by De Retz; a book which was written, according to a somewhat doubtful tradition, when its author was but eighteen years old, and which, by its clever perversion of history and its subtle insinuation of revolutionary ideas, is said to have drawn from Richelieu the comment: 'There is a dangerous man!'[1] In the sophisticated narrative of De Retz Fiesco appears as a modern Brutus, whose thought of personal aggrandizement was altogether subordinate to the thought of his country's welfare.   He is made much better than he really was, and the two Dorias much worse.

Further study of the subject, however, soon opened the eyes of Schiller to the other side of the question; for in Robertson's 'Charles the Fifth' he found Fiesco portrayed as an ambitious revolutionist who sought to overthrow the Dorias only in order that he might make himself the master of Genoa—in short as a Catiline instead of a Brutus.   The dramatic problem then turned from the first upon the character of Fiesco.   In the 'Dramaturgie' of Lessing the doctrine had been proclaimed that the dramatist is not bound by the so-called facts of history; that he may

---

[1] On the character of De Retz's work, and its relation to the original of Mascardi, consult the Notes and Introduction by Chantelauze in Vol, V of the 'Grands Ecrivains' edition of De Retz, p. 475 ff,

deal with them as suits his artistic purpose. But what was the purpose to be in this case? Should it be a tragedy of austere patriotism going down against a relatively bad order too strong to be resisted, or a tragedy of corrupt ambition dashing itself to death against a relatively good order too strong to be over-thrown? Either conception, if consistently worked out, might have sufficed for the groundwork of a good historical tragedy. What Schiller did, however, was to vacillate between the two, to blend them in a con-fusing way, and finally to let the interest of his play turn largely upon the hero's mental struggle between selfish ambition and unselfish patriotism.

The Catiline conception required an avenger of Genoa, for it was evident[1] that the accidental drowning of Fiesco in the moment of his triumph would never do in a play. It was necessary that his death appear as a punishment, a nemesis. So for the rôle of avenger Schiller invented a stern patriot to whom, without his-torical warrant, he gave the name of Verrina. Verrina is the real Brutus. To furnish the conspirators with a definite grievance Gianettino was made to violate the helpless Bertha, who was then provided with an avenger in the person of the young Bourgognino. Leonora, the wife of Fiesco, is historical. Robertson relates that on the night of the uprising Fiesco went to take leave of his wife, " whom he loved with

[1] It was evident, that is, to Schiller. In the dedication of 'Fiesco' to Professor Abel he wrote : " Die wahre Katastrophe des Komplotts, worin der Graf durch einen unglücklichen Zufall am Ziel seiner Wünsche zu Grunde geht, muszte durchaus verändert werden, denn die Natur des Dramas duldet den Finger des Ungefährs oder der unmittelbaren Vorsehung nicht."

tender affection.'' He found her ''in all the anguish of uncertainty and fear ''; and her terror was increased when she learned what was on foot. She endeavored by her tears and entreaties and her despair to divert him from his purpose. But in vain; he left her with the exclamation: '' Farewell! You shall either never see me more, or you shall behold to-morrow everything in Genoa subject to your power.'' On the other hand, the intrigue of Fiesco and Julia, the sister of Gianettino, is unhistorical. It was invented by Schiller as a part of the general scheme of duplicity and frivolity by which Fiesco should seek to quiet the suspicion of the Dorias. If this particular invention was upon the whole unfortunate—the matter will be discussed further on,—the same cannot be said of the Moor Hassan, who becomes Fiesco's factotum and ends his career on the gallows. The rascally Moor is the most picturesque figure and the most telling rôle in the whole piece.

Schiller introduces Fiesco as a seemingly frivolous *roué*, flirting desperately with the Countess Julia, to the great torment of his wife Leonora. We soon see, however, that the frivolity is only a mask: he has a serious purpose and that purpose is to make himself master of Genoa. At first, indeed, he toys with the idea of a nobler fame. In a soliloquy at the end of the second act he exclaims: 'To conquer a diadem is grand; to throw it away is divine. Down, tyrant! Let Genoa be free and me be its happiest citizen!' But this mood does not long withstand the intoxication of power. To rule, to rule alone, to feel that Genoa owes everything to him only,—this soon becomes his all-absorbing ambition.   At the last, when the revolution has succeeded, he puts on the ducal purple and the people are ready to acquiesce in the new régime. But old Verrina is not so tractable.   When he cannot prevail upon Fiesco to doff the hateful insignia, he pushes him into the sea and exclaims in disgust: ' I am going to Andrea! '

Such a scheme, it is evident, does not provide for a ' republican tragedy ', except in a very loose sense.   If we had a republican idealist pitting his strength against a tyrant and going down in the battle, either because of his adversary's superior strength or because of some weakness in his own character, that would be a tragedy of republicanism.   In Schiller's play, however, the conflict is not of that character.   At heart Fiesco is never a republican, though he sometimes takes his mouth full of fine republican phrases.   His mainspring of action is not the welfare of Genoa, but his own aggrandizement.   Old Andrea, whose power he plots to overthrow and whose magnanimity puts him to shame, is actually a better man than he.   If he has a measure of our sympathy in his feud with the younger Doria, that is only because Gianettino is portrayed as a vulgar brute deserving of nothing but the gallows. Politically there is little to choose between the two, so long as we regard virtue as consisting in an unselfish devotion to an ideal of republican liberty.

The character of Fiesco being what it is, his final catastrophe produces no very clear impression.   One does not see precisely what bearing it is to have on the political fortunes of Genoa.   At first blush the conclusion seems to mean that the state has been saved from the clutches of a tyrant who was about to subvert its liberties. But if we look at the matter in that light we have a tragedy, not of republicanism, but of the "vaulting ambition which o'erleaps itself and falls on the other." With the usurper Fiesco, and the brute Gianettino, out of the way, the state returns to the good regimen of Andrea, who represents the only republicanism then thinkable, democracy in the modern sense being nowhere in question. But it is doubtful whether Schiller intends Fiesco to be thus reprobated. The hot-blooded Italian has certain traits that win sympathy; and even his consuming ambition is so invested with a glamour of romantic enthusiasm that it is difficult to reckon him among the dangerous tyrants. If he is false to his better nature, we at any rate see that he has a better nature. One is thus tempted to regard Verrina's act as that of a madman who cares more for form than for substance and sees danger where there is none.

For Verrina, who plays the part of Brutus to his country's Cæsar and seems to represent the sternest type of republican virtue, is a repulsive fanatic. The horrible curse that he pronounces upon his daughter when he hears that she has been outraged is significant at once for his character and for the young Schiller's notion of tragic pathos. Throwing a black veil over her head he vociferates thus:

Be blind! Accursed be the air that fans your cheek! Accursed be the sleep that refreshes you! Accursed be every human trace that is welcome to your misery! Go down into the deepest dungeon of my house! Moan! Howl! Drag out the time with your woe. Let your life be the slimy writhing of the dying worm,—the obstinate, crushing struggle between being and not-being.   And this curse shall rest upon you until Gianettino has gasped out his last breath.

After this it is difficult to look up to Verrina as a competent savior of society, however much one may sympathize with him in his private feud.   His cynical tergiversation at the end makes his previous conduct ridiculous.   It seems to say that he has been participating in a tragic farce which is now ended.   One might almost get the impression that the whole play is only a satire upon republican clap-trap.

Satire, however, was very far from Schiller's thoughts.   His enthusiasm for liberty was much too genuine to permit any trifling with the sacred theme. There is no doubt that he began 'Fiesco' supposing that it would prove a convenient setting for those inspiring ideas of liberty which he had absorbed from the reading of ancient history and of modern revolutionary literature.   They were vague and tumultuous ideas, which had very little relation to a definite theory of government, but he was very much in earnest with them, especially after his rasping experience with the Duke of Württemberg.   No one can mistake the autobiographic note in the speech of Bourgognino which closes the first act: 'I have long felt in my breast something that would not be satisfied.   Now of a sudden I know what it was.   (Springing up heroically) I have a tyrant.'   But the young dramatist had not proceeded far before he discovered that his ideal requirement was out of tune with the facts.   To represent Fiesco as a would-be liberator of his country was impossible without a violent perversion of history for which he was not prepared. Out of deference to history he was led to abase his hero into something like a Catilinarian conspirator. But he could not give up the idea of a republican tragedy; so he tried to save it by depicting his hero as a man who had it in him to become a noble liberator, but is corrupted by the dazzling lures of power and so led on to ruin.

There are those who regard Fiesco's inconsistency as an artistic complexity of motive going to show that Schiller had progressed in the knowledge of life and become aware that human heroism is apt to be more or less mixed with base alloy. One writer [1] thinks it shows "how intelligently he had studied the Italian Renaissance and how correctly he had grasped its spirit." But this is to give him a credit that he does not fully deserve. The simple truth is that 'Fiesco' was written very hastily and that its author had spent precious little time in studying the Italian Renaissance, though it must be admitted that he possessed a remarkable gift for visualizing the little that he had read. Complexity of motive is all very well,—very human and very Italian; but the difficulty is that in this case it is not properly subordinated to a luminous dramatic idea. When a man's motives become so complex and contradictory that one does not know how to take him, he ceases to be available for the higher purposes of tragedy. That 'Fiesco' produces this bewildering effect is due to the fact that the inner logic of the piece had not been fully and consistently thought out when the writing began.

And this is not all. The author seems unable to

[1] H. H. Boyesen, in his biography of Schiller, Chapter III.

control and guide the unruly spirits whom he has
conjured into life. There is no lucid grouping of
historical forces. France, Germany and the Pope
stand dimly in the background like mechanical puppets, and we never learn what they severally represent
in relation to Genoese politics. Gianettino pulls a
string and has a sanction for the wholesale murder of
his countrymen. Fiesco pulls another string and gets
men and galleys ad libitum. We do not see an intelligible clash of great political ideas, but a wild
mêlée, in the outcome of which we have no reason to
be particularly interested. It is all as little tragic as
a back-country vendetta, or a factional fight in the
halls of a modern parliament.

How loosely the play is articulated, and how little
of logical compulsion there is in the catastrophe, is
shown with fatal clearness by Schiller's procedure in
revising his work for the Mannheim stage. By a few
strokes of the pen at the end he changed its entire
character. In the original draft his vacillating mind
had leaned more and more decisively towards the
Catilinarian conception of his hero, and the book-ver-
sion of 1783 was accordingly supplied with a motto
from Sallust's ‘ Catiline.’ The sentence runs: *Nam
id facinus imprimis ego memorabile existimo, sceleris
atque periculi novitate.* So the conspiracy was to be a
facinus and a *scelus*, and the hero, of course, another
‘ exalted criminal ’ in the style of Karl Moor. In the
stage version we observe that the motto from Sallust
has been dropped, and that while the title of ‘ tragedy ’
(*Trauerspiel*) is retained, the adjective ‘ republican ’ is
omitted. Furthermore, without any radical revision

of the preceding portraiture taken as a whole, a non-tragical conclusion has been substituted for the final catastrophe. Fiesco, hard pressed by the strenuous Verrina, declares that his heart has been right all along; only he was resolved that Genoa's freedom should be his work and his alone. So he breaks his scepter, concludes an eternal friendship with the amazed Verrina, and bids the people embrace their 'happiest fellow-citizen.' Thus the original version, which had called itself a republican tragedy and was a tragedy without being republican, became a play which is truly republican without being called so, but is no longer a tragedy.

This singular *volte-face* on the part of our dramatist has of course been the subject of infinite discussion. The most of the critics appear to regard it as a mistake, to say the least. One of them, Bellermann,[1] surmises that Schiller made the change against his will to meet the views of Dalberg. But of this there is no clear proof; and surely we cannot suppose that Schiller would have consented even reluctantly to a change which he himself felt to be utterly absurd because a complete stultification of the preceding plot. He must have felt that the new ending was artistically at least possible. And so it is. It is with ' Fiesco ' somewhat as with the Bible: the conclusion that one reaches must

[1] "Schillers Dramen," Berlin, 1898, I, 111 ff. Bellermann, who defends through thick and thin the unity and consistency of the original ' Fiesco', thinks that it is from first to last a tragedy of vaulting ambition,—not a political play at all, but a character play,—and that no other idea ever entered Schiller's mind. But his argument is anything but convincing and he carefully refrains from all discussion of the tell-tale phrase, 'a republican tragedy '.

depend upon the particular texts that one selects for emphasis. If we accent certain passages and pass lightly over others, we get the impression that it is a tragedy of selfish ambition doomed to disaster. If we accent a different set of passages, we are sure that it is a drama of republican idealism, sorely tempted by autocratic ambition, but destined to triumph finally over the baser motive. In the one view Verrina is a virtuous patriot; in the other he is a mad fanatic who does not understand the greatness of his chief. After Fiesco declares in soliloquy,—when a dramatic character is supposed to speak his real sentiments if anywhere,—that it is far nobler to renounce a diadem than to win it, we are certainly justified in expecting that he will seek the higher glory for himself. Thus either ending is possible, and which is the better is mainly a question of stage effect. Neither is historical, and neither gives a republican tragedy.

It would be pedantic indeed to have devoted so many words to a mere matter of name. If a drama is good it signifies but little what we call it, or whether its title be exactly appropriate. In this case, however, we have to do with a vital defect and not merely with a misnomer. A play may be good in different ways; and what the preceding criticism is intended to bring out is the fact that the strength of 'Fiesco', such as it has, does not lie in the intellectual organization of the whole. The mind of Schiller, but little trained hitherto upon historical studies, had not yet learned how to extract a clear poetic essence from a confused medley of recorded facts and opinions. Nature had endowed

him with a vivid imagination for details, but study had
not yet fitted him to exercise in a large and luminous
way the sovereignty of the artist. His facts confused
him and pulled him this way and that. And so we
miss in ' Fiesco ' that ' monumental fresco-painting ',
as it has been called, which constitutes the charm of his
riper historical dramas.

But average play-goers are wont to bother their
heads but little over these questions of higher artistic
import which are apt to bulk so large before the mind
of the literary critic. There are hundreds of literary
dramas that are impossible or deadly dull upon the
stage; and conversely dramatic talent will often make
an interesting play out of a succession of scenes that
lead the philosophic mind nowhither. If ' Fiesco '
remains a fairly good stage-play, it is because the
interest turns not upon its ultimate import, but upon its
elaborate intrigue, its exciting situations and its general
picturesqueness. The intrigue carries one along by
its very audacity, notwithstanding that in the light of
reason much of it appears rather absurd. Thus we
wonder how a mere brute like Gianettino can have
become such a power in the state right under the eyes
of the wise and good Andrea, who is subject to no
illusions with regard to him. No objection can be
made to Fiesco's mask of gayety and cynicism in the
first two acts, for that is historical. But was it necessary for him to deceive and torture the wife to whom
in the end he appears loyally devoted ? In any case
it is clear that the exposition should have hinted somehow at the true condition of affairs, for it is a good old
rule that while the people on the stage may disguise

themselves and befool one another as they will, the
audience must be kept posted.

As it is, there is no suggestion of make-believe in
Fiesco's courting of Julia.   When he exclaims in soliloquy that she loves him and he ' envies no god ', one
is justified in assuming that chivalrous devotion to
his wife is not among his virtues.   It is to be supposed, apparently, that he makes love to Julia in
order to be seen of men; but as a matter of fact
nothing comes of his flirtation except the torture of
his wife.   No one is deceived whom it was important
for him to deceive, and the whole incident serves only
to put his character in a dubious light.   Is this what
Schiller intended ?   Did he feel that his hot-blooded
Italian should not be made too much of an idealist in
his relation to women ?   Did he wish it to be understood that Fiesco is honestly infatuated with the
voluptuous Julia until he learns of her attempt to poison
his wife ?   These are queries to which the play gives
no very clear answer.   So far as the conspiracy is
concerned the whole affair with Julia is rather badly
motivated.

Still more dubious, from a rational point of view, is
Fiesco's relation to the Moor.   That a man having
large political designs requiring secrecy and fidelity
should, on the spur or the moment, choose as his confidential agent a venal scoundrel who has just tried to
murder him, is, to say the least, a little improbable.
Here Schiller was evidently trying to Shaksperize
again; trying, that is, to assert the poet's sovereign
lordship over the petty bonds of Philistine logic.   The
Moor's frank exposition of the professional ethics of

rascality, the dash with which he does his work, his ubiquitous serviceableness, and his rogue's humor make him a picturesque character and account for his having become on the stage the most popular figure in the piece; but that Fiesco should be willing to trust himself and his cause to such a scamp, and that such remarkable results should be achieved by the black man's kaleidoscopic activity, brings into the play an element of buffoonery that injures it on the serious side. The daring play of master and man excites a certain interest in their game, but it is impossible to care very much who wins. From a dramaturgic point of view, however, the Moor is a very useful invention, since Fiesco is thereby enabled to direct the whole conspiracy from his palace, and at the same time, in the person of his lieutenant, to be in every part of the city. Thus the action is concentrated and changes of scene are avoided.

As a portrayer of female character the author of ' Fiesco ' has clearly made some progress since his first lame attempt in ' The Robbers ', but the improvement is by no means dazzling. Both Leonora and Julia are singular creatures, and their unaccountableness is not of the right feminine kind that offers an attractive rôle to a good actress. Why should the Countess Fiesco, herself an aristocrat and a woman with heroic blood in her veins, submit so meekly in her own house to the coarse effrontery of the woman who has wronged her? We get the impression that she is only a crushed flower,—a helpless, wan-cheeked thing, with nothing womanly about her except her jealousy. And then, at the end, she suddenly develops into a heroine.

And what a strange heroine! No one will chide her for resorting on the fatal night to the protection of male attire,—a good enough Shaksperian device,—but how remarkable that a woman wandering crazily in the dark, and already sufficiently disguised, should borrow a tell-tale cloak and a worse than useless sword from a corpse that she happens to stumble upon! No wonder that Schiller in revising for the stage decided to let Leonora live rather than provide for her death by such a stagy *tour de force*. In the stage version, however, she does not reappear after the parting scene, and so we are left to wonder why she was introduced at all.

In Madame Julia we have a type of woman who was meant to be repulsive, and so far forth the young artist must be admitted to have wrought successfully. She is somewhat minutely described as a 'tall and plump widow of twenty-five; a proud coquette, her beauty spoiled by its oddity; dazzling and not pleasing, and with a wicked, cynical expression.' That such a woman should befool Fiesco and rejoice in her triumph is quite thinkable, but her qualities are those which usually go with a certain amount of discretion. That she should suddenly lose her head and throw herself away in a voluptuous frenzy hardly comports with the type. Nor is there anything in the inventory of her qualities that prepares us for her sudden assumption of the rôle of poisoner, when she is already, as she must suppose, the mistress of the situation. In her altercation with Leonora in the second scene of Act II she uses a number of coarse expressions befitting a woman of vulgar birth,—wherein some of the critics see an evidence of Schiller's unfamiliarity with the ways of refined ladies. It is quite possible, however, that we have to do instead with a realistic attempt to make her language match the essential vulgarity of her character. At any rate it is interesting to know that the scene was offensive to Schiller himself. He worked upon it with repugnance and was glad to be able to omit it entirely from the stage version.[1]

In respect of its diction ' Fiesco ' is in no way essentially different from ' The Robbers ', albeit some have imagined that a faint improvement is discernible. There is the same tearing of passion to tatters, the same predilection for florid rhetoric in the sentimental passages, and for frenzied talk and action in passages of more violent emotion. When Fiesco discovers that he has killed his wife, he first thrashes about him furiously with his sword. Then he gnashes his teeth at God in heaven and expresses himself thus: ' If I only had His universe between my teeth, I feel in a mood to tear all nature into a grinning monster having the semblance of my pain.' In his final expostulation with the would-be tyrant, Verrina delivers himself of this sentence: ' Had I too been such an honest dolt as not to recognize the rogue in you, Fiesco, by all the horrors of eternity, I would twist a cord out of my own intestines and throttle you with it, so that my fleeing soul should bespatter you with yeasty foam-bubbles.'

No wonder that critics and actors alike were offended by such insanity of rant and that Schiller himself soon saw the folly of it. He had got the idea that when a man is figuratively ' beside himself ', the most effective

[1] This appears from a letter of Sept. 29, 1783, to Dalberg.

way to portray his state of feeling is to make him talk and act like a veritable madman.   He had yet to learn the profound wisdom, for poets as well as actors, of Hamlet's rule to "acquire and beget, in the whirlwind of passion, a temperance that may give it smoothness."

CHAPTER V

The Fugitive in Hiding

Ich kann nicht Fürstendiener sein.—'*Don Carlos*'.

WHEN Schiller arrived at Mannheim, in the latter part of September, 1782, he was soon made aware that he had reckoned badly on the 'Greek climate of the Palatinate'. The friends to whom he showed himself were shocked at the audacity of his conduct; they could only advise him to conciliate the Duke of Württemberg and meanwhile to keep out of sight. So he wrote another very humble letter to his sovereign, explaining the desperate circumstances that had led to his flight and offering to return on condition of being allowed to continue his authorship. This letter he sent to his general, Augé, asking his mediation. In due time Augé replied, advising him to return, as the duke was 'graciously minded.' But this was not enough; Schiller knew his man too well and had probably never expected that his appeal would have any other effect than possibly to mollify the duke a little and thus avert trouble for Captain Schiller.

The fugitive had fixed all his hopes on the production of 'Fiesco' at the Mannheim theater. The manager, Meyer, was well disposed toward him, and it was soon arranged that Schiller should read his new play to a company of actors. The reading turned out a dismal failure. One by one the distressed auditors withdrew, wondering if what they heard was really the work of the same man who had written ' The Robbers '. The next day Meyer looked over the manuscript by himself and saw that it was not so bad after all; it had merely been murdered in the reading by its author's bad voice and extravagant declamation. But the decision did not rest with the friendly Meyer; it rested with Dalberg, who was just then away from home. Meanwhile, as reports came from Stuttgart to the effect that Schiller's disappearance had caused a great sensation and that there was talk of pursuit, or of a possible demand for his extradition, the two friends thought it best not to remain in Mannheim. Schiller did not actually believe that the duke would pursue him, but there was no telling; it was best to be on the safe side.

Accordingly ' Dr. Ritter ' and ' Dr. Wolf ' set out for Frankfurt. From there Schiller addressed a pathetic letter to Dalberg, setting forth that he was in great distress and asking for an advance of money against the first performance of ' Fiesco '. But the cautious Dalberg, who had just been in Stuttgart, replied coolly that ' Fiesco ' was unsuited to the stage and would need to be radically revised. So the luckless author, having no other recourse, returned to the village of Oggersheim, in the vicinity of Mannheim, and there, with the faithful Streicher to keep him company, he spent the next few weeks, partly upon the thankless revision of ' Fiesco ' and partly upon ' Louise Miller ', which interested him more. Having done his best with ' Fiesco ' he sent it to Dalberg, who curtly refused it a second time. His theatrical hopes thus completely baffled, Schiller turned over his play to the bookseller Schwan, who gave him eleven louis d'ors for it and immediately published it as a book for the reader.

In his extremity the exile now bethought him of the kind-hearted lady who had offered him an asylum in case of need. Frau Henriette von Wolzogen was a widow of humble means who had several sons in the academy at Stuttgart. She had conceived a liking for Schiller, and although there was some danger that her rôle of protectress might, if discovered, offend the Duke of Württemberg, she did not hesitate to keep her word. The necessary arrangements were soon made, and late in November Schiller bade farewell to Streicher and set out for Bauerbach, a little village near Meiningen, to occupy the vacant cottage that had been placed at his disposal. He still kept the name of 'Dr. Ritter',—not so much from the fear of arrest, probably, as from a natural desire to remain in obscurity until he had won a position which would justify his flight in the eyes of the world, and more particularly of his father. While at Oggersheim he had occasionally sent out misleading letters, in which he spoke of journeys here and there, of remarkable prosperity and of brilliant prospects in Leipzig, Berlin and St. Petersburg. But his family knew of his whereabouts, and before leaving the Palatinate he contrived a meeting with his mother and his sister Christophine, who drove over to a half-way village to see him. He arrived at Bauerbach on the 7th of December, and wrote thus to Streicher on the following day: 'At last I am here, happy and contented that I am actually ashore. I found everything in excess of my wishes; needs no

longer trouble me, and no annoyances from outside
shall disturb my poetic dreams and my idealistic illusions.'—And in this quiet retreat, well supplied by the
villagers with the necessaries of physical existence, he
did actually find for the next seven months all that he
needed.   There were books, friendship, leisure, peace,
—until the peace was disturbed by a maiden's eyes.

The books came from a man named Reinwald, who
was in charge of the ducal library at Meiningen and
to whom Schiller, foreseeing his own need, had made
haste to introduce himself.   Reinwald was some twenty-
two years older than Schiller, a bit of a poet and a man
of some literary ambition; but he had not got on well
in the world.   It was fated that he should marry
Christophine Schiller, become peevish and sour in the
course of time and lose the respect of his brother-in-
law.   For the present, however, he proved a very
useful friend; for he not only executed orders for books
and tobacco (Schiller had learned to smoke and take
snuff), but he served as general intermediary between
the mysterious Dr. Ritter and the outside world.
Schiller's nature craved friendship, and his imagination
easily endowed Reinwald with the qualities of an ideal
companion of the soul.   After a while we find him
writing in such a strain as this:

Your visit the day before yesterday produced a glorious effect.
I feel my spirits renewed and a warmer life courses through all
my nerves.   My situation in this solitude has drawn upon my
soul the fate of stagnant water, which becomes foul unless it is
stirred up a little now and then.   And I too hope to become
necessary to your heart.[1]

[1] Letter of March, 1783 ; in "Schillers Briefe", edited by Jonas, Vol.
I, page 101.

As for Reinwald, he had long since passed the effusive age, but it pleased him to receive the younger man's confidence. He wrote in his diary: ' To-day Schiller opened his heart to me,—a youth who has already been through the school of life,—and I found him worthy to be called my friend. I do not believe that I have given my confidence to an unworthy man. He has an extraordinary mind and I believe that Germany will some day name his name with pride.'— Which was not bad guessing in its way.

Excepting Reinwald and the villagers Schiller saw at first but little of his fellow-mortals. Both on his own account and for the sake of Frau von Wolzogen he wished that the persons who saw him should not know who he was. So he continued to scatter false reports with a liberal hand: he had gone to Hannover, was going to London, to America, and so forth. In the mean time, with no thought of leaving his nest at Bauerbach, he devoted himself to his work. For the first time in his life he was the master of his own movements; he had a chance to collect himself, to browse among his books, to meditate and to dream. And as for mankind in general, he felt that he had no cause to love it. ' With the warmest feeling ', so he wrote after a time, when the first bitterness had passed away, ' I had embraced half the world and found at last that I had in my arms a cold lump of ice.' [1] Withal the demands of work were imperious. He had risked everything upon his chances of literary success and it was necessary to win. He had broken for good and all with the Duke of Württemberg and there was

[1] Letter of Jan. 4, 1783, to Frau von Wolzogen.

nothing to be hoped for in that quarter. At the same time,—and the fact is characteristic of his large-mindedness,—he resolved not to air his personal griev-ance. To Frau von Wolzogen, who had been admonishing him never to forget his debt to the Stuttgart Academy, he wrote: 'However it may be with regard to that, you have my word that I will never belittle the Duke of Württemberg.'

Toward the end of December the wintry dullness of his Bauerbach cottage was brightened by the arrival of its owner and her daughter. Lotte von Wolzogen was a blond school-girl who had not yet passed her seven-teenth birthday. The records do not credit her with exceptional beauty, but she was sufficiently good-looking and her demure girlish innocence appeared to Schiller very lovable. Not that his plight was at all desperate; he hardly knew his own mind and was in no position to make love to any maiden, least of all to one with that menacing *von* in her name. Still he liked Fräulein Lotte very much, and the tenderness which now began to manifest itself in his letters to the mother must be credited in part to the daughter. Were this not so we could hardly account for such expressions as these, which are contained in a letter written after the ladies had left Bauerbach for a short sojourn in the neighboring Waldorf: 'Since your absence I am stolen from myself. To feel a great and lively rapture is like looking at the sun; it is still before you long after you have turned away your face, and the eye is blinded to all weaker rays. But I shall take great care not to extinguish this agreeable illusion.' And again after they had left the Meiningen region for

Stuttgart, with a promise to return in May: 'Dearest friend—a week behind me without you. So there is one of the fourteen got rid of. I could wish that time would put on its utmost speed until May, so as to move thereafter so much the more slowly.'

Such flutterings of the heart were not altogether favorable to that austere program of literary industry which the ambitious young dramatist had set for himself. When a man is in love other things seem more or less negligible, and it takes resolution to steer a firm course. Schiller was resolute—by spells. In the first list of books ordered from Meiningen we find noted, along with works of Shakspere, Robertson, Hume and Lessing, 'that part of the Abbé St. Réal's works which contains the history of Don Carlos of Spain.' From this we see that a second historical drama was already under way. At first, however, it was not 'Don Carlos' that claimed the most attention, but 'Louise Miller', which had made considerable progress in Oggersheim. By January 14, 1783, Schiller was able to pronounce the new play finished, though his letters show that the revision occupied him some time longer. Meanwhile we hear of other dramatic projects, —a 'Maria Stuart' and a 'Friedrich Imhof', whatever this last may have been. Nothing is known of it save that it was to deal with Jesuitical intrigue, the Inquisition, religious fanaticism, the history of the Bastille, and the passion for gambling.[1] By the end of March he had decided, after long vacillation between these two themes, to drop both of them and proceed with 'Don Carlos'.

[1] Undated letter of March, 1783; "Schillers Briefe", I, 101.

He began in prose, identifying himself completely with his hero and writing with joyous enthusiasm. A letter of April 14 to Reinwald deals at length with love and friendship and their relation to poetic creation. All love, we read, is at bottom love of ourselves. We see in the beloved person the sundered elements of our own being, and the soul yearns to perfect itself in the process of reunion. Thus love and friendship are of the nature of poetic imagination,—the waking into life of a pleasing illusion. Wherefore the poet must love his characters. He must not be the painter of his hero, but rather his hero's sweetheart or bosom friend. Then he makes the application to Don Carlos in these words:

I must confess to you that in a sense he takes the place of my sweetheart. I carry him in my heart,—*ich schwärme mit ihm durch die Gegend um*. . . . He shall have the soul of Shakspere's Hamlet, the blood and nerves of Leisewitz's Julius, and his pulse from me. Besides that I shall make it my duty in this play, in my picture of the Inquisition, to avenge outraged mankind . . . and pierce to the heart a sort of men whom the dagger of tragedy has hitherto only grazed.

But the 'bosom friend' of Don Carlos soon had his thoughts pulled in other directions. In the first place there came, very unexpectedly, a sugary letter from Dalberg. What led him to make fresh overtures to the man whom, a few months before, he had treated so shabbily, is not difficult to make out. He had become convinced that there was after all nothing to be feared from the Duke of Württemberg. Moreover, since the peremptory rejection of 'Fiesco' the Mannheim theater had been doing a very poor business. What more natural than that the shrewd intendant, with an eye to better houses, should bethink him of the pen that had written ' The Robbers ' ? From Schwan and from Streicher, who had remained in Mannheim, he knew of Schiller's address and occupation. So he wrote him a gracious letter, inquiring after his welfare and expressing particular interest in the new play.   It was now Schiller's turn to be foxy. He replied that he was very well, and that as for the play, ' Louise Miller ', it was a tragedy with a copious admixture of satirical and comic elements that would probably render it quite unfit for the stage. Dalberg replied that the specified defects were merits,—he would like to see the manuscript. The upshot of the correspondence was that Schiller, who had been negotiating with a Leipzig publisher but had been unable to make an acceptable bargain for the publication of ' Louise Miller ', now determined to revise it for the stage and meet the views of Dalberg if possible. So about the middle of April he laid aside ' Don Carlos ' and, for the third time in his life, devoted himself to the irksome task of converting a literary drama into a stage-play. On the 3rd of May he wrote to Reinwald:

> My L. M. drives me out of bed at five o'clock in the morning. Here I sit now, sharpening pens and chewing thoughts. It is certain and true that compulsion clips the wings of the spirit. To write with such solicitude for the theater, so hastily because I am pressed for time, and yet without fault, is an art. But I feel that my ' Louise ' is a gainer. . . . My Lady [Lady Milford in the play] interests me almost as much as my Dulcinea in Stuttgart [Lotte von Wolzogen].

Ere the revision of the new tragedy was finished Dulcinea herself arrived in Bauerbach; an event to which Schiller had looked forward with joyous palpitations and anxious forebodings. For back in March Frau von Wolzogen had written him that she and her daughter would be accompanied on their northward journey by a certain Herr Winkelmann, a friend of the family. Schiller at once divined the approach of a rival and wrote in great agitation that he would go to Berlin if Winkelmann came. In justification of his threat he made the diaphanous plea that his incognito was of the utmost importance to him, and that the inquisitive Winkelmann (whom he had known at the academy) would be sure to blab. To this Frau von Wolzogen sent some sort of soothing reply, hinting at the same time that she, the mother, would not interfere with her daughter's choice. So Schiller resolved to stand his ground. The ladies arrived in the latter part of May and soon thereafter he was given to understand that Lotte's affections were fixed upon the other man. There was nothing for him now but the rôle of lofty resignation. To his former schoolmate, Wilhelm von Wolzogen, he wrote as follows:

You have commended to me your Lotte, whom I know completely. I thank you for the great proof of your love. . . . Believe me, my best of friends, I envy you this amiable sister. Still just as if from the hands of the Creator, innocent, the fairest, tenderest, most sensitive soul, and not yet a breath of the general corruption on the bright mirror of her nature,—thus I know your Lotte, and woe to him who brings a cloud over this innocent soul ! . . . Your mother has made me a confidant in a matter that may decide the fate of your Lotte and has told me how you feel upon the subject. [It appears that Wilhelm disliked the young man.] I know Herr W—n and . . . believe me, he is not unworthy of your sister. . . . I really esteem him, though I

cannot at present be called his friend. He loves your Lotte and
I know he loves her like a noble man, and your Lotte loves him
like a girl that loves for the first time.

But the foolish dreams were not so easily to be given
their quietus, especially when he discovered that Lotte
was only half in love with Winkelmann after all. Then
there seemed hope for him and he surrendered himself
freely to the intoxication of his little summer romance.
What were the world and a poet's fame in comparison
with happiness? Still he did not declare himself.
He often called Frau von Wolzogen ' mother ', and
averred in letters that no son could love her better.
Probably a word from her might have led to an engagement. But the word was not spoken. She was a
sensible lady, who knew how to look into the future
and to guard the welfare both of her daughter and of
her protégé. She saw that if he was to make his way
in the world as a dramatist he must return to the world;
a prolongation of the Bauerbach idyl could lead to
nothing but disappointment and unhappiness. Besides,
his incognito had now become only a conventional
fiction; everybody knew who he was.

One day, accordingly, as they were walking together, she suggested that he pay a visit to Mannheim
and see what could be done with Dalberg. He resolved to follow her advice. Late in July he set out,
promising himself and her a speedy return. But it
was not so to be. Becoming absorbed in the business
of a new career he continued, indeed, to think of her
affectionately and to write to her, but at ever-increas-
ing intervals; and after a few months Bauerbach and
the Wolzogens were only a delightful memory. It is

true that after the lapse of nearly a year he one day took it into his head to suggest to the mother that she take him for a son-in-law. But the wooing went no further. After all he had not really been in love with Lotte in particular so much as with an ideal of domestic bliss.

Shortly before his departure from Bauerbach there had been some talk of his accompanying Reinwald on a contemplated journey to Weimar, where he might make the acquaintance of Karl August, Goethe and Wieland. In his excellent little book upon Schiller, Streicher expresses regret that his friend had not acted upon this suggestion instead of following the 'siren voice' that led to the Palatinate. But it is difficult to sympathize with this regret. He was not yet ripe for the rôle that fate held in store for him in Thüringen. His education was to proceed yet a while longer by the process of flaying. He was to suffer and grow strong; to battle further with the goblins of despair; to tread the quicksands of adversity and fight his way through to a firm footing among the sons of men. Who shall say that it was not better so?

The long-cherished hopes of a connection with the Mannheim theater were destined this time to be fulfilled. In the course of a few weeks Schiller entered into a contract which assured him, for a year at least, a respectable status in society and opened a new chapter in his life. Before we take up that chapter, however, it will be proper to consider the new play which he had brought with him as a passport to Dalberg's favor. Thus far he had called it by the name of its heroine, but when it was put upon the stage it was rechristened, at the suggestion of the actor Iffland, and has ever since been known as ' Cabal and Love '. The revision which he had undertaken, after the re-opening of correspondence with Dalberg, was even now not quite finished; so that the final touches had to be given at Mannheim.   It is probable that the political satire, which was based in part upon veritable history and contained transparent allusions to well-known personages, was more or less toned down in deference to the wishes of Dalberg.   Minor changes were also made at the behest of the actors.   But while it was not played and not printed until the spring of 1784, it belongs in its substance and its spirit, not to the Mannheim period of Schiller's life, but to the period which he had spent in hiding.   It is a freeman's comment upon high life as he had known it.   Scrupulously enough Schiller kept the letter of his promise not to use his pen in belittling the Duke of Württemberg.   But the *Wirtschaft* in Stuttgart was fair game, and there were other ways of masking a dramatic battery than to lay the scene in Italy.   In ' Cabal and Love ' the reigning prince does not appear upon the stage.

CHAPTER VI

Cabal and Love

Ich bin ein Edelmann—Lasz doch sehen, ob mein Adelbrief
älter ist als der Risz zum unendlichen Weltall; oder mein Wap-
pen gültiger ist als die Handschrift des Himmels in Louisens
Augen: Dieses Weib ist für diesen Mann.—*'Cabal and Love'*.

In 'Cabal and Love' Schiller found again, as he
had previously found in 'The Robbers', a thoroughly
congenial theme. More properly the theme found
him, took possession of him and would not let him go,
until the inner tumult had subsided and German literature had been enriched with its most telling tragedy of
the social conflict. 'Fiesco' had proved a disappointment; he had not been able to bring himself into perfect
sympathy with the subject, and at the best his Italian
conspiracy was a far-away matter. Now he set foot
again upon his native heath and all went better. In
spite of certain defects which led him to speak of it
later as rather badly designed, 'Cabal and Love' must
be pronounced the most artistic and the most interesting of his early plays.

It is the tragedy of two lovers, an honorable aristocrat and a girl of humble birth, who are done to death
through a vile intrigue which is dictated by the exigen-
cies of an infamous political régime. By means of a
compromising letter, which is not forged but extorted

under duress, the lover is made to suspect his sweet-heart's fidelity; and she, though innocent, is prevented by scruples of conscience from undeceiving him. In a jealous fury he gives her poison and then partakes of it himself. The mischief is wrought not so much by the wickedness of the great, albeit that comes in for a share of the responsibility, as by the obstinate class prejudice, amounting to a tragic superstition, of the heroine and her father. Many of the details were taken over by Schiller from his predecessors; but he so improved upon them, so vitalized the familiar conflicts and situations, and threw into his work such a power of genuine pathos, caught from the pathos of real life, that 'Cabal and Love' still stands out as a notable document of the revolutionary epoch. The epoch produced many bourgeois tragedies, but Schiller's is much the best of them all. Before we look at it more closely it will be worth while to glance at the history of the type in Germany.

The tragedy of middle-class life first took root, as is well known, in England. It was in 1732 that Lillo brought upon the Drury Lane stage his acted tale of George Barnwell, the London 'prentice who is beguiled by a harlot, robs his master, kills his uncle and ends his career on the gallows, to the great grief of the doting Maria, his master's daughter. The prologue tells how the experiment was expected to strike the public of that day:

> The Tragic Muse sublime delights to show
> Princes distrest and scenes of royal woe;
> In awful pomp majestic to relate
> The fall of nations or some hero's fate;

That scepter'd chiefs may by example know
The strange vicissitudes of things below. . . .
Upon our stage indeed, with wished success,
You've sometimes seen her in a humbler dress,
Great only in distress.   When she complains,
In Southern's, Rowe's, or Otway's moving strains,
The brilliant drops that fall from each bright eye
The absent pomp with brighter gems supply.
Forgive us then if we attempt to show
In artless strains a tale of private woe.

So it appears that 'Barnwell' was something new,
yet not entirely new.   The stately tragedy of solemn
edification, at which no one was expected to weep, had
already yielded a part of its sovereignty to the tragedy
of distress.   It occurred to Lillo that tears could be
drawn for the woes of the middle class, which had been
looked upon as suitable only for comedy.   The event
proved that he had reckoned well: the "brilliant
drops" fell copiously, the innovation crossed the
Channel, and soon the bourgeois tragedy, — whence by
an easy differentiation the lacrimose, pathetic, or
serious comedy, — had entered upon its European career.

The first German example was 'Miss Sara Sampson', written in 1755, wherein the daughter of a fond
English squire is lured away from her home, like
Clarissa Harlowe, by the profligate Mellefont, who
promises to marry her.   The pair take lodgings at a
low London inn, where Mellefont finds pretexts for
delaying the marriage ceremony.   Presently his former
mistress, Marwood, appears—a proud and passionate
woman of sin.   She claims him as the mother of his
child, but having now found out what true love is he
spurns her.   Bitter interviews follow, with spiteful

recriminations and awful threats. Marwood tells her
story to Sara and finally ends the tension by poisoning
her, whereupon Mellefont commits suicide. In writing
this play Lessing was in no way concerned with any
social question. He constituted himself the champion
of the bourgeoisie before the tribunal of Melpomene,
but not before the conscience of mankind. The woes
of hero and heroine are in no way related to class
prejudice or to the great democratic upheaval of the
century. Lessing's atmosphere is the moral and sentimental atmosphere of Richardson, though his literary
power is incomparably greater.

' Miss Sara Sampson ' did not long hold the stage,
but its influence is discernible in subsequent developments. The ' man between two women ' became a
regular feature of the new domestic tragedy. In play
after play we find a soulful, clinging, romantic creature
—usually the title-heroine—set over against a full-
blooded rival whose ways are ways of wantonness.
Lessing himself repeated the group in ' Emilia Galotti ',
which in its turn became the mother of a new brood.
The tragedy of lawless passion led by an easy step to
the tragedy of social conflict, which portrayed the
depravity of princes and nobles in their relation to the
common people, or called upon mankind to weep for
the woes of lovers separated by the barriers of rank.
In Germany the species was very timely. Nowhere
else in Europe had the nobility so little to be proud of,
and nowhere else was the pride of birth so stupidly
intolerant. That fruitful theme of earlier and later
poets, the love of nobleman for maid of low degree,
had been lost in the age of gallantry, save in lubricious

tales of intrigue and seduction. The appalling dissoluteness which characterized the French court during the first half of the eighteenth century, and was duly copied by the princelings of Germany, had poisoned the minds of high and low alike and led to a state of affairs in which there was little room for a noble or even a serious conception of love. Love was understood to be concupiscence. If an aristocrat stooped to a bourgeois girl, it was his affair and at the worst only an aberration of taste; her fate was of no importance.

When the inevitable reaction set in, it took the form of a debauch of sentimentalism. The poetry of real passion came back into literature and people wept for joy to find that they had hearts. Love was no longer a frivolous game played for the gratification of lust, but a divine rapture of fathomless and ineffable import. It was now the era of the beautiful soul, of tender sentiment, of virtuous transports and of endless talk about all these things. Love being natural,—a part of that nature to which the world was now resolved to return,—it was sacred, and superior to all human conventions. It belonged to the sphere of the rights of man. Its enemy was everywhere the corrupt heart and the worldly, calculating mind. Fortunately the new ecstasy associated itself with a strong enthusiasm for the simplification of life; for the poetry of nature and of rustic employments; for the sweetness of domestic affection. In Germany public sentiment had already been prepared for a certain idealization of the bourgeoisie. Enlightened rulers and publicists, here and there, were coming to feel that a virtuous yeomanry was the sure foundation of a state's welfare. Countless idyls and pastorals and moralizing romances had thrown a nimbus of poetry about the simple virtues and humble employments of the poor, and taught people to contrast these things with the corruption and artificiality of courts and cities. It was, however, the passionate eloquence of Rousseau which first gave to this contrast a revolutionary significance, and it was Rousseau who first stirred the reading world with a woeful tale of lovers separated by the prejudices of caste.

In ' The New Heloise ' it is the lady who is the aristocrat. Julie d'Etange, the daughter of a baron, wishes to marry the untitled St. Preux, to whom in a transport of passion she has yielded up her honor. But the Baron d'Etange is an implacable stickler for rank and she is a dutiful daughter; whence her marriage to the elderly infidel, Wolmar, and the well-known moral ending of the novel. The thought that concerns us here is best expressed by the enlightened English peer, Lord B., who thus expostulates with Baron d'Etange:

Let us judge of the past by the present; for two or three citizens who win distinction by honest means, a thousand knaves every day get their families ennobled. But to what end serves that nobility of which their descendants are so proud, unless it be to prove the robberies and infamy of their ancestor? There are, I confess, a great number of bad men among the common people; but the odds are always twenty to one against a gentleman that he is descended from a scoundrel. . . . In what consists then the honor of that nobility of which you are so proud? How does it affect the glory of one's country or the good of mankind? A mortal enemy to liberty and the laws, what did it ever produce, in the most of those countries where it has flourished, but the power of tyranny and the oppression of the

people ? Will you presume to boast, in a republic, of a rank
that is destructive to virtue and humanity ? Of a rank that
makes its boast of slavery and wherein men blush to be men ? [1]

This is of course the language of passion and prejudice (it would not else be Rousseau), but there was
enough of truth in it, as in the case of Rousseau's other
fervors, to rouse the revolutionary spirit. German
literature began to teem with novels and plays which
exhibit the sufferings of some untitled hero or heroine
at the hands of a vicious aristocracy. The theme is
touched upon in ' Werther ', but without becoming an
important issue. It appears in Wagner's ' Infanticide ',
wherein a butcher's daughter, Evchen Humbrecht, is
violated by a titled officer, runs away from home in her
shame, kills her child and is finally found by the
repentant author of her disgrace. We meet it again
in Lenz's ' Private Tutor ', the tragedy of a German
St. Preux who falls in love with his titled pupil and
dishonors her, with the result that she too runs away
from home and tries to commit suicide, while her lover
in his chagrin emasculates himself. These are grotesque
tragedies, not devoid of literary power, but devoid of
high sentiment and saturated with a woeful vulgarity.
We cannot wonder that the high-minded Schiller should
have condemned Wagner's malodorous play as a
mediocre performance. His incentive came rather from
Gemmingen's ' Head of the House ', which in turn
carries us back to Diderot.

In the hands of Diderot, democrat, moralist and
apostle of the *genre honnête*, it was natural that the
drama of class conflict should end happily. In his

---

[1] 'The New Heloise ', Part I, letter 62.

'Father of the Family', written in 1758 and first played in 1761, the contrast of high and low is vividly portrayed, but without bitterness. The aristocratic St. Albin d'Orbisson falls in love with a poor girl from the country who lives in an attic and earns her own living. Sophie's beauty and virtue make a man of him and he wishes to marry her, but is opposed by his kind-hearted, querulous father, who argues the case with him at great length, confronting passion with prudential common-sense. St. Albin is also opposed by his rich uncle, the Commandeur, from whom he has prospects. The uncle plots to get Sophie away by having her arrested, but is baffled by a counter-intrigue. Stormy scenes follow the revelation, and in the end it appears that Sophie is not a plebeian maiden at all, but the niece of the purse-proud Commandeur, who has neglected his poor relations. With the literary and dramatic qualities of this play, its absence of humor and of sparkling dialogue, its tedious moralizing, its hollow pathos and its general relation to Diderot's dramatic theory, we are not here directly concerned. What is important to observe is that, as a contribution to the burning social question, its point is blunted by the fact that its heroine is not what she seems to be. The whole matter reduces to a brief misunderstanding in an aristocratic family. Villainy is thwarted, true love comes into its own, and the foundations of society remain as they were.

Diderot's 'Father of the Family' enjoyed a short vogue in France and Italy and met with considerable favor in Germany. Most noteworthy among minor German plays that were influenced by it is Gemmin-

gen's ' Head of the House'.   Gemmingen was himself
an aristocrat, a baron by title, who was born in 1755.
After studying law he settled in Mannheim, where he
became deeply interested in the drama, so that in 1778
he was given the position of dramatist to the newly
established ' national theater '.   Two years later he
brought out his ' Head of the House ' with great success.   The piece is a pendant of Diderot's, but by no
means a slavish imitation.

Gemmingen's ' head of the house ' is an upright
German nobleman of the admirable sort, who returns
home after a long absence to find the affairs of
his family very much deranged. His eldest son,
Karl, has fallen madly in love with Lotte Wehrmann,
the daughter of an impecunious artist, gotten her
with child, and promised to marry her when his father
shall have returned and given his consent.   The
younger son, Ferdinand, an officer, has taken to
gaming, lost heavily and has a duel on his hands.
His son-in-law, Monheim, has become infatuated with
a dazzling widow, Countess Amaldi, grown cold
toward his wife Sophie, and the quarreling pair are
eager for a divorce.   The tangle is further complicated
by the fact that Amaldi, an excellent match, is in love
with Karl.   The perplexed father sets at work with
the tools of common sense and rational argument.   He
urges Karl to break with Lotte for his career's sake.
The irresolute and dutiful Karl consents, saying nothing
of Lotte's approaching motherhood, and the rumor of
his intended marriage to the countess is spread abroad.
When Lotte hears it she rushes to Amaldi and wildly
demands her lover in the name of her unborn child,

When the father hears the whole story he no longer thinks of rank but of honor. He bids Karl marry his true love and retire to the country, where, as overseer of a large estate, he will be less encumbered by a plebeian wife than in the career which had been planned for him. The magnanimous Amaldi furnishes the bride's dowry, the other domestic complications are easily adjusted and all ends happily.

Dramatically Gemmingen's play is rather tame, though its literary merit is considerable. He had a fair measure of constructive skill, but very little of poetic impulse or of dramatic verve. His best scenes interest us more for their good sense than for any more stirring qualities. His nearest approach to a strong character is the paterfamilias himself, who is certainly much less "woolly and mawkish"[1] than his pendant in Diderot. Next one may place the artist Wehrmann. Karl is a poor stick, Amaldi is rather colorless, and Lotte would be quite insipid but for her impending motherhood, on which everything is made to turn. Such as it was, however, the play excited the cordial admiration of Schiller, who read it soon after its appearance. Very likely it may have suggested to him the thought of trying his own hand upon a drama in the bourgeois sphere, but it was not until July, 1782, —just after he had finished reading Wagner's 'Infanticide ',—that the plan of ' Louise Miller ' began to take shape in his mind. Gemmingen's poor artist, Wehrmann, became the poor fiddler, Miller, and the daughter Lotte was rechristened Louise. The aristocratic lover, Gemmingen's Karl, was named Ferdinand von

---

[1] The adjectives are John Morley's; "Diderot", Chap. VII.

Walter, and Amaldi was converted into Lady Milford. One of Gemmingen's subordinate characters, the foppish nobleman, Dromer, who goes about making compliments to everybody, reappears in Schiller's play as the perfumed tale-bearer and exquisite ladies' man, Chamberlain von Kalb. The places represented are three in number and the same in both plays. Here, however, the parallel ends. Instead of Gemmingen's high-minded paterfamilias we have the rascally President von Walter, who, with his tool Wurm, reminds one of Lessing's Prince and Marinelli. And what is much more important, the relation of the lovers is so portrayed that we get the pure poetry of passion, such as it is, without any tinge of grossness.

In its earliest phase Schiller's plan looked toward a telling tragi-comedy for the stage, with a plenty of rough humor and caustic satire at the expense of 'high-born fools and scoundrels'. As he worked, the possibilities of his theme developed. An abstract enthusiasm for the rights of man was kindled by honest love of the common people, and by the lingering smart of a personal wrong, into a holy zeal of vengeance. President Walter was painted in colors which were taken largely from the political history and the *chronique scandaleuse* of the Württemberg court. As this court had its angel of light in soiled garments, Lady Milford was fitted out with the benevolent qualities of Franziska von Hohenheim; and as the portrait grew in firmness its author fell in love with it, like the young Goethe with his Adelheid. When he came to depict the jealousy of Ferdinand, he had the advantage of a personal acquaintance with the green-eyed monster. Thus the play was extracted from the book of life, as Schiller had been able to read it, and that accounts for its vitality. But in his details he is nowhere less original. Not only in the general conception of important characters, but in particular scenes, situations, motives, contrasts and forms of expression, we can see the influence of the literary tradition which he inherited.

To show the exact nature and the full extent of this indebtedness would be a tedious undertaking, which would require pages of quotation from works whose chief interest now is that they served as quarry for Schiller. Three or four illustrations will suffice. Our play begins with a scene which at once recalls what was originally the opening scene of Wagner's ' Infanticide '. In both there is a blustering father,—Lessing's Odoardo reduced to the bourgeois sphere,—discoursing with his silly wife upon the dangers that threaten their daughter from keeping aristocratic company. In both the domestic thunderer expresses himself in rough, strong language, and is only made the more furious by his wife's efforts to allay his fears. In Wagner's next scene Magister Humbrecht comes to woo Evchen, just as Schiller's Wurm comes to woo Louise, and we hear that the girl's head has been turned by reading novels. Just so Louise, whose father can scarcely find words to express his detestation of the young baron's infernal, belletristic poison. When Wurm arrives at Miller's and asks for Louise, he is informed that she has just gone to church. ' Glad of that, glad of that ', he replies, ' I shall have in her a pious Christian wife '. Here is a reminiscence of the scene in which Lessing's Count Appiani exclaims, on hearing that Emilia has

just been at church: ' That is right; I shall have in
you a pious wife '. The devout heroine was a hardly
less hackneyed figure in the dramatic literature of the
time than the blustering father of whom Goethe complained.[1] In Schiller's Louise we have the religious
sentiment sublimated into something quite too seraphic
for human nature's daily food. Her high-keyed sense
of duty to God, her natural filial piety and her superstitious reverence for the social order, combine to produce in her a curious distraction which is the real
source of the tragic conflict. She feels that her love is
holy but that marriage would be sinful; and so she
hesitates, responds to her lover's ardor with tremblings
and solicitudes, knows not what to do, does the foolish
thing and atones tragically for her weakness.

Not before Schiller's time had this conflict between
love and filial duty been so powerfully depicted, but it
is found in Wagner's ' Remorse after the Deed ' (1775),
wherein a coachman's daughter, Friederike Walz, is
loved by the aristocratic Langen, who is opposed by
his mother. Langen goes to his sweetheart, all courage
and resolution. He is prepared, like Leisewitz's Julius,
to defy his kin, renounce the lures of his rank and flee
to the ends of the earth with ' Rikchen '. To which
she replies: ' Langen, you are terrible. To marry
with the curse of parents is to make one's whole posterity miserable '. So Louise replies to Ferdinand's
similar entreaty: ' And be followed by your father's

---

[1] " La première fois que je la vis, ce fut à l'église ",—says Diderot's
St. Albin, in recounting the beginning of his infatuation for Sophie. So
with Faust and Margaret, and with Schiller's beautiful Greek lady in
' The Ghostseer '.

curse! A curse, thoughtless man, which even murderers never utter in vain, and which like a ghost would pursue us fugitives mercilessly from sea to sea.'

In the sentimental novel 'Siegwart', the heroine, Therese, loves a young squire, not for his blue blood, but for the nobility of his heart. Like Louise she renounces her love for this life, and bids him farewell. In writing to him she describes a scene between her father and his:

> Your father came dashing into our yard with two huntsmen. 'Are you the ——?' he called up to me. 'Is that Siegwart? He's a scoundrel, if he knows it. He wants to seduce my son. And this, I suppose, is the nice creature (here he turned to me again) who has made a fool of him. A nice little animal, by my soul!' . . . My father, who can show heat when he is provoked, told him to stop calling such names; that he was a decent man and I a decent girl.

Here we seem to have the suggestion of the stirring scene in which the irate old fiddler threatens to throw President von Walter out of doors for insulting Louise.

It would be very easy to give further examples of Schiller's talent for taking what suited his purpose, but such philology is not very profitable. After all, what one wishes to know is not where the architect got his materials, but what he made of them. And what he made was a play abounding in admirable scenes, but ending in a rather unsatisfactory manner. With even less violence to the inner logic of the piece than was necessary in the case of 'Fiesco', 'Cabal and Love' might have been given a happy ending. The whole tragedy hangs by a thread in the fifth act. Lady Milford has fled and is no longer a factor in the entanglement. The wicked president has relented and is ready to yield. Old Miller, released from prison, returns to his house and finds Louise brooding over her purpose of suicide. He preaches to her upon the sin of self-destruction and pleads with her to give up her aristocratic lover. She promises. Then Ferdinand comes and demands an explanation of the fatal letter. A word from her at this point, a momentary *accès* or simple common sense, would undeceive him and end the whole difficulty. Of course she must not break her oath; and one cannot blame her sweet simplicity for not taking refuge in the maxim that an oath given under duress is not binding. But her oath merely pledges her to acknowledge the letter as her voluntary act. There is no reason why she should not solemnly assure Ferdinand of her innocence, tell him that they are the victims of a plot and send him to his father for an explanation. Nothing prevents her from speaking in time the words that she actually does speak after she has taken the poison, but before she knows that she has taken it: ' A horrible fatality has confused the language of our hearts. If I might open my mouth, Walter, I could tell you things', etc.

If, out of filial piety, Louise is minded to give up her lover, there is at any rate no reason why she should wish him to despise her forever. Every natural girlish instinct requires her to clear herself. That she does not do this, but persists in a course which of all courses is the most unnatural,—seeing that she now has nothing to fear from any source,—produces a painful suspense which is anything but tragic. No skill of the actress can altogether save her from a cer-

tain appearance of fatuous weak-mindedness, or fore-
stall the cynical conclusion that she dies chiefly in
order that it may be fulfilled which was said unto himself by the author, namely: I will write a tragedy.

And yet such a conclusion would not be perfectly
just to Schiller. It is true that he was all for tragedy
and that a happy moral ending, in the vein of Diderot,
would not have been to his taste. But this does not
tell the whole story. The romantic lovers are sacrificed in order that the guilty president and his vile
accomplices may be brought to book and punished for
their sins. The heart of the matter for Schiller was
to free his mind with respect to the infamies of high life.
It was this that tipped his pen with fire.

Of course there are German critics who find Louise's
conduct in this last scene quite 'inevitable' and full of
a high tragic pathos. Thus Palleske says of her:

Her anxious piety, her touching and indeed so intelligible
devotion to her father, her lack of freedom, bring on her fate.
A veil of mourning rests upon all she says. Heroic liberty of
action, such as befits a Juliet, is made impossible to this girl by
her birth in the bourgeoisie; she has only the liberty to perish,
not the courage to be happy. Of guilt there can be no question
in this case: her anxiety, her filial devotion, are her whole guilt;
her virtue, her love for her father, become her ruin. Whoever
thoroughly knows the bourgeoisie, which had yet to recover from
these wounds,[1] will admit that this character is drawn with
terrible truthfulness.

---

[1] "Schillers Leben und Werke", 15. Aufl. (1900), p. 297. In earlier
editions of Palleske's work, which appeared originally in 1858-9, Louise
was further characterized as 'the crushed heart of the German people';
and the sentence, 'which had to recover from those wounds', read:
'which is beginning to recover'.

This, however, is putting too fine a point upon it; it implies, when closely analyzed, that Schiller deliberately made his heroine a little stupid,—a view of her that hardly comports with the rest of the play. To say that she *must* die because she belongs to the bourgeoisie is mere moonshine, for common sense can readily find a number of escapes. She may cleave to her father and send her lover packing, after proper explanations; or she may cleave to her lover in the face of her father's displeasure; or she may temporize in the hope of changing her father's mind. What she actually does is to goad her lover into a frenzy by her singular conduct and then come to her senses when it is too late. The effect is to cast doubt upon the intensity of her supposed passion for Ferdinand. One gets the impression that her previous sentimental ecstasies were not perfectly genuine; that she does not really know what it is to be in love, or how to speak the veritable language of the heart.

The truth seems to be that when Schiller wrote 'Cabal and Love', he had not progressed far enough in the knowledge of femininity to be able to draw a perfectly life-like portrait of a girl in Louise's station. She is a creature of the same order as Amalia and Leonora,—a sentimental *Schwärmerin*, very much lacking in character and mother-wit. From the first the expression of her love does not ring perfectly true. We suspect her of phrase-making,—she is quite too ethereal and ecstatic for a plain fiddler's daughter. No trace here of that homely poetic realism,—Gretchen at the wash-tub, or Lotte cutting bread and butter, —with which Goethe knew how to invest *his* bourgeois maidens.   For aught we can learn from her discourse Schiller's Louise might be a princess, brought up on a diet of Klopstock's odes.   That a girl, returning from church, should inquire of her parents if her lover has called, is quite in order.   That she should then confess that thoughts of him have come between her and her Creator, is pardonable.   But what are we to think when she goes on to say to her own parents:

> This little life of mine, oh that I might breathe it out into a soft caressing zephyr to cool his face!   This little flower of youth, were it but a violet, that he might step on it, and it might die modestly beneath his feet!   That would be enough for me, my father. . . . Not that I want him now.   I renounce him for this life.   But then, mother, then, when the barriers of rank are laid low; when all the hateful wrappings of earthly station fall away from us, and men are only men,—I shall bring nothing with me save my innocence; but, you know, father has so often said that pomp and splendid titles will be cheap when God comes, and that hearts will rise in price.   Then I shall be rich. Then tears will be counted for triumphs, and beautiful thoughts instead of ancestry.   I shall be aristocratic then, mother.   What advantage will he have then over his sweetheart?

What can one think, indeed, except that this supernal maiden has been reading Klopstock's famous ' Ode to Fanny'? [1]

Louise's passion, then, is no dangerous earthly flame, but a sentimental dream, a private revel in ecstatic emotion.   We opine that she does not really need her lover, as a mortal entity, at all, and are prepared to

[1] One strophe runs :
>   Dann wird ein Tag sein, den werd' ich auferstehn!
>   Dann wird ein Tag sein, den wirst du auferstehn!
>   Dann trennt kein Schicksal mehr die Seelen,
>   Die du einander, Natur, bestimmtest.

find her fearsome and irresolute in his presence. ' They
are going to separate us,' she exclaims, as if she herself had no voice in the matter, when really her own
timidity is the great obstacle. She is no Gretchen, or
Clärchen, ready to give all for love's sake and jump
the consequences; still less is she a bourgeois Juliet,
prepared to brave a family tempest provided only that
her Romeo's bent be honorable, his purpose marriage.
Those externalities of rank which she expects to drop
out of sight in heaven loom up very large in her earthly
field of vision. She fears her father's displeasure.
She pretends to fear the ruin of her Ferdinand's career,
albeit he assures her solemnly that she is of more importance to him than all else in the world. She is of
the opinion that her marriage to a man with a *von* in
his name and prospects in life would be ' the violation
of a sanctuary'; would ' unjoint the social world and
demolish the eternal, universal order '. Wherefore she
is minded to renounce him. ' Let the vain, deluded
girl '—so she sighs—' weep away her grief within lonely
walls; no one will trouble himself about her tears,—
empty and dead is my future,—but I shall still now and
then take a smell at the withered nosegay of the past.'
—No wonder that before she reaches this awful climax,
Ferdinand smashes the fiddle and bursts into laughter.

On the stage, the scene in which the agonized Louise
is compelled to write the compromising letter is one of
the most effective in the piece; and yet how futile and
absurd the whole intrigue would be if the conspirators
were not able to count upon her being a goose! One
cannot blame her, of course, for doing that which appears to be necessary in order to save her father's life.

One may pardon to her distress the solemn oath that she will acknowledge the letter as her voluntary act. But if she were really in love with Ferdinand as she has pretended to be, how easy it would be for her, without violating her oath, to put him on his guard against the trap that has been laid for him! In the scene with Lady Milford she appears as a pert little pharisee, caustic, sententious and philosophical beyond her years; so that one wonders why a girl that knows so much should not know more. She herself has just cast her lover off, after meeting his passionate entreaties with cool prudential argument. In a stagy paroxysm of jealousy she resigns her Ferdinand to Lady Milford, warning her, however, that her bridal chamber will be haunted by the ghost of a suicide. But why should Louise wish to quit this life? She has said farewell to Ferdinand, alleging that duty bids her remain and endure. She has chosen her part. All that separates her from her lover is her own chimerical sentiment of duty. Her virtue is intact. She has not the motive, say of Gemmingen's Lotte, for self-destruction. It is hard to take her seriously at this point, and we wonder that Lady Milford takes her seriously.

Truth to tell, Louise makes a rather tame and uninteresting tragic heroine. Notwithstanding all her fervid phrases, she is essentially cold. Did Schiller intend this effect, or is it due to the fact that he could not have portrayed her differently? Did it really spring from his limited observation of the feminine heart and of girlish ways, or from a deliberate artistic purpose to account adequately for Ferdinand's jealousy? Had he taken a lesson from the maidenly reserve of Lotte von Wolzogen and the prudential scruples of her mother? These are questions upon which one can only speculate. As matters stand, the whole catastrophe is made to hinge upon Ferdinand's suspicion. A little patience, a little faith in his sweetheart, would turn the course of fate. But her conduct makes faith difficult; so we understand his jealousy, but not so well his previous infatuation. He is in love with a beautiful soul and a pair of forget-me-not eyes, but the presuppositions are a little difficult. He is resolved to marry Louise for better or worse,—it is all understood, so far as he is concerned. Although there is no love-scene in the play, we do hear of precedent scenes of passionate self-surrender (always within the limits of virtue). One cannot help asking: Where were Louise's scruples then? Was she ignorant of her father's prejudice or resolved to brave it? Had she never reflected upon the august foundations of the social order? Had she resisted Ferdinand's suit and warned him that he must be content with a yearning friendship on earth and a union of souls in heaven? None of these suppositions can be said to prepare us fully for her actual conduct in the play, where she appears all along as a helpless bundle of tremors, vacillating between an alleged passion in which we do not fully believe and a sublimated sense of duty that we cannot fully understand.

In Ferdinand we have Schiller's favorite type of tragic hero,—the fervid young enthusiast whose calamity grows out of his own strenuous idealism. He is, however, a less weighty character than Karl Moor, or Carlos, or Max Piccolomini, because we see in him nothing more than the infatuate lover. In their case love is paired with the spirit of great enterprise; for him it is all in all, so far at least as the action of the play is concerned. His Louise sums up the entire macrocosm. If he thinks of doing anything in the world, it is only in order that he may marry her and live with her in a lover's paradise all his life. This is his way of talking:

Let obstacles come between us like mountains; I will make steps of them and fly to my Louise's arms. The storms of adverse fate shall inflate my feeling, danger shall only make my Louise the more charming. . . . I will guard you as the dragon guards the subterraneous gold. Trust yourself to me. You need no other angel. I will throw myself between you and fate, receive every wound for you and catch for you every drop from the cup of joy. On this arm shall my Louise dance through life, etc.

One can pardon some extravagance to a stage lover, since his intoxication is what makes him amiable. Who, for example, would abate a jot or tittle from the delicious nonsense of Romeo? When he says that carrion flies

                            may seize
On the white wonder of dear Juliet's hand
And steal immortal blessings from her lips,

he seems to have expressed himself appropriately. There is no suggestion of mawkishness in his discourse. Our Ferdinand, however, is distinctly spoony. There went no poetic irony to his creation, and he has no saving sense of humor. He never seems, like Romeo, to be toying with hyperbole in an artistic spirit, but it is all dead earnest. Such a love-lorn youth must expect to recruit his admirers chiefly from the ranks of the very young. And yet there are times, just as in

the case of Karl Moor, when Ferdinand's rhetoric
becomes impressive from sheer titanic force. Thus
when he says to Louise, who has just been reminding
him of his prospects: 'I am a nobleman,—we will see,
however, whether my patent of nobility is older than
the ground-plan of the eternal universe; whether my
escutcheon is more valid than the hand-writing of
heaven in Louise's eyes: This woman is for this man.'

It is undoubtedly in the scenes with his father that
Ferdinand appears at his best. Here at least there is
manly vigor. The contrast between the wicked father
and the good son is effectively brought out, although,
as in the case of Karl and Franz Moor, it is carried
beyond the limits of easy credibility. How unnatural
is the relation of the pair! One would think they had
never talked with each other before, and that each had
lived in complete ignorance of the other's character
and inclinations. The father, by way of founding a
claim to his son's grateful affection, declares that he
has 'trodden the dangerous path to the heart of the
prince' and killed his predecessor,—all for the sake
of his son. He admits that he is suffering the 'eternal
scorpion-stings of conscience', and yet he expects
Ferdinand to follow him without a whimper, and he is
angry when the young man indignantly renounces the
usufruct of his father's crimes. Although Ferdinand
is a major in the army, his marriage with Lady Milford
is arranged for him as if he had no claim to be con-
sulted. The president blurts out his plan with brutal
coarseness, and urges it in language which he knows
will rouse his son's anger. So when he appears in the
Miller house he makes himself as odious as possible.

Diplomacy and finesse are weapons not found in his
armory, though he is a courtier and a successful politician.   He is simply a cynical brute in high office.
In truth his conduct is so very inhuman as to convey
an impression of burlesque.   He seems copied from
some ogre in a fairy tale.

But if President von Walter appears now like a melo-
dramatic caricature, it is partly because times have
changed; for Schiller was not without his models in the
recent history of Württemberg.   During the period of
Karl Eugen's worst recklessness—the decade beginning
with 1755,—he was loyally abetted by two men, Rieger
and Montmartin, who made themselves thoroughly
odious.   Rieger was a man of talent and knowledge,
but without heart and without conscience.   It was he
who managed the cruel and lawless conscriptions
whereby Duke Karl raised the desired troops for
France.[1]   Young men were simply taken wherever they
could be found,—pulled from their beds at night, or
seized as they came from church,—and forced into the
army under brutal conditions of service.   Many a
Württemberg family could have told a tale of barbarity
essentially similar to that recounted by the lackey to
Lady Milford in the second act of Schiller's play.
Remorseless oppression of the people, for the purpose
of raising money to be spent on the duke's costly
whims, became the order of the day.

Still more brutal and cynical in his methods than
Rieger was Count Montmartin, who was made President
of the State Council in 1758.   A cunning and wicked
intriguer, he lent himself without scruple to the gratifi-

[1] See above, page 7.

cation of his master's lusts and caprices. The daughters
of the land were unsafe from his machinations if they
had had the misfortune to attract the wanton eye of
their sovereign. In 1762, wishing to be rid of his
powerful rival, Montmartin trumped up a charge that
Rieger was engaged in treasonable correspondence with
Prussia. The result was that Rieger was publicly disgraced. Meeting him one day on parade the duke
angrily tore off his military order, struck him with his
cane and then shut him up in the Hohentwiel, where
he lay for four years without light, table, chair or bed.
In like manner the patriotic publicist, Moser, was im-
prisoned for five years, without trial and without sentence, because he had withheld his consent to the
duke's high-handed proceedings.

Such was the political system that had afflicted
Württemberg during Schiller's childhood. It furnished
him with his dramatic 'mythology', as it has been
called. The name may be allowed to pass, only it
should be remembered that *this* mythology was simply
history. The rapier-thrusts of the dramatist were not
directed against wind-mills of the imagination, but
against political infamies that make one's blood boil in
the reading and that would have moved a more spirited
people to hang their rulers to the nearest tree. This
should be borne in mind by any one who, in the milder
light of a later and better era, is disposed to carp at
Schiller for caricaturing the nobility. He was not concerned with aristocracy in general, but with the particular kakistocracy that had disgraced his native land.
And all that he did was to exhibit it as it was, or lately
had been.

CHAPTER VII

Theater Poet in Mannheim

Die Schaubühne ist mehr als jede andere öffentliche Anstalt des Staats eine Schule der praktischen Weisheit, ein Wegweiser durch das bürgerliche Leben, ein unfehlbarer Schlüssel zu den geheimsten Zugängen der menschlichen Seele.—*Discourse on the Theater, 1784.*

MANNHEIM, famed for the geometric regularity of its streets, was in Schiller's day a city of about twenty thousand inhabitants. Since 1720 it had been the capital of the Bavarian Palatinate, and under the Elector Karl Theodor it had acquired some distinction as a nursery of the arts. We have seen that Schiller, coming thither from Suabia, imagined himself escaping from the land of the barbarians to the land of the Greeks. In the year 1777 the Upper and Lower Palatinate were united, and the Elector transferred his residence to München. For this withdrawal of the light of their ruler's countenance the Mannheimers were compensated in a measure by the establishment among them of a so-called National Theater. There was no German nation at the time, but there was a very general interest in the German drama. Lessing's famous experiment at Hamburg, though it turned out badly, had set people thinking. Playwrights and actors were learning to regard themselves no longer as purveyors of mere

137

amusement, but as the dignified representatives of a noble art having boundless possibilities of influence. The public was becoming interested in the principles of dramatic construction and in the criteria of excellence.   Scholars were beginning to inquire whether the stage might not again become what it had been for the ancient Athenians.   And so the way had been prepared for a serious conception of the theater and for experiments like that at Mannheim.

The management of the enterprise was placed in the hands of Baron Heribert von Dalberg, a young nobleman (born in 1750), who had given no evidence of unusual fitness for such an office, but was a connoisseur and a gentleman.   He devoted himself zealously to his work and soon made his theater famous.   He was courteous and hospitable, kept an eye open for promising talent and enjoyed the rôle of Mæcenas.   His system provided for regular meetings of his actors, at which plays were discussed, reports rendered and grievances ventilated.   For the rest he was not a man of ideas, but a follower of tradition.   He disliked to take risks and often missed the mark in his judgment of persons and of plays.   He continued until 1803 to act as intendant and occasionally tried his hand at dramatic composition, or the adaptation of a Shaksperian play.   All told, his services were such that the Mannheimers have deemed him worthy of a statue.

Among the actors whom Baron Dalberg's enterprise had assembled at Mannheim were three or four of notable talent.   Thus there was Iffland, of the same age as Schiller, who was destined to win fame as an actor, playwright and manager.   Like Diderot, Iffland

believed ardently in the moral mission of the drama.
He was himself a man of character who had taken to
the stage against the wish of his kinfolk, and now his
hobby was to refine the language of the stage and to
elevate the actor's profession.   He was an industrious
and thoughtful player, who gave careful attention to
the little matters of mimicry and personation and seldom
failed to please.   Another was Beil, a greater actor in
point of natural endowment, who relied more upon
vigorous realism than upon studied refinements.   Then
there was Beck, who was at his best as a portrayer of
youthful enthusiasm and sentiment.   His nature was
akin to Schiller's and a warm friendship sprang up
between the two.

When Schiller arrived in Mannheim, late in July,
1783, Dalberg was in Holland.   There was nothing
going on at the theater, and the sweltering town,
deserted by such as could get away, was suffering from
an epidemic of malarial fever.   But the faithful Streicher
was there and friend Meyer, the manager, and Schwan,
the publisher, whose vivacious daughter, Margarete,
gradually kindled in the heart of the new-comer another
faint blue flame which he ultimately mistook for love.
His first concern was to write to Frau von Wolzogen,
who had loaned him money for his journey, a detailed
report of his finances.   He was the possessor of fifteen
thalers, whereof he had reserved five for the return to
Bauerbach.   His friend Meyer had found him a nice
place where, by dispensing with breakfast, he could
eat, drink and lodge for about two thalers a week.
Hair-dresser, washerwoman, postman and tobacconist
would require, all told, one thaler.   So he hoped to

keep afloat in the great world at least three weeks, and then,—back to his heart's home in Saxony! The letter continues:

Oh, I shall long to be soon, soon, with you again ; and meanwhile, in the midst of my greatest distractions, I shall think of you, my dearest friend. I shall often break away from social circles and, alone in my room, sadly dream myself back with you and weep. Continue, my dear, continue to be what you have been hitherto, my first and dearest friend ; and let us be, all by ourselves, an example of pure friendship. We will make each other better and nobler. By mutual sympathy and the delicate tie of beautiful emotions we will exhaust the joys of this life and at the last be proud of this our blameless league. Take no other friend into your heart. Mine remains yours unto death and beyond that, if possible.

One sees that the writer of this letter had lived quite long enough in his idyllic retirement, and that his benefactress had judged the case wisely.

> Es bildet ein Talent sich in der Stille,
> Sich ein Charakter in dem Strom der Welt.[1]

We who do not live in an epoch of emotional expansion have the right to get what amusement we can out of this note of high-flown sentimentalism. At the same time its instructive aspect should not be lost sight of. When a youth of twenty-three, battling with the vulgar prose of life, falls into such a tone in writing to a middle-aged lady who has befriended him; when he lets his imagination brood upon the coming luxury of tears and of beautiful emotions; when he is so pathetically eager to reign without a rival in the heart of his

---

[1] A talent forms itself in solitude,
A character in the flowing tide of life.
—*Goethe's 'Tasso'*.

friend, and to assure her of his everlasting loyalty in the world to come,—how shall we expect him to express himself when he undertakes to speak the language of strong feeling in works of the imagination? Evidently we must be prepared for all things in the way of sentimental extravagance.

After two weeks of idle waiting Schiller was able to report that Dalberg had returned and was showing himself very friendly. The man was 'all fire',—only it was gunpowder flame that would not last long. The genial intendant insisted that Schiller should by all means remain in Mannheim. 'Fiesco', now in print as a tragedy, should be put upon the stage at once; 'Louise Miller' should be taken under consideration, a performance of 'The Robbers' be given for the author's special gratification, and so forth. At first Schiller was little disposed to bank upon this effusive kindness. His plans went no further than to effect a sale of the stage-rights of his two plays and then to return to Bauerbach. But the lures of Dalberg finally prevailed and in September he made a contract for a year's employment as dramatist of the Mannheim theater. He was to furnish one entirely new play, in addition to those he had on hand, and to have as compensation three hundred florins, the copyright of all the plays and the receipts of a single performance of each of them. For a moment the future looked tolerably bright. He saw in his mind's eye an assured income of more than twelve hundred florins, which would provide amply for his needs and enable him to pay his debts.

But his plans went all wrong. In the first place,

the pestilent fever, which he fought with giant doses
of quinine, proved very intractable and held him
in its grip for months.   He was unable to work and
fell into a sort of mental coma.   In a letter of November 13 he describes himself as eating Peruvian bark like
bread; and six weeks later he was still suffering from
the effects of his unlucky midsummer plunge into the
miasmatic air of Mannheim.   In other ways, too, the
new situation proved a disappointment.   Social demands
involved him in expenditures far in excess of his modest
calculations, while the intervals of relief from physical
incapacity were filled with a hundred distractions which
left him no time for sustained mental effort.   And
so he drifted into the winter without accomplishing
anything more notable than the final revision of
' Fiesco '.

About this time he was elected a member of the
so-called ' German Society ', a learned body which
enjoyed the protection of the Elector.   This little honor
was highly valued by Schiller, since it made him a
citizen of the Palatinate and gave him an assured social
status.   On the other hand, his emergence into the
light of day as a respectable functionary was not without its disadvantages, since his creditors now became
importunate.   There were pressing duns from Stuttgart
and from Bauerbach, but the debtor could not pay.
He became involved in a painful correspondence with
his father, who had undertaken to guarantee a small
debt of his son provided that another larger one be paid
so and so.   When this hope failed, the old captain lost
patience and began to deal out counsel, reproof and
warning with a lavish hand.   He recommended his son

to save the pennies and live more economically; to
return to medicine; to marry a wife; to remember his
Creator, and so on.   To all of which the perplexed
Friedrich could only reply with fresh promises, excuses
and recommendations of patience.   In like manner he
put off Frau von Wolzogen until she began to lose faith
in him.   A sharp letter from her brought him to his
knees with a humble apology, but it was years before
he could pay his debt to her.

The first performance of ' Fiesco ', the adaptation of
which to the stage had cost its author such a world of
trouble, took place on the 12th of January, 1784.   As
played it differed a good deal from the published version, and not alone with respect to the catastrophe.
Thus the painful episode of Bertha was worked over
into something less revoltingly horrible.   In the stage
version, instead of being brutally violated, she is
abducted by a tool of Gianettino, but rescued and
restored to her home unharmed.   With this change
made it would seem as if there were less reason than
ever for her being cursed and sent to a subterraneous
prison-vault.   Nevertheless Verrina's curse was allowed
to remain, — chiefly, as one cannot help surmising,
that the girl might be rescued with *éclat* in the fourth
act.   (The rescue scene in ' The Robbers ' had been a
great success.)   It has already been noted that the
offensive quarrel between Julia and Leonora was omitted
and that Leonora was allowed to live.   And there
were other such changes.   Schiller had been impressed
by an actor's criticism of his florid and violent language.   He accordingly removed or toned down a few
blemishes of this kind, but without making a radical

revision of the style.   Even in the stage version there
is quite too much of rant and fustian.

The Mannheimers took but little interest in ' Fiesco ',
—it was too erudite for them, as Schiller explained to
Reinwald some months later.[1]   Republican liberty, he
went on to say, was in that region a sound without
meaning; there was no Roman blood in the veins of
the Pfälzer.   In Berlin and Frankfurt, however, the
piece had met with good success.   We cannot blame
Schiller for trying to extract comfort from these bits
of evidence that the prophet was not without honor
save in his own country, though we may question his
implication that republican ideas were just then less rife
in the Palatinate than in Berlin and Frankfurt.   The
fact is that the lover of republican ideas must have been
the very person to feel the keenest dissatisfaction with
' Fiesco '.   Where it did succeed, its success was due
to causes having little to do with political sentiment.
The Berlin triumph was equivocal, being the triumph
not so much of Schiller as of one Plümicke, who took
high-handed liberties with the original text and made
it over, in both language and thought, so as to suit the
taste of the Berlin actors.   This northern version, thus
diluted with the water of the Spree, was presently
published by the enterprising pirate, Himburg, and
proved a formidable rival of the genuine edition.   The
play was tried at several theaters and with various
endings, — curiously enough Plümicke made Fiesco
commit suicide in the moment of his triumph,—but it
never became really popular.   It was translated into
English in 1796, into French in 1799.

[1] Letter of May 5, 1784.

Much more favorable was the reception given to 'Cabal and Love', which was first played at Mannheim on the 15th of April, 1784.[1] The part of the lackey who describes the horrors attending the exportation of soldiers to America was omitted; the satire was too strong for the politic Dalberg, who had all along been troubled by Schiller's drastic treatment of princely iniquity and his obvious allusions to well-known persons. Even Schwan, who was delighted with 'Louise Miller' from the first and readily undertook to publish it, described its author as an executioner. This time the Mannheimers had no difficulty of comprehension and they gave their applause unstintingly. After the great scene in the second act they rose and cheered vociferously,—whereat Schiller bowed and felt very happy. 'His manner', says honest Streicher, who has left a report of the memorable evening, 'his proud and noble bearing, showed that he had satisfied himself and was pleased to see his merit appreciated.'

A few days later the Mannheim players repeated their triumph at Frankfurt, where Schiller was lionized to his heart's content. 'Cabal and Love' now quickly became a stage favorite. Within a few months it was played successfully at nearly all the more important theaters of Germany. Even Stuttgart fell into line, but the Duke of Württemberg was not pleased, and a memorial of the nobility led to the prohibition of a second per-

---

[1] But this performance was not the first in order of time. 'Cabal and Love' had already been played on the 13th of April by Grossmann's company at Frankfurt. Grossmann was an intelligent theatrical man, who had conceived a liking for Schiller ; only he wished that the 'dear fiery man' would be a little more considerate of stage limitations.

formance. At Braunschweig it was tried with a happy ending, but this innovation, reasonable as it seems, took no root. A badly garbled English translation by Timaeus appeared in 1795; a better one by Monk Lewis, under the title of 'The Minister', in 1797. A French translation by La Martellière was hissed off the stage of the Théâtre Français in 1801.

From the Minerva press the new play got blame and praise. One writer saw in it the same Schiller who was already known as the 'painter of terrible scenes and the creator of Shaksperian thoughts'. A Berlin critic named Moritz, of whom we shall hear later, called the piece a disgrace to the age and wondered how a man could write and print such nonsense. The plot consisted, he declared, of a simpleton's quarrel with Providence over a stupid and affected girl. It was full of crass, ribald wit and senseless rodomantade. There were a few scenes of which something might have been made, but 'this writer converted everything into inflated rubbish'. Some one taxed Moritz with undue severity, whereupon he returned to the attack, insisting that this extravagant, blasphemous and vulgar diction, which purported to be nature rude and strong, was in reality altogether unnatural.[1]

And, to be candid, the critic was able to bring together an anthology of quotations which seemed like a rather forcible indictment of Schiller's literary taste. What Moritz failed to see was that the bad taste was only an excrescence growing upon a very vigorous stock. This was felt by another reviewer who declared

[1] Moritz's critique is reprinted in J. Braun's "Schiller und Goethe im Urteile ihrer Zeitgenossen", I, 103.

that high poetic genius shone forth from every scene of Schiller's works.   Many years later Zelter, the friend of Goethe, bore witness to the electric effect of the play upon himself and the other excitable youth who saw it in the first days of its popularity.   Like ' The Robbers ', it was a harbinger of the revolution.   It seemed to voice the hitherto voiceless woe of the third estate; and just because of that savage force which made it seem absurd to sedate minds, just because it rang out in such shrill and clangorous notes, it has continued to be heard.   Good taste is a matter of fashion.   It is never the most vital quality of literature.

If any one should be tempted to think that Schiller's youthful ideals of the dramatic art were not sufficiently exalted, he should read the lecture given before the Mannheim German Society, in June, 1784, on the question: ' What can a good permanent theater really effect ? '   It is an excellent, thoughtful essay, instinct with lofty idealism and at the same time full of sound observation.   Setting out from the postulate that the highest aim of all institutions whatsoever is the further-ance of the general happiness, the paper discusses the theater as a public institution of the state.   Its claims are examined, and the sphere and manner of its influ-ence discussed, along with those of religion and the laws.   Probably too much is made out of the moral and educational utility of the stage,—so at least it will be apt to seem to an American or an Englishman,— but the familiar arguments, the validity of which is now generally recognized in Germany, are marshalled with a fine breadth of view and with many felicities of ex-pression.   Toward the end there is a passage which shows that Schiller himself felt the shakiness of the utilitarian argument. He says: 'What I have tried to prove hitherto—that the stage exerts an essential influence upon morals and enlightenment—was doubtful'; and then he goes on to speak of a value not doubtful, namely, its value as a means of refined pleasure. This is the heart of the matter forever and ever; and one could hardly sum up the case more sagely than Schiller does in the sentence: 'The stage is the institution in which pleasure combines with instruction, rest with mental effort, diversion with culture; where no power of the soul is put under tension to the detriment of any other, and no pleasure is enjoyed to the damage of the community.'

The experience of Schiller at Mannheim illustrates the higher uses of adversity. Had he been well and happy, he might have written his third play, won the good will of Dalberg and then stuck fast for years in the Palatinate; which would have been a misfortune for him and for German letters. As it was, Mannheim gradually became odious to him. He had no buoyancy of spirit. 'God knows I have not been happy here', he wrote to Reinwald in May, 1784. His life was full of petty worries and distractions which weighted his imagination as with lead. As his year drew to an end he imagined that he had but to say the word to have his contract with the Mannheim theater renewed, but it was not so; Dalberg had quietly decided to get rid of him. From *his* point of view his poet had been a bad investment. Schiller had not kept his contract in the matter of the new play; he had done nothing but procrastinate and make excuses. 'Don Carlos' had

not even been begun.   There seemed to be no excuse
for such dawdling, when a man like Iffland could
always be relied upon to turn out a fairly acceptable
play in a few weeks.   No great wonder, therefore, that
Dalberg lost faith in Schiller and concluded that he
had exhausted his vein.   Through a friend he suggested a return to medicine.

Curiously enough Schiller grasped at the idea, pro-
fessing that a medical career was the one thing nearest
his heart.   He had long feared, so he wrote, that his
inspiration would forsake him if he relied upon literature for his living; but if he could devote himself to it
in the intervals of medical practice, good things might
be hoped for.   He accordingly proposed a renewal of
the contract for another year, with the understanding
that he devote himself principally to his medical studies
to the end of qualifying for the doctor's degree; in the
mean time he would undertake to produce one 'great
play' and also to edit a dramatic journal.   To this
amazing proposal Dalberg paid no attention; and when
the 1st of September arrived Schiller's connection with
the Mannheim theater came to an end.

It was a troublous, harassing time for him, that
summer of 1784, and the more since the woes of the
distracted lover were added to those of the disappointed
playwright and the impecunious debtor.   A German
savant observes that Schiller was not, like Goethe, a
virtuoso in love.   And so it certainly looks, albeit the
difference might perhaps appear a little less conspicuous
if he had lived to a ripe old age and dressed up his
recollections of youth in an autobiographical romance.
He did not lack the data of experience, but without

the charm of the retrospective poetic treatment his early love-affairs are not profoundly interesting. In the midst of his troubles it came over him that marriage might be the right thing for him; and so, one day in June, 1784, he offered himself to Frau von Wolzogen for a son-in-law. Nothing came of the suggestion; it was only a passing tribute to the abstract goodness of matrimony. About a year later he made, with similar results, an argumentative bid for the hand of Margarete Schwan. On the aforementioned visit to Frankfurt he met Sophie Albrecht, a melancholy poetess who had sought relief from the tameness of her married life by going upon the stage. Of her he wrote shortly afterwards:

> In the very first hours a firm and warm attachment sprang up between us ; our souls understood each other. I am glad and proud that she loves me and that acquaintance with me may perhaps make her happy. A heart fashioned altogether for sympathy, far above the pettiness of ordinary social circles, full of noble, pure feeling for truth and virtue, and admirable even where her sex is not usually so. I promise myself divine days in her immediate society.[1]

But all these palpitations were as water unto wine in comparison with his unwholesome passion for Charlotte von Kalb, whom he also met first in the spring of 1784. This lady, after a lonely and loveless girlhood, in which she had been tossed about as an unwelcome incumbrance from one relation to another, had lately married a Baron von Kalb. Her heart had no part in the marriage, which was arranged by

---

[1] From the letter of May 5, quoted above.

her guardian. In the pursuit of his career her husband left her much to herself. She was an introspective creature, very changeable in her moods and passionately fond of music and poetry. In Schiller she found her affinity. He acted first as her guide about Mannheim, then as her mentor in matters of literature. They saw much of each other; became intimately confidential and soon were treading a dangerous path,—though not so dangerous, peradventure, as has sometimes been inferred from the two poems, 'Radicalism of Passion' and 'Resignation', which belong to this period.

In the first of these poems our old friend, the lover of Laura, who is supposed to have married another man in the year 1782, resolves to fight no longer the 'giant-battle of duty'. He apostrophizes Virtue and bids her take back the oath that she has extorted from him in a moment of weakness. He will no longer respect the scruples that restrained him when the pitying Laura was ready to give all. Her marriage vow was itself sinful, and the god of Virtue is a detestable tyrant. In the other poem, which is a sort of antidote to the first, we hear of a poet, born in Arcadia, who surrendered his claim to earthly bliss on the promise of a reward in heaven. He gave up his all, even his Laura, to Virtue, though mockers called him a fool for believing in gods and immortality. At last he appears before the heavenly throne to claim his guerdon, but is told by an invisible genius that two flowers bloom for humanity,—Hope and Enjoyment. Who has the one must renounce the other. The high Faith that sustained him on earth was his sufficient reward and the fulfillment of Eternity's pledge.

Wer dieser Blumen eine brach, begehre
   Die andre Schwester nicht.
Geniesze wer nicht glauben kann.   Die Lehre
Ist ewig wie die Welt.   Wer glauben kann entbehre.
   Die Weltgeschichte ist das Weltgericht.[1]

When these poems were published, in 1786, their author saw fit to caution the public in a foot-note not to mistake an ebullition of passion for a system of philosophy, or the despair of an imaginary lover for the poet's confession of faith.   Thus warned one should not be too curious about the reality which is half revealed and half concealed by the verses.   Enough that it was not altogether a calm, Platonic sentiment, and that the torment of it was a factor in that uneasiness which finally became a burning desire to escape from Mannheim.   And the fates were preparing a way.

One day in June, when all was looking dark, Schiller received a packet containing an epistolary greeting, an embroidered letter-case and four portrait sketches.   The letter was anonymous, but he presently discovered that it came from Gottfried Körner, a young privat-docent in Leipzig, who had united with three friends in sending this token of regard to a Suabian poet whom they had found reason to like.   Schiller did not answer immediately and the skies grew darker still.   His relations with the Mannheim theater were presently strained to the point of disgust by the pro-

[1] In Bulwer's translation :
   "He who has plucked the one, resigned must see
      The sister's forfeit bloom :
   Let Unbelief enjoy—Belief must be
   All to the chooser ;—the world's history
   Is the world's judgment doom."

duction of a farce in which he was satirized.   He was in terrible straits for money.   To have something to do, after he was set adrift by Dalberg, he decided to go ahead with his project of a dramatic journal.   An attractive prospectus for the *Rhenish Thalia* was issued, and he began to prepare for the first number, which was to contain an installment of ' Don Carlos '.   The advance subscriptions fell far short of his sanguine hopes.   In these occupations the time passed until December.   Then one day he penned an answer to the Leipzig letter.   It was a turning-point in his destiny. A correspondence sprang up which presently convinced him that where these people were, there he must be.

Toward the end of the year there came another glint of good-will from the north.   The Duke of Weimar happened to be visiting at the neighboring Darmstadt, and through Frau von Kalb Schiller procured an introduction and an invitation to read the beginning of ' Don Carlos '.   The result was the title of Weimar Councillor.   This was very pleasant indeed; for while it put no florins in his purse, it gave him an honorable status in the German world.   He had been cast off by a prince of the barbarians to be taken up by *the* prince of the Greeks!   Henceforth he was in a sense the colleague of Goethe and Wieland.   He began to speak of the Duke of Weimar as *his* duke, and to indulge in day-dreams concerning the little city of the Muses in Thüringen.   For the rest there was an element of fate's amusing irony in the new title, seeing that he had just announced himself, in the prospectus of the *Rhenish Thalia*, as a literary free-lance who served no prince, but only the public.   The announcement con-

tained a sketch of his life and a confession of his sins,
—which he laid at the door of the Stuttgart Academy.
'The Robbers', he declared, had cost him home and
country; but now he was free, and his heart swelled at
the thought of wearing no other fetter than the verdict
of the public, and appealing to no other throne than
the human soul.

Owing to various delays the first number of the new
journal did not appear until the spring of 1785, and by
that time Schiller was all ready for his flight northward.
Matters had continued to go badly with him.   On the
22nd of February he wrote to Körner, 'in a nameless
oppression of the heart', as follows:

I can stay no longer in Mannheim.   For twelve days I have
carried the decision about with me like a resolution to leave the
world.   People, circumstances, earth and sky, are repulsive to
me.   I have not a soul to fill the void in my heart—not a friend,
man or woman ; and what might be dear to me is separated
from me by conventions and circumstances. . . . Oh, my soul is
athirst for new nourishment, for better people, for friendship,
affection and love.   I must come to you ; must learn, in your
immediate society and in intimate relations with you, once more
to enjoy my own heart, and to bring my whole being to a livelier
buoyancy.   My poetic vein is stagnant ; my heart has dried up
toward my associations here.   You must warm it again.   With
you I shall be doubly, trebly, what I have been hitherto ; and
more than all that, my dearest friends, I shall be happy.   I have
never been so yet.   Weep for me that I must make this confession.   I have not been happy ; for fame and admiration and all
the other concomitants of authorship do not weigh as much as
one moment of love and friendship.   They starve the heart.

To the worldly-wise such a perfervid sight-draft upon
the bank of love, made after a few weeks of epistolary
acquaintance, will no doubt seem a little risky.   One

is reminded of Goethe's Tasso, impulsively offering his friendship to a cooler man and getting the reply:

> In Einem Augenblicke forderst du
> Was wohlbedächtig nur die Zeit gewährt.[1]

But this time Schiller's instinct had guided him aright. Körner was no Antonio, and he did not recoil even when he learned that his new friend was very much in need of money and would not be able to leave Mannheim, unless a Leipzig publisher could be found who would take over his magazine and advance a few pounds upon its uncertain prospects. This was easily arranged, for Körner was well-to-do and had himself lately acquired an interest in the publishing business of Göschen at Leipzig. Göschen took the *Thalia* (dropping the ' Rhenish '), Schiller paid his more pressing debts, and early in April was on his way to Leipzig, panting for the new friends as the hart panteth after the water-brooks.

[1] Thou askest in a single moment that
Which only time can give with cautious hand.

CHAPTER VIII

The Boon of Friendship

Wem der grosse Wurf gelungen,
Eines Freundes Freund zu sein, . . .
Mische seinen Jubel ein.—' *Song to Joy*'.

GOTTFRIED KÖRNER, father of the more famous Theodor, was some three years older than Schiller and belonged to an opulent and distinguished family. His father was a high church dignitary, his mother the daughter of a well-to-do Leipzig merchant. The boy had grown up under austere religious influences and then drifted far in the direction of liberalism. After a university career devoted at first to the humanities and then to law, he had travelled extensively in foreign countries, and then returned to Leipzig, full of ambition but undecided as to his future course. Here, in 1778, he became acquainted with Minna Stock, the daughter of an engraver who had once been the teacher of Goethe. Stock died in 1773, leaving a widow and two daughters to battle with poverty. The elder daughter, Dora, inherited something of her father's vivacious humor and artistic talent, while the younger and handsomer, Minna, was of a more domestic temper. When Körner fell in love with the amiable Minna and wished to marry her, he met with opposition in his own family, who thought that the 'engraver's mamsell' was not good enough for him. This little touch of adversity converted him from a gentleman of leisure and a browsing philosopher into a man with a purpose in life. He set about making himself independent of the family wealth. To this end he offered himself as a privat-docent in law at the Leipzig university. When this expedient failed him through lack of students, he began to practice and soon received an appointment which took him to Dresden. This in 1783. Dresden now became his official residence, but he made frequent visits to his betrothed in Leipzig, and during one of these his memorable letter to Schiller was indited.

The other member of the quartette was Ludwig Huber, at that time the accepted lover of Dora Stock. Huber was three years younger than Schiller,—an impressionable youth, of some linguistic talent, who had his occasional promptings of literary ambition. But his soarings were mere grasshopper flights; steady effort was not his affair and he lacked solid ability. A doting mother had watched and coddled him until in practical affairs he was comically helpless. As the futility of his character became more apparent with the lapse of time, he lost the esteem of his friends, and the engagement with Dora Stock was broken off. So far as Schiller is concerned, the friendship of Huber was a passing episode of no particular importance.

Early in the year 1785 Körner lost both his parents and found himself the possessor of a considerable fortune. There was now no further obstacle to his marriage; so the time was fixed for the wedding and he set about preparing a home for his bride. Thus it came about that when Schiller arrived in Leipzig, on the 17th of April, 1785,—mud, snow and inundations had made the journey desperately tedious,—he did not at once meet the man whom he most cared to know. Huber and the two ladies, who seem to have expected a wild, dishevelled genius, were astonished to see a mild-eyed, bashful man, who bore little resemblance to Karl Moor and needed time to thaw up. But the stranger soon felt at home. He had explained to Huber minutely how he wished to live. He would no longer keep his own establishment,—he could manage an entire dramatic conspiracy more easily than his own housekeeping. At the same time he did not wish to live alone.

> I need for my inward happiness [he wrote] a right true friend who is always at hand like my angel; to whom I can communicate my budding ideas and emotions in the moment of their birth, without writing letters or making visits. Even the trivial circumstance that my friend lives outside my four walls; that I must go through the street to reach him, that I must change my dress, or the like, kills the enjoyment of the moment. My train of thought is liable to be rent in pieces before I can get to him. . . . I cannot live parterre, nor in the attic, and I should not like to look out upon a churchyard. I love men and the thronging crowd. If I cannot arrange it so that we (I mean the five-parted clover-leaf) may eat together, then I might resort to the table d'hôte of an inn, for I had rather fast than not dine in company.[1]

It is clear that, notwithstanding experiences which might have embittered a less genial nature, Schiller was in no danger of becoming a misanthrope. For him the throng upon the street was not the madding crowd of the English poet, nor the 'cursed race' of

[1] Letter of March 25, 1785.

Frederick the Great, but an inspiration; a spectacle to keep the heart warm and foster the sense of brotherhood. He felt the need of men, however shabbily they might treat him. And men enough were at hand; for the Leipzig fair was then on, and the town was full of strangers who were eager to gape at the author of 'The Robbers', to be introduced to him, to invite him here and there. So for a week he floated with the current of casual dissipation and then, caught for an hour by a refluent eddy of lonesomeness,—four parts of the pentamerous clover-leaf were paired lovers,— he penned a missive which might have changed much in his future career: He sent to Christian Schwan a formal proposal for the hand of Margarete. With characteristic optimism he urged that fortune had at last turned favorably. He had good prospects. He proposed to work hard upon 'Don Carlos' and the *Thalia*, and meanwhile quietly to return to medicine. Wherefore he now made bold to express a hope that he had long cherished but had not dared to utter.

The sequelæ of this wooing have never been cleared up in detail. Schiller's letter as preserved bears a marginal note by Schwan to the effect that Laura in the poem 'Resignation' was no other than his eldest daughter. 'I gave her this letter to read', the note says, 'and told Schiller to apply directly to her. Why nothing came of the affair has remained a riddle to me. Happy my daughter would not have been with Schiller.' The annotation is not dated. The identification of Laura with Margarete is obviously wrong. Was Schwan's memory also at fault? Did he imagine, long after the fact, that he had actually taken what

must have seemed to him, when Schiller had become
a famous poet, the reasonable course to have pursued?
Did he withhold the letter too long and then show it?
Or was Margarete herself disinclined,—piqued perhaps
by Schiller's neglect of her, or by his passion for
Charlotte von Kalb? Or did Schiller's own courage
fail him after he had received a hint of favor? A letter
to Körner, written May 7, tells of pleasant news from
Mannheim, and shortly afterward a rumor was in cir-
culation that Schiller was about to marry a rich wife.
The probability is that neither party was more than
half inclined to the match. The blue flame perished
naturally for lack of fuel.

Early in May, following the custom of well-to-do
Leipzigers, Schiller sought refuge from the incipient
summer heat of the city by taking rooms in the suburban village (such it was then) of Gohlis. Here, in a
little second-story chamber, which was provided with
an infinitesimal bed-room, he lived some four months,
—happy months, in the main, even if the famous
'Song to Joy', which local tradition ascribes to this
time and place, was in fact written a little later in
Dresden. Various friends were at hand. Besides
Huber there was Göschen, with whom he was soon on
terms of intimacy. The Stock sisters,—'our dear
girls', as he calls them in a letter to the absent
Körner,—had likewise quartered themselves in Gohlis;
and so had Dr. Albrecht and his wife, Sophie, the
actress. These with one or two others were enough
for converse and for jollity; and there were merry
evenings, with wine and talk, and cards and skittles
and nonsense. Though ordinarily he 'joked wi'

difficulty ', Schiller could be jovial enough in a company of congenial spirits.   Nevertheless there was but little of the bohemian about him.   That dignified seriousness which pervades all his later writings, and gave to Goethe the impression of a man dwelling habitually above the plane of vulgar things, was beginning even now to characterize him as a social being.

While living at Gohlis he received a visit from Moritz, the man who had written so savagely of ' Cabal and Love '.   If ever an author has been justified in giving the cut direct to a pestilent reviewer, this was the occasion.   But Schiller received his visitor with suave courtesy; an interchange of views followed and the two men parted with embraces and protestations of friendly esteem.   Schiller was not a good hater, except of hate.   His nature craved love and friendship. He was eager to learn of his critics and could not long cherish resentment over an honest expression of opinion.   Besides this he had now come to feel that his early writings were anything but invulnerable.

Notwithstanding his promise of steady industry, Schiller accomplished but little during his sojourn at Gohlis.   It was the old story: There were too many distractions, too many confusing images of what might be done.   The scheme of an antidote to ' The Robbers ', in the shape of a moral sequel, gradually dropped out of view, along with the medical studies.   The *Thalia*, originally planned with reference to the public at Mannheim, refused to bear transplanting to another soil without a season of wilting.   Instead of manuscript for the second number, Göschen was obliged to content himself for several months with excuses for postponement. And as for 'Don Carlos', the conception had so changed with the lapse of time that its author felt at a loss how to manage it. The play, with its wonderful pair of dreamers, was waiting for the inspiration of a real friendship at Dresden.

Long before they met in the body Schiller and Körner had given expression to their mutual trust in language of romantic enthusiasm. On the 2nd of May Körner wrote at length of his own life, character and aspirations. The letter reveals a noble nature conscious of an exceptional indebtedness to fortune and eager to pay the debt by solid work for mankind, but lacking the ability to decide and execute. Körner evidently felt that he was in some danger of becoming an intellectual Sybarite, and he hoped that Schiller's example would save him from this danger by spurring him to literary effort. In his reply Schiller expresses his admiration of a character to whom fortune's favor means not, as for most men, the opportunity of enjoyment, but the duty of more strenuous living; then he sends a jubilant Godspeed to the 'dear wanderer who wishes to accompany him in such faithful, brotherly fashion on his romantic journey to truth, fame and happiness.' The letter continues:

I now feel realized in us what as poet I but prophetically imagined. Brotherhood of spirits is the most infallible key to wisdom. Separately we can do nothing. . . . Do not fear from this time forth for the endless duration of our friendship. Its materials are the fundamental impulses of the human soul. Its territory is eternity ; its *non plus ultra* the Godhead.

Then, as if momentarily abashed by his own extravagance of expression, he protests that his *Schwärmerei*,

if such it be, is nothing but a 'joyful paroxysm anticipating our future greatness'.   For his part, he would
not 'exchange one such moment for the highest
triumph of cold reason'.   Enthusiasm, he declares, is
the greatest thing in life.

The two men did not see each other until July,
when a meeting was arranged at an interjacent village,
to which Schiller rode out with the Leipzig friends.
The next day he wrote a letter to Körner, who had
returned to Dresden, describing an incident of the
return journey,—a letter so full of instruction with
regard to the Schiller of this period that it deserves
to be quoted at some length:

Somehow we came to speak of plans for the future.   My heart
grew warm.   It was not idle dreaming.   I had a solid philosophic
assurance of that which I saw lying before me in the glorious
perspective of time.   In a melting mood of shame, such as does
not depress but rouses to manly effort, I looked back into the
past, which I had misused through the most unfortunate waste
of energy.   I felt that nature had endowed me with powers on a
bold plan, and that her intention with me (perhaps a great intention) had so far been defeated.   Half of this failure was due to the
insane method of my education, and the adverse humor of fate ;
the other and larger half, however, to myself.   Deeply, my best
of friends, did I feel all that, and in the general fiery ferment of
my emotions, head and heart united in a Herculean vow to make
good the past and begin anew the noble race to the highest goal.
My feeling became eloquent and imparted itself to the others
with electric power.   O how beautiful, how divine, is the con-
tact of two souls that meet on the way to divinity !   Thus far not
a syllable had been spoken of you, but I read your name in
Huber's eyes and involuntarily it came to my lips.   Our eyes
met and our holy purpose fused with our holy friendship.   It
was a mute hand-clasp—to remain faithful to the resolution of
this moment ; to spur each other on to the goal, to admonish

and encourage, and not to halt save at the bourne where human
greatness ends. . . . Our conversation had taken this turn when
we got out for breakfast. We found wine in the inn, and your
health was drunk. We looked at each other silently ; our mood
was that of solemn worship and each one of us had tears in his
eyes, which he tried to keep back. . . . I thought of the beginning of the eucharist : ' Do this as often as ye drink in memory
of me.' I heard the organ and stood before the altar. Suddenly
I remembered that it was your birthday. Unwittingly we
had celebrated it with a holy rite. Dearest friend, had you seen
your glorification in our faces, heard it in our tear-choked voices,
at that moment you would have forgotten even your betrothed ;
you would have envied no happy mortal under the sun. Heaven
has strangely brought us together, but in our friendship it shall
have wrought a miracle. Dim foreboding led me to expect
much, very much of you, when I first decided to come to Leipzig ; but Providence has more than fulfilled the promise, and has
vouchsafed to me in your arms a happiness of which I could not
form an image.

It tends to provoke a smile to read on in this letter
and find it suddenly turning from such ecstasies to a
straightforward confession that the writer is embarrassed
for lack of ready cash. He had met with disappoint-
ments. The Mannheim people had not treated him
handsomely, the subscribers to the *Thalia* were delin-
quent, and so forth. Could not Göschen be persuaded
to undertake a new and authentic edition of the published plays and to advance a sum of money on the
prospects ? Körner's reply was prompt and characteristic. He enclosed a draft for current expenses,
promised more against the time of need and bade his
friend have no further solicitude about money. He
knew very well, so he averred with politic delicacy,
that Schiller could easily earn enough by working for

money; but for a year at least he was to let himself
be relieved of that degrading necessity. They would
keep an account and all should be paid back with
interest in the time of abundance; but for the present
no more of pecuniary anxieties! Schiller, to whose
brief experience in a selfish world this sort of conduct
was something new, replied that he would not entrench
himself in a false pride, as the great Rousseau had done
on a similar occasion, but would accept the generous
offer; this being the best possible expression of his
gratitude. Körner was pleased to have the business
settled by letter. 'I have always despised money',
he wrote, 'to a degree that it disgusts me to talk
about it with souls that are dear to me. I attach no
importance to actions that are natural to people of our
sort, and which you would perform for me were the
conditions reversed.'

It was now arranged that after Körner's marriage
Schiller should make his home in Dresden. The
eagerly awaited migration took place in September,
and Schiller entered the Saxon capital, which was to
be his home for the next two years, in a flutter of
joyous anticipation. The Körners quartered him in
their charming suburban cottage at Loschwitz, in the
loveliest region he had known since his childhood.
The guest, who had seen but little of the quiet joys of
domestic life and was now received on the footing of
an adopted brother, felt very happy. His intercourse
with Körner gave him the very kind of intellectual
stimulus that he most needed. Körner was at this
time the more solid character of the two. He had
seen more of the world. While capable of warm affec-

tion and strong enthusiasm, he had adopted a profession which inevitably gave to his thoughts a practical bent. Besides this he had taken up the study of Kant with great earnestness and was thereby more than ever disposed to see all questions in the white light of pure reason. He was thus the very man to pour a cool Mephistophelean spray upon Schiller's emotional fervors. One can easily imagine the general drift of the philosophical discussions that took place during the lengthening evenings of September, 1785, when we find Schiller expressing himself to the absent Huber in such language as this:

The boyhood of our minds is now over, I imagine, and likewise the honeymoon of our friendship. Let our hearts now cleave to each other in manly affection, gush little and feel much ; plan little and act the more fruitfully. Enthusiasm and ideals have sunk incredibly in my estimation. As a rule we make the mistake of estimating the future from a momentary feeling of enhanced power, and painting things in the color of our transient exaltation of feeling. I praise enthusiasm, and love the divine ethereal power of kindling to a great resolution. It pertains to the better man, but it is not all of him.

But life at Loschwitz was not lived altogether in the upper altitudes of solemn philosophy. From this period dates the well-known ' Petition ',—one of the few glints of playful humor to be found among Schiller's poems. He had been left alone one day with ' Don Carlos ', and he found his meditations disturbed by the operations of the washerwoman. The result was a string of humorous stanzas bewailing the fate of a poet who is compelled by his vocation to fix his mind upon the love ecstasies of Princess Eboli, and listen at the same time to the swashy music of the wash-tub:

I feel my love-lorn lady's hurt,
   My fancy waxes hotter;
I hear,—the sound of sock and shirt
   A-swishing in the water.

Vanished the dream—the faery chimes—
   My Princess, pax vobiscum !
The devil take these wash-day rimes,
   I will no longer risk 'em.

When the Körners occupied their winter residence in the city, Schiller found rooms hard by, and was presently joined by Huber, who had secured a position in the diplomatic service. The time was now ripe for that jubilant song, more frequently set to music than any other of Schiller's poems, wherein we are introduced to a mystic brotherhood, worshiping in fiery intoxication at the shrine of the celestial priestess, Joy, whose other name is Sympathy. A mystic brotherhood; yet not an exclusive one, since the fraternal kiss is freely offered to every mortal on the round earth who has found one soul to love. The lines glorify Joy, just as the odes to Laura had previously glorified Love, as a mystic attraction pervading all nature and leading up to God; as that which holds the stars in their course, inspires the searcher after truth, sustains the martyr and gives a pledge of immortality. Wherefore the millions are exhorted to endure patiently for the better world that is coming, when a great God will reward. Anger and vengeance are to be forgotten, and our mortal foe forgiven. After these rapturous strophes, culminating in a health to the good Spirit above, one is just a little surprised to hear the singer urge, with unabated ardor, a purely militant ideal of life,—firm courage in heavy trial, succor to the oppressed, manly pride in the presence of kings, and death to the brood of liars. A final strophe, urging grace to the criminal on the scaffold, general forgiveness of sinners and the abolition of hell, was rejected by Schiller, who later characterized the song as a 'bad poem'. The 'Song to Joy' sprang from noble sentiment and has the genuine lyric afflatus; but its author had not yet emerged from that nebulous youthful sentimentalism according to which joy, sympathy, love, friendship, virtue, happiness, God, were all very much the same thing. And the thought is a trifle incoherent. If the good Spirit above the stars is to pardon everybody, what becomes of the incentive to a militant life? Why should one strive and cry and get into a feaze about tyrants and liars?

The 'Song to Joy', with music by Körner, was published in the second number of the *Thalia*, which, after hanging fire for months, finally appeared in February, 1786. It contained also the poems 'Radicalism of Passion' and 'Resignation', and a fresh installment of 'Don Carlos'. Of the prose contributions the most important was the story, 'The Criminal from Disgrace', later called 'The Criminal from Lost Honor'. It was based upon a true story, got from Professor Abel in Stuttgart, concerning the life and death of a notorious Suabian robber, named Schwan, who was put to death in 1760. Schiller changed the name to Christian Wolf and built out of the ugly facts a strumous tale of criminal psychology,—the autopsy of a depraved soul, as he called it. His hero is a sort of vulgarized Karl Moor; that is, an enemy of society who might have been its friend if things had not happened so and so. The successive steps of his descent from mild resentment to malignant fury, libertinism and crime, and the reaction of his own increasing depravity upon his own mind, are described in a manner which is fairly interesting from a literary point of view, whatever a modern expert criminologist might think of it. The *crux* of the ever difficult problem,— the precise division of responsibility between society and the wretch whom it spews out of its mouth,—is brought clearly into view, but without any attempt at an exact solution. The tale is not a homily, but an object-lesson designed to show how things go. It is too slight an affair to be worthy of extended comment, but it shows Schiller becoming interested in the psychological analysis of conduct. Moral goodness and badness are beginning to appear less simple concepts, and the tangle of human motive more intricate, than he had supposed.

Along with these contributions there also appeared in the second number of the *Thalia* a translation of the ' Précis Historique ', prefixed by Mercier to his recently published ' Portrait de Philippe Second '. The ' portrait ' itself was a dramatic picture, in fifty-two scenes, without division into acts. The work of Mercier, who paints the Spanish king in the darkest possible colors, furnished a few hints for ' Don Carlos ', but its influence was not very great. What chiefly concerns us here is to note Schiller's awakening interest in historical studies. In the spring of 1786, during an absence of the Körners which deprived him of his wonted inspiration, he found himself unable to work. Letter after letter tells of laziness and mental vacuity. As he could do nothing else he took to desultory reading, and this did not satisfy him. ' Really ', he wrote on the 15th of April:

Really I must turn over a new leaf with my reading. I feel with pain that I still have such an astonishing amount to learn ; that I must sow in order to reap. . . . History is becoming dearer to me every day. I have this week read a history of the Thirty Years' War, and my head is still quite feverish from it. That this epoch of the greatest national misery should have been at the same time the most brilliant epoch of human power ! What a number of great men came forth from this night ! I could wish that for the ten years past I had done nothing but study history. I believe I should have become a very different fellow. Do you think I shall yet be able to make up for lost time ?

One sees from this language by what particular hook the study of history had taken hold of Schiller's mind, and what kind of profit he was promising himself from further reading. He was interested in the evolution of great men. For him, as for the poets always, from Homer down, history resolved itself into the doings of the leaders.

For the time being, however, the new zeal seems to have been a mere flash in the pan, that set nothing in motion. Nor was Körner able, for some time to come, to induce his friend to make a serious study of Kant's ' Critique ', though every third word between them was of philosophy. Nevertheless their philosophic debates did bear literary fruit. The third number of the *Thalia*, which came out in May, contained the first installment of the ' Philosophical Letters ', a fictitious correspondence between two friends, Julius and

Raphael, who have arrived by different routes at the same way of thinking, and are resolved to tell the world how it all came about. Julius is Schiller; Raphael is Körner, who actually contributed one of the later letters. We learn that Julius was passing through a spiritual crisis. He was happy but he had not reflected. The little world of his rapturous emotions sufficed him. Now, however, Raphael has enlightened his mind, made him a citizen of the world and taught him to comprehend the all-sufficient majesty of reason; but he has won enlightenment at the expense of peace. He is miserable and demands back his soul. Raphael rebukes him gently for his faint-heartedness and asks for a history of his thinking. So Julius rummages through his papers and sends on a somewhat elaborate ' Theosophy of Julius ',—a sort of *précis*, it would seem, of Schiller's earlier views. It is religious mysticism set forth with warm eloquence. The universe is a thought of God. The highest aim of thinking is to read the divine plan. All spirits are attracted by perfection. The supreme perfection is God, of whom love is an emanation. Love is gain; hate is loss; pardon, the recovery of lost property; misanthropy a prolonged suicide; egoism the utmost poverty. If every man loved all mankind, every man would possess the world. If we comprehend perfection it becomes ours. If we plant beauty and joy, beauty and joy shall we reap. If we think clearly we shall love fervently.

To this ' theosophy ' Julius adds a few comments, evidently of later origin, which show that he has now become aware of its intellectual inadequacy. Still he does not repudiate it. He thinks it may do for a doctrine, if one's nature is adapted to it.—Herewith, so far as Schiller was concerned, the 'Philosophic Letters' came to an end; but in the spring of 1788, Körner surprised him with a letter by Raphael, which is, philosophically speaking, by far the best of the entire collection. But this book is not concerned with the writings of Körner.

Ere the third number of the *Thalia* appeared it had become evident that the enterprise would not be profitable, and its perplexed editor was in doubt whether to continue it. He finally decided to go on. When the fourth number came out, early in 1787, it contained the beginning of a novel, 'The Ghostseer', wherein a mysterious Sicilian, and a still more mysterious Armenian, dog the footsteps of a German Prince von * * * living at Venice, and do various things suggesting a connection with occult powers. The first installment of the story broke off at a very exciting point,—just when the Sicilian has produced his amazing ghost-scene, but has not yet been unmasked as a vulgar fraud. Schiller evidently began the novel in no very strenuous frame of mind. He wished to profit by the popular interest in tales of mysterious charlatanry which had been aroused by the exploits of Cagliostro. So he set out to spin a yarn in that vein, but he had no definite plan and did not himself know where he would bring up. The literary merits of 'The Ghost-seer', Schiller's most noteworthy attempt in prose fiction, will come up for consideration in connection with the conclusion, or rather the continuation, which he published some two years later, when he had left Dresden to seek his fortune in Weimar.

Even now the necessity of seeking his fortune somewhere was daily becoming more imperious.   The
Thalia did not pay, though the critics spoke well of
it, and he could not live forever upon Körner's friendly
advances of money.   The sense of his dependence
often galled him; and yet when a proposal, in itself
highly attractive, came to him from a distant city, he
could not pluck up courage to leave his friend.   Friedrich Schröder, the greatest German actor of the time,
wished to draw him to Hamburg.   Schiller looked up
to Schröder with genuine admiration and speculatively
promised himself great gain from association with 'the
one man in Germany who could realize all his ideas of
art.'   In Mannheim,—so he wrote in October, 1786,
—he had lost all his enthusiasm for the theater; it was
now beginning to revive, but he shuddered at the
treatment to which playwrights were exposed by
theatrical people.   Moreover he was living at Dresden
'in the bosom of a family to which he had become
necessary'.   So nothing came of the negotiations
except the preparation of a stage version of 'Don
Carlos' for the Hamburg theater.

An amusing glimpse of domestic conditions in the
Körner household is afforded by Schiller's dramatic
skit, entitled 'Körner's Forenoon'.   It belongs apparently to the year 1787, but was not published until
1862.   The busy councillor of the Dresden Consistory
sees a little leisure before him and squares off at his
desk for a solid forenoon's work.   He begins by ordering his man to shave him.   Then he is interrupted by
a procession of callers,—Schiller, in various rôles, and
Minna, and Dorchen, and Professor Becker and others,

—who keep the stream of babble flowing until one o'clock. Körner is too late for the consistory and all that he has accomplished is to get shaved. The piece is a slight affair, but there is enough of solemn fun in it to make one wish that its author had seen fit to work his lighter vein more frequently.

About the time when this facetious bagatelle was penned, or a little earlier perhaps, Schiller became the hero of a comedy in real life. In the winter of 1787 he attended a masked ball where he met a pretty domino—a plump voluptuous maiden—who fascinated him. Her name was Henriette von Arnim. He followed up the acquaintance and was soon quite seriously interested. As the Arnim family did not enjoy the best of reputations, the Körners were annoyed at Schiller's seeming lack of connoisseurship in women. They contrived to let him know that on the evenings when Henriette was not at home to him she was at home to a certain earthy Count Waldstein, or to a certain Jew banker, as the case might be. This was painful, but not immediately decisive, and miserable days ensued. In the spring he was persuaded to try a few weeks' outing in the country. Here he was at first frightfully lonesome,—a dejected Robinson Crusoe, who could neither work nor amuse himself. To his pathetic demands for reading-matter his friends replied with malicious humor by sending him Goethe's 'Werther' and Laclos's 'Liaisons Dangereuses'. After a while the Arnims followed him, but presently the count came also; and then the course of true love, thus awkwardly bifurcated, was more troubled than ever. After Henriette's return to Dresden there was an interchange of letters, wherein love fought a losing battle with doubt and suspicion.

This half-year of amatory perturbation was of course unfavorable to literary labor. No further numbers of the *Thalia* appeared, and ' The Misanthrope ', a new play of excellent promise, made no progress. But ' Don Carlos ' did at last get itself completed—after a fashion. It was published early in the summer. And now, with this burden lifted, the time seemed to have arrived for carrying out the long-cherished plan of a visit to Weimar. Who could tell what might come of it ? Körner was just as loyal as ever, but he was also wise enough to respect his friend's longing for a more assured and less dependent existence. And so in July Schiller set out for Thüringen,—to be seen no more in Dresden save as an occasional visitor. But the letters he wrote to the noble-minded friend who had done and been so much for him constitute, for several years to come, our best source of information concerning his outward fortune and his inner history. Before we follow him to Weimar, however, it will be in order to consider the play which remains as the most important achievement of his Dresden period.

CHAPTER IX

𝔇on Carlos

> Arm in Arm mit dir,
> So fordr' ich mein Jahrhundert in die Schranken.
> *'Don Carlos'*.

WITH the publication of 'Don Carlos' Schiller's literary reputation entered upon a new phase. Hitherto he had been known as a playwright in whom the passion for strong effects often obscured the sense of artistic fitness. Of his dramatic power there could be no doubt, but had he the higher gift of the great poet? Would he ever be able to clothe his conceptions in a form that would appeal permanently to the general heart because of high and rare artistic excellence? Doubts of this kind were quite justifiable up to the year 1787, but they were set at rest by 'Don Carlos'. However vulnerable it may be as a poetic totality, it has passages that are magnificent. Its sonorous verse, wedded to a lofty argument and freighted with the noblest idealism of the century, made sure its author's title to a place in the Walhalla of the poets.

Except 'Wallenstein' no other work of Schiller cost him such long and strenuous toil. 'Don Carlos', like Goethe's 'Faust', is a stratified deposit. The time that went to the making of it, only four years in all, was comparatively short, but it was for Schiller a time of rapid change; and the play, intensely subjective from the first, participated in the ripening process. The result is a certain lack of artistic congruity. Schiller himself, always his own best critic, felt this and frankly admitted it in the first of his 'Letters upon Don Carlos'.

It may be [he wrote] that in the first [three] acts I have aroused expectations which the last do not fulfill. St. Réal's novel, perhaps also my own remarks upon it in the first number of the *Thalia*, may have suggested to the reader a standpoint from which the work can no longer be regarded. During the period of elaboration, which on account of divers interruptions was a pretty long time, much changed within myself. . . . What had mainly attracted me at first, attracted me less later on, and at last hardly at all. New ideas that came into my mind crowded out the earlier ones. Carlos himself had declined in my favor, for no other reason perhaps than that I had outgrown him, and for the opposite reason the Marquis of Posa had taken his place. So it came about that I brought a very different heart to the fourth and fifth acts. Yet the first three were already in the hands of the public, and the plan of the whole could not be recast; I had either to suppress the piece entirely (for which very few of my readers would have thanked me), or else to fit the second half to the first as best I could.

Let us look somewhat closely at the process of evolution here alluded to in general terms.

The original impulse came from a work of romantic fiction, the 'Dom Carlos' of St. Réal, which was first read by Schiller in the summer of 1782 and drew from him the comment that the story 'deserved the brush of a dramatist'. St. Réal's novel begins by telling how Charles the Fifth arranged, just before his abdication, that his grandson Carlos should some day marry

Elizabeth of Valois; and how afterwards Philip determined to take the French princess for his own wife
instead of leaving her to his son. Meanwhile, however, by much gazing at the picture of his betrothed,
young Carlos had learned to love her, and she in turn
had conceived for him a ' disposition to love rather than
a veritable passion '. Arrived at the Spanish court
the young queen wins all hearts; even the white-haired
Philip falls in love with her, though he treats her with
stately reserve in the presence of others and surrounds
her with the restraints of Spanish etiquette. Thus the
queen comes to feel that she possesses ' only the body
of her husband, his soul being filled with the designs
of his ambition and the meditation of his policy '. As
for Carlos, his love-lorn eyes soon betray to her how
it is with him, but she can only pity him, though she
secretly returns his love, for she is as virtuous as she is
beautiful.

Not so the Princess Eboli, wife of Ruy Gomez, the
tutor of Carlos. Having tried to win the love of the
king and found her designs thwarted by the queen's
beauty, Eboli makes advances to Prince Carlos, who
lets her know that he cannot love her and thus makes
her angry. In this mood she bestows her favor upon
the king's half-brother, Don Juan of Austria, who
is also enamored of the queen and has been watching Carlos suspiciously. Having thus made enemies
of Eboli and Don Juan, Carlos next draws upon himself the hatred of the powerful Duke of Alva, of Ruy
Gomez, and of the Inquisition. This he does by his
outspoken criticism of their doings and his threats
of punishment to be meted out to them when he

shall have become king. Anxious for their own future Alva and Ruy Gomez conspire together and cause suspicions of Carlos to be whispered in the ear of the king. At first Philip is not greatly excited. When Carlos, importuned by Count Egmont, asks for a commission to the Netherlands, Philip does not refuse, but declares that he will go too and share the peril of his son. This, however, is a mere ruse to gain time. While they are waiting, the king meanwhile feigning illness, Carlos communicates freely with the queen through his bosom friend, the Marquis of Posa. Hearing of this intimacy the king now becomes really jealous, but of Posa not of Carlos. Maddened by suspicion he has the marquis murdered on the street and employs Eboli to watch the queen. After this Carlos resolves upon independent action and begins to negotiate with the Netherlanders. His operations are watched and reported by his enemies, and just as he is about to leave Spain he is arrested. The king places his case before the Holy Office, which decrees that he must die. Being allowed to choose the manner of his death he opens his veins while bathing.

With the actual Don Carlos, whose story bears but little resemblance to that of St. Réal's hero, we are not particularly concerned. The French Abbé's drift is to exalt the French princess and to give a telling picture of a pair of high-minded lovers who are brought to their death by a complicate intrigue begotten of jealousy, political hatred and religious fanaticism. After the death of Carlos the queen is poisoned and then, one after the other, all the conspirators meet with poetic justice. "Ainsi", the Abbé concludes,

" furent expiées les morts à jamais déplorables d'un
prince magnanime, et de la plus belle et de la plus
vertueuse princesse qui fut jamais. C'est ainsi que
leurs ombres infortunées furent enfin pleinement ap-
paisées par les funestes destinées de tous les complices
de leur trépas."

St. Réal's novel was published in 1672 and has been
a favorite quarry of the dramatist. Of the plays of
Otway (1676) and Campistron (1685) Schiller had no
knowledge, nor did he receive any suggestions from
the fierce and gloomy ' Filippo' of Alfieri, which appeared in 1783. He approached the subject in his
own way and his first thought was simply to dramatize
St. Réal, who is mainly interested in the love tragedy
and writes as a literary artist rather than as a political
or religious pamphleteer. We possess a prose outline[1] of ' Don Carlos', written probably at Bauerbach,
which shows exactly how the theme first bit into
Schiller's mind. The exposition was to show the
secret passion of the lovers and the dangers threatening
them from the jealousy of Philip, the political hostility
of the grandees and the malice of the slighted Eboli.
In the third act the king would become madly suspicious and resolve upon his son's death. Then there
was to be a gleam of hope : the ambition of Carlos
would awaken and begin to prevail over his love,
while Posa would divert the king's suspicion to himself
and fall a sacrifice to friendship. Then a new danger
would arise : the king would discover Don Carlos in a
seeming ' rebellion', and decree his death. The dying
declaration of Carlos would prove his innocence and

[1] It is printed in Sämtliche Schriften, III, 180.

the king would be left alone to mourn the havoc he had wrought and to punish the conspirators who had deceived him.

This sketch promises, it will be observed, not a political tragedy, but, as Schiller himself afterwards phrased it, a 'domestic tragedy in a royal household'. Springing up from the same soil and at the same time as ' Cabal and Love ', it was to be much the same sort of play. In both a pair of high-minded lovers belonging together by natural affinity, but separated by artificial barriers ; the rights of passion battling in the one case with social prejudice, in the other with the law of Rome and the malice of courtiers ; in both a court plot against the lovers ; the hero beset by a fair sinner who receives him in her private room, lays siege to him, and is angered by the slighting of her love ; in both a tyrannical and headstrong father at enmity with his son. Of the political ideas which the world associates with ' Don Carlos ' there is here no adumbration. We hear nothing of the Netherlanders, nor of the Inquisition, nor of the rights of man. Posa is only a friend of Carlos, not the ambassador of all mankind, and there is no room for his golden dreams of philanthropic statesmanship. And yet it is worth noticing that in three points (all in the third act) Schiller adds to his French source : Carlos's ambition was to waken and prevail over his love, Posa was to sacrifice himself, and the lovers were to rise superior to their passion.

However, no sooner did our playwright address himself seriously to his task than his imagination began to break over the bounds he had set for it.

Even at Bauerbach, as his letters show, his mind was occupied with the thought of 'avenging mankind' by scourging the gloomy despotism of Philip, the monstrous cruelty of Alva, the dark intrigues of the Jesuits and the hideous crimes of the Inquisition. That he made any progress in the spring of 1783, further than to cogitate upon his general plan and to fall in love with his hero, is not probable ; nor do his Mannheim letters allude to ' Don Carlos' until June, 1784. In a letter of that date he assures Dalberg,—mindful of that good man's trials in connection with ' Cabal and Love ', —that the new play will be 'anything but a political piece'. Whatever could offend the feelings was to be strictly avoided. August 24 he writes that ' Don Carlos' is a 'splendid subject', especially for himself. Four great characters, Carlos, Philip, the queen, and Alva (no mention of Posa) open before him a boundless field. He cannot forgive himself for having tried to shine in the bourgeois drama, where another may easily surpass him (this in allusion to Iffland), whereas in historical tragedy he need fear no rival. He adds that he is now fairly master of the iambic form and that the verse cannot fail to impart splendor and dignity.

So we see that by the end of his first year in Mannheim Schiller had indeed undergone a change. The *saeva indignatio* of the dramatic pamphleteer had given way to the serener mood of the poetic artist. This change would doubtless have come about under any circumstances, through the natural ripening of his mind and art, but it was hastened by the influence of Klein and Wieland, and by the example of Lessing's 'Nathan'. Anton von Klein, a Jesuit *bel esprit* liv-

ing at Mannheim, was a steadfast champion of the
regular heroic tragedy.   He had written a searching
review of ' The Robbers ', pointing out its many faults
and absurdities, but he recognized Schiller's talent and
saw in him a man worth converting.   At Mannheim a
friendship sprang up between the two, and Schiller
heard much talk about the superior merit of the noble
poetic style,—a region of thought in which he had
hitherto wandered but little.   He had written thus far
out of the fervor of his soul, and theory of any sort had
touched him but little.   From Rousseauite literature
he had caught a fantastic conception of ' nature ', and
this had led him to portray men and women who were
scarcely more natural than those of Gottsched himself.
In the rush of feeling he had enlisted among the young
revolutionists whose stormy and stressful tendency,
curiously enough, was regarded as ' English '.   And
now he found that there was after all something to be
said in favor of the classical French type.   The ' anglo-
maniacs ' were not in possession of the whole truth.
Might there not be, perhaps, a *tertium quid*,—a German
drama having a character of its own and combining the
literary dignity and artistic finish of the French with
the warmth and variety of the pseudo-English school ?
As if in answer to this query, Lessing's ' Nathan ', published in 1779, had already opened a vista of limitless
possibilities.   And ' Nathan ' was in blank verse.

To this was added the influence of Wieland, who had
lately published a series of ' Letters to a Young Poet ',[1]
in which he read his contemporaries a lecture on the
absurdity of their boasting over the French.   He

---

[1] In the *Teutsche Merkur* for October, 1782.

wanted to know where the German dramas were that could compare with the best works of Racine, Corneille and Molière. He insisted that a perfect drama no less than a perfect epic must be in verse. Even rime in his opinion was indispensable. Such doctrine coming from a man of Wieland's immense authority in literary matters could not fail to influence the groping mind of Schiller, though he could not stomach the demand for rime. The blank verse of Shakspere and Lessing seemed to promise best, and so he set about practicing upon it. At first the meter gave him great difficulty; he could not subdue his strong passion and his wild tropes to the even tenor of the decasyllabic cadence. Then followed his decision to publish his play piecemeal in the *Thalia*,—an unfortunate decision as it proved. His hope was to profit betimes by what his critics might say. He was in a mood of boundless docility and boundless confidence in the public. Resolved to write ' no verses that could not be submitted to the best heads in the nation ', he fondly imagined that the nation would be as eager to help him as he was eager to be helped. As a matter of fact he got but little assistance from the critic tribe, and his piecemeal publication only served to embarrass him when he came to the final redaction of the whole.

In the short preface which introduced the first installment to the public, Schiller ventured the opinion that the excellence of his tragedy would depend mainly upon his success in portraying the king. The situation of Carlos and the queen was interesting, he thought, but not tragically pathetic; it would be difficult to create sympathy for them. If, however, King Philip was to

be the center of tragic interest, it was evident that he
could not be depicted, in accordance with a one-sided
tradition, as a repellent monster. From these and other
expressions in the same essay we can see that Schiller
was growing cool toward his hero. He felt that
the troubles of Carlos and the queen could not be regarded under the Rousseauite scheme of natural passion battling with odious convention, but that the
passion was itself odious. He felt that a young prince,
pining and whining and plunging himself into disaster
all on account of an illicit and mawkish love for his
stepmother, was not a very inspiring personage to be
the hero of a great historical drama. The solution of
the problem seemed for the moment to lie in a 'rescue'
of King Philip. So the love-tragedy in a royal household began to take on more than ever the character
of a political tragedy, the promise to Dalberg being
quickly forgotten. When he began to publish, however, his political program was still rather vague and
negative ; it hardly went beyond the intention to bestow an incidental scourging upon the enemies of mankind in church and state.

Then came the influence of Körner, the effect of
which was to give great prominence to the character
of Posa as a positive champion of the right, and to
make him for a while the real hero of the play.
There seems at first blush but little resemblance
between the fanatical idealist of Schiller's imagination
and the sensible Dresden lawyer, but the Körner
strain in Posa is unmistakable. In his intercourse with
Schiller he was evermore insisting on the importance
of doing something for mankind. Enthusiasm, love,

friendship, sentiment of any kind, were valuable in his estimation only as sources of inspiration for telling activity. As matters of mere private ecstasy, of froth and foam rising and falling to no effect in the turmoil of the individual soul, they were for him objects of mild derision. And the idea that lay nearest his heart as a student of Kant was the idea of freedom. And so, as Schiller worked upon his play at Dresden, Posa was made the exponent of the new point of view. He became the teacher of the unripe Carlos, even as Körner had been the teacher of the unripe Schiller ; the subduer of unmanly emotionalism ; the apostle of renunciation ; the pointer of the way to great deeds ; the prophet of a free humanity to come. In the brilliant light thus thrown upon Posa the other heroes were somewhat obscured. The poet's original love, Don Carlos, and his second love, Don Philip, had to make way for a third passion that was stronger than either of the others.

The four installments of 'Don Carlos' that were printed in the *Thalia*, up to the end of 1786, comprised in all three acts. They carried the action to the point where the king, lonely amid sycophants and deceivers, sighs for a 'man' to counsel him. The great scene between Posa and Philip was yet to come in Act IV. The matter already in print contained more than four thousand verses, and several scenes had only been sketched in prose. At this rate it was evident that the play would reach twice the length of a regular tragedy and would be an impossibility on the stage. Schiller began to see that his impatience of stage restrictions and his subjective interest in certain situations had

done him an evil turn.   He had been deplorably long-
winded.   And just then came out a caustic review
which showed him that he had committed other sins
than those of prolixity.[1]   Nevertheless he did not now
have recourse to that drastic surgery whereby, in the
edition of 1801, he reduced the unwieldy play to more
manageable dimensions.[2] Without any radical revision
of the part already in print, he completed the last two
acts as best he could, with Minerva often unwilling.
Posa was made to gain the king's confidence, to become
seemingly omnipotent, and in the pride of his imagined
strength to enter upon that desperate game of intrigue
and double-dealing which involves himself and his
cause and his helpless friend, Don Carlos, in final
disaster.

Thus St. Réal's pathetic tale of love and intrigue
had been left far behind, and out of it had come a tragedy of amiable political idealism, growing insolent with
self-confidence and losing touch with present realities
in its dazzling dream of things to come.

'The soul of Shakspere's Hamlet, the blood and
nerves of Leisewitz's Julius, the pulse of Schiller himself ',—this, it will be recalled, was the original formula
for the composition of Prince Carlos.   But, alas, the
soul of one of Shakspere's heroes is not so easily pur-
loined, and Schiller did not succeed well in his proposed larceny.   What we find is not the soul but the

---

[1] In the *Neue Bibliothek der schönen Wissenschaften*, Vol. XXXII;
reprinted by Braun, "Schiller und Goethe im Urteile ihrer Zeitgenossen", I, 152 ff.

[2] The fragments published in the *Thalia* contained 4140 lines ; the
editio princeps of 1787, 6283 ; the edition of 1801, this being the form
in which the play is usually read, 5370.

situation of Hamlet : a young prince just returned from the university,—troubled by a strange melancholy,—a mystery to king and court,—beset by spies whom he sends packing,—visited by a dear academic friend,— called to a great work to which he feels himself unequal, and so forth. The parallel is obvious, but it hardly goes beyond externalities. Nor does the portrait of Carlos owe very much that is vital to Leisewitz. He gives us, to be sure, a love-sick prince whose illicit passion unnerves him, and like Carlos Julius has a friend who admonishes him to be a man. But there the resemblance ends ; he has not the strength to renounce and remains to the end a sentimental weakling.

The truth is that the soul, pulse, blood and nerves of Carlos are simply Schiller's own. There is no other creation of his into which he put so much of himself. That feeling of dark despair and dead ambition to which Carlos gives expression in his first dialogue with Posa is but a poetic echo of actual experiences.

> I too have known a Carlos in my dreams
> Whose cheek flushed crimson when he heard the name
> Of Freedom. But that Carl is dead and buried,—

sighs the Spanish prince. ' I might perhaps have become great, but fate took the field against me too early. . . . Love and esteem me for that which I might have become under more favorable stars ', — writes the actual Schiller.[1] And just as Carlos throws himself into the arms of Posa and thinks to find his all in friendship, so Schiller hoped ineffable things from Körner. Nowhere else in literature has the eigh-

---

[1] Letter to Reinwald April 14, 1783.

teenth-century cult of friendship found such fervid, and in the main such noble, expression as in ' Don Carlos '.

It may indeed be fairly objected that, in view of what is to come later, the Carlos of the first act is a little too soft even for the sentimental age. We are required to have faith in his heroic capacity for enterprises of great pith and moment. But after his first dialogue with Posa it is as difficult for the reader or spectator to trust him as it is for King Philip. His lacrimose raptures over so simple a thing as a youthful friendship ; his abject confession of despair and dependence ; his long-drawn-out revelation of a sick heart, and his morbid craving for sympathy in a passion which he himself feels to be abominable,—all this suggests a cankered soul of which there can be little hope. Hamlet greets the returning Horatio with the simple words :

> Sir, my good friend.   I'll change that name with you.

The corresponding passage in Schiller runs :

> Can it be ?
> Is't true ?   Is't possible ?   'Tis really thou.
> I press thee to my heart and feel the beat
> Of thine omnipotent against my own.
> Now all is well again.—In this embrace
> The sickness of my soul is cured.   I lie
> Upon my Roderick's neck.

One does not see how such pitiful weakness is all at once to be converted into manly strength by the mere arrival of a friend ; wherefore that fine saying of Carlos which closes the first act,

> Arm in arm with thee,
> I hurl defiance at my century,

sounds a trifle bombastic.

So again at his first meeting with Elizabeth, Carlos is distressingly mawkish. She pictures him, in pitying indignation, as succeeding to the throne, undoing his father's work and at last marrying herself. Then he exclaims in sudden horror:

> Accursed son! Yes, it is over. Now
> 'Tis over. Now I see it all so clearly,

and much more of the same purport. But how strange that he should have brooded for eight moons over his passion without ever having considered how it might appear to the object of it! His talk here suggests a mental inadequacy which one is hardly prepared to see change all of a sudden into heroic resolution.

To be sure it was a part of Schiller's design to represent in Carlos a process of evolution. Under the influence of manly friendship the puling sentimentalist was to have his fiber toughened into the stuff that great men are made of; and so it was quite in order that he should appear at first as a weakling. But he is too much of a weakling, and the reason is that Schiller did not foresee the end from the beginning. He thought of Carlos originally as a hapless youth having a sort of natural right to rebel. It was a part of the plan, moreover, that he should renounce and grow strong through renunciation. But this was to come later in the third act; in the beginning he was to dally with the morbid passion which was to be his tragic guilt. Now with this conception of the subject, the portrait of Carlos, just as we have it, fits in very well ; but when the main interest of the play had become political, when the lawless love had become of no account and the renunciation everything, —then it was surely an error to introduce Carlos in such a pitiful plight of soul that faith in him is next to impossible, and the next moment require us to accept him as a hero.

In fine, one may well wish that Carlos had a little more of the soul of Hamlet,—leastwise of Hamlet's rough energy of character and saving sense of humor. But the time is past for thinking to dispose of Schiller by saying that he was no Shakspere. Enough that he was himself. And nowhere was he more himself than in just this combination of infinite soft-heartedness with large manly ambition. When Carlos preaches to his father that 'tears are the eternal credential of humanity', he utters a genuine oracle of the senti-mental age. And when in the final scene he appears purified by suffering, master of his selfish passion and all intent upon that higher good of which he has caught a glimpse, he speaks again from the heart of Schiller. What a noble figure is Carlos in this last interview with his mother ! What matchless poetry in the lines ! And how genuinely, thrillingly tragic is the ending of the scene !

The teacher of Prince Carlos is the amazing Mar-quis of Posa. In a cynical foot-note of the year 1845 Carlyle quotes, with seeming approval, Richter's com-parison of Posa to the tower of a light-house,—" high, far-shining, empty ". But what would Jean Paul have had ? Is it not quite enough for a light-house to be high and far-shining ? One does not see how its usefulness would be enhanced by filling it with the beans and bacon of practical politics. Here surely one must side with Schiller and never think of criticising him for not making his Posa an exponent of political ideas that belong to a later time. Every age has its dream. Ours is of a people to be made happy by democratic legislation ; Schiller's was of a people to be made happy by the personal goodness and enlightenment of the monarch. That the one dream, seen *sub specie aeternitatis*, is any more empty and fatuous than the other, would be very difficult to prove.

The sentimental imagination of the eighteenth century was fond of dwelling upon the loneliness of the princely station. Standing above all other men, occupied habitually with weighty matters of state, surrounded by self-seeking flatterers and schemers, how was a ruler ever to hear the truth or to know the blessedness of disinterested friendship ? Awful fate to be thus cut off from tender human affection and compelled to tread the wine-press alone ! And if a prince should really find a friend, how fortunate for him and his subjects ! It was the simple theory of idealists under the Old Régime that the happiness of a people depended altogether upon the wisdom and goodness of the king ; and in an age when 'feeling was everything' it was natural that goodness of the heart should count for more than mere sagacity. What the king was believed to need pre-eminently, was to keep alive his human sympathies ; and how could he do this better than by having some one to love and confide in ?

So Schiller provides his Spanish prince with a friend. Our drama seems to wish to impute to Posa a lovable personality; else how account for the spell that he casts over all three of the royal personages ?[1] Looked at closely, however, and judged by his conduct rather than by his fine phrases, he appears anything but lovable. After his death it comes to light that he is deeply involved in a conspiracy for which the ordinary name is treason. He has been organizing a combination of European powers for the purpose of detaching the Netherlands by force from the Spanish crown. He returns to Spain as an arch-traitor,— with his pockets full of letters which if discovered would cost him his head. When one learns this and then thinks back in the light of this knowledge, his conduct throughout the play appears absolutely inconceivable; so that one is driven to the conjecture that Schiller did not think of him all along as an out-and-out traitor, but added this touch at the last, along with others, for the purpose of accenting his character as a Quixotic madman.

Up to the fourth act the impression produced by him is that of an amiable idealist, who has travelled

[1] Kuno Fischer, "Schiller-Schriften," I, 217, observes: "Freilich bedarf die Schauspielkunst um diese Scene [the great scene between Posa and Philip] so magisch wirken zu lassen, wie das Genie des Dichters sie erzeugt und gestaltet hat, eines Posa, dem die Natur die seltensten Gaben verliehen. Jede seiner Bewegungen, jede Geberde, jeder Ton, ist Anmut und Wohlklang. Er überzeugt den König nicht durch den Inhalt seiner Rede, er rührt ihn nicht durch seine Ideen, und doch gewinnt er ihn völlig, weil er ihn persönlich bezaubert." The natural effect of Schiller's words, however, is to give an impression that the king is moved not solely by Posa's personal charm, but in part by the idealism of his character.

extensively and acquired liberal ideas of government. He has been shocked by the régime of persecution and bloodshed in the Netherlands. He cares nothing for Protestantism as a creed, but he is an apostle of tolerance in the style of Frederick the Great. He returns to Spain intent upon securing for the Netherlands not political independence through revolution, but freedom of thought under the Spanish crown ; and this he thinks to accomplish by procuring the stadholdership for Prince Carlos. Now this being the presupposition, it was a great thought of Schiller to bring his humane dreamer face to face with the somber despot, Philip the Second. Let it be granted that Posa's views of statesmanship, which belong to the Age of Enlightenment, could hardly have found lodgment in the brain of a chevalier of the 16th century. The thing is perhaps supposable only in poetry ; but there it is supposable enough, and Schiller need not have troubled himself to argue away the anachronism. It is the poet's prerogative to mask himself and his own age in the forms of the fictitious past. He will do it anyway, no matter how hard he may strive after historical verisimilitude. It is just as well, therefore, for him to throw away his scruples and stand boldly on his rights.

From a dramaturgic point of view, indeed, the long political altercation between Posa and Philip is out of place ; it is magnificent, but it holds up the action to no purpose, and the play goes on as if it had not been. Schiller was evidently concerned to produce a pendant to the great scene in ' Nathan the Wise '. Saladin wants truth, Philip wants a man. Both the prophets

prepare themselves for their ordeal in a brief soliloquy.
Both monarchs get their wish, and a friendly relation
ensues. Both scenes' are purple patches of didacti-
cism,—the author preaching a sermon to his contemporaries. Unfortunately Schiller did not have at hand
a matchless fable to make his doctrine concrete and
give it human interest. In places his language is
abstract and difficult to follow, but taken as a whole
the scene is admirable in its denotation of Posa's
manly independence and humane philosophy. For a
moment the marquis dreams of accomplishing his purpose by an appeal to the goodness and enlightenment
of the king ; and into his appeal he pours all the
eloquence of eighteenth-century humanitarianism. All
that the literature of generations had garnered up ; all
that lay on the heart of the young Schiller, in the way
of fair hopes for mankind to be realized by humane
and enlightened rulership, finds here immortal expression through the mouth of Posa.

And then what a revulsion in the last two acts !
The great scene of the third act leaves an impression
that the world's affairs are not in such bad hands after
all. Posa does not convince the king's mind, but he
finds his heart and wins his confidence. One has the
feeling that, if he bide his time and use some tact, he can
accomplish all that he desires. But to our amazement
he gives up the king and enters upon a desperate game
of double-dealing in which he deceives everybody.
He forms the plan of sending Carlos to the Netherlands as the leader of a revolt. Of this plan he says
nothing to his friend, nor does he tell him of his own
new relation to the king. Instead he wraps himself

in mystery and asks Carlos for his letter-case. This he turns over to the king, and gets a warrant for the arrest of Carlos. The young prince, suspecting quite reasonably that he has been betrayed, goes to Eboli for enlightenment. Here Posa finds him and draws his dagger upon the woman, as if she were the possessor of some terrible secret,—which in fact she is not. Then he relents and arrests Carlos without explanation. He now writes a compromising letter which he knows will cause his own death. Then, after some delay, he goes to Carlos and tries to explain his strange conduct, and while he is telling his story the bullet of the king's assassin finds him. Carlos mourns the Great Departed as a pattern of unexampled heroic virtue, but one can have little sympathy with the panegyric, especially after one learns that Posa was a traitor from the beginning.

There would be little profit in discussing the last two acts of 'Don Carlos' with respect to their inherent reasonableness. It is possible to frame an intelligible theory of Posa's conduct, but not one which is perfectly coherent, and least of all one which shall harmonize with the impression produced by the first three acts. There we have an amiable idealist, whom we can at least understand ; here a madman smitten, like Fiesco, with a mania for managing a large and dangerous intrigue all in his own way, and accomplishing his ends by modes of action which seem to him heroic, but to the ordinary mind utterly preposterous. Thus he accounts for his failure to confide his plans to Carlos by saying that he was 'beguiled by false delicacy',—which seems to mean that his relation to the king was felt by

him as a breach of friendship. But how strange that
a man with public ends in view should feel thus under
the circumstances ! So too his self-sacrifice is nothing
but heroic folly, since his death in no way betters the
chances of Carlos for escape. The flight would have
had a better chance of success had Posa omitted his
heroics altogether and quietly planned to escape with
his friend. In fine, we have to do here with entirely
abnormal psychic processes. The reader and still
more the spectator is bewildered by Posa, and does
not know any better than Carlos and the king know
how to take him.[1]

Turning now to the portrait of the king we find
there too the traces of a wavering purpose. The
original conception was dark as Erebus. In the first
act, more especially in the first act as originally printed,
the King of Spain is painfully suggestive of a wicked
ogre swooping in upon a nursery of naughty children.
Such an insanely jealous, swaggering, domineering,
cruel fanatic is too loathsome to be interesting. Then
came the thought, suggested partly by the reading of
Brantôme and Ferrera, of presenting Philip's character
in a more favorable light and making him the center
of tragic interest,—a thought which was neither given
up nor consistently carried out. In October, 1785,
Schiller wrote to Körner that he was reading Watson
and that 'weighty reforms were threatening his own
Philip and Alva.' The Rev. Robert Watson's history
by no means idealizes Philip, but it credits him with

---

[1] Perhaps the best possible account of his death is that of Kuno
Fischer, " Schiller-Schriften ", I, 215 : " Er opfert sich für ein welt-
geschichtliches Ideal, das er idyllisch träumte."

sincerity, vigilance, penetration, self-control, administrative capacity and a 'considerable share of sagacity' in the choice of ministers and generals, — not an altogether mean list of kingly qualities. On the other hand, in Mercier's book [1] Philip appears as the embodiment of all those qualities which the Age of Enlightenment regarded as odious in a ruler. Thus, just as in the case of Fiesco, Schiller found himself pulled this way and that by his authorities ; and the result of his attempt to graft an impressive monarch upon the stock furnished by St. Réal's jealous husband is a Philip who does not fully satisfy either the historic sense or the poetic imagination.

For Schiller, of course, a truly great monarch needed to have a tender heart ; so Philip was given certain sentimental traits. He feels the loneliness of his station. In spite of his seeming coldness the pleading of Carlos for affection touches him, and he gives orders that henceforth his son is to stand nearer to the throne. For the purpose of exhibiting the king's magnanimity we have the anachronistic scene in which he is made to pardon Medina Sidonia for the loss of the great armada,—an event which happened twenty years later. Then he becomes suspicious of Domingo and Alva and longs for an honest man to tell him the truth. And when the man appears the king is most surprisingly open-minded. 'This fire', he says to Posa,

> Is admirable. You would fain do good,
> Just *how* you do it, patriot and sage
> Can little care.

[1] See above, page 169.

So Philip is a patriot and a sage, glowing with the holy fire of humanity ; and as such he even deigns to explain his policy and to enter into a contest of magnanimity with Posa. But the large-hearted monarch of whom we get a glimpse in this scene is soon reduced back to the jealous husband of St. Réal, and his jealousy is closely patterned upon that of Othello. The Philip of the last two acts is sometimes pitiable, some-times repulsive, never great. One is not very much surprised when he hires an assassin to kill Posa, instead of handing him over to the law.

Of the remaining characters the queen is the most interesting. In her Schiller for the first time depicts a woman convincingly. His Elizabeth is perhaps a shade too angelic,—she is an ideal figure like all his women,—but winsome she certainly is. One is a little startled by the readiness with which she approves Posa's treasonable plan of a revolution to be headed by Don Carlos, but in this play the sentiment of patriotism cuts no figure anywhere. The principal characters are all occupied with the idea of 'humanity', and are not troubled by any scruples arising out of national feeling.

Taken as a whole 'Don Carlos' is too complicated to yield an unalloyed artistic pleasure. It suffers from a lack of simplicity and concentration. There is material in it for two or three plays. The double intrigue of love and politics becomes toward the end very confusing. The confusion is increased by the unexpected turn given to the character of Posa, and reaches a climax when we learn from the Grand Inquisitor that *he* has been pulling all the strings from first to last, and that the entire tragedy was fore-ordained in the secret archives of the Holy Office. The unity of interest is marred by the fact that in the last two acts the real hero, Don Carlos, drops into the background as the helpless tool of the incalculable marquis. And Carlos, too, sometimes acts rather un-accountably; for example, when he supposes that the wanton *billet-doux* signed 'E.' can come from the queen, of whose purity and high-mindedness he has just had convincing evidence. Then again his conduct toward the Princess Eboli in the love scene is very sin-gular,—one might say amazing. And there are some other such defects, which concern the stage more than the reader and which, by skillful acting and judicious excision, can be reduced to insignificant proportions. When well played 'Don Carlos' produces a powerful impression. For the reader it is a noble poem con-taining a large ingredient of Schiller's best self.

CHAPTER X

Anchored in Thuringia

Ich musz ein Geschöpf um mich haben, das mir gehört.

Letter of 1788.

THE Weimar of Schiller's first acquaintance—he arrived there July 21, 1787—consisted of a petty provincial court plus an unsightly village. The inhabitants numbered about six thousand. Of the space built over about one-third was occupied by the buildings of the court, much of the outlying modern Weimar being then under water. The streets were narrow, muddy lanes, the houses plain and poor. And yet the sluggish little place, so unprepossessing in all material ways, was already beginning to assert that claim to glory which has since been conceded to it by all the world. Princely patronage of art and letters was by no means unknown elsewhere in Germany, but it was usually a matter of gracious condescension on the one side and grateful adulation on the other. Very different in Weimar, where Goethe was not only a member of the Council, but the duke's most intimate friend and trusted adviser. In his heart Karl August cared less for æsthetic matters than is often supposed, but his mother, the Dowager Duchess Amalie, patronized art for the real love of it. Poetry and music were as the

breath of life to her, and her taste in poetry had been
trained by the greatest living master. Aside from
Goethe, two other distinguished writers had found a
home in Weimar. The kindly but changeable Wieland,
not really one of the *dii majores*, but so regarded at the
time, had lived there since 1772 ; Herder, much more
nobly endowed, but less amiable and less popular,
since 1776.

At the time of Schiller's advent Goethe was still in
Italy, whither he had gone the previous autumn to find
relief from the miseries of duodecimo statesmanship.
Karl August and the reigning Duchess Luise were also
absent, but several minor notables of the court circle
had remained ' in town', and the dowager duchess was
giving æsthetic teas as usual in her easily accessible
' castle ' at Tiefurt. Wieland and Herder were likewise at home. On his arrival Schiller was taken charge
of by the Baroness von Kalb, who was awaiting her
soul's affinity with feverish eagerness. Her excitement
at seeing him again amounted to a ' paroxysm ' which
made her ill for a week. Then she grew better and
her emotions gradually found the level of a friendliness
too passionate to be called Platonic, but not sinful in
the lower sense. As for Schiller, he devotedly let
himself be loved and introduced to Weimar society,
the pair making no concealment of their liking for each
other. At first he felt some compunctions on account
of the absent husband, who might be annoyed by gossip. It pleased him to observe, therefore, that in
Weimar such a friendship was taken as a matter of
course and treated with delicacy.[1] 'Charlotte,' he

[1] Letter of July 28, 1787, to Körner.

wrote to Körner, 'is a grand, exceptional, womanly soul, a real study for me and worthy to occupy a greater mind than mine. With each forward step in our intercourse I discover in her new manifestations that surprise and delight me like beautiful spots in a broad landscape.'

For several months he played this unwholesome rôle of cicisbeo to Charlotte von Kalb. Then another and very different Charlotte crossed his path and quickly taught him the better way.

The story of Schiller's gradual adjustment to the Weimar *milieu* is told very fully in his frequent letters to Körner. He called upon Herder and Wieland, and was received with 'amazing politeness' by the one, with loquacious cordiality by the other. Herder knew nothing of his writings and regaled him with idolatrous talk about Goethe. Wieland knew all about him except that he had not yet seen 'Don Carlos'; criticised his early plays frankly as lacking in correctness and artistic finish, but expressed the utmost confidence in him nevertheless. He was received at Tiefurt, but did not like the dowager duchess: her mind, he reported, was very narrow; nothing interested her but the sensuous. A few days later he heard that 'Don Carlos' had been read to a select assembly at Tiefurt and had not made a good impression; there had been caustic criticism of the piece, particularly the last two acts, and Wieland, who was present, had not stood up for it. This led to a coolness toward Wieland. By the end of three weeks Schiller had despaired of Weimar and was miserable. He thought of leaving the place in disgust.

In August he spent a week at Jena as the guest of Professor Reinhold, who was about to begin lecturing upon Kant and was predicting that after a century the Königsberg philosopher would have a reputation like that of Jesus Christ.   Reinhold's enthusiasm led Schiller to read some of Kant's shorter essays, among which a paper upon universal history gave him 'extraordinary satisfaction'.   From Reinhold came also the assurance that it would be easy to secure a Jena professorship.   The idea did not at once take hold of him in the sense of becoming a definite purpose, but it tallied with his inclination.   His experience with 'Don Carlos' had left him in doubt whether the drama was after all his true vocation, and he had already begun to work fitfully upon a history of the Dutch Rebellion.

So he decided to remain a little longer in Weimar and devote himself to historical writing ; and, this resolution formed, life at once began to open more pleasantly before him.   He saw that he had made the mistake of taking the Weimar magnates too seriously ; of imagining that they were all sitting in judgment upon him, and that it was of the greatest importance to win their favor.   'I begin to find life here quite tolerable', he wrote early in September, 'and the secret of it—you will wonder that it did not occur to me before—is not to bother my head about anybody.'   And indeed he had no reason to be disgruntled.   Herder was pleased with 'Don Carlos' and came out in its favor before the æsthetic tribunal of Tiefurt.   Wieland noticed it favorably in the *Merkur*, spoke flatteringly of it in conversation and declared himself now convinced that Schiller's forte was the drama. Henceforth the two men were fast friends and presently Schiller was toying with the thought of marrying Wieland's favorite daughter. 'I do not know the girl at all', he wrote, 'but I would ask for her to-day if I thought I deserved her.'[1] His scruple was that he was too much of a cosmopolitan to be permanently contented with 'these people'. A simple-minded, innocent girl of domestic proclivities would not be happy with him.

The autumn passed in quiet work devoted mainly to his 'Defection of the Netherlands'. The Duke of Weimar came home for a few days towards the 1st of October, but immediately went away again to Holland. Schiller did not even see him. Evidently there was nothing to be hoped for immediately in that quarter; he would have to rely upon himself. But he was now in demand. The *Merkur* was eager for contributions from his pen, and so was the *Litteratur-Zeitung*, whose extensive review factory had been shown him during his sojourn in Jena. Then there was the comatose *Thalia*, which he determined to revive after New Year's.

In November he spent a few days at Meiningen, where his sister Christophine was now living as the wife of Reinwald. He saw Frau von Wolzogen and Lotte (who was about to be married), but Bauerbach had lost its charm. 'The old magic,' he wrote to Körner, 'had been blown away. I felt nothing. None of all the places that formerly made my solitude interesting had anything to say to me.' On his return

[1] Letter of Nov. 19, 1787.

fate was lurking for him at Rudolstadt, where his
friend, Wilhelm von Wolzogen, introduced him to
Frau von Lengefeld and her two daughters. ' Both
creatures ', Schiller wrote, ' are attractive, without being
beautiful and please me much. You find here considerable acquaintance with recent literature, also refinement, feeling and intelligence. They play the
piano well, which gave me a delightful evening.' The
elder daughter, Karoline, was married unhappily to a
Herr von Beulwitz, from whom she afterwards separated to marry Wilhelm von Wolzogen. She was a
woman of much literary talent, which found employment later in a novel, ' Agnes von Lilien ', and in her
excellent memoir of Schiller. The other daughter
was unmarried and bore the auspicious name of
Charlotte.

Lotte von Lengefeld, whose memory is cherished
with idealizing tenderness by the Germans, was now
twenty-one years old,—a demure maiden whose eyes
spake more than her tongue. She had long since won
the heart of the Baroness von Stein, who had introduced her at the Weimar court and held out to her the
hope of becoming a lady-in-waiting to the Duchess
Luise. Goethe was fond of her and did not omit to
send her affectionate greetings from distant Italy.
Some time before, she had spent a year with her
mother and sister in Switzerland for the purpose of
improving her French ; and on the way home, in the
summer of 1784, the party had caught a glimpse of
Schiller in Mannheim. Now the sisters were living in
a sort of idyllic solitude at Rudolstadt, cut off from the
great world, absorbed in their books, their music, and

the memories of that happy year in Switzerland. Karoline von Wolzogen writes, in speaking of this occasion :

My sister was seemingly in every respect a desirable match for Schiller. She had a very winsome form and face. An expression of purest goodness of heart enlivened her features, and her eyes flashed only truth and innocence. Thoughtful and susceptible to the good and the beautiful in life and in art, her whole nature was a beautiful harmony. Of even temper, but faithful and tenacious in her affections, she seemed created to enjoy the purest happiness.

Making all needful allowance for the partiality of a sister, one cannot wonder that the visitor went on his way with the feeling that Rudolstadt might be a good place in which to spend the summer.

The condition of his mind was certainly such as to facilitate the designs of Providence. In January, 1788, he wrote to Körner as follows :

I am leading a miserable life, miserable through the condition of my inner being. I must have a creature about me who belongs to me ; whom I can and must make happy ; in whose existence my own can grow fresh again. You do not know how desolate my soul is, how dark my mind ; and all not because of my external fortune,—for I am really very well off so far as that is concerned,—but because of the inward wearing out of my feelings. . . . I need a medium through which I can enjoy the other blessings. Friendship, taste, truth and beauty will produce a greater effect upon me when a continual succession of sweet, beneficent, domestic feelings attune me to joy and warm up my torpid being.

In mid-winter Lotte von Lengefeld came to Weimar for the social season and Schiller saw her occasionally with steadily increasing interest. Their famous correspondence, beginning in February, 1788, is at first very reserved, very formal and decorous, but soon begins to bewray the beating of the heart. 'You will go, dearest Fräulein', writes Schiller on the 5th of April, as Lotte was about to return to Rudolstadt, 'and I feel that you take away with you the best part of my present joys.' A month later she had found him lodgings in the neighboring village of Volkstedt, and then came a delightful summer idyl, which prolonged itself until the middle of November,—an idyl not of love-making, for Schiller could not yet pluck up the courage for that, but of spiritual comradeship. To quote Karoline again:

A new life began for Schiller in our house. He had long been denied the delight of a free, friendly intercourse, and he always found us susceptible to the thoughts that filled his soul. He wished to influence us, to teach us what might serve our turn of poetry, art, and philosophy, and this effort gave to himself a gentle harmonious disposition. . . . When we saw him coming to our house in the shimmer of the sunset, a bright ideal life disclosed itself to our inner sense. Lofty seriousness and the light gracious winsomeness of a pure and open soul were always present in Schiller's conversation; in listening to him one walked as among the changeless stars of heaven and the flowers of the earth. . . . Schiller became calmer, clearer; his appearance and his character more winsome, his mind more averse to those fantastic views of life which he had hitherto not been able to banish. A new hope and joy dawned in the heart of my sister, and I returned, in the happiness of a new inspiring friendship, to a true enjoyment of life. Our whole social circle shared in the pleasure of this kindly magic.

The discourse of these amiable truth-seekers turned partly at least upon the Greeks. Up to this time Schiller had remained virtually ignorant of the Greek

poets, thus missing the best of all sanative influences.
He had absorbed indirectly something of the Hellenism that had been diffused through the air by Winckel-
mann, Lessing, Herder and Goethe, but his knowledge
of the Greek language was very rudimentary, and good
translations had not been easily procurable. Thus the
glory that was Greece now came to him with the
charm of a new discovery. The poem, ' The Gods of
Greece ', contributed to the *Merkur* in March, 1788,
marks the beginning of his Hellenizing. A little later
Homer fascinated him. A letter written in August
runs thus :

> I now read almost nothing but Homer. I have got Voss' trans-
> lation of the Odyssey, which is in truth excellent, aside from the
> hexameters, which I cannot endure. . . . For the next two years
> I have made up my mind to read no more modern authors. . . .
> Not one of them benefits me. They all lead me away from
> myself, and the ancients now give me true enjoyment. At the
> same time I need them most urgently to purify my own taste,
> which through subtlety, artificiality and smartness was begin-
> ning to depart from true simplicity. You will find that familiar
> intercourse with the ancients will benefit me exceedingly, per-
> haps give me classicity. I shall first study them in good trans-
> lations and then, when I almost know them by heart, read the
> Greek originals. In this way I expect to play at the study of the
> Greek language.

On the 7th of September, 1788, an event occurred :
Goethe, who had now returned from Italy, came to
visit the Lengefelds, and Schiller was introduced to
him. For a year he had heard Goethe idolized on
every hand and felt his spirit brooding over the
Weimar atmosphere. What he heard did not please
him. The local Goethe-cult, so he wrote to Körner,

was characterized by a proud, philosophic contempt of all speculation and investigation. This 'child-like simplicity of mind', this 'resigned surrender to the five senses', seemed to him a sort of affectation. Besides this he was irritated by Goethe's prosperity and lordly independence. At the same time he could not help admiring him as a poet. The new 'Iphigenie' gave him a 'happy day', though his pleasure was somewhat marred by the depressing thought that he himself would never be able to produce anything like it. And so he waited with eager expectation to see what a personal acquaintance would bring forth. It brought forth pleasure mixed with dubiety. After that first interview with the great man he wrote to Körner thus:

On the whole, my idea of him, which was in truth very great, has not suffered from this personal acquaintance; but I doubt whether we shall ever come very close to each other. Much that is still interesting to me has had its day with him. He is so far in advance of me,—not so much in years but in self-development and experience of life,—that we shall never come together. And then his whole being is differently organized from mine. His world is not mine; our ways of looking at things seem essentially different. Nevertheless one cannot draw a sure conclusion from such a meeting. Time will tell.

Upon Goethe the meeting made no impression at all. For him Schiller was the author of 'The Robbers', a work whose popularity annoyed him. He did not know, and he took no pains to find out, that Schiller was no longer in sympathy with the ideas that had found expression in the detested play. So he held himself aloof and six years passed ere the two men came together in a friendly intimacy. At the same time there was nothing like ill-will on Goethe's part.

He recognized Schiller's talent, praised ' The Gods of Greece ' and was half pleased with the review of ' Egmont', which might well have nettled a less Olympian temper. In the fall of 1788 'The Defection of the Netherlands ' was published and favorably received. About the same time a vacancy occurred in the Jena faculty, and Schiller's friends proposed him for the position. Goethe took the matter up with the various governments concerned and met with no opposition. And so it came about, one day in December, that Schiller, who had meanwhile taken to translating Euripides and was planning a whole Greek theater in German, was interrupted by an official notice that he had been appointed professor of history at Jena and would be expected to enter upon his duties in the spring. It was only an ' extraordinary' professorship without salary, but its possibilities as a stepping-stone were alluring. He decided to accept.

Now came a short season of helpless and comical dismay. 'I would take a thrashing', he wrote to Körner, 'if I could have you here for four-and-twenty hours. Goethe quotes his *docendo discitur*, but these gentlemen do not seem to know how small my learning is.' To Lotte he declared that he should feel ridiculous in the new situation. ' Many a student will perhaps know more history than the professor. Nevertheless I think like Sancho Panza with respect to his governorship : To whom God gives an office, to him he gives understanding ; and when I have my island I shall rule it like a nabob.' It was not pleasant to drop his fascinating studies of the Greek poets and bury himself in learned sawdust, but the thing was not to be helped. So the winter and spring were devoted mainly to historical reading. At the same time, however, 'The Ghostseer' was carried along in the now resuscitated *Thalia*, and the long poem, 'The Artists', was slowly and with infinite revision got ready for publication in the *Merkur*.

During this period he saw little or nothing of Goethe and steadily nursed a splenetic determination not to like the man. Passages in his letters are almost comical in their perversity of misjudgment. He was exasperated by Goethe's reticence, composure and self-sufficiency,—qualities which seemed to him to spring out of calculating egotism. Goethe, so the arraignment ran, was a man who went on his way serenely dispensing favors, winning love and admiration and putting people under obligation, but always like a god, —without ever giving his intimate self or surrendering his own freedom. For his part, he, Schiller, did not wish to live near such a man, much as he admired his intellect and valued his judgment. This attitude of his was a great trial to the Lengefeld sisters, who did not fail to expostulate with him. But it was of no use. 'I have not time', he declared, 'in this short and busy life, to attempt a decipherment of Goethe's enigmatic character. If he is really such a very lovable being, I shall find it out in the next world, when we shall all be angels.' In fine he was not yet ripe for an understanding of the Weimar sovereign. He did not see that Goethe's method was after all a giving of himself, and that the self thus given was not the worse but the better for having outgrown the effusive raptures of sentimentalism.

In May the lectures at Jena began with great *éclat.*
On the first day students to the number of five or six
hundred flocked to hear the author of ' The Robbers '
expound the difference between the philosophic scholar
and the bread-and-butter professor.   It was an inspiring discourse, full of high idealism and well fitted to
inspire the souls of ingenuous youth, even though they
might not quite understand it.   The students were enthusiastic and gave the new professor the unusual
compliment of a serenade.   Having decided to begin
with a course of free public lectures upon universal history, he took his duties very seriously, and even after
curiosity had abated he continued, during the first term,
to address a large audience.   He had hoped only for
prestige, and the game was quickly won.   He was the
most popular professor in Jena.   All this time, however, his heart was in Rudolstadt,—with the two sisters
to whom, for a year and a half, he had been writing
letters of impartial Platonic devotion.   Late in July he
received a hint from Karoline to the effect that her
sister was very much in love with him and that an
understanding might be desirable.   Then at last the
timorous, cunctatory worshiper of femininity in the
abstract declared himself and prayed to know if the
good news could be true.   Lotte assured him that it
was ; if she could make him happy she was willing
to devote herself to the enterprise during the remainder of her days.

Now the millennium began.   Our celestial dreamer,
who had thus been gently pushed over the threshold
by a friendly hand, found himself in a human paradise
much more grateful to the soul than the court of

Venus Urania. He was very, very happy. The
black phantoms that had beset his pathway hitherto,—
the depressing sense of loneliness, of having missed
the great prize, of being *de trop* at the banquet of life,
the occasional promptings of pessimism and misanthropy, the baleful pull of illicit passion, the selfish
hugging of an illusory freedom,—all these took their
flight to return no more. He had found what he
needed—salvation from self through a woman's love.
But he did not behave like other sons of Adam. He
continued to address his love-letters to both sisters
impartially, as if the possession of Lotte were after all
to be only a subordinate incident in the preservation
of a triangular spiritual friendship. Sometimes it is
'my dearest, dearest Karoline', again 'my dearest,
dearest Lotte', most frequently 'my dearest dears'.

At first the trio agreed to keep their momentous
secret from *chère mère*. Schiller was poor and his
prospects all uncertain. When he began, in the fall
of 1789, to give lectures that were to be paid for, he
found that his income from students' fees would be insignificant. Lotte had but a slender portion, and then
there was that dreadful *von* in her name. To meet this
difficulty Schiller procured the title of 'Hofrat' from
the Duke of Meiningen. Then he laid the case before
Karl August of Weimar, who was very sympathetic
but also very poor. The best he could do was to
promise shamefacedly a pittance of two hundred thalers by way of professorial salary. This, with love,
was enough. In one of the noblest letters he ever
wrote Schiller now addressed himself to *chère mère*,
who made no objections; and on the 22nd of February,

1790, the impecunious Hofrat Professor Schiller and his courageous, aristocratic sweetheart were married.

The work of Schiller in the historical field will be considered by itself in the next chapter. Before passing on to that subject, however, let us glance at the more important of the minor writings produced during the period just traversed.

In 'The Gods of Greece' he strikes with almost clangorous emphasis the note of pagan æstheticism. The poem sees the world under the aspect of the Beautiful and regards that as its most important aspect. The Greek religion, we hear, peopled earth and sky and sea with lovely forms that gave warmth and color to life and fed the imagination with sensuous poetry. Nature appeared living, spiritual. Rock and stream and tree had each its tale to tell, its tale of passionate personal history. The gods were near, intelligible, sympathetic ; and divine gifts were more precious for being shared by the giver. And as the gods were more human, so man was more divine. In comparison our modern monotheism is cold, abstract, mechanical. Instead of a radiant Apollo, we have the law of gravitation. We have lost the many fair gods of old to enrich One who is remote, unfathomable, self-sufficient.

> Where art thou, beauteous world of story ?
> Fair morning of a vanished day !
> Alas ! the magic of thine ancient glory
> Lives only in the poet's lay.[1]

[1] In the original, lines 145-8, of the earlier version :
> Schöne Welt, wo bist du ?—Kehre wieder,
> Holdes Blütenalter der Natur !
> Ach ! nur in dem Feenland der Lieder
> Lebt noch deine goldne Spur.

It was inevitable that such a frank eulogy of the old gods at the expense of the Christian Demiurgus should give offense. Count Leopold von Stolberg put himself at the head of a vociferous opposition by denouncing the poem in a Leipzig journal as blasphemous, and lamenting that the author of the noble 'Song to Joy' should have fallen so low. The modern reader finds it easy to acquit him on the religious arraignment, since he did not profess to present the claims of monotheism completely. We are quite willing to judge of poetry as poetry and to leave it its ancient privilege of passionate overstatement. Of this privilege Schiller availed himself in the fullest measure, going quite beyond the bounds of sanity in his idealization of the Greeks. Well might the indignant Stolberg ask him if he really believed that the 'eternal bonds of the heart were gentler and holier when Hymen tied them'. Whatever else may be said of them, the amours of the Greeks (gods and men) were not remarkably strong on the side of gentleness, holiness and fidelity.

In respect of poetic merit Schiller certainly had the right to his opinion that 'The Gods of Greece' surpassed his earlier efforts. To please Wieland he aimed at Horatian correctness, and he came near hitting the mark. There is no progress toward lightness of touch or melody of phrasing,—Schiller was not the man for tuneful titillation of the ear,—but the poem is tolerably free from the bizarre hyperboles that mar its predecessors. It is intellectual, argumentative, but suffused at the same time with genuine feeling, and the stanzas have a stately impressive swing. Goethe was pleased with the poem, but thought it too long,—a well-founded criticism, since many of the stanzas merely brought fresh illustrations of the same thought. In his revision Schiller reduced the twenty-five stanzas of the original version to sixteen, and at the same time omitted or toned down the lines that had given offense. In its revised form it is in every way a better poem.

In ' The Artists ' we have a sonorous panegyric of Art as the great teacher and refiner of mankind. The poem shows the influence of Herder's evolutionary speculations, being in reality nothing less than a condensed history of civilization. The old Rousseauite point of view is here completely abandoned. No more girding at the degeneracy of the ' ink-spattering century '! The opening lines glorify the modern man as the ' ripest son of time, free through reason, strong through laws, great through gentleness '. Then the sublime creature is admonished not to forget the goddess who made him what he is:

> In industry the bee may scorn thy merits,
> In cleverness a worm thy teacher be ;
> Thy knowledge thou must share with happier spirits,
> But Art, O Man, is all for thee.[1]

After this we hear that man entered the land of knowledge through the morning gate of the beautiful; it was his inchoate art-sense that developed his understanding. The heavenly goddess Urania, whom we know here as Beauty and shall one day known as Truth,

[1] In the original :

> Im Fleisz kann dich die Biene meistern,
> In der Geschicklichkeit ein Wurm dein Lehrer sein,
> Dein Wissen teilest du mit vorgezogenen Geistern,
> Die Kunst, O Mensch, hast du allein.

accompanied him into the exile of mortality and became his loving nurse, teaching him to live by her law, free from wild passion and from the bondage of duty. To aid her in this work she chose a select body of priests, the artists, and taught them to imitate the fair forms of nature. In the contemplation of their work savage man was lifted to the heights of spiritual joy and forgot his gross appetites. He became acquainted with ideals and made gods and heroes for himself. Then he began to weigh and compare these ideals and thus arose philosophy and science, which aim in their slow and halting way to explain the full import of the primeval revelation. All truth was given in symbols at the beginning, and the artists still remain the conservators and prophets of the highest spiritual things.

In case of such a metrical disquisition it is not easy to separate the poetry, which in places is very good, from the intellectual content, which is not so good from a modern point of view. By the joint aid of several sciences laboriously piecing together bits of knowledge that have nothing to do with the goddess Urania, we have learned something of primitive man, and what we have learned is very much out of tune with Schiller's dream. He assigns to the æsthetic thrill a larger rôle than it has actually played in human history. This, however, is unimportant. What is more important is that by investing his subject with a nimbus of poetic mysticism he became one of the founders of the modern Religion of Art. For the theological revelation of truth he substitutes a secular revelation of beauty, which, however, was regarded by him as containing the germs of all truth and virtue. We see him moving toward a theory that Truth, Beauty and Goodness are one, and that Beauty is the one. To-day these abstractions, even when written with a capital initial, have no power to turn the heads of any but a few of the hyperæsthetical. For Schiller's contemporaries, aweary of rationalistic narrowness and reaching out after new sources of inspiration, the Religion of Art had the great advantage of novelty. It laid hold of them powerfully, remaining, however, a dignified intellectual cult which was quite compatible with plain surroundings. It was a very different thing from the later decorative æstheticism.

As poetry ' The Artists ' may be said to come under the head of metrical rhetoric. It quite lacks the simplicity and sensuousness of Milton's canon, and as for passion, it is florid rather than passionate. It is however strong in Schiller's strength,—in its vastness of outlook, its splendid sweep of thought, its magnificent phrase-making. At first indeed the reader is disturbed and perplexed by the argument. He is lifted up into the blue mists, far above the plane of the verifiable, and borne along hither and thither by successive gusts of the poetic afflatus. Presently he is lost; there is no north and no south. By dint of review and cogitation he gets his bearings (if he is lucky), but only to lose them again as he is wafted on through the empyrean. Not until he has read the poem many times, knows where he is going and is no longer pestered by the necessity of thinking, can he hope to enjoy the voyage.

The beginning of ' The Ghostseer ', published while Schiller was still in Dresden, was spoken of in Chapter VIII. His general idea, it would seem, was to describe an elaborate and fine-spun intrigue devised by mysterious agents of the Romish Church for the purpose of winning over a Protestant German prince. But the details had not been very fully excogitated, and his foremost thought, after all, was simply to popularize the *Thalia*, which was largely caviare to the general. The experiment proved moderately successful. Curiosity was excited and inquiries began to be made. When, therefore, he was ready to resume the publication of the *Thalia*, in the spring of 1788, he had reason to regard ' The Ghostseer ' as his most valuable asset. He set about continuing the story, feeling that it was 'miserable daubing' and a ' sinful waste of time '.[1] In this temper he wrote and published a second installment, which carried the story through what was subsequently known as the first book. In this installment the hoax of the ghost scene is cleared up, but the Armenian remains a mystery. The Prince maintains a sensible, rationalistic attitude, asks many questions, puts this and that together and finally concludes that Armenian and Sicilian are two charlatans working in collusion.

Up to this point ' The Ghostseer ' is a well-told and readable yarn, with only just philosophizing enough to give it a touch of dignity. In the second book it runs off into a quagmire of abstruse speculation. Schiller had got the idea—and it interested him for personal reasons—of carrying his hero through a debauch of skepticism. This he thought would give weight and distinction to the book. So the Prince's philosophic demoralization is described at tedious length and the

[1] Letter of March 17, to Körner.

story drops out of sight for a long time. Then it is taken up again and the Prince falls in love with a beautiful Greek *réligieuse*. The portrayal of this woman aroused another flicker of interest on Schiller's part, though she too was finally to be unmasked as one of the conspirators. Then he seems to have tired of 'The Ghostseer' altogether; at any rate he choked it off suddenly with a 'Farewell', in which nothing is concluded save that the Prince goes over to the Catholic Church.

From this description it is evident that Schiller's one attempt at novel-writing is of no great account as a contribution to artistic fiction. It is a torso consisting of two heterogeneous parts. It is not a study of life based upon the observation of life, but a tale of marvelous happenings which are recounted for the purpose of showing their subtle reaction upon the plastic mind of the Prince. The hero is taken over a route that was to become very familiar,—the route from a narrow and gloomy type of Protestantism through liberalism, rationalism, skepticism, Pyrrhonism, and mental exhaustion to the repose of the Catholic Church. Of course the story was not to end there, but what the further developments were to have been one can only guess. Schiller himself did not think it worth while to enlighten the public, even after his 'Ghostseer' began to call out imitations and continuations.

In the 'Letters upon Don Carlos', published in 1788, in Wieland's *Merkur*, Schiller undertook to defend himself against his critics and to correct some misapprehensions. In temper and style they are admirable, even when they do not convince. They begin by admitting and accounting for that seeming incongruity between the first three and the last two acts, which has always been the gravamen of critical objection to ' Don Carlos '.   After this they attempt to show that such a character as Posa might very well have existed in the sixteenth century at the Spanish court.   Then we are told that it was not the author's purpose to depict Carlos and Posa as a pair of ideal friends.   For Carlos, indeed, friendship is everything, but not for Posa. In him the passion for friendship is everywhere subordinated to the passion for humanity.   He is not to be blamed, therefore, for belying the character of a true friend, since that is not his dominant and essential character.   He regards Carlos merely as an indispensable tool for his political designs.   In his interview with the king he is carried away by a momentary enthusiasm,—what he says there is of no importance, his hopes being really fixed upon Don Carlos.   At the beginning of the fourth act he sees not his personal friend, but the instrument of his political plans, in awful danger.   He resolves to save him for Flanders and for humanity by sacrificing himself.   This is no more unnatural or inconceivable than the self-sacrifice of Regulus.   But Posa wishes to save his friend like a god and not like a common level-headed Philistine. He has the soul of a Plutarchian hero, and where two ways present themselves, the most natural is for him the most heroic.   Hence his desperate procedure and its disastrous consequences.

To all of which one can give but a qualified assent, the difficulty being that the play is not so constructed as to bring out its author's intention.   The character of Posa in Act IV is a surprise, and a disagreeable surprise. His conduct may harmonize with a theory of antique heroism, but it does not grow naturally out of what precedes. There is no exigency that calls for his heroic foolhardiness. The reader or the spectator can hardly be supposed to know that the famous tenth scene in the third act, the longest and most carefully elaborated in the whole play, does not count. One naturally supposes that it does count, and the only way it can count is to create a hopeful situation of which Posa is absolute master. When, therefore, he throws away his advantage and deliberately plunges his friend into a needless danger, in order to make an opportunity for rescuing him at the cost of his own life, one inevitably associates him mentally not with antique heroes but with modern lunatics.

A man capable of conceiving such a hero as Posa, and defending the conception as true to life, could hardly be expected to adjust his mind easily to such a work as Goethe's 'Egmont'. In his review of the play, published in 1788, Schiller found, indeed, much to praise; but his general praise was so mixed up with general fault-finding as to produce upon the Rudolstadt people the impression of a naughty *lèse-majesté*. He divined correctly enough that 'Egmont' was to be regarded as a drama of character, rather than of plot or of passion. But Egmont's character seemed to him painfully lacking in 'greatness'. Egmont, so the criticism runs, really does nothing extraordinary. He is idolized by the people, but the deeds upon which his fame rests have all been done before the curtain rises. In the play he appears as a light-hearted cavalier who affronts us by persistently refusing to take serious things seriously. In particular the review objected to Goethe's perversion of history in representing Egmont not as a married man with a large family of children but as a bachelor with a bourgeois sweetheart. Not that Schiller regarded the departure from history as reprehensible in itself. The dramatist has a right to pervert facts for the purpose of exciting sympathy for his hero; but in this case, Schiller argued, the effect is to degrade the character of Egmont and thus to alienate sympathy. Finally the review took exception to Egmont's vision of Freedom in the form of Clärchen; this, Schiller thought, was a deplorable plunge into opera at the end of a serious drama.

To adjudicate the issue thus sharply drawn between the two great German poets would require some preliminary attention to their fundamental difference of artistic method,—a subject that will concern us in a subsequent chapter. Here suffice it to remark that Schiller was not entirely in the wrong. While Goethe was incomparably the more subtle psychologist, Schiller had the better eye, or rather he cared more, for that which is dramatically effective, average human nature being such as it is. His dramatic instinct told him that Egmont was not a very powerful stage-play. Its subtle psychology did not impress him so much as its lack of 'greatness'. And then he had his pique against Goethe and wished to show the Weimarians that *he* at least could perceive the spots on the sun. Goethe's serene comment upon reading the critique was to the effect that the reviewer had analyzed the moral part of the play very well indeed, but in dealing with the poetic aspect of it he had left something to be done by others.[1]

The dramatic fragment, ' The Misanthrope Reconciled ', which Schiller fished up out of his drawer in 1790 and used, *faute de mieux*, to fill space in the eleventh number of the *Thalia*, was begun, as we have seen, in Dresden. Possibly the theme may have been suggested at Mannheim by the problem of staging Shakspere's ' Timon '. At any rate the theme was congenial for a man who had ' embraced the world in glowing passion and found in his arms a lump of ice '. At Weimar he returned to it several times, puzzled over the general plan, added a little here and there, but finally gave it up as a bad subject for dramatic treatment. The published fragment is certainly of no great account. It introduces a misanthrope, Hutten by name, who, as feudal lord, treats his dependents handsomely out of sheer contempt for them. When they come to thank him on his birthday, he spurns their gratitude and scolds them, having made up his mind never to be duped again by any show of human emotion. He has brought up his beautiful and dutiful daughter to be an angel of mercy and a paragon of perfection, but he insists that she too shall be a misanthrope like himself. He makes her swear that she will never marry, but she shrewdly tacks on the proviso, ' except with papa's consent '. The exposition shows her duly in love with a cheerful and estimable youth named Rosenberg; and the problem is: How will Rosenberg manage the misanthrope ? That he was to win somehow is evident from the title.

[1] Letter of Oct. 1, 1788, Goethe to Karl August.

In his translations from Euripides, which also belong
to the period under consideration, Schiller aimed partly
at the improvement of his own taste.　He hoped to
familiarize himself with the spirit of the Greeks and to
acquire something of their manner.　He thought that
they might teach him simplicity both in expression and
in the construction of dramatic plots; and he felt that
his style was in need of their chastening influence.　Of
' The Phœnician Women ' he translated about one-
third, but omitted the choruses entirely; of the ' Iphi-
genia in Aulis ' he translated nearly the whole text,
rendering the choruses very freely in rimed lines of
uneven length and varying cadence.　His work reads
smoothly and gives the general effect of Euripides, but
cannot count as good translation.　It was not only that
his Greek scholarship was deficient, but he lacked
patience,—an indispensable virtue for the translator.
His real original was not the Greek text at all, but the
Latin version of Joshua Barnes; and when this appeared
to him jejune and unpoetic he sometimes created an
original of his own.

The other minor writings of the years 1788 and 1789
may be passed over as of little significance.　On the
poetic side there were three or four occasional poems,
and also the rimed epistle called ' The Celebrated
Wife ', in which the unfortunate husband of a literary
lady pours out the tale of his domestic woes.　In prose
there were several perfunctory reviews contributed to
the *Litteratur-Zeitung*, and also an anecdote—exhumed
from an old chronicle and retold for the *Merkur*—relating to a breakfast given to the Duke of Alva by the
Countess of Schwarzburg in the year 1547.　To these

may be added, finally, the short story entitled ' Play of Fate ', also published in the *Merkur*, which describes, under a thin disguise of fictitious names, the rise and fall and rehabilitation of Karl Eugen's former minister, P. H. Rieger.[1]

[1] See above, page 135.

CHAPTER XI

𝕳istorical 𝕎ritings

Der Mensch verwandelt sich und flieht von der Bühne, seine Meinungen verwandeln sich und fliehen mit ihm; die Geschichte allein bleibt unausgesetzt auf der Bühne, eine unsterbliche Bürgerin aller Nationen und Zeiten.—First lecture at Jena.

SCHILLER'S merit as a writer of history has been much discussed and very differently estimated by high authorities. In general one may say that his historical writings have fared at the hands of experts very much like the scientific writings of Goethe; both being treated as the rather unimportant incursions of a poet into a field which he had not the training or the patience to cultivate with the best results. Niebuhr's adverse opinion is well known and has often been echoed in one form or another by later critics. On the other hand, lovers of the poet are very apt to overestimate the historian, who would probably be seldom heard of to-day if he had not achieved immortal fame by his plays and poems. As it is, his historical writings have become, for better or worse, a part of the classical literature of Germany, and as such we have to reckon with them.

And the best way to reckon with them is to describe them as objectively as possible and to consider them in relation to the intellectual tendencies of Schiller's own time. We shall see that he began a history of the Dutch Rebellion without knowing Dutch or Spanish, and without spending any time in a preliminary study of the original sources of information.[1] His 'History of the Thirty Years' War' was a bread-winning enterprise, hastily executed for a ladies' magazine. For neither work did he draw a full breath. To compare him, therefore, with the modern giants of research, would be quite absurd; and the more absurd since Schiller the historian, unlike Goethe the scientist, was extremely modest in his self-estimate and fully aware of his limitations on the side of scholarship.

Of the qualities that go to the making of a great historian he had two,—the philosophic mind and the vivid imagination. But he lacked the spirit of the investigator and had not a sufficient reverence for the naked fact. History interested him for the sake of his theories and his pictures, and rhetoric was his element. This being so it is not strange that we get from him now and then a distorted image. Great movements and prominent characters are depicted by him in accordance with his freedom-loving, cosmopolitan preconception; and his study was not to correct this preconception by a survey of all the evidence, but rather to select that which would confirm his view in a striking manner. On the whole, however, the tale of his positive error, as brought to light by the critics, is not as large as one might expect. This chapter will not

[1] It is to be taken into consideration that the 'sources', as the word is now understood, were for the most part inaccessible in the eighteenth century.

deal with it at all, but rather with his general method and point of view.[1]

'The Defection of the Netherlands' was begun in the summer of 1787 and grew out of the reading of Watson's 'Philip the Second'. This book impressed Schiller strongly and he attributed its fascination to the working of his own imaginative faculty. He wished that others might see and feel what he had seen and felt. So he began to retell the story in his own way, intending at first only a brief sketch. As he proceeded, he found gaps and contradictions and isolated facts of obscure import. He began to consult the authorities, not so much to increase his store of information as to clear up his doubts. In this way the intended sketch expanded ideally into a six-volume treatise which should present the history of the Netherlands from the earliest times down to the establishment of their independence. Of the *magnum opus* thus planned the first volume, the only one that was ever written, appeared in the autumn of 1788, in three books. The first book sketched the history of the Low Countries down to the Spanish domination; the second dealt with the regency of Margaret of Parma, and the third with the conspiracy of the nobles, ending with the supersession of Margaret by the Duke of Alva, in 1567. Thus the most dramatic period of the great struggle was not reached. Subsequently, however, the narrative was supplemented by two separate pictures, 'The Death of Egmont' and

[1] The subject which is here necessarily treated in a general way is discussed much more fully and with admirable balance by K. Tomaschek, "Schiller in seinem Verhältnis zur Wissenschaft", Wien, 1862. Another excellent book, if used with some care, is J. Janssen's "Schiller als Historiker", Freiburg, 1879.

' The Siege of Antwerp ', which in the edition of 1801 were first printed with the history.

Letters of Schiller indicate that for a while at least he was very enthusiastic in his new pursuit. He found in the seeming capriciousness of history a constant challenge to the philosophic mind, and he enjoyed the imaginative exercise of investing the dry bones with muscles and nerves. It struck him that the inner necessity was much the same in history as in a work of art. He even went so far as to contend that the fame of the historian was on the whole preferable to that of the poet, and to express the opinion that his own nature was more akin to that of Montesquieu than to that of Sophocles. He felt that he was getting new ideas and expanding his soul at every step. ' Really,' he wrote to Körner in 1788, ' I find each day that I am pretty well suited to the business I am now carrying on. Perhaps there are better men, but where are they? In my hands history is becoming something in many respects different from what it has been.'

And so it really was. In point of readableness ' The Defection of the Netherlands ' is vastly superior to any previous historical writing in the German language. The stately march of its paragraphs, each bearing the impress of a serious and lofty mind; the care with which seemingly small matters are logically connected with great issues, the mingling of philosophic reflection with the narrative,—all this gave to the work an air of literary distinction. It was actually interesting, and this was much in a land that had no historical classics whatsoever. To be interesting was what Schiller frankly aimed at; he wished to ' convince one portion

of his readers that history might be written with fidelity
to the facts, but without becoming a trial to the
reader's patience; and another portion that it might
borrow something from a kindred art without becoming
romance'.   And he succeeded. · In reading him it is
easy to see that the poetic habit of conceiving his
characters to fit a preconceived scheme, his vivid imagination, his love of sharp contrasts, telling analogies
and broad generalizations, occasionally distort the true
relation of things.   He was an artist rather than a
scholar, and one must e'en accept him as such.   A
letter to Karoline von Beulwitz puts the matter thus:

> I shall always be a poor authority for any future investigator
> who has the misfortune to consult me.   But perhaps at the ex-
> pense of historic truth I shall find readers, and here and there I
> may hit upon that other kind of truth which is philosophic.   His-
> tory is in general only a magazine for my fancy, and the objects
> must content themselves with the form they take under my
> hands.

The animating idea of 'The Defection of the Netherlands ' is the same that Goethe found running through
all the writings of Schiller—the idea of freedom.   From
the days of his youth 'freedom', however unphilosoph-
ically he might think about it, had connoted for his
imagination the highest and holiest interest of mankind;
and when he began his first historical work his enthusiasm had not yet been sicklied o'er by the events
of the Paris Terror.   He saw in the Dutch revolt a
glorious battle for liberty; the struggle of a small
trading population against the proudest, richest and
most powerful monarch of the century; a cause seemingly hopeless at first, but growing stronger through

pluck, union, tenacity and wise leadership, until the Spanish Goliath was completely beaten. It was magnificent and Schiller desired that his countrymen should feel its magnificence and take to heart its lesson. So he adorned his title-page with an emblem of freedom, —a broad-brimmed hat and a feather upon a pole,— and began his treatise with a bugle-blast that left no doubt of his purpose: ' I have thought it worth while to set up before the world this fair monument of civic strength, in order to waken in the breast of my people a joyous self-consciousness, and to give a fresh and pertinent example of what men may venture for a good cause and may accomplish by united action.'

A remarkable passage of the introduction runs as follows:

Let no one expect to read here of towering, colossal men, or of amazing deeds such as the history of earlier times offers in such abundance. Those times are past, those men are no more. In the soft lap of refinement we have allowed the powers to languish which those ages exercised and made necessary. With humble admiration we gaze now at those gigantic forms, as a nerveless old man at the manly sports of youth. Not so in the case of this history. The people that we here see upon the stage were the most peaceful in this part of the world, and less capable than their neighbors of that heroic spirit which gives sublimity to even the most paltry action. The pressure of circumstances surprised this people into a knowledge of their own strength, forcing upon them a transitory greatness which did not belong to them and which they perhaps will never again exhibit. So then the strength they manifested has not vanished from among us, and the success which crowned their desperate adventure will not be denied to us if, in the lapse of time, similar occasions call us to similar deeds.

One sees from this that Schiller is halting between

the poetic and the scientific view of the past, uncertain which way to set his face. The poet in him is inclined to idealize the brave days of old and to mourn that the ancient giants are no more. At the same time he finds that the struggle of the Low Countries, while not 'heroic', was very remarkable, very instructive and very inspiring. From this observation it is but a step to the recognition of the truth that it is his own conventional notion of 'heroism' that needs revising; that the giants of yore were no taller than those of to-day and that the world's supply of courage and devotion is not running low. It is an interesting fact that the sentence beginning, 'So then the strength they manifested', was omitted by Schiller from the edition of 1801, possibly because the horrors of the Revolution had put him out of humor with fighting. But he might well have allowed the words to stand. Their truth was soon to be memorably proved by the German uprising against Napoleon.

A German writer [1] remarks correctly that Schiller occupies with Kant a middle stage between the older pragmatic historians, upon whom Faust [2] pours his scathing ridicule, and the later school of Ranke, whose principle was to extinguish self and simply tell what happened and how. He does not moralize like his predecessors, nor is he guilty of treating the distant past with patronizing condescension. At the same time he wishes to instruct and does not hesitate to point

[1] Otto Brahm, "Schiller", II, 209.
[2] Was ihr den Geist der Zeiten heiszt,
Das ist im Grund der Herren eigner Geist
In dem die Zeiten sich bespiegeln. — 'Faust', lines 577–8.

out where the instruction is to be found. He aims to be impartial to the extent of giving both sides a hearing, but he imputes motives freely and does not pretend to extinguish self. Probably the effort to do so would have seemed to him absurd. His sympathy is of course with the Netherlanders, but he writes as a philosophic champion of freedom rather than as a partisan of Protestantism. His concern is not to excite indignation at the colossal wickedness of Philip and Alva, but to show up their colossal folly. As we should expect he devotes his best powers to his portraits, some of which,—as those of Margaret, Granvella, Egmont and Orange,—are deservedly famous. At the same time they are subject to correction from the documents. Thus the crafty politician, William the Silent, in whom there was very little of the strenuous idealist, is presented as a 'second Brutus, who, far above timid selfishness, magnanimously renounces his princely station, descends to voluntary poverty, becomes a citizen of the world and consecrates himself to the cause of freedom '.

From what has been said it is clear that Schiller regarded the writing of history as essentially an exercise of the creative imagination. And such in a sense it really is and always must be, since no historian can divest himself of his own personality. He will inevitably see the events with his own eyes and put his own construction upon them. His very arrangement of his materials, his distribution of lights and shades, his selection of the matters to be recorded and commented upon, will involve a subjective coloring of his narrative. This being so, one cannot reasonably criticize Schiller for having his point of view, but only for taking too little trouble in the gathering and verification of his facts. He did not think it important to study his subject from first-hand sources of information. He quotes more than a score of authorities in Latin, French and German, but he uses them quite uncritically, and chiefly, it would seem, to give his work a semblance of learning. The facts were for him nothing but the raw material of history; the important thing was their philosophic truth, that is, the intellectual formula that should explain them. In our day we have grown distrustful of the 'philosophy of history', especially of any philosophy that does not rest upon a basis of long and thorough investigation.

'The Defection of the Netherlands' was very favorably received by the German public. Its merits lay on the surface, while its defects were not patent to the casual reader. Every one felt that Schiller had set a new pattern for historical composition. In his hands history had become literature. With such an achievement to his credit it was natural that his *début* in Jena should be looked forward to in academic circles as a great occasion. Feeling that much would be expected of him he prepared with great care his inaugural discourse upon the study of universal history. The address, which was subsequently published in the *Merkur*, begins with a vigorous elucidation of the difference between the bread-and-butter scholar and the philosophic thinker. The former is depicted in caustic terms as a narrow, selfish, timorous time-server. He is the enemy of reform and discovery, because he is forever dreading that the enlargement of the human outlook may disturb his little private routine. He cares for truth only so far as it can be turned to his personal gain in the form of money, praise or princely favor. The philosophic thinker, on the other hand, is a joyous lover of his kind. Feeling the essential solidarity of all knowledge he seeks ever for the unifying principle. He loves truth for its own sake. Every advance of knowledge is welcome to him, and he willingly sees his private edifice go to ruin for the joy of building a new and better one. Then the lecture proceeds to describe the splendid progress of the human race. The task of universal history is declared to be the explanation of this evolutionary process. It must show how all things hang together, and, selecting for description those portions of the record which have a more obvious bearing upon the present form of the world, it must seek to bring home to the modern man the full import of his heirship.

In this address we begin to trace the influence of Kant, whose 'Idea of a Universal History in a Cosmopolitan Spirit', published in 1784, was read by Schiller with great interest. The leading thoughts of this memorable paper, new then but very familiar now, are that the race and not the individual is nature's concern in her scheme of man's perfectibility; that the only perfection and happiness possible to him are those which he creates for himself by the progressive triumph of reason over instinct; that the fighting-spirit, antagonisms, wars, the madness and the calamity of the individual, are the necessary condition of race-progress; that the goal is a just civil society, which in turn, since man is an animal that needs a master, is inseparable from the idea of a law-governed state. Thus, while Herder's formula for the great evolutionary process was the upbuilding of the individual man to humanity, that of Kant was the preparation of man for a free citizenship which should ultimately embrace the world.

By the general bent of his mind Schiller was nearer to the humane idealism of Herder than to the law-governed collectivism of Kant. At the same time we can see from many a sentence in his inaugural address that the far more rigorous logic of the Königsberg philosopher had had its effect upon him. In particular he was captivated by the idea that the individual exists for the sake of the race, and that the gruesome antagonisms of history are therefore to be regarded with composure as the birth-pains of the modern man. A striking passage of the lecture runs thus:

History, like the Homeric Zeus, looks down with the same cheerful countenance upon the bloody works of war and upon the peaceful peoples that innocently nourish themselves upon the milk of their herds. However lawlessly the freedom of man may seem to operate upon the course of the world, she gazes calmly at the confused spectacle ; for her far-reaching eye discovers even from a distance where this seemingly lawless freedom is led by the cord of necessity. . . . History saves us from an exaggerated admiration of antiquity and from a childish longing for the past. Reminded by her of our own possessions we cease to wish for a return of the lauded golden age of Alexander or of Cæsar.

From this way of thinking it seems but a span to the modern scientific point of view; for that, however, neither Schiller nor Kant was ripe, since both thought it necessary to assume that human history began about six thousand years ago and began substantially as reported in Genesis, however the original authentic tradition might have been incrusted with spurious supernaturalism. The explanation of society thus resolved itself for them into the problem of a rational interpretation of the Bible. Kant believed, like Rousseau, in an original paradisaic condition, in which man had lived as a happy, peaceful animal. But while man's emergence from that state was regarded by Rousseau as a disaster, the selfish passions, with their resulting antagonisms, were conceived by Kant as the *sine qua non* of rational development. This thought, with its corollaries, was set forth by Kant in an essay of the year 1786, entitled 'Conjectural Beginning of Human History'. The Fall is there explained as a good thing, the story in Genesis being interpreted as a symbol of the emergence of man from the estate of a peaceful but instinct-governed animal to that of a quarrelsome but rational being. Kant's line of reasoning interested Schiller deeply, and in 1790 he published in the *Thalia* a paper upon the same general subject. It was entitled 'Something about the First Human Society on the Basis of the Mosaic Record'.

Portions of this essay, with its naïve license of affirmation, would make a modern anthropologist shudder. It begins with a description of the original paradise, from which the infant man was to be led forth into life by Providence, his watchful nurse. To quote a few words:

By means of hunger and thirst She showed him [let us keep the feminine providence of the German] the need of nourishment ; what he required for the satisfaction of his needs She had

placed around him in rich abundance ; and by the senses of smell
and taste She guided him in his choice. By means of a mild
climate She had spared his nakedness, and through a universal
peace round about him She had secured his defenceless existence. For the preservation of his kind provision was made in
the sexual impulse. As plant and animal man was complete.
. . . If, now, we regard the voice of God which forbade the tree
of knowledge as simply the voice of instinct warning man away
from this tree, then the eating of the fruit becomes merely a defection from instinct, that is, the first manifestation of rational
independence, the origin of moral being ; and this defection
from instinct, which brought moral evil into the world, but at
the same time made moral good possible, was incontestably the
happiest and greatest event in the history of mankind.

It has seemed worth while to linger a moment over
these two rather unimportant productions for the sake
of the light they throw on Schiller's general attitude.
One sees that remote antiquity has lost in his eyes
something of its old poetic glamour. He is content to
explain it like any rationalizing professor. The past
interests him mainly for the sake of the present, and of
the present he now has a very good opinion,—especially
of the Goddess of Reason. He did not know what a
terrible trial was preparing for this goddess and her
self-complacent worshippers. Ere long he himself was
destined to lose a little of his buoyant faith in her and
to become in part responsible for the apostasy of many.
For the present, however, it was no inchoate Romanticism, but a publisher's enterprise, that led him into the
study of the Middle Ages. He had undertaken to edit
a great 'Collection of Historical Memoirs'. There
were to be several volumes each year for an indefinite
time ; the volumes to consist of translations from various

languages and to cover European history from the
twelfth century down. Schiller was to supervise the
undertaking and furnish the needful introductions. His
plans were presently thwarted by illness and then by
his increasing interest in philosophic studies; so that
after the first few volumes had appeared he withdrew
and left the continuation of the 'Memoirs' to other
hands.

Of his various contributions to the initial volumes of
the 'Historical Memoirs' a part are mere hack-work
and therefore devoid of biographical interest.   Somewhat different is the case with an elaborate account of
the crusades, in which he attempts to show that that
great medieval madness,—so it was regarded by the
Age of Enlightenment,—was 'in its origin too natural
to excite our surprise and in its consequences too beneficent to convert our displeasure into a very different
feeling'.   The general argument is that the ancient
civilizations were dominated by the idea of the state;
they produced excellent Greeks and Romans but not
excellent men.   The prestige of the despotic states
was destroyed by the great migrations, but it was the
crusades which first taught the nations to subordinate
patriotism to a higher and broader sentiment.   It was
then that men learned to fight for an idea of the reason,
—for the truth as they saw it.   And thus the crusades
prepared the way for the Reformation.   The interest
of the essay lies not in the vigor of its logic, which is
lame here and there, but in the evidence it affords of
Schiller's increasing respect for the Middle Ages.
And he went further still.   In a preface which he wrote
in 1792, for a German translation of Vertot's work on

the Knights of Malta, we find a passage which sounds very much like inchoate Romanticism:

The contempt we feel for that period of superstition, fanaticism and mental slavery betrays not so much the laudable pride of conscious strength as the petty triumph of weakness avenging itself in unimportant mockery for the shame wrung from it by superior merit. . . . The advantage of clearer ideas, of vanquished prejudice, of more subdued passions, of freer ways of thinking (if we really can claim this credit), costs us the great sacrifice of active virtue, without which our better knowledge can hardly be counted as a gain. The same culture that has extinguished in our brains the fire of fanatical zeal has also smothered the glow of inspiration in our hearts, clipped the wings of our sentiment, and destroyed our doughty energy of character. . . . Granted that the period of the crusades was a long and sad stagnation of culture, and even a return of Europe to its former barbarism; still, humanity had clearly never before been so near to its highest dignity as it was then,—if indeed it is a settled doctrine that the essence of man's dignity is the subordination of his feelings to his ideas.

We see that Schiller, though he was in no danger of becoming a renegade on the main issue, had his moods of disgust, as Goethe and Herder had had before him, at the shallow self-complacency of the Age of Enlightenment.

In comparison with these disconnected and more or less perfunctory studies, the ' History of the Thirty Years' War ' seems like a large undertaking. But it was not so conceived at first. While ' The Defection of the Netherlands ' is the fragment of a great project, the ' Thirty Years' War ' is the expansion of a small one. We first hear of it in a letter of December, 1789, wherein Schiller, just then casting about eagerly for

possibilities of income, informs Körner that he is to
have four hundred thalers from Göschen for an ' essay '
upon the Thirty Years' War, to be published in the
' Historical Calendar for Ladies '.   He felicitates himself that the labor will be light, since the material is so
abundant and he is to write only for amateurs.   The
following spring he took up his task, which then grew
upon his hands as he proceeded.   Two books were
printed in the ' Calendar ' for 1791, a third in 1792,
the fourth, and also a separate book-edition, in 1793.
It met with great favor, the sales running up to seven
thousand, and the author winning the name of Germany's greatest historian.

And, indeed, it does exhibit Schiller's historical style
at its best, there being here, in comparison with his
earlier work, somewhat less of heavy philosophical
ballast.   The narrative moves more lightly.   There is
this time not even a pretense of erudite scholarship.
He does not quote authorities, rarely indulges in
polemic, avoids tedious ' negotiations ' and all political
disquisitions which might be dull reading to the ' female
fellow-citizens ' for whom he writes.   He endeavors
merely to tell his complicated story in a lucid and
interesting manner.   The third book, which describes
the career of Gustav Adolf from the great battle of
Breitenfeld, in 1631, to his death at Lützen in the following year, is an admirable specimen of vivid historical
writing.   It may well be doubted whether any suc-
cessors of Schiller have surpassed him in the art of
narrating, though they may have been able to correct
him here and there in matters of fact.   What a telling
description, for example, is that of the desperate

charge at Lützen just after the death of the Swedish king!

In his last historical work, just as in his first, the burden of Schiller's thought is evermore the idea of freedom. The Thirty Years' War is conceived by him as the successful struggle of German liberty against Hapsburg imperialism. Upon the abstract merits of the religious controversy he has little to say; the subject evidently does not interest him. He does indeed make himself the champion of Protestantism, but only because Protestantism is identified in his mind with the august cause of liberty. The Protestant princes fought, he tells us, for what they took to be the truth, —whether it really was the truth does not matter. Their motives were not always lofty and their historian is not in the least concerned to hide or to gloss over their frequent venality and selfishness. His point of view is that they fought for a higher good than that which their eyes were fixed upon, and this higher good was the advancement of free cosmopolitanism. 'Europe', he writes in his introductory reflections, 'emerged unsubdued and free from this terrible war in which, for the first time, it had recognized itself as a connected society of states; and this interest of the states in one another, to which the war first gave rise, would alone be a sufficient gain to reconcile the citizens of the world to its horrors. The hand of industry has gradually obliterated the evil effects of the struggle, but its beneficent consequences have remained.'

Our historian, it is plain, was very firmly convinced that his own cosmopolitanism was a European finality and was worth all that it had cost. What would he have said if he could have looked ahead a hundred years and beheld the nations still snarling at each other's heels in the same old way!

It is pertinent to observe in this connection that Schiller's enthusiasm for liberty is quite unaffected by the 'ideas of 1789'. Neither in his letters nor elsewhere does he manifest any strong sympathy with the revolutionary aims of the French democracy. Liberty is for him the perfect fruitage of the benevolent despotism. It is something that concerns the prince in his relation to some other prince, rather than in relation to his own subjects. Of the German people at the time of the Thirty Years' War he has but little to say, his thoughts being fixed always upon the leaders. His great hero is Gustav Adolf, whom he regards at first as the unselfish champion of German freedom. Little by little, however, the portrait of the king undergoes a change: the ideal knight of Protestantism shades off into the earthy politician and selfish conqueror. And when at last death overtakes him his historian is prepared to admit that the event was fortunate for his own royal renown and for the welfare of Germany. A part of his final estimate runs thus:

Unmistakably the ambition of the Swedish monarch aimed at such power in Germany as was incompatible with the freedom of the Estates, and at a permanent possession in the heart of the Empire. His goal was the Imperial throne; and this dignity, supported and made efficient by his activity, was in his hands liable to far greater abuse than was to be feared from the race of Hapsburg. A foreigner by birth, brought up in the maxims of absolutism, and in his pious enthusiasm a declared enemy of all papists, he was not the man to guard the sanctuary of the German constitution, or to respect the freedom of the Estates.

After the death of Gustav Adolf the focus of interest is Wallenstein, and when Wallenstein is disposed of the history soon becomes a lean and hurried summary, the perfunctory character of which is quite obvious to the reader.

CHAPTER XII

Dark Days Within and Without

1791-1794

Zu einer Zeit, wo das Leben anfing, mir seinen ganzen Wert zu zeigen, wo ich nahe dabei war, zwischen Vernunft und Phantasie in mir ein zartes und ewiges Band zu knüpfen, . . . nahte sich mir der Tod.—*Letter of 1791.*

THE year 1790 was the happiest of Schiller's life. For a little while, at last, fate became supremely kind to him. The reality of wedlock more than fulfilled his dreams, and it seemed as if all his vague *malheur d'être poète* were about to be buried in the deep bosom of connubial beatitude. 'We lead the blessedest life together', he wrote to Christophine Reinwald in May, 'and I no longer know my former self.' And a month later to Wilhelm von Wolzogen: 'My Lotte grows dearer to me every day; I can say that I am just beginning to prize my life, since domestic happiness beautifies it for me.' His income, indeed, was pitifully small, but his courage was great, his fame well grounded, and there were prospects here and there. From the first he had regarded the Jena professorship only as a makeshift. To bring variety into his academic routine he began, in the summer term of 1790, to lecture upon the theory of tragedy, developing

the subject from his own brain and paying little attention to the authorities.   In the autumn these lectures
were resumed, and soon the æsthetic philosopher
began to prevail over the historian.

And now came his great calamity.   In reading the
later writings of Schiller, whether philosophical or
poetical, it is difficult to imagine them the work of an
invalid, produced in the intervals of physical suffering
such as would utterly have broken the courage of a less
resolute man.   But so it was.   The early winter of
1791 brought with it a disastrous illness which shattered
his health, doomed him for the rest of his days to an
incessant battle with disease and finally carried him
away prematurely at the age of forty-five.

Among the acquaintances that he had made through
his connection with the Lengefeld family was a little
group of people in Erfurt.   There were Karoline von
Dacheröden and her lover, Wilhelm von Humboldt,
who was destined to become Schiller's intimate friend
and also his faithful comrade in the field of æsthetic
philosophizing.   Then there was the influential Baron
Karl Theodor von Dalberg, a brother of the Mannheim
intendant.   This elder Dalberg, who some years later
became dubiously prominent in connection with Napoleon's Confederation of the Rhine, was now residing
at Erfurt as Coadjutor to the Elector of Mainz and expecting to become Elector himself on the death of his
superior.   He was an energetic, good-natured man,
not free from ostentatious fussiness, and he enjoyed the
rôle of Mæcenas.   In Schiller and Lotte he took a
deep interest, promising to do something handsome for
them when he should come to power at Mainz.   While

spending his vacation with these Erfurt friends, at the close of the year 1790, Schiller took a cold which brought on an attack of pneumonia. An Erfurt doctor treated the case lightly and unskillfully and sent him back half cured to Jena, where he resumed his lectures. Now came a second and sharper attack, with hemorrhage and other alarming symptoms. The doctors operated upon him as best they knew, with leeches and phlebotomy and purgatives and vomitives, and came very near killing him. For days he lay at the point of death, a few faithful students sharing the young wife's anxious vigil at his bedside. His convalescence was slow and in the end imperfect, leaving him with wasted strength, a pain in the right lung and a serious difficulty in breathing. Of course it was all up with his lecturing; but he easily obtained a release for the summer term from the sympathetic Duke of Weimar. In March he was well enough to take up the reading of Kant's then recently published ' Critique of the Judgment ', and a little later to try his hand at translating from the Æneid in stanzas and to write a rejoinder to the ' anticritique ' of the aggrieved Bürger.

This unfortunate feud with Bürger grew out of a magisterial review published by Schiller in 1791 ; a review which, while dignified in tone and purporting to speak solely in the interest of the lyric art, amounted to a scathing condemnation of Bürger's character. After expatiating upon the high vocation of the poet, the necessity of his thinking and feeling nobly, and the importance of his giving only his idealized self, the anonymous critic proceeded to comment upon Bürger's frequent lapses from good taste, his crudities, indecencies and vulgar ding-dongs, and to refer these things with remorseless directness to personal defects. The criticism was just and had all the other merits save discretion and urbanity. Goethe was pleased with it before he knew who wrote it,[1] and eleven years later Schiller saw nothing in it to change. In writing it, as a matter of fact, he was only breaking the rod over his own early self; for in his Stuttgart 'Anthology' he had committed nearly every sin for which now, from the serene heights of a better artistic insight, he castigated his victim. To poor Bürger, whose life was just then bitter enough at the best, the review was a terrible blow. He at once published a reply, which is also very good reading in its way, but might have been made much more spicy had he known the name of his adversary. Schiller's final rejoinder added nothing of importance to the discussion.[2]

This short digression leads naturally to another. While still at Weimar Schiller received a visit from Bürger, and the two agreed to vie with each other in a translation from Vergil. Schiller chose for his experiment the eight-line stanza which he was proposing to use in an epic upon Frederick the Great. This 'Fredericiad' was much on his mind in the spring of 1789. His plan was to center his story about some ominous juncture in Frederick's career (say the battle of Kollin), and write a poem which should exhibit in lightly-flowing stanzas the 'finest flower' of eighteenth-

---

[1] So, at least, Schiller states in a letter of March 3, 1791, to Körner.

[2] The original review, together with Bürger's reply and Schiller's rejoinder, are printed in Sämmtliche Schriften, VI, 314 ff.

century civilization.[1]   Albeit intensely modern it was to have the indispensable epic ' machinery '.   Nothing came of the project, but a year later he was still ruminating upon it and declared that he should not be truly happy until he was again making verses.

Instead of attempting an original epic, however, he now began to translate from the Æneid, and this light and congenial labor continued to occupy him for a year or more after the break-down of his health.   He finally completed two books, the second and fourth. The translation is sonorous and otherwise readable, but it is not Vergil and does not produce the effect of Vergil.   The breaking up of the matter into stanzas, each having a unity of its own, led to additions, omissions and perversions,—there are 2104 lines in the translation to 1509 in the original,—and substituted an interrupted romantic cadence for the stately continuous roll of the hexameter.

The opening lines of the second book will serve as well as any others to illustrate Schiller's method as a translator:

> Conticuere omnes, intentique ora tenebant.
> Inde toro pater Aeneas sic orsus ab alto :
> ' Infandum, regina, jubes renovare dolorem,
> Trojanas ut opes et lamentabile regnum
> Eruerint Danai; quaeque ipse miserrima vidi
> Et quorum pars magna fui.'

Schiller's version runs thus:

> Der ganze Saal war Ohr, jedweder Mund verschlossen,
> Und Fürst Aeneas, hingegossen

[1] The plan is very fully discussed in a letter of March 10, 1789, to Körner.

Auf hohem Polstersitz, begann :
Dein Wille, Königin, macht Wunden wieder bluten,
Die keine Sprache schildern kann :
Wie Trojas Stadt verging in Feuerfluten,
Den Jammer willst du wissen, die Gefahr,
Wovon ich Zeuge, ach, und meistens Opfer war.

As for the 'Fredericiad', it never got beyond the status of a plan. By November, 1791, Schiller had concluded that Gustav Adolf would be a better subject for an epic,—he could get up no enthusiasm for Unser Fritz and shrank from the 'gigantic labor of idealizing him'. Soon after this he seems to have dropped altogether the idea of writing an epic.

In the spring of 1791, when he had grown strong enough to think of attacking the second installment of the 'Thirty Years' War', Schiller took up his abode in Rudolstadt; and there, in May, he was prostrated by a second illness which was worse than the first. His life was despaired of, he bade his friends farewell and the report went out from Jena that he was dead. After the crisis was past came weary weeks of lassitude and pain, with no possibility of writing or reading. In July he took the waters at Karlsbad, with some slight benefit. By autumn he was well enough to do the promised continuation of his history and to lay plans with Göschen for a *New Thalia* to begin with the next year. But he was now in desperate straits for money. His illness had been very costly and the cessation of work had brought a cessation of income. He was in debt to various friends, and the Duke of Weimar was too poor to help him. Saddest of all, his beloved wife's health was broken with anxiety and watching. 'It is a joy to me', he wrote to Körner in October, 'even when I am busy, to think that she is near me. Her dear life and influence round about me, the childlike purity of her soul and the warmth of her love, give me a repose and serenity that would otherwise be impossible in my hypochondriac condition. If we were only well we should need nothing else to live like the gods.'

It was a dark juncture, darker far than that of 1784, and now as then help came unexpectedly from afar. It came this time from Denmark.

The Danish author Baggesen had visited Jena the previous year and returned home a fervid admirer of Schiller. At Copenhagen he had imparted his enthusiasm to Count Schimmelmann and the Duke of Holstein-Augustenburg, who, with their wives, proceeded to found a sort of Schiller-sect. Full of the time's generous ardor for high and humane ideas, they were just about to give a rustic fête in honor of their great German poet, when the news of his death arrived. They met with heavy hearts and sang the 'Song to Joy', with an added stanza by Baggesen, wherein they pledged themselves to 'be faithful to Schiller's spirit until they should meet above'. When they learned a little later that the author of the 'Song' was alive, after all, and very much in need of money, the two noblemen immediately wrote him a joint letter, offering him, in language of admirable delicacy, a gift of a thousand thalers a year for three years, with no conditions whatever. He was simply to give himself needed rest and follow the bent of his mind, free from all anxiety. Should he choose to come to Copenhagen they assured him that he would find loyal friends and admirers, and a position in the government service if he desired it.

This timely windfall 'from the clouds' put an end to the misery of distress about money. For the first time in his life Schiller found himself free to consult inclination in the forming of his plans and the disposition of his time. Without hesitation he gratefully accepted the gift and resolved now at last to take up the study of Kant and fathom him, though it should require three years. A strange resolution, it would seem, for a sick poet! Many have judged it unwise and have deprecated that long immersion in Kantian metaphysic. But Schiller was the best judge of his own needs, and how he felt about the matter appears very clearly from a letter that he wrote to Körner a few months later:

I am full of eagerness for some poetic task and particularly my pen is itching to be at 'Wallenstein.' Really it is only in art itself that I feel my strength. In theorizing I have to plague myself all the while about principles. There I am only a dilettante. But it is precisely for the sake of artistic creation that I wish to philosophize. Criticism must repair the damage it has done me. And it has done me great damage indeed ; for I miss in myself these many years that boldness, that living fire, that was mine before I knew a rule. Now I see myself in the act of creating and fashioning ; I observe the play of inspiration, and my imagination works less freely, since it is conscious of being watched. But if I once reach the point where artistic procedure becomes natural, like education for the well-nurtured man, then my fancy will get back its old freedom, and know no bounds but those of its own making.

And so it was destined to be. His philosophic

studies, pursued with tireless zeal for a period of three or four years, gave him the self-assurance that he hoped for. They created for him at least, if not for all men everywhere, a poetical *modus vivendi* between natural impulse and artistic rule. ' Nature ' learned to wear the fetters of art without feeling them as fetters. At last he grew weary of theorizing; but his later plays, produced in rapid succession, each unlike the other and all characterized by a remarkable imaginative breadth and freedom, bear witness to the quantity of artistic energy stored up during this period of artistic self-repression.

A few words of biography will suffice for the goings and comings of this Kantian period, which was for Schiller a period of quiet study, eager discussion and laborious authorship. At first he continued to reside in Jena. Early in 1792 he started the *New Thalia*, and this he used for the publication of his earlier æsthetic lucubrations. With the perfunctory conclusion of the ' Thirty Years' War ', in September, his work as a historian virtually came to an end. He now began to lecture again, but gave only an æsthetic *privatissimum* in his own room. He went out of the house hardly five times during the whole winter, and when spring came his health was again very precarious. He now determined to try the effect upon body and soul of the milder climate of his native Suabia. He set out in August and took the precaution to halt in Heilbronn, not knowing what brutality the Duke of Württemberg might still be capable of. On receiving the blessed assurance that his Highness would ' ignore ' him, he continued on his way to Ludwigsburg, where a son was born to him in September. He remained in Ludwigsburg during the winter in pleasant intercourse with his family and friends. In October Karl Eugen went to his reward. 'The death of the old Herod', Schiller wrote to Körner, 'does not concern me or my family, except that all who have to do directly, like my father, with the head of the state, are glad that they now have a man before them.' [1]

One of the first important official acts of the new duke was to abolish the Karlschule; but this did not happen until after Schiller had visited the scene of his former woes, in the rôle of distinguished son, and had received the enthusiastic plaudits of the four hundred students. It was here in Ludwigsburg that his ripest philosophic work, the 'Letters upon Æsthetic Education', came into being. In the spring he spent some weeks in Stuttgart, where Dannecker began to model the famous bust that now adorns the Weimar library. In Stuttgart he made the acquaintance of the enterprising publisher Cotta, who wished him to undertake the editorship of a great political journal. But another plan lay nearer to Schiller's heart, and before he left Suabia he had arranged with Cotta to edit a high-class

[1] On the other hand, Wilhelm von Hoven, who was with Schiller at the time, represents him as deeply touched by the death of Duke Karl and as expressing himself thus : "Da ruht er also, dieser rastlos thätig gewesene Mann. Er hatte grosze Fehler als Regent, gröszere als Mensch, aber die ersteren wurden von seinen groszen Eigenschaften weit überwogen, und das Andenken an die letzteren musz mit dem Toten begraben werden ; darum sage ich dir, wenn du, da er nun dort liegt, jetzt noch nachteilig von ihm sprechen hörst, traue diesem Menschen nicht : er ist kein guter, wenigstens kein edler Mensch." Cf. Kuno Fischer, "Schiller-Schriften", I, 153, and Karoline von Wolzogen, "Schillers Leben", Achter Abschnitt.

literary magazine to be known as *Die Horen*.   In May,
1794, he returned to Jena, glad to have escaped at last
from his dear, distracting fatherland and to be once
more at home.   His health had not improved, and he
had now become reconciled in a measure to the doom
of the invalid.   But although he knew that the death-
mark was upon him, the knowledge only spurred him
to more eager activity.[1]   He felt that he had a great
work to do and that the time might be short.   By this
time his acquaintance with Humboldt had ripened into
a warm friendship.   'What a life it will be', he wrote
to Körner, 'when you come here and complete the
triad.   Humboldt is for me an infinitely agreeable and
at the same time useful acquaintance; for in conversation with him all my ideas move happily and move
quickly.   There is in his character a totality that is
rarely seen and that, except in him, I have found only
in you.'

After his return to Jena he lectured no more, but
threw all his energy into the new journal.   He prepared an alluring prospectus and invited the coöperation of all the best writers in Germany.   Among these
was Goethe, who sent a favorable reply.   And thus
began a correspondence which presently led, as all the
world knows, to an ever memorable friendship.   The
activities centering in the *Horen* ushered in a new
literary epoch, the epoch of Germany's brief leadership
in modern literature.

Thus the period of his Kantian studies, a time of

---

[1] A letter of May 24, 1791, contains the brave words : "Ich habe mehr
als einmal dem Tod ins Gesicht gesehen, und mein Mut ist dadurch
gestärkt worden."

tremendous political excitement in Europe, was for Schiller a quiet period of intense thinking and of eager debate with like-minded friends, upon the abstruse questions of æsthetic theory.   The turmoil of the revolution affected him hardly at all.   There was nothing of the democrat about him.   With all his devotion to liberty and with all his poetic fondness for republicanism, he remained at heart a devoted monarchist.   All his life, nearly, he had lived with aristocrats, and he himself had the temper of an aristocrat.   There is no evidence in his letters that he ever really sympathized with the French people, even during the early days of the revolution, in their practical program of 'liberty, equality and fraternity'.   His notion of liberty was at no time a definite political concept, but always a rainbow in the clouds,—something to rave and philosophize over.   Of human brotherhood he had sung most affectingly in the 'Song to Joy', but it was only a poetic kiss that he had ready for all mankind.   He would have been amazed if any plebeian stranger had proposed to take him at his word.   As for equality, there is no evidence that it entered as a factor or an ideal into his scheme of man's better time to come.

It was thus perfectly natural, when the proceedings were instituted against the ill-fated Louis the Sixteenth, that Schiller should take the part of the accused.   The fierce determination of the French democracy to exact a reckoning from their sovereign, not so much for what *he* had done as for ages of accumulated wrong, appeared to him the very madness of injustice.   In December, 1792, he planned to write a book or a pamphlet in defence of the king, and have it translated into French

for the purpose of influencing public opinion in Paris.[1]
He seems actually to have begun the work, but the fate
of the unlucky Bourbon was swifter than the pen of his
German defender.   Schiller's horror of the regicide
knew no bounds.   'These two weeks past', he wrote
on February 8, 1793, 'I can read no more French
papers, so disgusted am I with these wretched executioners.'   The ensuing events of the Terror intensified
this feeling.   In speaking of the year 1793, Karoline
von Wolzogen has this to say of her brother-in-law:

He regarded the French Revolution as the effect of passion
and not as a work of wisdom, which alone could produce true
freedom.   He admitted, indeed, that many ideas which had previously been found only in books and in the heads of enlightened
men, were now matters of public discussion ; but, he said, the
real principles which must underlie a truly happy civil constitution are not yet so common among men ; they are found (pointing to a copy of Kant's 'Critique' that lay on the table) nowhere
else but here.   The French Republic will cease as quickly as it
has come into being.   The republican constitution will give rise
to a state of anarchy, and sooner or later a capable strong man
will appear from some quarter and make himself master not
only of France but also, perhaps, of a large part of Europe.[2]

If this remarkable prediction of Napoleon is rightly
reported and rightly dated by the Baroness von
Wolzogen, one can hardly suppose that Schiller was
very much elated when he read in a paper, towards the
close of the year 1792, that he had been made an
honorary citizen of the French Republic.   Under a law
passed in August of that year,—*l'an premier de la
liberté*,—the name and rights of a French citizen were

---

[1] Letter of December 21, to Körner.
[2] "Schillers Leben", Achter Abschnitt.

bestowed upon a number of foreigners who had 'consecrated their arms and their vigils to defending the cause of the people against the despotism of kings'. A motley band of heroes had been selected for this honor,—the names of Washington and Wilberforce and Kosciusko being put to pickle in the same brine with those of Pestalozzi, J. H. Campe, Klopstock and Anacharsis Cloots,—and the bill was about to pass when a deputy arose,—he must have been an Alsatian,—and proposed to add the name of M. Gille, *publiciste allemand*. The amendment was accepted, and a few weeks later Minister Roland transmitted to 'M. Gille' an official diploma of French citizenship. It took the postal authorities of Germany some six years to deliver the letter, and when at last they succeeded, its recipient was less than ever in a mood to be overjoyed at the well-meant distinction that had been conferred upon him by the French republicans.

The progress of the Revolution appeared to Schiller to endanger the higher interests of civilization. He was too close to it for a serenely impartial view. Had it been an occurrence of the sixteenth century, he would have been just the man to philosophize over it and to show that in this case, again, "the frenzy of the nations was the statesmanship of fate". As it was, the unrest of the people, and their increasing absorption in questions of mere politics, disgusted him. He felt that a counteragent was needed. And so, declining Cotta's offer anent the political journal, and thus leaving the famous *Allgemeine Zeitung* to begin its career a few years later under other hands, he chose instead to found the *Horen*, which was to exclude politics altogether and induce people, if possible, to think of something else. He saw that the times were unpropitious for his enterprise, but felt that it was for that very reason the more urgently needed. In announcing the *Horen* to the public in 1795 he wrote:

The more the minds of men are excited, shut in and subjugated by the narrow interests of the present, the more urgent is a general and higher interest in that which is purely human and superior to all influences of the time ; an interest which shall set men free again and unite the politically divided world under the banner of truth and beauty. This is the point of view from which the authors of the *Horen* wish it to be regarded. The journal is to be devoted to cheerful and passionless entertainment, and to offer the mind and heart of its readers, now angered and depressed by the events of the day, a pleasant diversion. In the midst of this political tumult it will form for the Muses and Graces a little intimate circle, from which everything will be banished that is stamped with the impure spirit of partisanship.

Many a modern reader will be inclined, perhaps, to smile at this deliverance and to see in it a fatuous misjudgment of the relative importance of things. The French Revolution versus a spray of æsthetic rose-water! But we must not be too hasty. Posterity has no better criterion for judging great men than the criterion of service. And service is a question of vocation. As the matter is put by Goethe, who himself a little later took refuge from the *misère* of the Napoleonic epoch in the contemplative poetry of the Orient: ' Man may seek his higher destiny on earth or in heaven, in the present or in the future; yet for that reason he remains exposed to constant wavering within and to continual disturbance from without, until he once for all makes up his mind to declare that that is right which is in accordance with his own nature.'[1]　It was not in Schiller to be a political journalist or a pamphleteer. In that field he would have wasted his splendid energy. He knew what he could do best; and it was well for his country and for the world that he chose to withdraw from the turmoil of the Revolution and prepare himself for ' Wallenstein ' and ' William Tell '.

[1] "Dichtung und Wahrheit", Elftes Buch.

CHAPTER XIII

Æsthetic Writings

Es ist gewisz von keinem Sterblichen kein gröszeres Wort gesprochen als dieses Kantische, was zugleich der Inhalt seiner ganzen Philosophie ist : Bestimme dich aus dir selbst.

Letter of 1793.

FROM a quotation in the preceding chapter we have seen what Schiller hoped for when he resolved to grapple with the Kantian philosophy. He was in pursuit of that which would help him as a poet. He felt that a little philosophy had done him harm by quenching his inner fire and destroying his artistic spontaneity. The rules were continually coming between him and his creative impulses. His hope was that more philosophy would repair the damage by making the principles of art so clear and so familiar that they would become as second nature, and therefore cease to be felt as a clog or an interference.

This expectation, looking at the matter *a priori*, was reasonable enough. Looking at it retrospectively, Goethe came to the conclusion, as is well known, that Schiller's philosophic bent had injured his poetry by teaching him to ' regard the idea as higher than all nature '. Goethe thought it ' depressing to see how such an extraordinarily gifted man had tormented himself with philosophic modes of thought that could be of no use to him'.[1] But this does not tell the whole story, notwithstanding the greatness of the authority. To assert that all philosophy is always harmful to a poet would be to assert the most patent nonsense. Goethe himself at one time found help and inspiration in Spinoza, the dryest and most abstract of thinkers;[2] and after all, 'nature' comes off about as well in 'Wallenstein' as in 'Faust'. It is a question of personal endowment, of what the mind can assimilate and turn to account. There are many kinds of the poetic temper, the intellectual element blending variously with the emotional, the instinctive and the visional. For Schiller poetry was not 'somnambulism', but a very deliberate process; wherefore it was quite natural for him to expect that a season of philosophic study would be good for him. So he set out to fathom the laws of beauty; assuming, of course, that there must be such laws and that they must be, in some sense or other, laws of human nature.

To follow him critically in all the by-ways of his theorizing would require a treatise; and the treatise would be dull reading, except, peradventure, to such as might be specially interested in the history of æsthetic discussion. In the end, too, it would shed but little light upon Schiller's later plays, which were in no sense the offspring of theory and were influenced only in a very general way by their author's previous philosophical studies. To understand the poet's development it is nowise necessary to lose one's self

[1] Eckermanns "Gespräche", under date of November 14, 1823.

[2] He also admitted that he himself had profited from the study of Kant; cf. Eckermann, under date of April 11, 1827.

with him in the Serbonian bog of metaphysic. On the other hand, it *will* be useful to know what the problems were that chiefly interested him, and to see how he attacked them and what conclusions he arrived at. With the soundness of his reasoning and the final value of his contributions to the literature of æsthetics we need hardly concern ourselves at all; since the scientific questions involved are differently stated and differently approached at the present time.[1]

The pre-Kantian stage of Schiller's æsthetic philosophy is of quite minor importance. He obtained his original stock of ideas at the Stuttgart academy from Ferguson's 'Institutes', as translated by Garve. In Ferguson, who rested strongly upon Shaftesbury, no line was drawn between the moral and the æsthetic domain. It was taught that all truth is beauty and that 'the most natural beauty in the world is honesty and moral truth'. Perfection was made to depend on harmony and proportion; and moral beauty upon the harmony of the individual soul with the general system of things. Wrong action was regarded as discord, imperfection. Virtue, being a disposition toward the general harmony, necessarily meant happiness. Thoughts of this kind, mixed up with vague ideas of a pre-established harmony, constituted the staple of Schiller's early philosophizing. The identity of the good, the true and the beautiful, was for him the highest of all generalizations, though more a matter of pious emotion than of close thinking.

---

[1] Schiller's æsthetic writings, and especially his relation to Kant, have been much discussed in recent years. For a list of the more important works consult the Appendix.

Nor do we observe any noteworthy change of attitude in the minor philosophic writings, such as the letters of Julius and Raphael, and the second book of 'The Ghostseer',—which he published prior to his acquaintance with Kant. In these it is always the moralist that speaks, and the great question is the bearing of skepticism on individual happiness. But by the end of his first year in Weimar the moralist had begun to retreat before the æsthetic philosopher. For the author of 'The Gods of Greece' and 'The Artists', it is evident that the beautiful has become the corner-stone of the temple. He saw before him all at once a new region that invited exploration. If art had played such a commanding rôle in the history of the world, it was evidently of the greatest importance to understand it. It was this feeling for the dignity of art, as the greatest of factors in human perfectibility, that led him to devote the leisure afforded by his Danish pension to a thorough study of Kantian æsthetics.

He began quite independently, as we have seen, with a course of lectures upon the theory of tragedy. The lectures were never published, but the cream of them is probably contained in two essays, 'On the Rational Basis of Pleasure in Tragic Themes', and 'On the Tragic Art', which were contributed to the *New Thalia* in 1792. In the former Schiller first combats the idea that art has any higher aim than the giving of pleasure. Its aim, he argues, is not morality but 'free pleasure', the 'free' meaning subject to no law but its own. If morality is made its final aim, it ceases to be 'free'. Then the essay goes on to discuss

the *crux* of our feeling pleasure in painful representa-
tions. All pleasure, we read, comes from the percep-
tion of *Zweckmäszigkeit*, that is, the quality of being
adapted to the furtherance of an end. Since man is
meant to be happy and naturally seeks happiness,
human suffering affects us primarily as a 'maladapta-
tion', and so gives us pain. But in this very pain our
reason recognizes a higher 'adaptation', since we are
incited by it to activity. We know that it is good for
us and for society; and so we take pleasure in our own
pain. The total effect of tragedy depends upon the
proportion in which this higher sense of adaptation is
present.

The important thing to notice in this argument is
that æsthetic judgments are made to depend upon concepts of the mind. The reason, with its abstractions
of 'fitness' and what not, is regarded as the prior and
the dominating factor. In the second of the two
essays, however, we find a distinct recognition of the
fact that emotional excitement may give pleasure in
and of itself. Illustrations are brought in,—such as
the passion for gaming and for dangerous adventure,
and the general love of ghost stories and tales of
crime,—which go to show that Schiller by no means
overlooked the non-rational element in the pleasure
afforded by tragedy. Nevertheless he seems to have
attached very little importance to that element, for he
goes on to observe that we know only two sources of
pleasure, namely, the satisfaction of our bent for happiness (*Glückseligkeitstrieb*), and the fulfillment of
moral laws. As the pleasure we take in acted or
narrated suffering cannot proceed from the former, it

must spring from the latter and do its work by gratifying the 'bent for activity' (*Thätigkeitstrieb*), which is a moral bent.—After a long tussle with such hazy abstractions the essayist attempts a working definition and practical discussion of tragedy. This part of the essay is still eminently readable, but need not be analyzed here. Sufficient to say that Schiller regards the excitation of 'sympathy' as the sole aim of tragedy. He has nothing to say of the Aristotelian 'fear' or 'katharsis'; in fact he did not make the acquaintance of Aristotle until 1797.[1]

It would be next in order to consider the lectures of 1792–93, but unluckily they are known only from the notes of a student.[2] As published in 1806 they bear the impress of Schiller's mind, but are too brief and summary to be counted among his works. They show that by 1793 he had come to feel at home in the field of æsthetic speculation. He had read Kant and Moritz and Burke, and was ready with his criticisms. In particular, he had found what he regarded as a weak point in the system of Kant, who had not only made no attempt to establish an objective criterion of beauty, but had summarily dismissed the whole problem as obviously hopeless. Schiller felt that, if this were so, there was no firm foundation anywhere, and all æsthetic judgments were reduced to a matter of taste,—which was of course a very unwelcome conclusion. In the belief that he had found the missing link he planned,

---

[1] An oft-repeated assertion to the contrary, which goes back to Karoline von Wolzogen, "Schillers Leben", Achter Abschnitt, is contradicted by a letter of Schiller to Goethe, written May 5, 1797.

[2] They are reprinted in Sämmtliche Schriften, X, 41 ff.

toward the end of 1792, a treatise to be known as
' Kallias, or Concerning Beauty '. It was to take the
form of a dialogue, to be written in a pleasing style,
with a plenty of illustration,—merits to which Kant
could lay no claim,—and to review the whole history
of æsthetic theorizing.

This plan was finally given up, but a series of rather
abstruse letters to Körner, beginning in January, 1793,
may be regarded as preparatory studies for the contemplated treatise. Schiller's idea was, evidently, to
blaze a private trail through the jungle of Kantian
theory, with Körner's critical assistance, and then to
return and convert the trail into an agreeable road for
the general reader. In the end he chose a different
form than that of the Socratic dialogue for the literary
presentation of his doctrine, but what he wrote subsequently was based partly at least upon conclusions that
he had reached through his correspondence with
Körner; wherefore it will be well to look a little more
closely, at this point, into his quarrel with the Königsberg philosophy.

As is well known, Kant placed the æsthetic faculty
under the jurisdiction of the ' judgment ', which he
regarded as a sort of connecting link between the pure
reason and the practical reason, that is, between cognition and volition. A judgment is teleologic, according to his scheme, if it implies a pre-existing notion to
which the object is expected to conform; it is æsthetic
when pleasure or pain is produced directly by the
object itself. In the good and the agreeable we have
an interest,—we will the former and desire the latter.
The beautiful, on the other hand, is that which pleases

without appealing to any interest (*interesseloses Wohlgefallen*). This is its character under the category of quality. Under that of quantity it is a universal pleasure; under that of relation, a form of adaptation (*Zweckmäszigkeit*), with no end present to the mind. Finally, under the fourth category—modality—it is 'necessary', being determined not by any objective criterion, but by the *sensus communis* of mankind, that is, their agreement in taste.

For Kant, then, the whole matter of æsthetics is a subjective matter. He does not inquire what it is that makes objects beautiful, but how it is that we 'judge' them to be beautiful. While his predecessors made the impression of the beautiful to depend upon objective attributes of form, proportion, harmony, completeness and the like, he insisted that the essence of beauty was to please without reference to any such intellectual concept whatever. His terminology was not very happy, since a judgment that has nothing to do with the intellect is not a judgment at all, but a feeling; nevertheless his system brought out clearly,—and this is perhaps his most important merit in the domain of æsthetics,—the necessity of distinguishing more sharply between the beautiful, on the one hand, and the good and agreeable, on the other. But in expounding his central doctrine, that beauty cannot depend upon a mental concept, he is not quite consistent; for he recognizes 'adaptation' as a form of beauty, and adaptation is a concept of the mind. To meet this difficulty he makes a distinction between free beauty (*pulchritudo vaga*) and adherent beauty (*pulchritudo adhærens*), the latter being mixed up with the good or the desirable.   Even a generic or a normative concept was for him fatal to the idea of pure beauty.   Thus pure beauty could not be affirmed of a horse, because one inevitably has in his mind an antecedent notion as to how a horse ought to look.   Again, there could be no such thing as pure beauty,—at the best only adherent beauty,—in a moral action, since a moral action does not please in and of itself.   At the same time Kant held that the highest use of beauty is to symbolize moral truth, and in illustrating the possibilities of this symbolism he indulged in some rather fanciful speculations.

Now we can easily understand that Schiller, notwithstanding all his admiration of Kant and his prompt recognition of the far-reaching importance of Kant's doctrine, could not be perfectly satisfied with a philosophy which decreed that an arabesque is more beautiful than any woman, and that morality cannot be beautiful at all, except in some mystical poetic sense. Nor could he be content with Kant's *sensus communis æstheticus*, which seemed to leave the beautiful finally a matter of taste.   His mental attitude is clearly brought to view in a letter of February 9, 1793, to the Prince of Augustenburg.   After speaking warmly of Kant's great service to philosophy, he describes thus the problem which Kant regarded as impossible of solution and which he himself, Schiller, was bold enough to attempt:

When I consider how closely our feeling for the beautiful and the great is connected with the noblest part of our being, it is impossible for me to regard this feeling as a mere subjective play of the emotional faculty, capable of none but empirical rules. It seems to me that beauty too, as well as truth and right, must rest upon eternal foundations, and that the original laws of the reason must also be the laws of taste. It is true that the circumstance of our feeling beauty and not cognizing it seems to cut off all hope of our finding a universal law for it, because every judgment emanating from this source is a judgment of experience. As a rule people accept an explanation of beauty only because it harmonizes in particular cases with the verdict of feeling; whereas, if there were really such a thing as the cognition of beauty from principles, we should trust the verdict of feeling because it coincides with our explanation of the beautiful. Instead of testing and correcting our feelings by means of principles, we test æsthetic principles by our feelings.

So then Schiller attacked his problem in the afore-mentioned letters to Körner and was soon able to announce his solution: Beauty is nothing else than freedom-in-the-appearance (*Freiheit in der Erschei-nung*).

To make clear the steps by which he arrived at that formula and the wealth of meaning that it contained for him would require a fuller analysis of his argument than there is space for in this chapter. Suffice it to say that he now fully accepts the dogma of Kant that beauty cannot depend upon a mental concept,—the feeling of pleasure is the prior fact. At the same time he has an unshakable conviction that beauty must somehow fall under the laws of reason. He gets rid of the *crux* by taking the æsthetic faculty away from the jurisdiction of Kant's rather mysterious 'judgment', and turning it over to the 'practical reason'. His argument is that the practical reason demands free-dom, just as the 'pure' or theoretic reason demands rationality. Freedom is the form which the practical reason instinctively applies upon presentation of an object. It is satisfied when, and only when, the object is free, autonomous, self-determined. He then propounds his theory that beauty is simply an analogon of moral freedom. On the presentation of an object the practical reason (*i.e.*, the will) may banish for the time being all concepts of the pure reason, may assume complete control and ask no other question than whether the object is free, self-determined, autonomous. If, then, the object appears to be free, to follow no law but its own, the practical reason is satisfied; the effect is pleasurable and we call it beauty. Schiller is careful to point out that it is all a question of appearance: the object is not really free,—since freedom abides only in the supersensual world,—but the practical reason imputes or lends freedom to it. Hence beauty is freedom in the appearance.

In a letter of February 23, 1793, he applies his dogma to an exposition of the relation between nature and art. The problem of the artist in the representation of an object, so the theory runs, is to convey a suggestion of freedom, that is, of not-being-determined-from-without. This he can only do by making the object appear to be determined from within, in other words, to follow its own law. It must have a law and obey it, while seeming to be free. The law of the object is what is disclosed by technique, which is thus the basis of our impression of freedom. Starting from Kant's saying that nature is beautiful when it looks like art, and art beautiful when it looks like nature, Schiller gives a large number of concrete illustrations of his theory. Thus a vase is beautiful when, without prejudice to the vase-idea, it looks like a free play of nature. A birch is beautiful when it is tall and slender, an oak when it is crooked; the shape in either case expressing the nature of the tree when it follows nature's law. 'Therefore', he concludes his illustrations, 'the empire of taste is the empire of freedom; the beautiful world of sense being the happiest symbol of what the moral world should be, and every beautiful object about me being a happy citizen who calls out: Be free like me.'

It did not escape our theorist that his hard-won criterion of beauty was after all, apparently, an idea of the reason. He was however prepared to meet this difficulty and promised to do so in a future letter. But the æsthetic correspondence with Körner was not continued beyond February. The project of the 'Kallias' continued for some time longer to occupy Schiller's mind, but a fresh attack of illness intervened, and when he was again able to work he turned his mind to an essay upon 'Winsomeness and Dignity' (*Anmut und Würde*). It was written in May and June, 1793, and printed soon afterwards in the *New Thalia*. In this essay we can observe a growing independence of thought and an amazing gift for the analysis of subtle impressions. In the main it is lucid enough, especially when one calls in the aid of the preceding letters to Körner; but portions are hard reading. To give the gist of it in a few words is next to impossible, because it is so largely taken up with superfine distinctions in the meaning of words for which our language has at best but rough equivalents.

It will be recalled that Kant had denied pure beauty to the human form, on the ground that the human form

expresses the moral dignity of human nature, which is
an idea of the reason.   Schiller was piqued by this
dictum to test *his* theory of beauty on the human form.
He begins, in a manner fitted to make old Homer
smile, with a rationalizing account of the girdle of
Venus,—the girdle which Venus lends to Juno when
the latter wishes to excite the amorous desire of Jove.
Venus, we are told, is pure beauty as it comes from
the hand of nature.   Her girdle makes her ' winsome '.
So winsomeness is something distinct from beauty;
something transferable, movable.   It is then further
defined as beauty of motion; as the special prerogative
of man; as the element of beauty which is not given
by nature but is produced by the object.   The essay
then goes on to make a distinction between architec-
tonic and technical beauty.   The former is defined as
a beautiful presentation of the aims of nature, the latter
as referring to the aims themselves.   The æsthetic
faculty is concerned with architechtonic beauty.   In
contemplation of an object it isolates the appearance
and is affected by that alone, irrespective of any ideas
of purpose or adaptation.   At the same time the
reason imputes freedom to the object, and when the
object is a human form, this imputed freedom, whereby
the object seems to assert its own autonomous personality, this which is superadded to the beauty that
nature creates by the law-governed adaptation of means
to ends, is winsomeness.—All of which seems to mean
substantially this: That while Pygmalion's statue was
still ivory *it* was beautiful; but when it became a
woman with winsome ways *she* was winsome.

Having demonstrated to his satisfaction that beauty

is really compounded of two elements, first the sensuous pleasure caused by the play of personality, and secondly the rational gratification caused by the idea of adaptation to an end, Schiller takes up the questions of moral beauty and of the ideal of character. He deprecates Kant's strenuous insistence upon the categorical imperative of duty. A man, he urges, must be free; and the slavery of duty is no better than any other slavery. Virtue is inclination to duty, and the ideal is to be found in the perfect equipoise of the sensuous and the rational nature; in other words, when 'thou shalt' and 'I would' pull steadily and harmoniously in the same direction. So he defines 'dignity' (*Würde*) as the expression of a lofty mind, just as winsomeness is the expression of a beautiful soul. Control of impulses by moral strength is intellectual freedom, and dignity is the visible expression of this freedom. Dignity is manifested rather in suffering ($\pi\acute{a}\vartheta os$), winsomeness in behavior ($\mathring{\eta}\vartheta os$). Each acts as a check upon the other. We demand that virtue be winsome and that inclination be dignified, and where winsomeness and dignity are present in harmonious equipoise in the same person, there the expression of humanity is complete.

In the essay just spoken of reference is made more than once to a contemplated 'Analytic of the Beautiful', which was to clear up this and that. Instead of attempting a treatise, however, Schiller chose to go on settling his account with Kant through the medium of contributions to the *New Thalia*. Those published immediately (1793–4) were the essay 'On the Sublime', which included a special chapter 'On the Pathetic'; and 'Scattered Reflections on Various

Æsthetic Subjects'. Two other papers of kindred import, dating from this period, were not published until 1801. These were: 'On the Artistic Use of the Vulgar and the Low', and a second disquisition 'On the Sublime'.

Following Kant Schiller defines the sublime as the impression produced by an object which excites in man's sensuous nature a feeling of weakness and dependence, and at the same time in his rational nature a feeling of freedom and superiority. He objects, however, to the Kantian nomenclature. For the two kinds of sublime which Kant called the mathematical and the dynamic, he proposes the names of the theoretical and the practical; meaning by the former that which tends to overawe the mind, by the latter that which tends to overawe the feeling. Then follows a long and juiceless *Begriffszergliederung*, which may be passed over as containing little that is of importance for the understanding of Schiller's individuality. At last he comes to the subject of tragic pathos, as the most important phase of the practical-sublime. Here he lays down the dogma that the final aim of art is the representation of the supersensuous. The essence of tragic pathos is declared to be the representation of moral superiority under the stress of suffering. The hero's sufferings must seem to be real that he may obtain due credit for his moral triumph. In connection with this thought Schiller takes occasion to deride the genteel sufferers of the French classic tragedy and to commend the Greeks for their fidelity to nature. At the same time he utters his word of warning to those poets who think to gain their end merely by the spectacle of great suffering. The sensuous, he insists, has in itself no æsthetic value; it is the moral resistance that counts, and the suffering is needed only to show that there really was something to resist. The latter part of the essay is directed against those who would try the creations of the poet by the standards of the moral judgment. It is argued that the moral and the æsthetic spheres of interest are separate and distinct. The poet is concerned with the latter. What he needs for his purpose is the manifestation of strength; whether the strength is put forth to a good or an evil purpose is, in itself, a matter of indifference. The poet cannot serve two masters.

In all these discussions of the sublime and the pathetic, et cetera, Schiller exhibits a pathetically sublime faith in the possibility of settling the questions at issue by the analytic method. He writes as if the human mind were composed of air-tight compartments, wherein the various operations of reason, understanding, taste, feeling and what not, are carried on under immutable laws growing out of the nature of man. His philosophy is also dualistic. He regards ' man ' as consisting of two parts joined like the Siamese twins. The one part, sensuous man, which is like unto the animals, is a part of ' nature '; the other part, the rational man, which is dowered with the birth-right of ' freedom ', is outside of nature and above it. The untenableness of this conception has become since Schiller's time increasingly evident. Moreover, we have learned to look upon all things under the aspect of development and to know that man's reason, like the rest of him, is very much the creature of time and place. This being so, one finds it difficult, nowadays, to read the philosophic lucubrations of Schiller with that patience which their well-meant seriousness really deserves. Indeed he himself seems to have felt all along that there was some danger of his being carried too far away into the region of barren speculation; wherefore it was necessary, as he thought, not only to present his ideas in a popular form, but also to prove their relevancy to the practical concerns of human life.

It was with this thought in mind that he finally began, instead of the ' Kallias ', a series of letters to his benefactor, the Prince of Augustenburg. In a long letter of July 13, 1793, he explained his point of view. The political dream of the century, he declared, that is, the dream of recreating society upon a foundation of pure reason, had come to naught. ' Man ' had shown himself unfit for freedom. His chains removed, he stood revealed as a barbarian and a slave,—the slave of unruly passion. And this notwithstanding all that the century had done for the enlightenment of his mind! Evidently the need of the hour and of the future was not so much enlightenment of the mind as discipline of the feelings. In a number of subsequent letters, admirable in style and spirit, Schiller set forth his theory of æsthetic education and his vision of the great good to be accomplished by it in the redemption of mankind from the dominion of the grosser passions. Objections were duly considered, especially the discouraging fact that, historically, æsthetic refinement has too often coincided with supineness of character and moral degeneracy. This consideration made it an important part of the problem to show how the dangers of æsthetic culture could best be counteracted.

The letters to the Danish prince formed the basis of the 'Letters on Æsthetic Education', which were published in 1795 in the *Horen*, and constitute the ripest and most pleasing expression of Schiller's æsthetic philosophy. In the first ten of the 'Letters' he discusses the spirit of the age, for the purpose of showing that some sort of educational process is needed in order to fit mankind for the high calling of the freeman. The problem is to transform the state-ruled-by-force into a state-ruled-by-reason. To this end man must learn to resist and subdue the two inveterate enemies of his nobility, namely, the tyranny of sense which leads to savagery, and the inertness of mind which leads to barbarism. Schiller defines the savage as a man whose feelings control his principles, the barbarian as a man whose principles destroy his feelings. At present, he declares, the mass of men still oscillate between savagery and barbarism, but the man *comme il faut* must establish and preserve a perfect equipoise between his sensuous and his rational nature. Whither shall he look for help? The state cannot aid him, for it treats him as if he had no reason; nor can philosophy save him through the mere cultivation of the reason, for it treats him as if he had no feelings. His only redeemer is the æsthetic sense, the love of beauty.

The 'Letters' then take up the desperate task of showing how the æsthetic sense can do this wonderful work. Descending to the lowest nadir of abstraction, —Schiller calls it rising to the highest heights,—he

brings up two ultimate instincts or bents of mankind,
to which he gives the appalling names of the 'thing-
bent' and the 'form-bent' (*Sachtrieb* and *Formtrieb*).
The former impels to a change of status, the latter to
the preservation of personality. The one is satisfied
with what is mutable and finite, the other demands the
immutable and the rational. To harmonize these two
instincts, to take care that neither gets the better of the
other or invades the other's territory, is the problem
of culture. For a driver of the ill-matched team
Schiller calls in the *Spieltrieb*, or play-bent, which is
only a new name for the æsthetic faculty. His idea is
that in the moment of æsthetic contemplation the
sensuous and the rational instinct both find their
account. In the act of escaping from the serious pull
of thought and feeling to a mental state which satisfies
both without succumbing completely to either, he
finds an analogy to the act of playing. At the same
time he is careful to point out that this kind of play is
different from the sports of common life. As he uses
the word, it means surrender to the illusion of art.
Play is thus the symbol of the highest self-realization.
Only in playing is man completely man.

The last ten letters are devoted to what Schiller,
following Kant, calls 'melting beauty' (*schmelzende
Schönheit*), which is opposed to 'energizing beauty'
(*energische Schönheit*). The former is the natural corrective to the emotional excess which leads to savagery,
while the latter (the sublime, the stirring,) is the antidote to the mental inertness which leads to barbarism.
It is admitted that the æsthetic state is perfectly neutral
so far as concerns the influencing of the will. A good

work of art should leave us in a state of lofty serenity and freedom of mind. If we find ourselves influenced to a particular course of action, that is a sure sign that the art was bad. Nevertheless,—and here lies the kernel of the whole discussion, so far as it bears upon education,—the æsthetic state is a necessary stage in the restoration of imperilled freedom. It is valuable morally simply because it *is* neutral ground. When a man is under the too exclusive domination of either principles or feelings, he is in danger of becoming a slave, and needs to be pulled back to the neutral belt of freedom, in order that he may start afresh. ' In a word ', says Schiller, ' there is no other way of making the sensuous man rational except by first making him æsthetic.' Finally the ' Letters ' take up the evolution of man from the state of savagery and attempt to show argumentatively and in detail how his progress has been determined by the development of his æsthetic sense.

Such are the ' Letters on Æsthetic Education ', which Schiller regarded, in the year 1795, as a tract for the times. Years agone he had made Karl Moor talk of poisoning the ocean; now he himself was thinking to sweeten a poisoned ocean with a bottle of æsthetic syrup. We see that the gist of the whole matter is simply this: That sanity and refinement are pressing needs; that good art makes for these things and in so doing makes indirectly for progress in right living and right thinking. This looks like a painfully small result to have been reached by such long and laborious logic-chopping; so that one is reminded of Carlyle's cynical observation that the end and aim of the

Kantian philosophy "seem not to make abstruse things simple, but to make simple things abstruse". It is to be remarked, however, that the real value of the 'Letters' is not to be found in the logic-chopping, for which their author apologizes again and again; not in the "dreadful array of first principles, the forest huge of terminology and definitions, where the panting intellect of weaker men wanders as in pathless thickets and at length sinks powerless to the earth, oppressed with fatigue and suffocated with scholastic miasma",[1] —but in the incidental flashes of luminous and suggestive comment.

Having himself conquered the Kantian dialect and learned to write it, Schiller had little patience with those who supposed that philosophic truth could and should be set forth in the easy manner of a fireside yarn. It was to free his mind on this subject that he published, in one of the early numbers of the *Horen*, an essay 'On the Necessary Limits of the Beautiful'. Here the burden of his thought is that the philosopher, aiming at truth, must not yield to the seduction of trying to write beautifully. His concern is with fact and logic; imagination and feeling have no place in his domain. The lure of beauty may relax the mind and endanger truth, just as it may relax the will and endanger morality. This last thought contained the germ of his further essays, 'On the Dangers of Æsthetic Culture' and 'On the Moral Benefit of Æsthetic Culture'. These, however, are only an amplification of ideas contained in the 'Letters'.

There remain for consideration, to complete our

---

[1] Carlyle's "Life of Schiller", page 137 (edition of 1845).

survey of Schiller's philosophical writings, his short essay on Matthison's poems and his long disquisition upon ' Naïve and Sentimental Poetry '. In the review he discusses the subject of landscape poetry, thus touching upon a question that had occupied Lessing in the ' Laokoön '. But instead of arguing like Lessing that detailed description of objects is necessarily out of place in poetry, Schiller defends it as capable in a high degree of giving pleasure. The poetic effectiveness of a description he finds to consist, first, in the truthfulness of the description; secondly, in its power, analogous to that of music, to excite vague emotion; and finally, in its power to awaken ideas by the law of association. He distinguishes between ' true ' nature and ' actual ' nature. We arrive at true nature when we take away from actual nature whatever is accidental, peculiar or unnecessary. This process is precisely what is described in one of the ' Kallias ' letters as ' idealization '.

To idealize an object is, then, in Schiller's vocabulary, not to beautify it, or to make it in any way other than it is, but to portray the ' idea ' of it, that is, its essential truth, apart from all that is accidental or individual. He lays down the general rule that poetry is only concerned with true (or ideal) nature in this sense; never with actual (or historical) nature. ' Every individual man ', he declares, ' is by just so much less a man as he is an individual; every mode of feeling is by just so much less necessary and purely human as it is peculiar to a particular person. The grand style consists in the rejection of all that is accidental and the pure expression of the necessary.'

Of the essay upon 'Naïve and Sentimental Poetry', contributed to the *Horen* in 1795, the first part is devoted to the 'Naïve', which is defined as nature in felt contrast with art. To be naïve an action must not only be natural but must put us to shame by suggesting a contrast with our own sophisticated standards. From this it follows that our pleasure in the naïve, being connected with an idea of the reason, is not purely æsthetic, but partly moral. The *naïveté* of children appeals to us because they are what we were and what we should again become. They represent an ideal, a theophany. Though we may look down upon the childish, we can only look up to the childlike. A naïve action always implies a triumph of nature over art: if it is unintentional (naïve of surprise) we are amused; if deliberate (naïve of character) we are touched. Genius is always naïve. Both in its works and in social intercourse, it manifests the simplicity and directness of nature. It is modest because nature is modest; but cares nothing for decency, for decency is the offspring of corruption. It is sensible, but not shrewd. It expresses its loftiest and deepest thoughts with naïve grace: they are divine oracles from the mouth of a child.

These thoughts duly expounded, the essay goes on to consider the modern man's feeling for nature. This results, according to Schiller, from our imputing *naïveté* to the non-rational world. We are conscious of having wandered away from the state of innocence, happiness and perfection. 'Nature' represents this state to our imaginations; it is the voice of the mother calling us back home, or whispering to us of boundless happiness and perfection. Poetry which expresses this boundless longing for the ideal is 'sentimental', while that which reflects nature herself, in some definite part or phase, is 'naïve'. The naïve poet *is* nature; the sentimental poet seeks a lost nature. The Greeks are prevailingly naïve, the moderns prevailingly sentimental, but neither in any exclusive sense. The words are to be understood as expressing only a mode of feeling. The same poet, the same poem, may be naïve at one moment and sentimental at another. All sentimental poetry, then, is concerned with the disparity or contrast between reality and the ideal. If the poet is mainly interested in the real, we have, in the broad sense, satire, which may be pathetic or humorous. If he dwells more upon the ideal, we have elegiac poetry—elegiac in the narrower sense, if the ideal is conceived as a distant object of longing, idyllic if it is portrayed as a present reality. The second part of the essay is devoted to a review of the sentimental poets of modern Germany.

In the third part the naïve and sentimental poets are contrasted. The former, Schiller contends, is concerned with the definite, the latter with the infinite. From the realist we turn easily and with pleasure to actual life; the idealist puts us for the moment out of humor with it. The one follows the laws of nature, the other those of reason. The one asks what a thing is good for, the other whether it is good. Withal, however, Schiller is careful to insist that even the naïve poet, the realist, is properly concerned only with true nature, and not with actual nature. Everything that is,—for example, a violent outbreak of passion,—is actual nature; but this is not true human nature, because that implies free self-determination. True human nature can never be anything but noble. 'What disgusting absurdities', exclaims Schiller,—and the words might well be taken to heart by some of our modern naturalists—'have resulted both in criticism and in practice from this confusion of true with actual nature! What trivialities are permitted, yea even praised, because unfortunately they are actual nature!' It is a part of Schiller's theory that the true realist and the sane idealist must finally come together on common ground.

CHAPTER XIV

The Great Duumvirate

Nun kann ich aber hoffen, dasz wir, so viel von dem Wege noch übrig sein mag, in Gemeinschaft durchwandeln werden, und mit um so gröszerem Gewinn, da die letzten Gefährten auf einer langen Reise sich immer am meisten zu sagen haben.

Letter of 1794.

THE coupled names of Goethe and Schiller denote a literary epoch as well as a peculiarly inspiring personal friendship. What a vista opens before the mind's eye when one thinks of all the influence that went out from them into the wide world during the nineteenth century! The visitor to Weimar who goes to look at Rietschel's famous statue in front of the theater has a sensation like that of standing at the source of a mighty river. Of course the men and their time have been greatly idealized; like the sculptor, the imagination of posterity has lifted them above the level of the earth, joined their hands and given them the pose of far-seeing literary heroes. We think of each as increased by the whole strength of the other. As Herman Grimm puts it algebraically, the formula is not $G + S$, but $G(+ S) + S(+ G)$.[1]

And all this hits an essential truth, albeit the student of the documents—the letters and journals of the

[1] "Goethe", einundzwanzigste Vorlesung.

duumvirs, and of their friends and enemies—has great difficulty at times to imagine himself in an atmosphere of heroism. No nation, no public life of any account; a complete lack of interest, apparently, in many matters that now bulk very large in the minds of men; a small theater, equal to none but very modest demands; a few engravings and plaster-casts and paintings—many of them very poor—to serve as a basis for theories of art; a little optical apparatus, a few minerals and plants and bones, to aid in the advancement of science; everything material on a small scale,—this was Weimar a hundred years ago. Truly a restricted outlook upon this spacious world as it appears to us to-day!

And then the duumvirs had their struggle with the infinitely little, and they fussed over this and that. This is especially true of Goethe. His journals produce upon the reader now and then not so much an impression of glorious many-sidedness as of precious time wasted in futile puttering. But who shall dare to say that it was so in reality? The genius of life tells every great man what he can do, and it is for posterity to accept him and understand him as he was, without complaint and without sophistication. What Goethe and Schiller did in the midst of all their other doings, was to set their stamp upon the culture of their time; to create a new ideal of letters and of life, and to enrich their country's literature with a number of masterpieces which have since furnished food and inspiration to countless myriads. This is quite enough to justify a perennial curiosity concerning the details of their alliance.

For six years the two men, though living as neighbors with many friends and many interests in common, had steadily held each other aloof. That they did so was Goethe's fault, at least in the beginning. We may be very sure that a friendly advance from him would have melted Schiller's animosity as the sun melts April snow. But he did not say the word. He looked upon Schiller as the spokesman of a new and perverse generation that knew not Joseph; and so he went his own way, serenely indifferent to the personality of the man whose talent he had recognized by helping him to a Jena professorship. He paid some attention, it is true, to Schiller's philosophic writings, but what he read did not altogether please him. When the essay upon 'Winsomeness and Dignity' came out, it seemed to him that Schiller, in his enthusiasm for freedom and self-determination, was inclined to lord it all too proudly over mother Nature. Goethe was no less interested in 'ideas' than Schiller, but he had not the same fondness for abstract reasoning from mental premises. His starting-point was always the external fact, and he regarded ideas as possessing a sort of objective reality. His homage was paid to nature and the five senses; Schiller's to the deductive reason.

Nevertheless, the whole trend of Schiller's æsthetic speculations brought him steadily nearer to Goethe's way of thinking. His intense Hellenism; his insistence upon the immense importance of art as an element of culture; his fervid championship of art for art's sake; his practical identification of the ideal with the typical; his doctrine of genius in its relation to abstract dogma, and above all his great earnestness, as of one striving with all his powers towards the better light,—this and much more could not fail to meet Goethe's approval. And then came the great project of the *Horen*, which was to unite all the best writers of Germany in a common effort for the advancement of letters and the elevation of the public taste. This was an opportunity not to be despised, for Goethe was at last beginning to be weary of his isolation at Weimar. Although at heart very desirous of exerting a large influence, he had well-nigh lost touch with the literary public. For four years he had done nothing worthy of his great name. People took little interest in his scientific studies, his ' Grosz-Cophta ', and his ' Citizen-General '. He felt the need of rehabilitating himself. So when he received Schiller's polite invitation anent the *Horen*, he accepted with alacrity; declaring himself ready not only to contribute, but to serve on the editorial committee. And a few days later,—it was on June 28, 1794, before he had seen Schiller or exchanged further letters with him,—he wrote to Charlotte von Kalb that ' since the new epoch Schiller too was becoming more friendly and trustful towards us Weimarians '; whereat he rejoiced, ' hoping for much good from intercourse with him '. So we see that, as the matter then lay in Goethe's mind, it was Schiller who was the distant and distrustful party.

Thus the way was all prepared for the ' Happy Event ', as Goethe called it in an oft-quoted bit of reminiscence published many years later. It chanced that he and Schiller were both present at a meeting of naturalists in Jena. As they left the room together Schiller let fall a remark to the effect that such piecemeal treatment of nature as they had been listening to was dull business for the layman. Goethe replied that there were experts who could not approve it either. Then he proceeded to explain his own views. They reached Schiller's house in earnest conversation, and Goethe went in to continue his demonstration with the aid of a drawing—probably of a typical plant. Schiller listened with seeming comprehension and then shook his head, saying: 'But that is not an experience; that is an idea.' Goethe was disappointed, perplexed. All his labor had gone for naught, and the awful chasm was still yawning. He replied that he was glad if he had ideas without knowing it and could actually see them with his eyes. Schiller defended himself suavely as a good Kantian, and the men separated, each in a docile mood with respect to the other.

Herman Grimm will have it that Schiller now entered upon a crafty campaign for the conquest of Goethe; and really the facts give some color to such a view, albeit, as we have seen, the battle was more than half won before a shot was fired. Schiller had his magazine very much at heart, and besides that he had always been a very sincere and ungrudging admirer of Goethe's poetic genius. Very likely he looked upon him as a weakling in philosophy. To talk of seeing ideas with the bodily eye! Evidently there was no profit in bombarding such a man with syllogisms. But it might be useful to show that one understood him. So Schiller sat him down and wrote out, in the form of a letter, a little essay upon Goethe's individuality, attributing to him a wonderful intuition whereby he saw in advance all that philosophy could prove:

Minds of your sort seldom know how far they have advanced, and how little reason they have to borrow from philosophy, which can only learn from them. . . . For a long time, though at a considerable distance, I have been watching the course of your mind and noticing with ever-renewed admiration the way that you have marked out for yourself. You seek the necessary in nature, but by the very hardest path,—a path which weaker minds would take good care not to attempt. You take all nature together, in order to get light upon the particular. In the totality of her manifestations you hope to find the rationale of the individual. . . . Had you been born a Greek or even an Italian, and thus surrounded from infancy with exquisite scenery and idealizing art, your way would have been infinitely short-ened, perhaps rendered unnecessary. . . . As it was, having been born a German, you had to refashion the old inferior nature that was thrust upon your imagination, after the better pattern which your imagination had created ; and this could only be done by means of leading principles. But this logical direction which the reflecting mind is compelled to take does not tally well with the æsthetic direction of the creating mind. So you had another task ; just as you passed previously from intuition to abstraction, you had now to convert concepts back into intui-tions, and thoughts into feelings ; for only through these can genius create.

For Goethe, whose nature really craved friendship hardly less than Schiller's, there was something very grateful in this frank homage combined with rare perspicacity. He saw that Schiller understood him or was at least concerned to understand him. With all their differences they were spiritual congeners, and much might be hoped for from this new connection. So he sent a very cordial reply to the man who had thus 'with friendly hand struck the balance of his existence '; averring that he too dated a new epoch from their meeting in Jena; expressing the hope that

they might soon find opportunity for a further interchange of views and that, having mutually cleared up
their past course of thinking, they might proceed on
their way together. A few weeks later Schiller spent
two weeks as Goethe's guest in Weimar, where long
discussions, spun out on one occasion from noon to
midnight, begot a perfect understanding and laid the
foundation of a lifelong friendship. It was a friendship
based upon mutual respect and mutual need, full of
high advantage on both sides and cherished loyally to
the end.

Between then and now many and many a writer has
compared Goethe with Schiller and undertaken to
reckon up the balance of their respective merit. The
task is not easy, even though the world is now well
agreed that Goethe's was the rarer genius. No doubt
he, much more than Schiller, was destined to be a
bringer of light to the coming century; but the immense
prestige of his name is due partly to the happy fate that
gave him a long life and invested his old age with the
glamour of literary kingship. If we compare the actual
production of the two men during the eleven years of
their association, it is not at all clear that the palm
should be given to Goethe. The five plays of Schiller,
with the ' Song of the Bell ', and the best of his shorter
poems, will bear comparison very well, in the aggre-
gate, with ' Wilhelm Meister ', ' Hermann and Dorothea ', the ' Natural Daughter ' and those portions of
' Faust ' which were written at this time. Unquestionably Goethe at his best was a far greater poet than
Schiller; but he was less steadily at his best, and his
artistic conscience was more lax than Schiller's. He

envisaged life more largely and more truly, and he wrote with his eye upon the object. His nature inclined to placid contemplation; he was no orator, though something of a preacher. He did not care so much to stir the depths of feeling as to inform and liberalize. In his imaginative work he let himself go *mit holdem Irren* and preferred to avoid artificial surprises and stagy contrasts. Wherefore his work is the more illuminative, the more suggestive,—he is the poet of the literary class. Schiller, on the other hand, was an orator who never lost sight of the effect he wished to produce. He worked more intensely, more methodically, and was less dependent upon mood. He is thus the poet of those who care less for delicacy of workmanship than for sonorous diction, elevated sentiment and telling effects. There is room in the world for both kinds of endowment.

It is quite probable that Goethe and Schiller would sooner or later have come together in a friendly relation even if the *Horen* had never been thought of; and in that case their friendship would have lacked the militant tinge that it presently took on. It was the magazine that leagued them together as allies against the forces of Philistia and made Thuringia the storm-center of a new literary movement. But for this it would probably never have occurred to any one to dub them ' the Dioscuri '.

Prior to the appearance of the first number, in January, 1795, the new journal had been well advertised. Cotta was prepared to spend money on it freely; the contributors were to be handsomely paid, and twenty-five of the best known writers in Germany had promised their coöperation. There was every reason to hope for a dashing success; and to make assurance doubly sure Schiller arranged for 'cooked' reviews of the *Horen* to be paid for by its publisher. But when the time came to launch his enterprise the hopeful editor found himself left very much in the lurch. 'Lord help me, or I perish,' he wrote ruefully to Körner, on December 29; 'Goethe does not wish to print his 'Elegies' in the first number, Herder also prefers to wait, Fichte is busy with his lectures, Garve is sick, Engel lazy and the others do not answer.'

And so it came about that the first number of the *Horen* was largely made up of rather abstruse reading. Schiller did not fully realize that the philosophy on which he had been feeding with satisfaction for three years was not a palatable diet for the general literary public. He regarded his own 'Letters on Æsthetic Education' as a model of lucid popular exposition,— as indeed they are in comparison with Kant. But the number was further freighted with a deep-diving article by Fichte, while Goethe's poetic 'Epistle' in hexameters, and the beginning of his 'Conversations of German Emigrés', though in a lighter vein, were not of thrilling interest to seekers after entertainment. The public, which had expected something different, was disappointed; and when succeeding numbers brought further brain-racking profundities, there was a large ebullition of disgust. Cotta began to write of complaints and cancelled subscriptions; and ere long it looked as if the *Horen* would prove a big fiasco.

Schiller, who should have been inured by this time to the consequences of editorial misjudgment, was dis-

gruntled, vexed.   He began to feel that the German
public was an indolent, long-eared beast that needed
the education of the scourge rather than of æsthetic
letters.   He made some effort, it is true, to enliven his
columns with more entertaining matter, but the
abstruse, in prose and verse, continued to preponderate.
By autumn he was minded to give up the whole undertaking, but was persuaded by Cotta to go on.   Meanwhile he had begun to grow weary of theorizing and
to feel the homesickness of the poet.   ' Wilhelm
Meister ', as it began to issue from the press, excited
his unbounded enthusiasm.   ' I cannot tell you ', he
wrote to his new friend,

I cannot tell you how painful it is to me oftentimes to turn
from a work of this character to philosophy.   There everything
is so bright, so living, so harmonious and humanly true ; here
everything is so strict, so rigid, so very unnatural. . . . This
much is certain : the poet is the only true human being, and the
best philosopher is only a caricature beside him.

So, in the summer of 1795, he began once more to
poetize,—' not venturing out upon the high sea of invention ', as he expressed it, ' but keeping close to the
shore of philosophy '.   In other words he wrote a
number of philosophic poems, partly for the *Horen*
and partly for the new poetic ' Almanac ' that he had
undertaken to edit, in addition to the *Horen*.   This
return to poetry was a joy to him, notwithstanding the
ill health which confined him to the house and cut him
off from the exhilarations of the external world.   It
must never be forgotten that those philosophic poems
are the effusions of a lonely thinker who was compelled
to draw his inspiration from within, and was not

entirely unaware of the fetters he had forged for himself by his long addiction to philosophy.

There was, however, one more subject, of literary as well as philosophic interest, which he was minded to treat before turning his back finally upon the arid wastes of theory, — the subject of realism versus idealism, or, as he decided to phrase it, of naïve and sentimental poetry. This essay, published in 1796, was briefly analyzed in the last chapter. It marks the end of Schiller's one-sided glorification of the Greeks. In more than one passage he comes to the rescue of the modern poet—the sentimentalist—as the poet of the infinite, of the ideal. His contention is that while the realist may be the more admirable in a limited sphere, the idealist has a larger sphere, and his perfection is a higher thing. This attempt of Schiller's to describe, in a scientific spirit, the different kinds of artistic endowment, and to do full justice to all, grew naturally out of his intercourse with Goethe. He admired Goethe more and more. The fifth book of 'Meister' produced in him a 'veritable intoxication'; yet its quality was strikingly unlike that of 'Werther' or 'Iphigenie', and totally different from anything that he himself had done or could possibly do. Perhaps he may have been further influenced by A. W. Schlegel's sympathetic papers upon Dante, which had been published in the *Horen* and which revealed to him a new poetic genius of the highest order, yet not at all Homeric. So he wrote his famous disquisition, —next to Lessing's 'Laokoön' the most thoughtful and the most influential piece of criticism produced anywhere in the eighteenth century, —and endeavored to make it as readable as possible. Goethe, who read the manuscript in November, 1795, wrote of it thus:

Since this theory treats me so well, nothing is more natural than that I should approve its principles and that its conclusions should seem to me correct. I should be more distrustful, however, if I had not at first found myself in an attitude of opposition to your views; for it is not unknown to you that, from an excessive predilection for the ancient poets, I have often been unjust to the modern. According to your doctrine I can now be at one with myself, since I no longer need to contemn that which, under certain conditions, an irresistible impulse compelled me to produce; and it is a very pleasant feeling to be not altogether dissatisfied with one's self and one's contemporaries.

Thus the two men were drawn closer together in mutual sympathy and appreciation, and found in each other more and more a bulwark against the whips and scorns of hostile criticism. Of such criticism there was no lack. The *Horen* was making enemies rapidly and had become, as Schiller put it, a veritable *ecclesia militans*. One Jakob in Halle made an assault upon Schiller's æsthetic writings. Dull old Nicolai in Berlin complained of the ravages of Kantism in German literature. Pious souls like Stolberg were scandalized by the lubricity of Goethe's 'Elegies' and 'Wilhelm Meister'. The famous philologist, Wolf, pounced violently upon one of Herder's Homeric essays. Schiller had now fallen out with his old friend Göschen, who was a center of contemptuous opposition at Leipzig. And Goethe, too, had his quarrel with the world: he felt absurdly sore over the neglect by scientific men of his optical theories in opposition to Newton. Friendly voices were scarcely heard anywhere. There was little opportunity for indulging that pleasant emotion of 'being satisfied with one's contemporaries'.

And so it came to pass that the two friends waxed wroth and determined to strike back. At first they thought of a withering review in the *Horen*, but this idea was given up in favor of another. Goethe had taken a great fancy to the ancient elegiac meter and for some time past it had been his favorite form of poetic expression. Schiller, originally a hater of the hexameter, had caught the fever from Goethe, and used the elegiac form in a number of poems. In December, 1795, Goethe suggested that they amuse themselves by making epigrams, in the style of Martial's 'Xenia', upon the various journals against which they had a grudge, devoting a distich to each. His plan was that each should make a large number; then they would compare, select the best and publish them in the second volume of the 'Almanac'. Schiller was captivated by the idea, and 'Xenia' now became the order of the day. It was soon decided not to restrict them to the offensive journals, but to take a shot wherever there was a mark. Both conspirators took great delight in the proposed *Teufelei*,—it would be such sport to stir up the vermin and hear them buzz. They gave the milder 'Xenia' pet names such as 'jovial brethren', 'little fellows', 'teasing youngsters', while the harsher ones were likened to stinging insects, or to the foxes of Samson:

> You with the blazing tails, away to Philistia, foxes!
> Spoil the flourishing crops, crops of paper and ink.

As Goethe was still preoccupied with 'Wilhelm Meister', it happened at first that Schiller was the more active in the production of these 'kitchen presents', especially such as had pepper in them. With the lapse of time Goethe's share increased. The two were frequently together, for days or weeks at a time, and the mass of Xenia grew rapidly. They determined to swell the number to a thousand and to give the collection a sort of artistic completeness; to make it, that is, a sort of general confession of faith. They agreed furthermore that they would publish the epigrams as a joint production and treat their separate authorship as an inviolable secret. As a matter of fact, some of them really were joint productions. One would suggest the idea or the title, and the other write the verses; or one write the hexameter and the other the pentameter.

During the first half of 1796 Schiller wrote little else than Xenia. By the arrival of summer the joint output amounted to nearly a thousand, but less than half that number found their way into the famous 'Xenia Almanac' of 1797. Of these the targets were legion and the merit various. Some few of them were very good, others little short of atrocious, particularly in the matter of form. As for the general mass, their piquancy is not so great as to superinduce in the reader of to-day a dangerously violent cachinnation. Neither Goethe nor Schiller can be credited with a large vein of sparkling wit. Some of the Xenia are far-fetched and operose, while others sound rather vacuous. The form of the monodistich was in itself a safeguard against diffuseness, but not against the equal peril of inanity.

It would be impossible here to do more than glance at the personalities involved in this rather inglorious squabble. Many of the Xenia were personal pin-pricks. Thus several were directed against the musician Reichardt, who, as editor of two journals, had shown strong sympathy with the Revolution. Goethe, the courtier, and Schiller, who had no democratic proclivities, came to the defense of the gentry thus:

Aristocratical dogs will growl at beggars, but mark you
How little democrat Spitz snaps at the stockings of silk.

And again:

Gentlemen, keep your seats! for the curs but covet your places,
Elegant places to hear all the other dogs bark.

A whole broadside was aimed at the garrulous Nicolai, who deserved a better fate. As the champion of lucidity and reasonableness he stood in reality for a very good cause,—no preachment more necessary in Germany then or since. But in his old age he had fallen a prey to the *cacoethes scribendi;* he insisted upon having his say about everything, yet his stock of ideas had long since run out. So he became the bogey of the Weimar-Jena people. The Xenia assailed him with frank brutality, thus:

What is beyond your reach is bad, you think in your blindness,
Yet whatever you touch, that you cover with dirt.

Other objects of attack were the brothers Stolberg, for their narrow religiosity; Friedrich Schlegel, for his bumptious self-conceit; and various small fry for this and that peccadillo.[1]

---

[1] All the extant Xenia, nine hundred and twenty-six in number,— many of them previously unknown,—were published in 1893 by Erich Schmidt and Bernhard Suphan, with copious introduction and notes, as Volume 8 of the "Schriften der Goethe-Gesellschaft" in Weimar.

A large part of the epigrams, however, were of the 'tame' variety, that is, stingless outgivings of a jocund humor, or grave pronunciamentos upon religion, philosophy, art and so forth. The authors did not wish to appear before the world as mere executioners, but as men with a positive creed, comprising things to be loved as well as things to be hated. They pleaded for sanity, clearness and moderation, and frowned upon the fanatics, hypocrites, vulgarians and cranks. The well-known distich entitled 'My Creed' is representative of many which were directed against the spirit of blind partisanship:

Which religion is mine? Not one of the many you mention.
'Why', do you venture to ask? Too much religion, I say.

Even virtue was to be cherished temperately,—without too much talk about it:

Nothing so hateful as Vice, and all the more to be hated,
Since because of it, now, Virtue is really a need.

And so on in endless variety, on all sorts of subjects. Further illustration shall be dispensed with, seeing that the ancient distich is a poetic form for which the English language has, at the best, but little sympathy. In German it goes much better; and for Schiller in particular, with his natural love of antithesis, it proved a convenient setting for his opinions.

The effect of the Xenia was to set literary Germany agog with curiosity. Two editions of the 'Almanac' were quickly bought up and a third became necessary. There was infinite guessing, speculating, interpreting, and among those who had been hit there was wailing and gnashing of teeth. A very few friends of Goethe and Schiller, such as Körner, Humboldt and Zelter, watched the commotion with solemn glee. Others were shocked or grieved at such a mode of warfare. Wieland mildly regretted that he had come off well in the Xenia, seeing that many other honest people had fared so badly. Herder was much more outspoken and declared that he hated the whole accursed species. The replies, protests and counter-attacks were legion, some in brutal belligerent prose, others in more or less clever Anti-xenia. Some of the latter were grossly abusive, and even indecent; a few contained very pretty home-thrusts, as when in allusion to a well-known poem of Schiller's he was advised to trouble himself less about the ' Dignity of Women ' and more about his own; [1] or where his ' Realm of Shades ' was declared to be so very shadowy that one could not see the shades for the shadow. [2] But the best of all perhaps was the oft-quoted gem:

> In Weimar and in Jena they make hexameters like this,
> But the pentameters are even more excellent. [3]

Historians of German literature are probably right in believing that the Xenia fusillade produced on the whole a salutary effect, although many of the objects of attack seem, at this date, to have been hardly worth

---

[1] Lasz doch die Frauen in Ruhe mit ihrer Würde, und sorge
Für die deine, mein Freund. Ihre bewahren sie schon.

[2] Nun, was denkt ihr vom Reiche der Schatten? Es schattet und schattet
Dasz man vor Schatten umher nichts von den Schatten erkennt.

[3] In Weimar und in Jena macht man Hexameter wie der;
Aber die Pentameter sind doch noch excellenter.

the ammunition. But the explosion cleared the muggy air like a thunder-storm and defined many an issue that it was well to have defined. Writers of every ilk were shaken out of their somnolence and compelled to look in the direction of Weimar; and when it was a question of taking sides, where was the force that could hope to make headway against the combined strength of Goethe and Schiller ? The odds were too great; there was nothing to do but to grumble a little and then—acquiesce in the new leadership. As for the Dioscuri, they had the wisdom to see that one sharp campaign was enough; that for the rest they could further the good cause much more effectively by admirable creation than by peppery epigrams. Prod a man for his bad taste or his foolish opinions, and you harden his heart and provoke him to retaliate; give him something to admire, and you make him a friend in spite of himself.

In the autumn of 1796 Schiller addressed himself to ' Wallenstein ', and from that time on dramatic poetry continued to be his chief concern. He led a quiet, laborious life, battling often with disease and depression, but sustained by high resolution and finding joy enough in domestic affection and the friendship of Goethe. The *Horen* lasted three years and then died an easy death by the mutual consent of editor and publisher. Of the ' Almanac ' five numbers appeared, beginning with 1796. In these small annual volumes a large part of Schiller's best poems were originally published. His work upon the ' Almanac ' was usually done in the summer, other activities being then temporarily laid aside. From the time of his connection with Cotta, who took over the ' Almanac ' after the first number had appeared, Schiller usually had money enough for his needs. But his needs were very modest, the demands of social life in Jena—or even in Weimar under the fiercer but still not very fierce light of the court — being extremely simple. He had not to reckon with the Persian apparatus that disturbed the soul of Horace.

The further relations of Goethe and Schiller, so far as they have any important bearing upon the works of the latter, will be touched on in subsequent chapters. Here let it be remarked in passing that their friendship was not, as it has sometimes been represented, a mere relation of master and disciple. It was rather a spiritual copartnership of equals, each recognizing the other's strength, respecting the other's individuality and eager to profit by discussion. In the beginning, it is true, Schiller looked up to Goethe as to a great and wise teacher who was to give everything and receive little or nothing in return. Every one will recall his saying that he was a mere poetic scalawag in comparison with Goethe. But it is worth remembering that this remark was made after the reading of ' Wilhelm Meister ',—a work which, notwithstanding his admiration, he criticised very sharply. And the justice of his criticism was admitted by Goethe; whereupon Schiller drily observed in a letter to Körner that Goethe was a man who could be told a great deal of truth. As time passed, Schiller dropped the tone of humble docility and became more and more independent. If he deferred to the superior wisdom of Goethe in dealing with the plastic arts and with natural science, there were other matters,—phi-

losophy, poetic theory and the dramatic art,—upon
which he felt that he could speak as one having
authority.   And his authority was respected by Goethe,
especially after the completion of ' Wallenstein '.
Goethe saw that Schiller, along with his poetic gift,
possessed a practical dramatic talent,—an eye for effect
and a power of appealing to the general heart,—such
as he, Goethe, could by no means claim for himself.
And so the nominal director of the Weimar theater
leaned heavily upon his friend and looked to him as
the best hope of the German drama.

CHAPTER XV

Later Poems

So führt zu seiner Jugend Hütten,
Zu seiner Unschuld reinem Glück,
Vom fernen Ausland fremder Sitten
Den Flüchtling der Gesang zurück,
In der Natur getreuen Armen
Von kalten Regeln zu erwarmen.

'*The Power of Song*'.

THE dominant note of Schiller's later poetry is intellectual seriousness; wherefore, if there be those for whom intellectual seriousness is not a quality of poetry at all, for them he has not written. The element of reflection is nearly always prominent in his verse, though there are a few of his poems, notably his best ballads, in which it is conspicuously lacking. What we usually hear is the man of culture commenting upon life, and everywhere he makes his appeal to universal sentiments. The spontaneity, or seeming spontaneity, of the great lyrists was no part of his gift. To catch a fleeting fancy, or some eccentricity of private emotion, and fix it in musical verse of a vague suggestiveness, was not in his line. If he had ever, like Heine, imagined himself joining his sweetheart in the grave and defying the resurrection in a rapturous embrace, he would probably have thought it beneath his dignity to

versify the whimsy.   Of course his verse is self-revela-
tion, without which poetry cannot be; but it is the
revelation of a soul dwelling habitually in the upper
altitudes of thought and emotion, and always assuming
that fellow-mortals who care for poetry at all will be
capable of a serious joy in the things of the mind.

One may say that his art as a poet consists not so
much in the direct expression of feeling in sensuous and
passionate language, as in the transfiguration of thought
by means of impassioned imagery.   In his poems as
elsewhere he is a good deal of a rhetorician, but he is
never insincere.   His verse came from the heart, only
it was the expression of character and convictions
rather than of moods and fancies.   It seems intended
to edify rather than to portray; to impress rather than
to delight.   Some of it, too, is occupied with ideal
sentiments so abstract and sublimated as to possess but
languid interest for normally constituted lovers of
poetry.   For a while, at least, after his return to
poetry, he may fairly be said to have cared a little too
much for the white radiance of eternity, and not quite
enough for the colored reflection beneath the dome.[1]

This last observation has in view more particularly
the poems he wrote in the year 1795, while still
'hugging the shore of philosophy'.   Take for example
'The Veiled Image at Sais', which tells in rather
prosaic pentameters of an ardent young truth-seeker
who is escorted by an Egyptian hierophant to a veiled

[1] "The One remains, the many change and pass,
     Heaven's light forever shines, earth's shadows fly;
 Life, like a dome of many-colored glass,
     Stains the white radiance of Eternity."

—*Shelley's "Adonais".*

statue and told that whoso lifts the veil shall see the Truth. At the same time he is warned that the veil must not be lifted save by the consecrated hand of the priest himself. Moved by a curiosity which can hardly seem anything but laudable,—unless one is prepared to take the side of the sacerdotal humbug,—the young man returns in the night and raises the veil. In the morning he is found pale and unconscious at the foot of the statue. Soon afterwards he dies, leaving to mankind the message:

Woe unto him who seeks the Truth through Guilt.

This has an unctuous sound, and one gets a vague impression that the old story has been dressed up for the sake of some modern application. One is piqued to reflect upon it; but the more one reflects the more clearly one sees that there is no real instruction in it. But if there is no instruction, there is nothing at all; since the mysticism is of a kind that appeals solely to the intellect.

Far more interesting is the poem which was at first called ' The Realm of Shades ' and later ' The Ideal and Life ',—a difficult production, which resembles ' The Artists ' in its suggestion of a voyage through the imponderable ether. We begin with the blessed gods in Olympus and end with the apotheosis of Hercules; and the intervening stretch is like the vasty realm of the Mothers in ' Faust '. The poem is intellectual, in the sense that its theme is a concept of the mind, and its structure logical throughout; yet every strophe is surcharged with feeling, and the diction presents a marvelous wealth of imagery. It must be conquered by study before it can yield any great pleasure; but the conquest once made, one finds a noble delight in the gorgeous coloring with which Schiller invests his idealistic rainbow in the clouds. Good critics, favorable to Schiller's genius, regard ' The Ideal and Life ' as the greatest of his philosophic poems and the most characteristic expression of his nature. He himself felt a sort of reverence for it. ' When you receive this letter ', he wrote to Humboldt, ' put away everything that is profane and read this poem in solemn quiet. ' And Humboldt replied: ' How shall I thank you for the indescribable pleasure that your poem has given me ? Since the day on which I received it, it has in the truest sense possessed me; I have read nothing else, have scarcely thought of anything else. '

The general drift of the wonderfully pregnant verses is that man attains peace only by renouncing the things of sense and living in the realm of shades, that is, among eternal ideals.   Here he is free—like the gods.

> The Weavers of the Web—the Fates—but sway
> The matter and the things of clay ;
>   Safe from each change that Time to Matter gives,
> Nature's blest playmate, free at will to stray
> With Gods a god, amidst the fields of Day,
>   The FORM, the ARCHETYPE, serenely lives.
> Wouldst thou soar heavenward on its joyous wing ?
>   Cast from thee Earth, the bitter and the real,
> High from this cramped and dungeon being, spring
>   Into the Realm of the Ideal. [1]

Throughout the poem ' Beauty ' is put for ' the Ideal '; and we get a reflex of the philosophic doctrine that

[1] Bulwer's Translation.

only the æsthetic faculty can resolve the eternal conflict between the sensuous and the rational man.   Life
is and must be struggle, that being its very essence;
but by taking refuge in the Realm of the Ideal, man
anticipates his apotheosis.   There he escapes from the
tyranny of the flesh and the bondage of nature's law.
The misery of struggle and defeat no longer vexes him.
The warring forces are reconciled and he sees their
conflict under the aspect of eternal beauty.   Thus, like
the new-born god, Alcides, taking leave of the terres-
trial battle-ground, he mounts into heaven, while the
nightmare of the earthly life ' sinks and sinks and
sinks '.

> Behold him spring
> Blithe in the pride of the unwonted wing,
>   And the dull matter that confined before
> Sinks downward, downward, downward, as a **dream** !
>   Olympian hymns receive the escaping soul,
> And smiling Hebe, from the ambrosial stream,
>   Fills for a God the bowl.[1]

All this may seem, at first blush, to attach excessive
importance to the attainment of inward peace and
harmony,—as if one's private comfort were the greatest
thing in life.   It *seems* to recommend a quietistic, contemplative life; for how else shall one escape from the
actual into the ideal ?   Nevertheless it would be a great
mistake to read into the poem anything like a recom-
mendation of quietism.   The ultimate goal is described
in terms which suggest now the mythology of Homer,
now the Platonic realm of ideals, and again the Christian heaven; but however the blessed existence is

---

[1] Bulwer's Translation.

imaged, it is always thought of as attainable only through a strenuous grapple with the realities of this life. Thus the essential spirit of the poem is the spirit of energetic, hopeful endeavor. Its doctrine is, to quote the words of Kuno Francke, that "only through work are we delivered from the slavery of the senses"; that "the very trials and sufferings of mankind bring out its divine nature and insure its ultimate transition to an existence of ideal harmony and beauty".[1]

The doctrine, in its essence, was dear to Goethe, as well as to Schiller, and takes us into the holy-of-holies of their joint philosophy. What else did Goethe mean by his oft-reiterated preachment of renunciation, and by his well-known verses about 'weaning oneself from the half and living resolutely in the whole, the good and the beautiful'? In his excellent book upon Diderot Mr. John Morley speaks somewhere of "that affectation of culture with which the great Goethe infected part of the world". Let it not be forgotten, however, in our latter-day contempt of culture, that the Weimar poets were great workers, and also, in their way, great fighters. They did not turn their attention—at least not directly—to the crushing of the Infamous, nor to any battle against social or political wrong. They fought rather for sanity, for good art, for philosophy; for those things which go to enrich and broaden the life of the individual. It was a good fight,—the best which, at their time, with their gifts, they could possibly have engaged in.

Schiller's fervid verses, recommending an escape from the bondage of sense to the free realm of the

---

[1] "Social Forces in German Literature", p. 376.

mind, correspond of course to nothing that is humanly feasible. The shackles of the flesh are upon us and there is no way to get rid of them. It is only an ideal, a poet's dream. Nevertheless the subject has a practical aspect which is definable in plain prose. It is found in the following passage from Goethe:

We put one passion in place of another ; employments, dilettantisms, amusements, hobbies,—we try them all through to the end only to cry out at last that all is vanity. No one is horrified at this false, this blasphemous saying ; indeed it is thought to be wise and irrefutable. But there are a few persons who, anticipating such intolerable feelings, in order to avoid all partial resignations, resign themselves universally once for all. Such persons convince themselves with regard to the eternal, necessary, law-governed order of things, and seek to acquire ideas which are indestructible and are only confirmed by the contemplation of that which is transient.[1]

Other poems of the year 1795 were ' The Partition of the Earth ', wherein Zeus takes pity on the portionless poet by giving him a perpetual *entrée* to the celestial court; the mildly humorous ' Deeds of the Philosopher ', a bit of persiflage on the art of proving what everybody knows, and also several pieces in the elegiac form.

Of these last the weightiest is the one at first called simply ' Elegy ', and later ' The Walk '. Just as Goethe had used the elegiac meter for his reminiscences of Rome, so Schiller employs it for his impressions of such small travel as fate permitted him,—a summertime walk in field or forest. The verses will bear comparison very well with the ' Roman Elegies '.

---

[1] "Dichtung und Wahrheit", sechzehntes Buch.

Instead of paintings, statues, marble palaces and the troublesome Amor, we have the aspects of nature, —the music of bird and bee, and the toil of the husbandman 'not yet awakened to freedom'. As our sauntering poet comes in sight of a city,—the locus of the poem is the neighborhood of Jena, with reminiscent and imaginative touches here and there,—he is moved to reflections upon the more eager life of the townspeople. This leads to a retrospective survey of the origins of civilization,—of agriculture, the mechanical crafts, trade, letters, art, science and the social sentiments. Then the darker side of the picture is developed,—the evils, inhumanities, corruptions and vices of civilized life. For some time the wanderer pursues his way completely lost in these sad contemplations; then suddenly he returns to the present and finds himself alone with nature, from whose 'pure altar' he receives back again the joyousness of youth. Thus the poem ends, like 'The Ideal and Life', upon an idyllic note; the one pointing forward, beyond the warfare of life, to an unimaginable Elysium, the other pointing backward to a happy golden age of which Mother Nature is the living reminder:

> Ever the will of man is changing the rule and the purpose,
> Ever the genius of life alters the form of his deed.
> But in eternal youth, in ever varying beauty,
> Thou, O Mother of Men, keepest the ancient law. . . .
> Under the selfsame blue, over the same old green,
> Wander together the near, and wander the far-away races,
> And old Homer's sun, lo! it shines on us now.

The inner form of 'The Walk'—loving contemplation of nature, giving rise to general reflections upon

life—is essentially Goethean; one may safely regard
it as a conscious experiment in Goethe's manner. As
such it is very good indeed, although its exotic meter
has stood in the way of its attaining the popularity of
the ballads and the ' Song of the Bell '. ' The Walk '
and ' The Ideal and Life ' are the noblest gifts of
Schiller's didactic muse.

Coming now to the poems of the year 1796, and
regarding them first in a general way as a group by
themselves, we can observe that Schiller has made
progress in weaning himself from abstract modes of
thought. The stanzas entitled ' The Power of Song '
tell of a fugitive in strange lands lured back to warm
himself in the embrace of nature from the chill of ' cold
rules '. Another reminds the metaphysician, who
boasts of the great height to which he has climbed, that
his altitude can do nothing for him except give him a
view of the valley below. ' Pegasus in Harness ' is a
humorous apologue intended to enforce the truth that
the winged horse is of no use for drudgery and exhibits
his proper mettle only when ridden by a poet. Of
much greater interest than any of these is ' The
Ideals '. Here the middle-aged poet recalls the fervid
dreams of his youth and thinks of them under the image
of airy sprites attending his rushing chariot, like the
Hours in Guido's picture. Midway in his course he
finds that they have all dropped away, save Friendship
and Work,—Friendship that lovingly shares the bur-
dens of life, and Work that only brings grains of sand
one by one to the Builder,

> Yet from the debt-book of the ages
> Erases minutes, days and years.

Most noteworthy in this group, however, is unquestionably that famous tribute to womanhood which goes by the name of ' Dignity of Women '. Looked at with the scientific eye it is sheer gyneolatry,—the chivalrous sentiment inflated with poetic wind, like a bubble, to the utmost possible degree of iridescent tenuity. Man is depicted as a wild creature, ever tossing on the sea of passion, or chasing phantoms in the empyrean. Reckless and vehement, he lives by the law of force, or, at the best, by the law of reason and logic. Woman, on the other hand, follows the better light of feeling and gently lures the daring wanderer back to present realities. In her little sphere of intuition she is richer and freer than he in his boundless kingdom of thought and imagination. Her sovereignty is that of a child or an angel, making always for peace, gentleness and goodness.—All of which is extremely interesting as a classical expression of an old-fashioned sentiment that good men used once to believe in. Schiller believed in it ardently, and one loves him none the less for that. The most cogent objection to his verses is their generality. For ' man ' it is necessary to read ' Friedrich Schiller ', and for ' woman ', his wife.

In its metrical form the poem attempts to express the lovableness of the ' eternal-womanly ' by means of a lightly flowing dactylic measure, while a heavier trochaic cadence is employed to denote the nature of man:

> Ehret die Frauen ! Sie flechten und weben
> Himmlische Rosen ins irdische Leben,
> Flechten der Liebe beglückendes Band. . , .

> Ewig aus der Wahrheit Schranken
> Schweift des Mannes wilde Kraft,
> Und die irren Tritte wanken
> Auf dem Meer der Leidenschaft.[1]

Such a scheme, in the hands of a Schiller, leads inevitably to a crescendo of rhetorical contrasts, which in the end sound somewhat flighty and forced. The poem was an object of ridicule to the Romanticists, and the elder Schlegel wrote a saucy parody of the first two strophes.[2]

The few poems that found a place in the 'Almanac' of 1797, along with the luxuriant crop of Xenia, are relatively unimportant. The difference between the sexes, a subject which Wilhelm von Humboldt had discussed in the *Horen*, was expounded anew by Schiller in distichs. It is very much the same story as the 'Dignity of Women', the distich form lending itself beautifully to those antitheses which were Schiller's delight. Then there was a poetic riddle, called 'The Maiden from Afar',—a slight affair, but pretty in its

---

[1] Bulwer translates the lines, somewhat lamely, thus :
> Honour to Woman !   To her it is given
> To garden the earth with the roses of Heaven !
> All blessed, she linketh the Loves in their choir. . . .
>> From the bounds of Truth careering,
>> Man's strong spirit wildly sweeps,
>> With each hasty impulse veering
>> Down to Passion's troubled deeps.

[2] Ehret die Frauen !   Sie stricken die Strümpfe,
> Wollig und warm, zu durchwaten die Sümpfe,
> Flicken zerriss'ne Pantalons aus. . . .
>> Doch der Mann, der tölpelhafte,
>> Find't am Zarten nicht Geschmack ;
>> Zum gegohrnen Gerstensafte
>> Raucht er immerfort Taback.

way; a 'Lament of Ceres', in trochaic tetrameters,
and a 'Dithyramb', wherein a poet is visited by all the
Olympian gods and cheered with a draught of Hebe's
joy-giving nectar. These classicizing poems, which
purport to express modern feeling in the terms of Greek
mythology, sound now a little hollow and conventional.
The vein had been worked to excess even in Schiller's
day, and it is no wonder that the Romanticists pined
for something new. The best of them all is 'The
Eleusinian Festival', called originally 'Song of the
Citizen', in which Schiller returns to his favorite theme
—the origin and progress of civilized society. The
climactic thought of the twenty-seven sonorous stanzas
is contained in the Kantian oracle of Ceres:

> Freiheit liebt das Tier der Wüste,
> Frei im Äther herrscht der Gott,
> Ihrer Brust gewalt'ge Lüste
> Zähmet das Naturgebot;
> Doch der Mensch, in ihrer Mitte,
> Soll sich an den Menschen reihn,
> Und allein durch seine Sitte
> Kann er frei und mächtig sein.[1]

In the spring of the year 1797, as 'Hermann and
Dorothea' was approaching completion, Goethe and
Schiller were led to an interchange of views concerning

[1] " In the waste the Beast is free,
    And the God upon his throne!
    Unto each the curb must be
    But the nature each doth own.
    Yet the Man—betwixt the two—
    Must to man allied belong;
    Only law and Custom thro'
    Is the Mortal free and strong."
    —*Bulwer's Translation.*

the distinctive qualities of epic poetry. Their discussion begot an interest in the kindred type of the ballad, which may be regarded as a miniature epic in a lyrical form. The result was that both poets began to make ballads for the next year's 'Almanac'. Schiller contributed five: 'The Diver', 'The Ring of Polycrates', 'The Cranes of Ibycus', 'The Errand at the Furnace' and 'The Knight of Toggenburg'. In subsequent years he wrote three others: 'The Pledge', 'Hero and Leander' and 'The Count of Hapsburg'. To these may be added 'The Glove', which was not called a ballad because not written in uniform stanzas, and 'The Fight with the Dragon', which was called a 'romanza'.

These poems, taken as a whole, owe nothing whatever to the folk-song. The popular ballad, which had once fascinated Goethe and Herder and Bürger, and the Göttingen poets generally, seems never to have appealed to Schiller in any notable degree. If we except 'The Count of Hapsburg', his ballad themes are all exotic, that is, they do not deal with German legend or history or superstition. The suggestions came generally from out-of-the-way reading, and in one or two cases his exact source has not been certainly identified. The tales have no odor of the soil, no local color. They make no use of the supernatural, the gruesome or the uncanny. They are not wild roses, but jaqueminots cultivated with an æsthetic end in view. Their aroma is distinctly literary, and they are all eminently serious. Not a smile is provided for in the whole list. There is no element of mystery about them. The passions and sentiments illustrated are of the universal kind. And just as vague, uncanny and bizarre feelings play no part, so there is no resort to verbal tricks, such as meaningless repetitions, or onomatopoetic jingles. The language is dignified and classical. Their great merit is the vivid and strong imaginative coloring with which situations and actions are portrayed. While in no sense folk-songs, they have always been great favorites with the German people.

In 'The Diver' the stress falls upon the portraiture of the raging deep and its awful horrors. It is a rhetorical *Prachtstück*, which has done good service to many an elocutionist and declaiming schoolboy. Schiller himself had never seen the sea, nor any body of water remotely resembling the Charybdis of the poem. Observation, as he humbly confessed, had given him nothing more awesome than a mill-dam,— the rest was Homeric and imaginative; wherefore it no doubt gratified him when Goethe reported from Schaffhausen, after a visit to the cataract, that the line

Und es wallet, und siedet, und brauset, und zischt,

was scientifically correct. 'The Glove' merely versifies a simple incident of a brave knight whose courage is put to an inhuman test by his lady-love; he brings her glove from among the 'horrible cats', and then contemptuously cuts her acquaintance. In these two, the earliest of the ballads, description of the situation preponderates over the epic element, and there is no 'idea' except to narrate an extraordinarily brave action. In 'The Ring of Polycrates' one can discern progress in the mastery of the ballad form, though the subject was none of the best. Based upon a story in

Herodotus, it is a poetic setting of the ancient idea that excessive good fortune provokes the anger of the gods and portends disaster. Strangely enough Schiller's poem breaks off with the recovery of the ring from the fish's belly, and the consequent warning and departure of the Egyptian guest. One would expect an additional stanza or two, showing how the forebodings of Amasis were presently realized.

Much better than any of the foregoing is 'The Cranes of Ibycus'. In the composition of this ballad Goethe took a deep interest, giving several suggestions which were adopted by Schiller to the great advantage of the poem. The Greek legend does not explain, or explains variously, just why the murderers in the theater call out the name of Ibycus when they see the cranes flying over. Schiller supposes that the spectacle just then going on was a solemn chorus of the Eumenides. Thus the unaccountable exclamation of the murderers is connected with the mysterious power of the avenging Furies. It is this use of the nemesis idea that makes the merit of the ballad.

'The Knight of Toggenburg' is a sentimental tale of romantic love, while 'The Pledge'—a captivating and powerful version of the Damon and Pythias story —is a heroic ballad of loyal friendship. 'The Errand at the Furnace', wherein a spiteful tale-bearer meets the horrible fate he has prepared for the innocent and devout Fridolin,—may be styled a ballad of pious edification. Here, as a critic observes, Schiller purposely essays a tone of childlike *naïveté* which was foreign to his nature.[1] 'The Battle with the Dragon'

---

[1] Otto Harnack, "Schiller", page 274.

has for its theme the moral majesty of self-conquest. With ' The Cranes of Ibycus ' and ' The Pledge ', it forms a triad which may be regarded as the choicest fruitage of Schiller's interest in the ballad. The later ones, ' The Count of Hapsburg ' and ' Hero and Leander ', are no less finished in the matter of form, but have more of a lyric tinge.

We see that as a balladist Schiller got his inspiration mainly from two sources: the traditions of Greek antiquity and the traditions of chivalrous romance. He dwelt habitually in the idealisms of the past, and his controlling purpose was to make these idealisms live again in stirring poetic pictures. The present time, with its fierce national conflicts, the larger meaning of which was not yet apparent, seemed to him barbarous and depressing. In the prologue to ' Wallenstein ', it is true, he was able to survey the situation with a calm artistic eye and to see in the ' solemn close of the century ' a period in which ' reality is becoming poetry '. But this is an isolated deliverance. His habitual mood was one of aversion, from which he sought relief by an escape into the kingdom of the mind. Thus, in some stanzas on the opening of the new century, he laments that the English-French war has overspread sea and land and left no place on earth for ' ten happy mortals '. Then he bids the friend to whom the verses are addressed take refuge in the holy temple of the heart, seeing that Freedom and Beauty dwell only in dreamland. A similar sentiment finds expression in ' The Words of Illusion ', published in 1801, as a sort of pendant to the earlier ' Words of Faith '. The words of faith are Freedom, Virtue and

God. Men are exhorted to cling steadfastly to these eternal verities, whereof only the heart gives knowledge. The other poem is directed against the superstition of believing in a golden age, or in any external realization of the right, the good and the true. The final stanza runs:

> And so, noble soul, forget not the law,
> And to the true faith be leal;
> What ear never heard and eye never saw,
> The Beautiful, the True, they are real.
> Look not without, as the fool may do;
> It is in thee and ever created anew.

These last-named poems belong to a type which the Germans sometimes call the 'lyric of thought', — a name which is fairly appopriate to a goodly number of Schiller's shorter effusions. Other examples—to mention a few of the best—are 'Light and Warmth', 'Breadth and Depth' and 'Hope'. They might be called lyrics of culture, since they regard the perfection of the individual,—the equipoise of heart and head, steadfast seriousness as opposed to showy sciolism, the preservation of hope and faith,—as a noble object of emotion. They are not intellectual in the opprobrious sense of the word as applied to poetry; they are suffused with warm feeling and their language is simple and natural. On the other hand they *are* argumentative: they state propositions and draw conclusions the value of which must in the end be gauged by the mind. For this reason one who has no sympathy with Schiller's idealism,—one who either never felt it or has lost it in the stress of life,—will not be touched by these poems, but will regard them as hollow. Yet they are no more hollow than the lyrics of Goethe or Heine or Shelley, though the illusion of sincerity is less perfect than in the work of these great lyrists.

A pure lyric effusion, of the kind that seems to sing itself without help or let from the brooding philosopher, was not often attempted by Schiller. Perhaps his very best achievement in this sort is ' The Maiden's Lament ', of which the first two stanzas, translated as closely as possible with reference to both substance and form, run as follows:

> The oak-wood moans, the clouds float o'er,
> The maiden sits by the green sea-shore.
> The waves are breaking with might, with might,
> And she breathes out a sigh in the gloom of the night,
> And her eyes are dim with weeping.

> ' My heart is dead, the world is naught,
> It brings nothing more to my longing thought,
> I have lived and loved,—earth's fortune was mine,
> Thou Holy One, take this child of thine,
> Take her back into thine own keeping.' [1]

Such verses, and one might adduce further the admirable songs in ' William Tell ', show that Schiller had in him, when he could find it and let it have its

---

[1] Der Eichwald brauset, die Wolken ziehn,
> Das Mägdlein sitzet an Ufers Grün,
> Es bricht sich die Welle mit Macht, mit Macht,
> Und sie seufzt hinaus in die finstere Nacht,
> Das Auge von Weinen getrübet.

> "Das Herz ist gestorben, die Welt ist leer,
> Und weiter giebt sie dem Wunsche nichts mehr.
> Du Heilige, rufe dein Kind zurück,
> Ich habe genossen das irdische Glück,
> Ich habe gelebt und geliebet."

way, a lyric gift of a high order. As a rule, however, when he attempted to sing, the attempt resulted in a philosophic evaluation of the feelings expressed. Thus in his well-known 'Punch Song', he is mainly concerned with the ethical symbolism of the four elements, —the lemon-juice, the sugar, the water and the spirits. In other cases he suggests an allegorical symbolism, and leaves the reader puzzling over an intellectual query that may or may not be worth puzzling over. Examples are 'The Maiden from Afar', 'The Youth at the Brook', 'The Mountain Song'. He even wrote a number of professed poetic riddles,—which may be left without commentary to those who like that sort of poetry.

The cultural poems of Schiller have always enjoyed a high degree of popularity. A large number of his lines and couplets have become familiar quotations that come readily to the tongue or pen of the educated German. There is probably no modern poet who has taken a deeper hold upon the intellectual life of his countrymen. This is partly attributable to the fact that his idealistic sentiments appeal especially to the youthful. No poet that ever lived is better adapted to the needs of the school; none more infallibly safe and inspiring to the young of both sexes. For the riper mind and the larger experience his oracles are apt to lose somewhat of their impressiveness; for it is not to be denied that his poetry at its best is seldom supremely good. The divine spark that fuses rare thought and waiting expression in the white heat of the imagination and gives one the sense of artistic perfection is not often there. His verse is never cold, never trivial; but it does lack artistic distinction. Its highest claim is to give expression to the maxims of a ripe culture in tuneful verses and pleasing imagery that impress themselves readily upon the general heart. This is what he does in the most famous of all his poems, 'The Song of the Bell'. It is not great poetry, but it is a pleasing production which well deserves its popularity.

'The Song of the Bell' was first given to the world in the 'Almanac' of 1800, after several years of incubation. Its germ-idea is similar to that of the 'Punch Song'; that is, we have a mechanical process,—in the one case the mixing of a glass of punch, in the other the casting of a bell,—accompanied at its various stages by reflections of an ethical character. The bell-founder is an idealist with a feeling for the dignity of man and of man's handiwork. As he orders his workmen to perform the successive operations involved in the casting of a bell, he delivers, from the depths of his larger experience, a little homily, suggested, in each case, by the present stage of the labor. The master's orders are given in a lively trochaic measure, while the homilies move at a slower gait in iambic lines of varying length. The fiction is handled with scrupulous attention to technical details, and is made to yield at the same time a series of easy and natural starting-points for a poetic review of life from the cradle to the grave.

The great charm of the 'Song' lies in its vivid pictures of the epochs, pursuits and occurrences which constitute the joy and the woe of life for an ordinary industrious burgher. Childhood and youth; the passion of the lover, sobering into the steadfast love of the husband; the busy toil of the married pair in field and household; the delight of accumulation and possession; the calamity of fire that destroys the labor of years; the blessedness of peaceful industry; the horrors of revolutionary fanaticism; the benediction of civic concord,—these are the themes that are brought before us in a series of stirring pictures that are irresistibly fascinating. To have felt and expressed so admirably the poetry of every-day life, and that at the very time when the Romanticists were beginning to fill the air with noise about the prosaic dullness of the present time as compared with the Middle Ages, was a great achievement, and all the greater as Schiller himself had not remained unaffected by the Romantic doctrine. He could Hellenize and philosophize, and, on occasion, he could Romanticize; but 'The Song of the Bell' shows how deeply, after all, his feeling was rooted in the life of the German people.

The 'Almanac' for 1800 was the last volume that appeared, and after the removal of this exigency Schiller's lyrical production diminished. His best strength was devoted to his plays, which in themselves, however, contain a large lyric element. The choral parts of 'The Bride of Messina' show the final phase of his art in its perfection. Like these, the few independent poems written by him during the last years of his life are characterized by great beauty of diction and of rhythmic cadence, but in their substance they hardly compare with the best of his previous work. Most noteworthy are 'Cassandra', devoted to the pathos of foreseeing calamity without being able to prevent it, and 'The Festival of Victory', wherein the Greek heroes, assembled for departure after the sack of Troy, discourse amiably and profoundly upon the finer issues of life. In some of the shorter and more subjective poems there is discernible a note of sadness, as of a drooping spirit unreconciled, after all, to the stress of this earthly existence. This is heard, for example, in ' Longing ' and ' The Pilgrim '. But from such sporadic utterances no large inference should be drawn respecting Schiller's mental history. They proceeded from a sick man whose days were numbered.

CHAPTER XVI

Wallenstein

> So hab' ich
> Mit eignem Netz verderblich mich umstrickt,
> Und nur Gewaltthat kann es reiszend lösen.
>
> *'Wallenstein'*.

THE great play which signalizes the return of Schiller to dramatic poetry must be accounted upon the whole his masterpiece. To be sure it is less popular than 'Tell' and less immediately effective than 'Mary Stuart'. It has not the romantic soulfulness of 'The Maid of Orleans', nor the splendid diction of 'The Bride of Messina'. On the stage, too, its effectiveness is somewhat impaired by its great length. But in the imaginative power whereby history is made into drama; in the triumph of artistic genius over a vast and refractory mass of material, and in the skill with which the character of the hero is conceived and denoted, 'Wallenstein' is unrivaled. Well might Goethe pronounce it 'so great that nothing could be compared with it'. Its chief figure is by far the stateliest and most impressive of German tragic heroes.

Since the completion of 'Don Carlos' Schiller had written nothing of any moment in the dramatic form. For nine years he had been occupied with historical and philosophic studies which he himself regarded as preparatory to some new and nobler flight of artistic creation. Of course he had been aware all along, none better than he, that great poetry cometh not by theorizing; that theory could have at the best only a general regulative value. At the same time, with the example of Lessing before him, he could not but feel that this regulative value might be very great. And so he had gone resolutely on his way, even after the dread truth had come home to him that he had not long to live and might never be able to reap the fruit of what he was sowing.

He had studied certain epochs of history very carefully and had acquired a deeper insight into that tangled interplay of inward motive and outward circumstance which determines the course of events. Philosophy had only deepened his early conviction that man's dignity, his heroism, consists in his free self-determination; but who knew better than he the infinite pathos of the battle between ' will ' and ' must ' ? He had become familiar with the spirit and the technique of the Greek drama and learned to admire its simple and stately architecture. Latterly, however, he had been drawn toward the moderns and had found in the expression of the modern spirit—with all its idealisms, its heights and depths and mysteries of feeling—a higher artistic goal than antiquity had ever imagined. Finally, his association with Goethe had taught him the importance of looking fairly at life and portraying it not indeed just as it is, but in its essential human spirit. This, for him, was to idealize.

Two themes had been suggested by his historical studies, and both had haunted his thoughts for years,

—'The Knights of Malta' and 'Wallenstein'. The former, if his plan had been carried out, would have yielded a play of the classical type, with few characters and a severely simple structure. In the final balancing of the two subjects 'Wallenstein' prevailed, no doubt because it seemed in advance the easier and the more promising. It pointed to a familiar field where history itself had already shaped in the rough a stupendous and fascinating tragedy. To reproduce the form and pressure of the Thirty Years' War, at one of its most exciting moments, was an alluring problem to a dramatist who had written a history of the struggle, and who had always felt that his strength lay in the historical drama.

Serious musings upon 'Wallenstein' began, as we have seen, in the autumn of 1796.[1] The first great problem was, of course, the general plan of the piece, —how to select, dispose and concentrate. To quicken his imagination Schiller commenced reading again upon the history of the period and soon perceived that what he already knew would be quite inadequate; that it would be necessary to go over the whole ground anew and more thoroughly. He found the material dry, chaotic and abstract; in short, lacking in nearly all the poetic elements which he would have thought indispensable a few years before. He could not treat it in his earlier manner. He had no love for any of his personages except Max and Thekla, whom he had invented for the purpose of infusing a little warm blood

[1] Let it be said once for all (to avoid frequent references), that the following account of the genesis of 'Wallenstein' is based upon Schiller's letters—chiefly to Körner and to Goethe—beginning in November, 1796.

into an action which would otherwise have been dominated altogether by the cold passions of ambition, vindictiveness and fear. Wallenstein was not great or noble; at best he could only be made terrible. The basis of his power was his army, and this—so it seemed to Schiller at first—was too large and complex a thing to be effectively portrayed. Then, too, his enterprise failed chiefly because of bad management, and he himself rather than fate was to blame for his catastrophe. This Schiller regarded as the weak point of the whole subject; but he took some comfort from the example of 'Macbeth'.

Notwithstanding these difficulties, however, he worked at his task with great eagerness, feeling that just such a subject as 'Wallenstein' would prove the crucial test of his powers. His old theory that love is what makes the artist was now completely outgrown, and he was gratified to observe that he had learned to keep himself out of his work. So much for the influence of Goethe, to whom he wrote, in November, 1796, as follows :

With the general spirit of my work you will probably be satisfied. I might almost say that the subject does not interest me at all. I have never combined such coolness toward my theme with such a warmth of feeling for my work. My principal character, and the most of my subordinate characters, I have treated up to this time with the pure love of the artist.

After some hesitation between prose and verse he began in prose, being led thereto partly by the advice of Wilhelm von Humboldt and partly by his own desire to produce this time an acceptable stage-play. His

progress was at first very slow. There was endless
reading to be done and endless rumination over the
plot. In the winter season, with its close confinement
and its lowered vitality, the invalid could accomplish
but little. He fixed his hopes longingly upon the
return of spring and decided to buy a house with a
garden, so that he could muse and write in the open
air. In May, 1797, the purchase was made, but by
this time work on ' Wallenstein ' had completely stag-
nated and other interests were at the fore. He was
back among the Greeks. Renewed study of Sophocles,
particularly of the ' Trachiniæ ' and the ' Philoctetes ',
had convinced him that everything hinges upon the
invention of a poetic fable. To quote again from a
letter to Goethe:

The modern poet wrestles laboriously and anxiously with accidental and subordinate matters and, in his effort to be very
realistic, loads himself down with the vacuous and the trivial.
Thus he runs a risk of losing the deep-lying truth which constitutes the real nature of the poetical. He would fain imitate an
actual occurrence, and does not consider that a poetic representation can never coincide with actuality, because it is absolutely true.

A little later he took up the study of Aristotle's
' Poetics ' and was delighted to find that the dread
Rhadamanthus was after all so very liberal and sensible. He had now reached a firm footing and was not
to be dislodged even by Aristotle, whose whole body of
doctrine, as he did not fail to observe, was deduced
empirically from concrete specimens of a particular type
of play. It could not be canonical for all the world,
but it was very instructive. Schiller was glad that he

had finally discovered Aristotle, but glad also that he had never read him before.

On returning to 'Wallenstein' in October, after the summer claims of the 'Almanac' had been satisfied, he noticed that what he had written was characterized by a certain dryness. It was evident that, in his strenuous effort to avoid his besetting sin of rhetoric, he was in danger of becoming trivial. He had still a sustaining faith in the goodness of his subject, but the great problem would be to make it poetical. It was necessary to find the middle way between the rhetorical and the prosaic. The practical result of these cogitations was a decision to write 'Wallenstein' in verse. In versifying the completed scenes he found himself, so he wrote to Goethe, before a different tribunal. Much that had seemed very good in prose would not do at all; for verse tended to invest everything with an imaginative nimbus which rendered triviality and mere logic intolerable.

But the new form brought with it a new danger—that of prolixity. It was necessary that the exposition account for Wallenstein's conduct by exhibiting the sources of his power. This meant a dramatic picture of his wild and irresponsible soldatesca. The theme was boundless and Schiller was a facile verse-maker. Ere long he reported ruefully to Goethe that his first act was already longer than three acts of 'Iphigenie'. He was in doubt whether his friend had not infected him with a 'certain epic spirit' which tended to diffuseness. In his embarrassment of riches he decided to give the preliminary picture the form of a dramatic prologue having but a loose connection with the play proper, which was still conceived as a five-act tragedy.

During the winter of 1797–8 he worked as he could, steadily upborne by the friendly encouragement of Goethe. When summer arrived the last two acts were still unfinished, and the first three had grown to portentous dimensions. It was now that he decided to divide his unmanageable tragedy into two parts, 'The Piccolomini' and 'Wallenstein's Death'; his idea being that 'The Piccolomini', preceded by the dramatic prologue, which was now christened 'Wallenstein's Camp', would fill up an evening and prepare the way for the real tragedy of 'Wallenstein's Defection and Death'. This plan, involving a reconstruction of the whole, was carried out in the ensuing months. At the urgent request of Goethe, preparations were made to reopen the newly-renovated Weimar theater with a performance of the 'Camp' alone. As the piece was too short for this purpose, Schiller hastily amplified it to a sufficient size and wrote for it a noble prologue, which ranks among the best of his poems. When played at Weimar, in October, 1798, the 'Camp' was well received as a picturesque novelty, but that was all. It gave no clew to what was coming, and there was nothing in it to stir the depths of human nature.

'The Piccolomini' was completed in December and put upon the Weimar stage, under Schiller's personal direction, on January 30, 1799. As then performed it included two acts of 'Wallenstein's Death'. The first performance was a great success. The Weimarians, with Goethe at their head, were enthusiastic; and Schiller, who had of late known but little of popular favor, found himself suddenly invested with a new renown. He was pleased, elated; from this time on he felt sure of his vocation as dramatic poet. Returning to Jena he applied himself steadily to ' Wallenstein's Death ', completing it finally in March. It was first played on the 20th of April, preceded at short intervals by the ' Camp ' and ' The Piccolomini '. And great indeed was the poet's triumph, now that his achievement could be judged as a whole. He had given his best after years of preparation, and the world saw at once that it was very good. The animosities aroused by the Xenia lingered for a while in a few small minds, but it was of no use to fight genius with the missiles of petty malice. The Germans had accepted Schiller as their great dramatist.

To form a right estimate of ' Wallenstein ' one must first look at it in a large way, remembering that structurally it forms a class all by itself. The name ' trilogy ', in the technical sense of the Greeks, does not apply to it, seeing that the ' Camp ' is not an integral part of the whole, but a dramatic prelude in an entirely different key. In a loose sense, to be sure, it forms a part of the exposition; but it can be omitted entirely, if one chooses, since everything technically necessary to be known is repeated in ' The Piccolomini '. Its characters are different and nothing is said or done that is vitally related to the ensuing complication. Its purpose is to show the nature of Wallenstein's soldiers and the grounds of their attachment to their commander. Their loyalty is of course the great factor in Wallenstein's position; it is because he relies upon their fidelity that he dares to dally with the thought of treason. But this fidelity of theirs, their sturdy *esprit du corps*, their unwillingness to be separated, could have been indicated in a scene, or in the report of a messenger; in fact it *is* indicated in the memorial which they place in the hands of Max Piccolomini.

The ' Camp ', then, with its eleven-hundred verses, is to be regarded as a military genre-picture, elaborated for its own sake into an independent piece. As a prelude it transports us into the *milieu* of the tragedy, but without anywhere striking its key-note; for the tragedy is intensely serious, while the note of the ' Camp ',—notwithstanding an undertone of seriousness without which it could not have been the work of Schiller,—is that of jovial humor. And the poet's scheme required just this effect in the prelude. One can hardly assent, therefore, to the suggestion of Harnack [1] that it would have been well if the sentiment of loyalty to the emperor had been made more prominent and given a more worthy champion than the stolid Tiefenbachers, who have nothing to say. Had this been attempted it must have led to an adumbration of the coming tragic conflict,—which is what Schiller wished to avoid. He wished that spectator and reader should accept the prelude as a thing of its own kind, complete in itself. It was for this reason that he gave it a distinctive meter, having convinced himself that meter of some kind was essential if he would avoid banality. With a wise instinct he chose the old free-and-easy tetrameter, which Goethe had used with excellent effect in some of his early plays. In German this meter lends itself beautifully to the bluff, off-hand

[1] "Schiller", p. 286.

discourse of soldiers. It gives an illusion of realism while preserving the effect of poetry.

Particularly admirable is the art with which Schiller has contrived to denote the motley variety of human types gathered under Wallenstein's banner, while giving to each of his figures a fairly distinct individuality. With a little study of costume a painter could paint them all. There is the wretched Peasant, who has been reduced to beggary and is willing to retrieve his fortunes by gambling with loaded dice; the sagacious Sergeant, who always knows more than other people, and prides himself upon 'the fine touch and the right tone' that can only be acquired near the person of the commander; the depraved Chasseur, who glories in fighting for its own sake, cares not for whom or what, and objects to discipline; the philosophic Cuirasseur, who argues for a higher ideal and pities the woes of the producing class, but cannot help matters; and the fiery Capuchin, who pronounces his wordy anathema against the whole godless crowd. What a picturesque assembly they make and how admirably they bring out the lights and shadows of the Wallenstein régime! One wonders how an invalid recluse, a bookish philosopher like Schiller, should ever have been able to write such scenes.

The total effect of the prelude is to put one in a very good humor with the personages who figure there. One indeed feels sub-consciously that they are detestable—not a whit better than the angry friar paints them. One sympathizes intellectually with his fierce denunciation and pities the land that is exposed to such a scourge. And yet—such is the poetic glamour thrown over them—feelings of this kind never become dominant. It is like the squalid slums of a great city, when seen through the sun-lit morning mist. The reality is horrible, revolting. The soul of the philanthropist is pained—but not so the eye of the artist. Schiller contrives that we see his vagabonds with the artistic eye and are drawn to them by their very picturesqueness. We quickly impute to them more virtue than their ways betoken; and when in their lusty final song they break out in a strain of lofty idealism:

> Und setzet ihr nicht das Leben ein,
> Nie wird euch das Leben gewonnen sein,

one is hardly conscious of the incongruity.

The dramatic fable devised by Schiller for the tragedy proper carries us back to the winter of 1634. Events extending over several months are concentrated by poetic fiat into the four days preceding the assassination of Wallenstein, which took place on the 25th of February. The prominent characters fall into two groups,—the abettors of Wallenstein in his treason, and the imperialists who work his ruin. The first group consists of historical personages, mainly officers, whom he had bound to him by one or another tie of selfish interest. Foremost among these are Illo, the Count and Countess Terzky, and General Butler, who turns against his chief and becomes the agent of his taking-off. The central figure of the other group is Octavio Piccolomini, whom Schiller converts from a young officer of thirty into an elderly man with a grown-up son. Octavio, in reality the trusted agent of the emperor, is regarded by Wallenstein with a superstitious infatuation as his own most faithful friend. Between these two groups stand the ingenuous lovers, Max and Thekla, imaginary characters who can make their perfect peace with neither side and are done to death in a pathetic struggle between love and duty.

As we have already seen, Schiller found it no easy task to mould the historical Wallenstein into a satisfactory tragic hero. The character was lacking in nobility. To be sure it was not necessary to make him out an infamous traitor; for his character, his motives, the measure of his guilt, were subjects of debate among the historians, and the evidence was, as it still is, inconclusive. It was therefore quite within the license of a dramatic poet to take the part of Wallenstein, so far at least as to throw into strong light all the palliating circumstances that could be urged in his favor. Such were, for example, that he was a prince of the empire and as such had a right to conduct negotiations and to make peace; that he wished to give rest to a torn and bleeding Germany; that he had been ignobly treated by the House of Austria, and so forth. By laying stress upon these things and passing lightly over others, it was easily possible to save Wallenstein from the detestation that is wont to associate itself with the idea of a traitor.

But for an interesting tragic hero it is not enough to fall short of infamy. He must have some sort of distinction. He must be a towering personality. One does not go to the theater to be convinced in a moral or political argument, but to be carried along with a rush of feeling, for which the old term sympathy is perhaps as good a name as any other. A magnificent

criminal will serve the purpose very well, as Schiller
had discovered in his early years, but he must be
magnificent. Now it was precisely this element of
greatness that was lacking in the character of the historical Wallenstein. No lofty idealism of any kind
could be imputed to him. He was not a religious
zealot, like Cromwell or Gustav Adolf, nor was he a
strenuous German patriot, like Frederick the Great.
He was not even a great soldier; for while, as the head
of a great host of marauding mercenaries, he made
himself the scourge and the terror of Germany, he
never won a decisive battle against an equal enemy.
The history of his fighting is largely a history of
futilities. And when he formed the plan of a separate
peace, — a plan which if promptly and vigorously
executed might possibly have succeeded and have
caused him to be numbered with the benefactors of
Europe,—he dallied with the thought until it was too
late, fell into the pit which he had digged for himself,
and, in trying to flounder out, met his death at the
hands of an assassin who had a grudge against him.
Thus even his death was pitiful rather than tragic. It
does not appear to be the work of that high Nemesis
which Schiller noticed as dominating the career of
Shakspere's Richard the Third.

To have succeeded as Schiller did succeed, in the
face of such difficulties, is a memorable triumph of the
poetic art. By purely æsthetic means, without any
appeal to political or religious passion, without requiring us to take sides in any debatable cause, but simply
by the skill and subtlety of his drawing, he has invested
Wallenstein with an impressiveness such as belongs

only to the great creations of the great tragic poets. His overruling trait is ambition; and in the denotation of this, as of his whole relation to the Countess Terzky, the influence of ' Macbeth ' is obvious. And yet he is very far from being a copy of Shakspere's hero, or a mere embodiment of ambition. On the contrary, he is the most complicate of all Schiller's creations, and the most difficult to portray on the stage in a thoroughly satisfactory manner. As a good critic observes, he is ' fascinating and repulsive, admirable and contemptible, fantastic and cunning, cautious and frivolous, a mighty organizer and a helpless child, false and true, touching and terrible, a mixture of all possible qualities, and yet a unity, a totality '.[1] The promise of the Prologue is admirably fulfilled:

> But art shall show him in his human form
> And bring him nearer to your eyes and hearts ;
> She sees the man in all the stress of life,
> And for the greater portion of his guilt
> She blames the working of malignant stars.

The last two lines, be it observed, involve much more than a mere allusion to Wallenstein's superstitious belief in astrology. Schiller's idea, schooled as he had been for years upon Sophocles and Shakspere, was to blend the fate-tragedy of the ancients with the modern tragedy of character. The two things were not incompatible, since in a broad view of the matter a man's character is his fate. It is to be observed also that the peculiar effect of Greek tragedy does not depend upon the way in which the external $\mu o \hat{\imath} \rho \alpha$ was conceived, but upon the fact that the hero seems to be

---

[1] Bulthaupt, "Dramaturgie des Schauspiels", I, 288.

battling, and was by the audience known to be battling, against the inevitable. The situation is not what he supposes, and the event will not be what he intends. He is the subject of an illusion, an infatuation; and this ἄτη is the principal factor in the tragic effect.[1]

Now Wallenstein's ἄτη takes the form of a blind and overweening self-conceit. He has the 'great-man-mania' hardly less than Karl Moor. Accustomed to follow his own light, to command and to be obeyed, and to look with contempt upon the interference of priests and courtiers in the business of war, he thinks himself omnipotent. There is no power that he fears save that of the stars; and even that he imagines he can bend to his will by studious attention to astrologic portents. He has found it possible to raise and maintain a great army by taking good care of his officers and men; and appealing thus constantly to the lower motives of human nature, he comes to think at last that there are no others. When the Swede Wrangel suggests a suspicion of his Chancellor that it 'might be an easier thing to create out of nothing an army of sixty thousand men than to lead a sixtieth part of them into an act of treachery', Wallenstein replies: 'Your Chancellor judges like a Swede and a Protestant.' And when he finds that this sentiment of loyalty—*die Treue*, one of the most ancient and powerful of motives—is still a real force in human affairs, he can only account for it as a curious superstition:

[1] Notwithstanding frequent references to occult powers and overruling destiny, the Greek idea of fate is quite foreign to "Wallenstein". It is essentially a modern character-drama. Cf. Fielitz, "Studien zu Schillers Dramen", page 9 ff.

'Tis not the embodiment of living strength
That makes the truly terrible.   It is
The vulgar brood of all the yesterdays,
The eternally recurring commonplace,
That was and therefore is and hence will be.
For man is fashioned of the trivial
And customary use he names his nurse.[1]

It would seem as if such a blind and superstitious self-worshiper could have but little chance of winning sympathy, and the less chance for the reason that he really does nothing in the play to justify his grand airs. His mighty deeds are a matter of hearsay.   We are obliged to take his greatness on trust, as something growing out of the past.   And yet Schiller contrives, with splendid artistic cunning, that we do take him from first to last at his own estimate.   His assumption of superiority appears perfectly reasonable; and even in the ticklish astrological scenes, about which Schiller himself was in doubt until reassured by Goethe, he never becomes ridiculous.   His belief in destiny and his unctuous palaver about the occult connection of events do not detract from his dignity.   One understands that his oracles are fallacious, that it is all a humbug; but so perfect is the illusion that instead of smiling one mentally associates him with other men undoubtedly great,—men like Cæsar, Cromwell and

[1] Nicht was lebendig, kraftvoll sich verkündigt,
Ist das gefährlich Furchtbare.   Das ganz
Gemeine ist's, das ewig Gestrige,
Was immer war und immer wiederkehrt,
Und morgen gilt, weil's heute hat gegolten !
Denn aus Gemeinem ist der Mensch gemacht,
Und die Gewohnheit nennt er seine Amme.

Napoleon,—who were haunted by more or less similar hallucinations.

This is effected, in part at least, by bringing Wallenstein into contrast with vulgar and commmonplace natures. In the presence of a real hero he would be a pigmy,—even under the searchlight of the ardent young Max his effulgence pales somewhat,—but surrounded by the Illos, the Terzkys, Isolanis and the rest of them, he is a moral and intellectual giant. One does not wish to belong to *their* company or to believe in their arguments; and so when they urge him to act one is quite prepared to credit the mysterious oracles which assure him that the time is not yet ripe. Thus even his indecision,—most damning of weaknesses in a great soldier,—does not seem to belittle him. One enters into the spirit of his self-defense, is half inclined to believe in his innocence and to sympathize with him, when the psychological moment arrives and the capture of Sesina compels him to translate a traitorous thought into a traitorous deed. And even after this, when he stands forth as a declared traitor; while his trusted friends are secretly turning against him, and his unsuspected enemies are quietly plotting his doom; when, with a futile energy, he is making the plans that are yet, as he believes, to leave him master of the situation; and when, finally, in his bereavement and isolation, he is brought to face his miserable fate, —everywhere he looms up as a grand figure. Schiller has taken good care that one shall not think of his treason or of his weakness, but rather of his imposing personality.

That Wallenstein produces such an impression is

largely due to the character of his chief antagonist.
Octavio Piccolomini is certainly one of Schiller's most
notable minor studies. It is he who stands for the
cause of loyalty to which one naturally leans; but he
is so portrayed that one soon distrusts and in the end
almost despises him. And yet he is no villain of the
extreme type so dear to Schiller in his early years.
Octavio's conduct and his sentiments are technically
correct. He is a faithful servant of the empire, a far-
sighted and energetic commander and an affectionate
father. The groundwork of his character seems much
better entitled to sympathy than that of Wallenstein.
In the play, however, from the moment we hear of the
secret order making him temporary commander-in-
chief, we begin to suspect that he too is playing a
game for profit. And when he lays his secret plans
against Wallenstein, while openly appearing as his
friend; when he craftily works upon the vanity of
Butler, and instils into Butler's small soul the poison
of a murderous hate, one is not drawn to the cause
which needs such championship.

Rationally and before the bar of politics, Octavio's
conduct is unimpeachable. He does his duty in baffling
a powerful traitor in the most effective way. It is not
his fault that Wallenstein is deceived in him, and nothing requires that he go and undeceive him. He resorts
to no tricks, he feigns no sentiments that are not his.
He but tells the truth to Butler in regard to the ancient
matter of the title. It is no part of his plan that Butler
shall murder his former chief. And when Wallenstein
falls, not so much because of his present treason as
because of his former duplicity, Octavio is technically

guiltless of the deed. And yet so skillfully is the portrait drawn, so subtly are the lights and shadows managed, that when the curtain falls one is little disposed to sympathize with him in his triumph. There is a world of ironical pathos in those last words of the play: ' To Prince Piccolomini '.

A very important element in the impression produced by Octavio, as also in that produced by Wallenstein himself, is the fact that we are made to try them not at the bar of worldly ethics, but before the tribunal of the heart as represented by the young idealist, Max. It is a weak criticism of Wallenstein which objects to the love-story or regards it as a mere concession to the sentimental demands of the average play-goer. For the reason just stated it must rather be looked upon as a vital element of the plot. No doubt the play can be imagined without it and would in that case be more in accordance with history. But what a relatively cold affair it would be! The tragedy of the lovers is an important part of the Nemesis that follows Wallenstein from the moment of his taking the fateful step. It is this which makes in no small degree the real impressiveness of his final isolation. Without it we should see in Wallenstein a masterful spirit, like Macbeth, playing fast and loose with the higher law and meeting an ignoble fate at the hands of enemies meaner than himself. In a sense the moral law would be vindicated, but how much more effective is the vindication when this masterful spirit first makes havoc of all that should be dearest to him as a man!

It is quite true that the figure of Max, like that of Posa, is out of harmony with the general *milieu*.

Schiller was a lover of contrast, and in his skillful use
of it lies a large part of his effectiveness as a playwright. To a certain extent his contrasts are made to
order; that is, they proceed from the vision of the artist
calculating an effect, rather than from the observation
of life as it is. Partisans of realism tell us that this
propensity is a weakness, a fault; and such it is, beyond
question, whenever it leads to forced and stagy contrasts. But surely no general indictment can lie
against Schiller for taking advantage of a principle
which is perfectly legitimate in itself and has been employed more or less freely by the dramatists of all ages,
including realists like Ibsen and Hauptmann. After
all life does really offer contrasts of character as glaring
as any that poet ever imagined, only they are not apt
to be found in juxtaposition. The artist, however, has
a perfect right to juxtapose them if it suits his purpose;
that is, if it will really enhance the effect that he wishes
to produce. If ever he departs too far from the
familiar verities of life, he pays the penalty; for the
judicious, instead of being thrilled by his pathos (or
whatever it may be), are annoyed by his artificiality.
This is the whole law of the matter, so far as its
general aspect is concerned.

As for Max Piccolomini, he is a perfectly thinkable
character—in the time of the Thirty Years' War or
at any other time. There is nothing supernal about
him; he is simply the type of a brave and honorable
young soldier who tries to walk by the higher law of
conscience. There are always such men in the world,
and Schiller cannot be blamed for locating one in the
camp of Wallenstein, though history omitted to hand

down his name. It is perhaps a little surprising that such a youngster as Max should be in command of the great Pappenheim's regiment; that, however, is a part of the presupposition which one must mentally adjust as best one can. Within the limits of the play everything follows naturally. As a soldier he loves his commander and sides with him instinctively against the courtiers and politicians. His enthusiasm increases the ' mighty suggestion ' that goes out from Wallenstein; one feels that the object of such idolatry from such a worshiper must indeed be great. In the love-scenes Max is always a man,—no trace here of sentimental weakness, or of any leaning to Quixotic folly. In his relation to Wallenstein, to Octavio, and to Thekla, his character is firmly and naturally drawn. And when his great disillusionment comes and he is forced to choose between love and duty, he makes a man's choice and his career ends as it must end—in a tragic drama.

The drawing of the female characters in ' Wallenstein ' bears witness, like all the rest of the play, to the ripening power of the years that had intervened since the writing of ' Don Carlos '. That indefinable something that infects the earlier heroines of Schiller and gives them an air of sentimental futility, or else of schematic unnaturalness, has disappeared. The Countess Terzky, in particular, is a strong portrait which one can admire without reservation. As for Thekla, while her essence is an all-absorbing love for Max, she has at the same time a will and an energy of resolution which make her the worthy daughter of her father. Upon the whole she is the most lovable of all the heroines of Schiller. It is her tragedy of the heart which renders ' Wallenstein ' perennially interesting to the young. And this is much; for does not Goethe's shrewd Merry-Andrew declare that the great object of dramatic art is to please the young,—that *die Werdenden* are the very ones to be considered ? [1]

It is true that critics, speaking more for *die Gewordenen*, have often objected that the love-story in ' Wallenstein ' is unduly expanded and that the lines have here and there, for a historical tragedy, rather too much of a sentimental, lyrical coloring. In the first of these objections, at any rate, there is some force. It was Schiller's personal fondness for his pair of lovers that led him to spin out his material until it became necessary to divide it into two plays of five acts each. This, from a dramatic point of view, was unfortunate, albeit the reader who knows the entire work will hardly find it in his heart to wish that any portion of it had remained unwritten. Properly speaking, the entire ' Piccolomini ' should constitute the first two acts of a five-act tragedy. It has no distinct unity of its own, but it takes an entire evening with what is properly the exposition and the entanglement of a play relating to Wallenstein's defection and death. The result of a separate performance is that the climax of what should be the third act—Wallenstein's momentous decision —comes right at the beginning of the second evening,

[1] Dann sammelt sich der Jugend schönste Blüte
Vor eurem Spiel und lauscht der Offenbarung,
Dann sauget jedes zärtliche Gemüte
Aus eurem Werk sich melanchol'sche Nahrung. . . .
Wer fertig ist, dem ist nichts recht zu machen ;
Ein Werdender wird immer dankbar sein.—' *Faust* '.

and is thus not adequately led up to, save as one carries over the impressions of a preceding occasion. The effect is like that of dividing any other play between the second and the third act. One could wish, therefore, that Schiller had seen fit in his later years to prepare a stage version which would have made it possible to present the entire play in a single evening. It would have been a difficult task,—hopeless for an ordinary theatrical man working by the process of excision,—but for Schiller it would have been possible. And if he had attempted it, we may be quite certain that the love-story would have been very much abbreviated.

As regards the lyrical and softly-sentimental passages, the cogency of the critical objection is not so clear. Any opinion grounded upon an abstract theory of historical tragedy as such can have but little weight. Schiller had no models for ' Wallenstein '; and if he had had, there is always more merit in finding new paths than in following the old. Historical tragedy without tender sentiment is possible, but it presupposes a public politically awake and an author upborne and inspired by a vigorous national life. Schiller could appeal to no such public, and his instinct told him that a play based upon cold passions must itself be cold. So he chose to sentimentalize history, at the expense of detracting somewhat from its dignity, rather than to make frigid plays which no one would care to see or to read. And if we grant a *raison d'être* to the sentimentalized historical drama, no fault can reasonably be found with lyrical passages like that at the end of the third act of ' The Piccolomini '. Schiller found the

soliloquy at hand as an accepted convention of the
stage and he converted it occasionally into a lyric
monologue, as Goethe had done before him in ' Iphigenie ' and ' Faust '. This looked toward opera,
toward Romanticism, toward a mixture of types; but
it was effective as a mode of portraying states of feeling.
The lyric monologue is of course out of tune with the
modern naturalistic dogma, but so is Hamlet's soliloquy. And then it must be remembered that the
naturalistic dogma was no part of Schiller's creed.

A noteworthy characteristic of ' Wallenstein ', as of
all the plays that followed it, is its pervading seriousness. Humor plays no part. There are no Dogberries
or grave-diggers, no quips or quibbles. Schiller had
but little of the far-famed quality of ' irony '. It did
not lie in his nature to take a position aloof from the
moving panorama of life and depict it impassively as it
runs, with its sharp contrasts of grave and gay, of high
and low. He is always a part of the world that he
creates. For the other and higher method, as exemplified by Shakspere and also by Goethe in ' Wilhelm
Meister ', he showed a keen appreciation, and for a
little while he imagined that he himself was catching
the trick. That he did not altogether deceive himself
is abundantly proved by ' Wallenstein's Camp '. After
that, however, the ingrained seriousness of his temperament reasserted itself with all-controlling power. The
gift of humor was not denied him, but the use of it in a
grave drama was repugnant to his sense of style. In
this respect he was more a disciple of the French and
of the Greeks than of Shakspere.

CHAPTER XVII

𝔐ary 𝔖tuart

Wohlthätig heilend nahet mir der Tod,
Der ernste Freund ! Mit seinen schwarzen Flügeln
Bedeckt er meine Schmach—den Menschen adelt,
Den tiefstgesunkenen das letzte Schicksal.—'*Mary Stuart*'.

AFTER the completion of 'Wallenstein', in the spring of 1799, Schiller was not long in selecting a new dramatic theme. The unwonted leisure was irksome to him, so that he felt like one living in a vacuum. At first, being weary of war and politics, he was minded to try his hand upon something altogether imaginary, some unhistorical drama of passion. But the aversion to history and the balancing of attractions did not last long. On the 26th of April he wrote to Goethe as follows:

I have turned my attention to a political episode of Queen Elizabeth's reign and have begun to study the trial of Mary Stuart. One or two first-rate tragic motives suggested themselves straightway, and these have given me great faith in the subject, which incontestably has much to recommend it. It seems to be especially adapted to the Euripidean method, which consists in the completest possible development of a situation ; for I see a possibility of making a side issue out of the trial, and beginning the tragedy directly with the condemnation.

This time the historical orientation proceeded very rapidly. By the 4th of June he was ready to begin the

first act, which formed his principal occupation during
the next two months. From a letter to Goethe, written
June 18, it is clear that he was then thinking especially
of the danger of sentimentalizing his heroine. She
was to excite sympathy, of course, but, so he averred,
it was not to be of the tender, personal kind that
moves to tears. It was to be her fate to experience
and to arouse vehement passions, but only the nurse
was to 'feel any tenderness for her'. As we shall
see, he did not remain entirely faithful to this early
conception of Mary's character. In August, the
second act was completed and the third begun. Then
came a long interruption, occasioned by the demands
of the 'Almanac', the dangerous illness of Frau
Schiller,—a lingering puerperal fever following the
birth of her third child, Caroline, on the 11th of
October,—and finally by the distractions incident to a
change of residence. For Schiller had now decided
to make his winter home in Weimar, so that he might
be near the theater. He was heart and soul in the
business of play-making, and looked forward to devoting the next six years of his life to that kind of work.
To Körner he did not confide his new plan at first,
though he wrote of it often to Goethe.

The removal to Weimar took place early in December, having been made possible by an increase of
stipend amounting to two hundred thalers. In grant-
ing this increase Karl August intimated that it might
be of advantage to Schiller as a dramatic poet if he
were to take the Weimarians into his confidence and
discuss his plays with them. 'What is to influence
society', he sagely remarked, 'can be better fashioned

in society than in isolation '; and he added a very gracious expression of his own personal friendliness. Schiller thus found himself once more virtually a theater poet. The Weimar stage, with its little and large problems, became the focus of his activity. As a good repertory was of prime importance, much of his time went to the making of translations and adaptations. Thus he began a version of Shakspere's 'Macbeth', and had not finished it when he was again prostrated by a fresh and dangerous attack of his malady. After the completion of 'Macbeth', in the spring of 1800, he returned to 'Mary Stuart', but found his progress impeded by manifold interruptions. To escape these he retired to the quiet of Ettersburg, and there, early in June, he finished his tragedy of the Scottish queen. A few days later, June 14, it was played at Weimar, and from that time to this it has been one of the accepted favorites of the stage. One who saw the second performance has left it on record that the spectators unanimously declared it to be 'the most beautiful tragedy ever represented on the German boards '. Madame de Staël characterized it as the most moving and methodical of all German tragedies.

Schiller conceives Mary Queen of Scots as a beautiful sinner who has repented. Her sins are grievous and she does not deny or extenuate them. But they are in the distant past; so far as the present is concerned, she is in the right. She has come to England seeking an asylum, but instead of being treated as a queen she has been confined in one prison after another and finally brought to Fotheringay, where she is subjected

to petty indignities and denied the consolations of the
Catholic religion. She has been charged with a crime
of which she declares herself innocent, has been brought
to trial before a commission of judges whose jurisdiction
she indignantly repudiates, and has even been denied
the common right to confront the witnesses testifying
against her. At the opening of the play she does not
yet know the verdict of the court.

This is the substance of Schiller's masterly exposition; and the effect of it, upon the reader or spectator
who has not prejudged the case, is to create an attitude
of compassion for the prisoner. But the sympathy that
one feels for the passive victim of political or legal
injustice is not the kind which Schiller regarded as
'tragic'. There had to be some sort of 'guilt', and
it was also necessary that this guilt should grow out
of the free act of the individual. But what was to be
done with a helpless captive who was not free to shape
her own fate? From the above-quoted letter to
Goethe, of April 26, 1799, it is inferable that Schiller
at first thought of representing the trial of Mary. He
soon saw, however, that this would make the effect of
the drama turn upon political, religious and legal considerations of an abstruse and doubtful character. It
would be with the play as it always had been with the
historical controversy: the devout Catholic would
regard Queen Mary as the victim of brutal tyranny,
while the Protestant would think her deserving of her
fate. Schiller did not wish to take sides boldly in a
partisan controversy, but to make a tragedy the effect
of which should grow out of universal human emotions.
So he felt happy when a 'possibility' occurred to him

of dispensing altogether with the trial and beginning with the last three days of Mary's life.

The expedient that had suggested itself to him involved three unhistorical inventions: first, an attempt to escape, in which Mary and her cause would become involved in the guilt of the murderous fanatic, Mortimer; secondly, a supposititious love for Leicester, who would use his influence with Elizabeth to bring about a meeting of the two queens; and, finally, the meeting itself, in which Mary's long pent-up passion would get the better of her and betray her into a deadly insult of her rival. After this her fate would appear inevitable and incurred by her own act. This concentration of the action brought with it certain other departures from history which are of minor importance. Mary was beheaded in February, 1587, in the forty-fifth year of her age. At the time of her death her captivity in England had lasted about nineteen years. In order to account for the infatuation of Mortimer and the still lingering passion of Leicester, our drama imagines her some twenty years younger than she actually was.[1]

As thus made over by Schiller, Queen Mary is a pathetic rather than a tragically imposing figure. She appeals, after all, to the sentimental side of human nature and does not produce that effect of tragic sublimity which is produced by ' Wallenstein '. The sympathy that she excites is like that one feels for a martyr. We see in her a royal *réligieuse* who is persecuted by powerful and contemptible enemies and is

---

[1] In a letter to Iffland, written June 22, 1800, Schiller directed that his Queen Elizabeth be represented as a woman thirty years old, Mary as twenty-five.

unable to help herself.   Her death is decreed from the
beginning and there is no way of averting it.   The
object of fierce contentions on the part of others, she
herself does nothing, and can do nothing, to change
the predestined course of events.   She is never placed,
as the real tragic hero must be, before an alternative
where the decision is big with fate.   When the end
comes there is nothing to do but let her renounce all
earthly passion and face the headsman as a purified
saint.   So far as she is concerned, there is no action
at all, but only the dramatic development of a situation.[1]

For, after all, the expedients just spoken of do not
hit the mark exactly, in the sense of making the heroine
responsible for her own fate.   They bring in some new
and exciting complications, which, however, do not
affect the course of events at all.   The catastrophe
would have been just the same without them.   This,
nevertheless, is something that one does not see until
we reach the end and look back.   Before the two
queens come together it seems as if the meeting might
be a turning-point in Mary's fate; and this appearance
is all that Schiller aimed at.   In a letter to Goethe he
spoke of this scene as ' impossible ', and he was curious
to know what success he had had with it.   By this he
meant, seemingly, that the futility of the scene, as
affecting Mary's fate, was predetermined by the nature
of the subject.[2]   Mary was to die; it was impossible to

[1] The thought is expressed thus by Harnack, "Schiller", page 324 :
" Der eigentliche tragische Konflikt, der den Helden vor grosze Ent-
scheidungen stellt und endlich in sein Verhängnis hinabreiszt, *fehlt* in
' Maria Stuart '.   Die gefar gene Königin befindet sich im Konflikt mit
ihrer unwürdigen äuszeren Lage, aber nicht mit sich selbst."

[2] Compare, however, Fielitz, " Studien zu Schillers Dramen ", page 49.

make Elizabeth pardon her or treat her claims with
indulgence. And yet it was necessary to create the
illusion of great possibilities hanging upon this interview of the two queens. This was a very pretty
problem for a playwright, and the skill with which it is
solved by Schiller is the most admirable feature of the
whole piece. The scene is not great dramatic poetry,
for there is too little of subtlety in it,—we are simply
placed between light and darkness, as one critic says,
—but it is the perfection of telling workmanship for the
stage.

The preparation for the scene begins back in the
first act, where Mary declares to Mortimer that Leicester
is the only living man who can effect her release.
When she produces her picture and sends it to him for
a token of her love, we begin to share her premonition
that something may indeed be hoped for if her cause
is taken up by the powerful favorite of Elizabeth. The
lyric passages at the beginning of the third act fix
attention altogether upon Mary's longing for mere
physical freedom. There is no room for the suspicion
that she wishes to use her liberty for any political purpose whatever. She appears as a noble sufferer whose
whole being is absorbed in the delirious joy of breathing once more the free air of heaven. She surmises
rightly that her unwonted liberty to walk in the park
is due to Leicester, and she imagines that greater
favors are in store for her:

> They mean to enlarge the confines of my prison,
> By little favors to lead up to greater,
> Until at last I see the face of him
> Whose hand shall set me free forevermore.

And the hope seems reasonable. May not the queen of England—so one is inclined to speculate—be moved to pity? May she not be persuaded that policy is on the side of mercy? May she not at least postpone the execution of the death-sentence and gradually increase her prisoner's liberty?

When Elizabeth appears it is quickly made evident that these hopes are vain. Mary humbles herself to no purpose. Her enemy, a consummate hypocrite herself, sees in her self-abasement nothing but hypocrisy. Mary's earnest pleading, her offer to renounce all for the boon of freedom, are met with bitter taunts and accusations which culminate in the galling insult:

> To be the general beauty, it would seem,
> One needs but to be everybody's beauty.

Then Mary loses her self-control and throws discretion to the winds. In a wild outburst of passionate hate she accuses Elizabeth of secret incontinence and calls her bastard and usurper. Thus she triumphs in the war of words, for her enemy retreats in speechless amazement; but there is no more room for hope in the clemency of Elizabeth. The prisoner's fate is sealed even without the murderous attempt of the fanatic Sauvage.

It must be repeated that the whole famous scene is better contrived for the groundlings in a theater than for the lover of great dramatic poetry. Mary's crescendo of feeling, from humble supplication to reckless defiance, gives an excellent opportunity for a tragic actress, but the whole thing is rather crass. The effect is produced by confronting Mary with a vain and spiteful termagant bearing the name of the great English queen. One could wish, not only in the interest of historical truth, the obligation of which Schiller denied, but also in the interest of poetic beauty, the obligation of which he regarded as paramount, that Elizabeth had been painted here in less repulsive colors. She might have been allowed to show a trace of human, or even of womanly, feeling. She might have been represented as touched for the moment by Mary's entreaty, and as holding out to her some small hope of life and liberty, under conditions which it would have been reasonable to discuss. If she had been so portrayed and then later brought back to a sterner mood by the attempt upon her own life and the discovery of Mortimer's conspiracy, the final result would have been just the same; the meeting of the two queens would have served even better the dramatic purpose which it was meant to serve, and we should have had from it a noble poetic effect instead of a crass theatrical effect. The pathos of Mary's position would have been increased, because it would have been made evident that, whatever her own inner thoughts and purposes might be, she was a standing menace to the English monarchy. Thus her death would have appeared in the play what it was in fact,—a measure of high political expediency with which petty female spite had nothing to do.

It is natural to raise the query whether these considerations, which are so obvious and are of the very kind that would have appealed to Schiller, were overlooked by him or were set aside for reasons of his own. Virtually he takes the Catholic side of the controversy. The ugly traits of Mary's character, while we cannot say that they are concealed with partisan intent, are so wrought into the picture that they do not impress the imagination as ugly at all. They are consigned to the dim limbo of the past and have the effect of winning for her that sympathy which human nature is always ready to bestow, in art if not in life, upon the Magdalen type. On the other hand, the ignoble traits of Queen Elizabeth are brought into the foreground and made the most of, while her great qualities are hardly more than adumbrated in the picture. The result is a canonization and a caricature; and one cannot help wondering how Schiller was brought thereto, when it would seem that his Protestant sympathies, as we have known him hitherto, should have led him in the contrary direction.

The key to the riddle is, no doubt, that he had begun to feel the influence of the Romantic movement, which was well under way when 'Mary Stuart' was written. The influence is difficult to prove, because Schiller always maintained ostensibly a very cool and critical attitude toward the efforts of the new school. His relations with its leaders were not intimate, and one of them at least, the younger Schlegel, was his particular aversion. Nevertheless he read their works; and while he always professed to be but little edified, there is abundant evidence that his ideas of literary art were considerably affected by the new propaganda. So, too, Goethe was never a partisan of the Romanticists, and he often spoke derisively of them; yet when he published the Second Part of 'Faust', the world saw that he had learned from them all there was to be learned. An author is not always most influenced by that which he consciously approves.

As for Schiller there was much in common between him and the Romanticists. He had worked out an æsthetic religion which completely satisfied him. In religious dogma of any kind he had ceased to take a practical interest. His ethical ideal was an ideal of harmony, of equipoise. His critical studies had cured him of his one-sided Hellenism, and his historical studies had taught him that the Middle Ages were not without their own peculiar greatness. It was thus natural enough that the Catholicizing drift of the Romantic school should appeal to his æsthetic sympathies. When a man of poetic temper drifts away from his theological moorings and becomes indifferent to positive dogma, he is apt to value the historical religions according to their æsthetic qualities. That is best which has the most warmth and color and makes the strongest appeal to the imagination.

It is along this line of reflection that we must seek the explanation of Schiller's Catholicizing tendency in ' Mary Stuart '. Her creed, if reduced to dogma, would have offended his intellect, just as her political claims would have been rejected by his historical judgment. But he saw in her character that which could be poetically transmuted into a type of the noble sufferer, burdened with remorse, fated to contend with injustice, and betrayed by her own rebellious nature; but triumphing at last in the peaceful assurance that her death is the divinely appointed expiation of her sins. The drama was to represent a process of inward purification,—the attainment, after fierce storms and buffetings, of a calm haven for the soul. Queen Mary was to appear at last as the embodiment of all the

Pathos of the Conclusion

qualities that seem most noble and enviable in one who
"feels the winnowing wings of death ". And of this
idea what better dramatic setting can be imagined than
the ceremony of confession and absolution in accordance with the forms of the Catholic Church ? The
solemn searching of the heart gives to Mary's character
a saintly dignity, as of one already beatified, and
invests the whole scene with an incomparable pathos.[1]
Swinburne makes his Mary declare, in angry scorn of
woman's weakness, that

> Even in death,
> As in the extremest evil of all our lives,
> We can but curse or pray, but prate and weep,
> And all our wrath is wind that works no wreck,
> And all our fire as water.

Schiller's Mary meets her fate in a nobler mood. She
sees in death the 'solemn friend' who comes to lift the
ancient burden from her soul. Not only does she forgive and bless her enemies, but she sees in the very
injustice of her death a part of the divine benediction:

> God deems me fit, through this unmerited death,
> To expiate my heavy guilt of yore.

Such a sentiment, it must be admitted, is rather too
sublimated to harmonize perfectly with the political
complications that precede. We seem to have come
suddenly into another world; and so we have in truth,
—the world of medieval mysticism. That which begins

[1] Even Macaulay, who was certainly not the man to be captivated by
anything in the scene save its poetry, thought the "Fotheringay scenes
in the fifth act . . . equal to anything dramatic that had been produced in Europe since Shakspere."—Trevelyan, "Life and Letters of
Lord Macaulay", II, 182.

as a drama of conflicting political passions, ends as a drama of mystical edification. The rationalist does not see how the divine order can be vindicated by the triumph of gross injustice; nevertheless he recognizes that the ways of God are inscrutable, and he knows that such ideas, of the winning of peace through blood-atonement, were once intensely real to the Christian world. Schiller requires the rationalist to return in his imagination to this time and place himself in the emotional *milieu* of the medieval church.

Returning now, in the light of these considerations, to the famous quarrel-scene in the third act, we see that a more favorable portrait of Elizabeth, while it would have had the advantage pointed out, would have weakened the final effect which Schiller wished to produce. It was necessary that Mary appear as the victim of injustice in order that her saintly triumph might shine with the greater luster. Moreover, Mary's outburst of passion, for which there would have been no room if her enemy had been given a nobler character, was needed in order to make her earlier sins credible. Without that scene we should have difficulty in believing that so excellent a lady could ever have committed those crimes of hot blood which weigh upon her soul. All this means that a noble-minded Elizabeth would not have fallen in with Schiller's artistic idea, but it hardly justifies him in making her the monster that she appears. In making her heartless he might at least have left her head in the possession of ordinary common sense. Her off-hand employment of the stranger, Mortimer, as an assassin; her stagy signing of the death-warrant, after a speech indicating that she acts from pusillanimous motives of personal spite; her silly comedy with Davison about the execution of the death-sentence; her coquettish airs with the wretched Leicester,—these are repulsive touches which are difficult to justify on any æsthetic grounds, and the total effect of which approaches perilously near to caricature.

'Mary Stuart' may be described, then, as a tragedy of self-conquest in the presence of an undeserved death. The stage climax is the meeting of the two queens in the third act, but the psychological climax occurs in the fifth act, when Queen Mary gives up her hopes of freedom and of life and welcomes the 'solemn friend' who is to lift the burden from her soul. In working out this conception Schiller did not trouble himself greatly about the historical verisimilitude of his chief personages. One who looks for the real Mary, Elizabeth, Burleigh and Leicester, will not find them in his pages. The principal figures are drawn with less impartiality than in 'Wallenstein', the subjective presence of the author is more noticeable. And yet, looked at in a large way, the play is an excellent piece of historical fresco-painting. The whole spirit of the time with its warring passions, its intrigues of fanaticism, is vividly and powerfully brought before us. The author's partisanship is æsthetic only, not religious or political. The many counts in the long indictment of Queen Mary, the motives and arguments of the English government, even the higher traits of Queen Elizabeth, are all brought out in the course of the play. Nothing of importance is neglected, and the whole complicated situation is made admirably clear. The historical background, with its luminous vistas of European politics, really leaves very little to be desired.

Masterly, too, in the main, is the constructive skill with which all this history is brought to view in a dramatic action concentrated into the last three days of Queen Mary's life. The great difficulty which always besets the 'drama of the ripe situation',—to use a modern phrase for a thing as old as Euripides, —is the difficulty of explaining the past without forcing the dialogue into unnatural channels; in other words, of orienting the public without seeming to have that object in view. As regards this merit of good craftsmanship, 'Mary Stuart' is here and there vulnerable. For example: in the fourth scene of the first act, the nurse, Hannah Kennedy, recounts to her mistress at great length the latter's past sins and sufferings, describing her motives, her infatuation, her heart-burnings and much else that the queen must know far better than any one else in the world. Such passages, obviously intended for the instruction of the audience, were permitted by the traditions of the drama, but they are bad for the illusion. In 'Wallenstein' they are much less noticeable,—a fact which indicates that Schiller was now disposed to make his labor easier by availing himself of conventional privileges. In most respects, however, the technique of 'Mary Stuart' is excellent. The scenes are lively, varied and very rarely too long. Everything is well articulated. Dramatic interest is not sacrificed to any sort of private enthusiasm or special pleading.

One who reads the history of Mary Queen of Scots in any good historian, and endeavors to follow the maze of intrigues, uprisings, plots, assassinations and what not, is impressed by no other characteristic of the age more strongly than by its complete dissociation of religion from humane ethics. The religion of love to one's neighbor, though the neighbor be an enemy, had become a fierce fanaticism which scrupled at nothing and recognized no fealty higher than the supposed secular interest of the church. In his 'Mary Stuart in Scotland' Björnson makes the queen put to Bothwell the question: 'You are surely no gloomy Protestant, you are certainly a Catholic, are you not ?' To which Bothwell replies: 'As for myself, I have never really figured up the difference, but I have noticed that there are hypocrites on both sides.' For the modern man this is an eminently natural point of view, and we might have expected, from all we know of Schiller, that he would introduce into his play some representative of this sentiment. Or if not that, we might have expected some representative of the religion of love. Instead of either we have a romantic youth who has forsworn the Protestant creed on purely æsthetic grounds.

Mortimer is on the whole the most interesting of the subordinate characters. He was obviously suggested by Babington, but the coarse fanatic of history was too repulsive for a proper champion of Schiller's idealized heroine. So the name was changed, and we get an imaginary youth who has been intoxicated by the glamour of the Catholic forms as he has seen them at Rome. The description of Mortimer's conversion, —his sudden resolve to abjure the dismal, art-hating religion of the incorporeal word, and to go over to the communion of the joyous,—is one of the telling declamatory passages of the play.   With the sentiment expressed Schiller can have had, in the bottom of his heart, but little sympathy; but his artistic nature had begun to respond to the Romantic propaganda.   For the rest, Mortimer is not a very convincing creation. One is a little surprised that a youth who purports to be so very soft-hearted, so very susceptible to the religion of the beautiful, should undertake so jauntily the rôle of murderer.   As for his amorous passion, that is credible enough if, in accordance with Schiller's direction, we think of Queen Mary as twenty-five years old.   But in that case one's imagination has difficulty with that perspective of years which have accumulated the ancient burden of guilt.

CHAPTER XVIII

The Maid of Orleans

Die Schönheit ist für ein glückliches Geschlecht; ein un-
glückliches musz man erhaben zu rühren suchen.—*Letter of
July 26, 1800.*

IT was well observed by Wilhelm von Humboldt
that Schiller's plays are not repetitions of the same
thing, such as talent is wont to produce when it has
once met with a success, but the productions of a spirit
that ever kept wrestling anew with the demands of art.
With each fresh attempt he essayed a really new theme,
and taken as a whole his works exhibit a remarkable
variety of substance. Each one has its own individuality, its own atmosphere. And he himself
wished that this should be so; it was a part of his study
to avoid repeating himself. ' One must not become
the slave of any general concept',—so he wrote to
Goethe in July, 1800,—' but have the courage to invent
a new form for each new matter and keep the type-idea
flexible in one's mind.'

These words were penned with direct reference to
' The Maid of Orleans ', which was begun very soon
after the completion of ' Mary Stuart '. Whether
Schiller then had in mind all those elements which
subsequently led to the sub-title, ' a romantic tragedy ',

is not at all certain; it would be natural to surmise that he may have thought at first of a drama within the lines of authentic tradition. However, we know very little in detail about the genesis of this particular play. The letter just quoted tells of the usual initial difficulty in concentrating the action, the interesting occurrences being so widely separated in time and place. Later letters hardly do more than occasionally to report progress; they do not discuss artistic questions, nor give any information as to books read. Three acts were finished by mid-winter, and the whole on the 15th of April, 1801. Schiller had now learned his routine; he felt confidence in himself and went ahead in his own way, with but little discussion of his plans. What he finally gave to the world is a tragedy in which he proceeds still further along the path of romantic idealization,—proceeds indeed so far that one can no longer follow him without some rather serious misgivings.

The French peasant girl becomes an ambassadress of heaven, gifted with second sight and the power of working miracles. She not only leads the French troops in battle, but she herself fights with a magic sword and kills English soldiers with the ruthlessness of a veteran in slaughter. Through it all, however, she is supposed to remain a tender-hearted and lovable maiden, such as the highest officers of France may wish to marry. By the command of the Holy Virgin, from whom her mission and power derive, she is bound to refrain from all earthly love. A momentary tenderness for the English general, Lionel, which leads her to spare his life, presents itself to her conscience as an infraction of the divine command. She is overwhelmed

with remorse and loses all her power. Arm and soul
are paralyzed. Taxed by her superstitious father with
witchcraft, she cannot find speech to defend herself
and imagines that a thunder-clap is heaven's testimony
against her. Then she wanders about as a helpless
and disgraced fugitive and is captured by English
soldiers. With fettered hands she is compelled to
witness a new battle, in which her countrymen,
deprived of her aid, are about to be worsted. But
through adversity she has been purged of her sin.
Her self-confidence returns, and with it her miraculous
power. By the efficacy of prayer she breaks her
chains and rushes into the fray. Her reappearance
brings victory to the French arms, but she herself is
mortally wounded and dies in glory on the battle-field.

It is evident that such a conception carries us back
into the dreamland of pious romance. It presupposes
a world in which things did not happen as they happen
now; in which the incredible is assumed to be real and
the course of events is shaped by miracle. To be sure,
miracle is but sparingly used in the dramatic action
itself, and the totality of the play is only a little more
wonderful than the Maid's actual history as given by
authentic records. Johanna's vision of the Virgin is
merely described retrospectively and is parallel to the
Voices of the historical Joan. So too her recognition
of the King, whom she has never seen before; her
reading of his mind; her wonderful influence over the
French army, and much more of the kind, are part of
a well-authenticated tradition with which the skeptical
mind must make its peace as best it can. And the feat
is not altogether easy. The modern rationalist will

say, and is no doubt right in saying, that if we knew all the pertinent facts accurately from first to last, the Maid's story would fit perfectly into our scheme of scientific knowledge and would appear no more mysterious than other stories of obsession, genius and devotion. Still the fact remains that upon ordinary human nature, without regard to religious prepossessions, the record of the Maid's life, as brought out at her trial, makes an impression of the marvelous. This is quite enough for the purposes of a dramatic poet. But when Schiller introduces a magic sword; when he makes his heroine talk with a ghost upon the battlefield, and break her heavy fetters by the power of prayer; and when we not merely hear these things reported, but see them,—then we are clearly in the realm of pure miracle.

Schiller's ultra-romantic treatment of the Maid's story has often been sharply criticised, even by those who are in the main friendly to his genius; while those who are not friendly have always seen in it the complete flowering of his worst tendencies. Critics have debated at great length the question whether he was 'justified' in introducing the supernatural at all. They have fallen back upon the ghost in 'Hamlet' for a precedent and have tried to illuminate the subject with the light of Lessing's famous comparison of Shakspere's ghost with Voltaire's in 'Semiramis'. Others have been shocked by Schiller's bold departure from history at the close. On a first reading of 'The Maid of Orleans', Macaulay recorded in his journal an opinion that "the last act was absurd beyond description. Schiller might just as well have made Wallenstein dethrone the emperor and reign himself over Germany—or Mary become Queen of England and cut off Elizabeth's head—as make Joan fall in the moment of victory.'' [1]

Now opinions of this kind have a certain interest for the student of literature, but it is best not to take them too seriously.   A dramatist is 'justified' if his intention is good and he succeeds in it.   The proof of the pudding is not in the cook's recipe.   If any dramatist in the wide world chooses, for reasons of his own, to experiment with an imaginary reversal of the verdict of history, there is no abstract reason why he should not do so.   It is just as well, as Schiller said, to 'keep the type-idea flexible in one's mind', — especially when we know that his experiment was received with ecstasy at its first performance and has ever since held its place in the affection of German play-goers.   They are not troubled by its irrationalities, but receive them with pious awe, as Schiller intended.   For the reader, too, 'The Maid of Orleans' has a deep and perennial fascination.   Theorize about it as we may, it is a great popular classic, which has exerted an enormous educative influence and proves how thoroughly its author knew the heart of the German people.

It is perfectly safe to conjecture, even without documentary evidence, that when Schiller began to think of Joan the Maid as the possible heroine of a tragedy, his first perplexity related to the question of her 'guilt'.   This was for him an indispensable ingredient of the tragic, whatever later theorists may think of it.

---

[1] Trevelyan, "The Life and Letters of Lord Macaulay", II, 249.

Althougn, as we have seen, he contemned the bondage
of general concepts, he never came to the point of
imagining a tragedy without 'tragic guilt'.   But the
story of Joan offers no suggestion of guilt in any sense
whatever,—she was the innocent victim of groveling
superstition playing into the hands of insane political
hate.   For modern sentiment, Catholic and Protestant
alike, and quite independently of the view one may
take of her claims to divine illumination, her death at
the stake was simply a horrible and revolting wrong.
In comparison with those who put her to death she was
an angel of light.   To follow the lines of history here
was for Schiller unthinkable, since the end would have
been a mad fatality, leaving no room for any feeling
of acquiescence in the wise ordering of the world.   If
the story of Joan was to yield a tragedy at all, it was
necessary to have recourse to some bold invention
which should bring her fate into harmony with the
central rightness of things.[1]

Schiller solves the problem in the terms of religious
mysticism: he endows his Johanna with a supernatural

[1] According to Böttiger, whose statements are not always trustworthy
in matters of detail, Schiller said to him in November, 1801, that he had
at one time planned three different plays on the subject of the Maid of
Orleans, and that he would have executed all three if he had had time.
One of these was to have been a historical tragedy, with Johanna dying
at the stake in Rouen.—This can hardly mean anything more than that
Schiller was in doubt for a while as to the best treatment of his theme.
The idea of his actually making three different plays on the same subject is quite too preposterous.   His promise, in a letter of March 1,
1802, that *if* he should write a second 'Maid of Orleans', Göschen
should publish it, is only an author's playful 'jollying' of a friendly
publisher.   The passage from Böttiger is quoted at length by Boxberger
in his Introduction to 'The Maid of Orleans' (Kürschners Deutsche
National-Litteratur, Vol. CXXII, second part, page 211).

power dependent upon her renunciation of earthly love, and then makes her fall in love contrary to the divine command. In one of her lonely vigils under the ' holy oak ' the Virgin appears to her and bids her go forth and destroy the enemies of her country and crown the king at Rheims. When Johanna asks how a gentle girl can hope to accomplish such a work, Mary replies,

> A maiden chaste
> Can bring to pass all glorious things on earth
> If only she renounces earthly love.

Thus far we are close enough to tradition; for the historical Joan, who habitually called herself the Maid, knew very well that love and marriage would be fatal to her mission. Moreover, the idea of a non-natural power attaching to the state of virginity is sufficiently familiar both to Christian and to Pagan story. From this conception it is no very far cry to the idea that the very thought of love, bringing with it a sense of guilt, might cause an impairment of the maiden's divinely bestowed strength. These are mystical ideas, but the mysticism is of a kind familiar to the imagination of medieval Europe and therefore quite permissible to a poet who had set out to romanticize. If, therefore, Schiller had made his heroine fall in love in human fashion, and had then connected this lapse from virginal ideality a little more clearly with the final catastrophe, there could be no reasonable objection to his fundamental idea, and we should have, probably, the best imaginative basis for a romantic tragedy on the story of Joan of Arc. One has no right to play the rationalist in such a matter and argue that falling in love is no sin and cannot be felt as a sin by the modern mind. It can be so felt by the modern imagination, and that is quite enough.

As the play stands, however, it must be allowed that the demand made upon the imagination is quite too severe. The love-incident is preposterous in itself and a mere episode at that, serving no purpose finally but that of a picturesque contrast. It is a sort of thing which one can put up with very well in a romantic opera, but not so well in a serious drama. To begin with, Schiller makes his heroine a supernatural being. His Johanna is not a peasant girl who imagines herself the bearer of a divine mission, and by the human qualities of purity, bravery, devotion and self-confidence, exerts a *seemingly* magic influence upon the French army,—but she is actually endowed with superhuman powers. She carries a charmed sword which, against her will, guides itself miraculously in her hand to the work of slaughter. No enemy can withstand her. To all Englishmen she is incarnate Death. In the full frenzy of combat she meets Lionel—for the first time. They fight and she strikes his sword from his hand. Then, as he closes with her, she seizes his plume from behind, lifts his helmet and draws her sword to cut off his head. As his comely face is bared her heart fails her, her arm sinks and the whole mischief is done. No wonder that an early critic objected to a tragedy turning thus upon the weak fastening of a helmet!

It is difficult to justify such a scene upon any theory of poetic art. The romantic drama since Schiller's time has served up many a greater marvel than this; but it produces a truly poetic effect only by keeping within the limits of tradition. The poet who deals with Siegfried and Brunhilde, or with Lohengrin or Faust, may very properly require us to accept the miracles which pertain in each case to the saga. But such a being as Schiller's Johanna is found in no saga; she is a purely arbitrary creation. A very thoughtful German critic, Bellermann, attempts to defend our love-episode by showing how Schiller took good care in the preceding scenes to depict his heroine as susceptible to the tender emotions of her sex; in other words, to depict her as a maiden who might conceivably love and be loved. But earthly maidens do not suddenly fall in love with their mortal enemies upon the battle-field; and when a celestial amazon like Johanna does so, one can only imagine that she has been mysteriously forsaken by her Protectress in the skies. In that case, however, the fault lies with heaven. It is really quite futile to discuss the artistic reasonableness of this scene, since Johanna's supernatural character takes her outside the range of human psychology. If one likes it and is touched by it, very well; but a prudent poet might well have had some regard for the very large number of people who would find such a scene ridiculous rather than touching.

One could wish, in fine, that Schiller had omitted his disturbing supernaturalism altogether. If it was necessary that his heroine fall in love, one could wish that he had let her affections fasten humanly upon the good Raimond or some other honest Frenchman. And he might well have spared us the Black Knight, —that revenant ghost of Talbot, who comes to frighten Johanna but does not succeed, and whose function in the economy of the play remains in the end somewhat mysterious. Had he left out these things, the real greatness of the play would have suffered not a whit, and the artistic idea which kindled his imagination would have found a no less noble expression. That idea was to reproduce the spirit of the epoch which saw the birth of French patriotism. He wished to bring before his rationalizing contemporaries a picture of the Middle Ages as a time when, to quote the words of a recent American writer, '' life was lived passionately and imaginatively under haunted heavens ''.[1]

What thoughts were agitating him at the very time when ' The Maid of Orleans ' was taking shape in his mind can be seen from an interesting letter which he wrote to a certain Professor Süvern, who had favored him with a critique of ' Wallenstein '. Schiller answered under date of July 26, 1800, and one paragraph of his reply runs as follows:

I share your unconditional admiration of the Sophoclean tragedy, but it was a phenomenon of its time, which cannot come again. It was the living product of a definite, individual present; to force it as a standard and a pattern upon an entirely different epoch would be to kill rather than to quicken art, which must always come into being and do its work as a living dynamic influence. Our tragedy, if we had such a thing, has to wrestle with the time's impotence, laziness and lack of character, and with a vulgar mental habit. It must therefore exhibit force and character. It must endeavor to stir and uplift the feelings, but not to resolve them into calm. Beauty is for a happy race ; an unhappy race one must seek to move by sublimity.

These words, which contain implicitly the whole Romantic confession of faith, give the right point of

[1] Lewis E. Gates, "Studies and Appreciations."

view from which to judge ' The Maid of Orleans '. Schiller felt that the need of the hour was to escape from the banality of conventional ideas and feel the thrill of sympathy with great, overmastering emotions. To-day this seems a very simple and obvious matter, because we have learned to think of the imaginative appeal of poetry as the corner-stone of the temple. But a hundred years ago the outlook was different. Notwithstanding the revolt which Goethe and Schiller had themselves led against the self-complacent rationalism of the century, the old spirit was still potent even in Germany, where the reaction first gathered force. Among the intellectual classes religion had well-nigh ceased to be reckoned with as a mystic passion of the soul. Several decades of tolerance,—practically an excellent method for keeping the sectaries from one another's throats,—had produced a public sentiment which looked with mild contempt upon all religious fervors. When Schleiermacher published his famous ' Discourses on Religion ', in the year 1799, he addressed them ' to the cultivated among its despisers ', —which was only his phrase for what we should call the general public.

Nor was the case very different with respect to another mystic passion, which derives from the tribal instinct of the primitive savage and which the civilized man calls patriotism. The lesson of Frederick the Great had not been entirely forgotten, but it was lying inert,—waiting to be kindled into fiery zeal by the humiliations of Jena and Tilsit and Wagram. Schiller was no mystic, nor was he, in our narrow sense, a patriot; but he had a poet's feeling for the sublimity of great and passionate devotion. He was a man of the eighteenth century, and as thinker he understood full well its imperishable claims to honor; but as poet it was not for him to fall into that cynical, vulgarizing drift which had led the greatest Frenchman of his day to make Joan of Arc the butt of his lewd wit. Voltaire saw in her one of the pious frauds of that Infamous he was bent on crushing; for her national mission he had little feeling, because of his fixed idea that nothing good could have come from the ages of superstition.[1] Schiller saw in her, and was the first great poet to see what all the world sees now, the heroic deliverer of her country from a hated foreign invader. And so he threw down the gauntlet to his century and lifted the *ludibrium* of the French wits to the pedestal of an inspired savior of France. It was a great deed of poetry; in the presence of which a right-minded critic, after duly airing his little complaints, as critics must, will be disposed to doff his hat and say Bravo! Well might Schiller declare in the stanzas entitled ' The Maid of Orleans ':

> The world brooks not nobility,—disdaining,
>   Defaming, smirching, goes its vulgar gait ;—
> But fear thou not, true hearts are still remaining,
>   To love thee for the heart that made thee great.

In its inmost essence, then, ' The Maid of Orleans ' is a drama of patriotism. It is Johanna's love of country that gives her a measure of human interest, in spite of the supernaturalism that invests her. Were she not thus the representative of a passion that is intensely real, and that has come to be regarded, for

[1] Compare Morley's " Voltaire ", Chapter III.

better or for worse, as preëminently noble, she would now possess but very languid interest for the sublunary mind. Her mystical attributes and her unthinkable love-affair would place her beyond the range of natural sympathy. As it is, one is made to forget, or at least to pass lightly over, everything else but her love for France. She wins favor by her patriotic devotion, and when the end comes one thinks of her under the familiar rubric of the hero dying for his country. The episode with Lionel and the humiliation of the Cathedral scene have all been forgotten, and one does not mentally connect these things with Johanna's death in any way whatsoever. Her death is sufficiently provided for from the beginning in her own fatalistic prevision:

> Johanna goes and never shall return.

It must be admitted that a heroine who excites interest chiefly by virtue of her patriotic sentiments and the bravery of her conduct does not represent the highest type of poetic creation. The muse will always lend virtue and bravery to any common poetaster for the mere asking; but she does not so readily vouchsafe a convincing semblance of complex human nature. A distinctly human Johanna, with a definite girlish individuality and a character all her own,—such as Goethe might have given us had he turned his thoughts in that direction,—would have been a higher and a more difficult achievement than the schematic creature of Schiller's imagination. Such a Johanna, however, would hardly be thinkable on the stage: the final horror of her fate would be intolerable in the visible representation, while to leave it unrepresented would be to admit the reasonableness of Schiller's departure from history. Shall we then take refuge in the position that the Maid's story is not adapted to dramatic treatment at all ? Such a position is at once rendered absurd by the perennial popularity and effectiveness of Schiller's play. Until some great realistic poet shall prove the contrary by deeds, the mere critic is certainly justified in holding that, whatever may be thought of his love-episode, the ghost and the miraculous escape from bondage, the general requirements of the theme are best met by Schiller's romantic treatment.

Turning from the heroine to the other characters, one finds but little that invites discussion. Johanna is the central sun of the system, and in the romantic light that goes out from her the others seem rather pale and uninteresting. Father Thibaut impresses one in the Prologue as a little too refined, intelligent and far-sighted for the rôle of besotted superstition and mis-understanding which he subsequently plays in the cathedral scene. La Hire and the Duke of Burgundy and the Bastard of Orleans, who preserves only a sug-gestion of the rugged soldier that once bore his name, are there only to illustrate the divine magic of the Maid. Two of them wish to marry her, and when we add the Englishman, Lionel, and the French peasant, Raimond, we have a quartet of lovers. Verily the little god Cupido would seem to be something too prominent and ubiquitous for a military drama. His-tory required that the Dauphin should be a weakling, and such he is in the play; but he too is romanticized through his devotion to the tender and soulful Agnes.

More strongly drawn, if not exactly more lifelike,
than any of these, are the sensual old fury, Isabeau,
and the English general, Talbot, whose fierce valedic-
tory to this folly-ridden earth is deservedly famous:

> Soon it is over, and to earth go back—
> To earth and the eternal sun—the atoms
> Erstwhile combined in me for pain and joy.
> And of the mighty Talbot, whose renown
> But now filled all the world, nothing remains
> Except a handful of light dust.   So ends
> The life of man—and all we bear away,
> As booty from the battle of existence,
> Is comprehension of its nothingness
> And sovereign contempt of all the ends
> That seemed exalted and desirable.

In short, the characters of ' The Maid of Orleans '
leave much to be desired on the score of verisimilitude.
One has the feeling all along, as in the case of Goethe's
' Helena ', of being in an artificial world made to order
by an imaginative fiat.   To enjoy the play it is necessary to put aside one's rationalism and surrender oneself to the illusion one knows that the author wishes to
produce.   ' The Maid of Orleans ' does not compel the
surrender like ' Wallenstein ' ; one must meet the poet
half-way.   That done, however, everything is in order,
for the technique of the play is faultless.   It is not easy
to point to a better piece of dramatic exposition than
the scenes which precede the appearance of Johanna
in the French army.   The Prologue is perhaps a trifle
too long, but serves admirably to give the tragic key-
note, by picturing the shepherd-girl of Dom Remi
leading a life apart from that of her family, given to
strange brooding, and at last receiving the sign from

Heaven, which she prophetically feels to be the call of death. And then the desperate plight of France; the helpless weakness of the king; the disgust and discouragement of the generals; and after this the news of a long unwonted victory, followed quickly by the appearance of Johanna and the magic change of the military situation,—how vividly it is all brought before one! And what a fine scene is that at the end of the second act, in which Burgundy is won over! One who is not touched by this portion of the play; who does not return to it with ever-renewed pleasure after each sojourn in the choking air of naturalism, is—to state the case as gently as possible—unfortunately endowed.

CHAPTER XIX

Ʈhe Ɓride of Ɱessina

Das Leben ist der Güter höchstes nicht,
Der Übel grösztes aber ist die Schuld.
'The Bride of Messina'.

AFTER the completion of ' The Maid of Orleans ',
in the spring of 1801, Schiller found himself once more
the unhappy victim of leisure. A new task was needed
to make life tolerable, but what should it be ? ' At
my time of life ', he remarked in a letter to Körner,
' the choice of a subject is far more difficult; the levity
of mind which enables one to decide so quickly in
one's youth is no longer there, and the love, without
which there can be no poetic creation, is harder to
arouse.' Ere long, having a mind to try his hand
upon a tragedy in ' the strictest Greek form ', he was
musing upon that which in time came to be known as
' The Bride of Messina '.

For the present, however, and for some time to
come, he did not advance beyond very general planning. In the summer he spent several weeks with
Körner in Dresden, during which literary labor was
suspended. After his return to Weimar, in September,
he found the conditions without and within unfavorable
to a serious creative effort, so he undertook a German
version of Gozzi's ' Turandot '. This occupied him

until January, 1802.   Then it was a question whether his next theme should be ' The Knights of Malta ', or ' Warbeck ', or ' William Tell ', the last having begun to interest him because of a persistent rumor that he was working upon a play of that name.   But none of the four projects carried the day immediately, and the winter and spring passed without bringing a decision. He began to be worried over the ' spirit of distraction ' that had come upon him.   In August, however, the long vacillation came to an end, and ' The Bride of Messina ' began to take shape on paper.   He found it more instructive than any of his previous works.   It was also, he remarked in a letter, a more grateful task to amplify a small matter than to condense a large one.   Once begun, the composition proceeded very steadily,—but little disturbed by the arrival, one day in November, of a patent of nobility from the chancellery of the Holy Roman Empire,—until the end was reached, in February, 1803.

The play may be described as an attempt to treat a medieval romantic theme in such a manner as to convey a suggestion of Greek tragedy.   Although written with enthusiasm it is not the bearer of any heartfelt message and must be regarded as a study of theory rather than of life.   The highly artificial plot does not reflect any past or present verities of human existence upon the planet earth.   Nor can we call the play an imitation of the Greeks, its general atmosphere being anything but Greek.   The dialogue is not written in classical trimeters, but in the modern pentameter; while the speaking chorus, divided into two warring factions and going about here and there as the scene changes, has little resemblance to anything found in the Greek drama. On the other hand, there *is* a chorus, and there are dreams which take the place of oracles. There is also a further suggestion of the antique in the pervading fatalism of the piece.

Of all Schiller's works ' The Bride of Messina ' has been the most variously judged by the critics. Some have seen in it the very perfection of art, others the climax of artificiality. Schiller himself reported, after seeing it performed at Weimar, in 1803, that he had ' received for the first time the impression of true tragedy '. There is also an authentic record to the effect that Goethe was inexpressibly delighted with it and declared that ' by this production the boards had been consecrated to higher things '. Wilhelm von Humboldt wrote that nothing could surpass the majesty of the play, and Körner assigned it a high rank among Schiller's productions. On the other hand it was spoken of by the satellites of the disgruntled Herder as a ' singular *fata morgana*, and a ' shocking mon-strosity '; while F. H. Jacobi characterized it as a ' disgusting spook made by mixing heaven and hell '. And these discordant voices, in all their vehemence of expression, have been echoed by later critics; so that in the case of this particular drama, as Bellermann observes, it is hardly possible to speak of a settled average opinion. On one point, nevertheless, there is very general agreement: namely, that the diction of the choruses is magnificent in its kind. Nothing finer in German poetry anywhere.

From the outset critical discussion of ' The Bride of Messina ' has turned mainly upon its antique elements, that is, upon its chorus and its treatment of the fate-idea. There has been endless comparison of Sophocles' 'King Œdipus' and endless logomachy about free-will and predestination in their relation to guilt. And such discussion is pertinent, because we have Schiller's own word that he wished to vie with Sophocles. An oft-quoted passage from a letter to Wilhelm von Humboldt runs as follows:

My first attempt at a tragedy in the strict form will give you pleasure. From it you will be able to judge whether I could have carried off a prize as a contemporary of Sophocles. I do not forget that you have called me the most modern of modern poets, and have thus thought of me in the sharpest contrast to everything that is styled antique. I should thus have reason to be doubly pleased if I could wrest from you the admission that I have been able to make even this strange spirit my own.

At first blush this looks like an abandonment of the position stated so clearly and emphatically in the letter to Süvern (page 380). In reality, however, it is not so. Schiller was not concerned to imitate Sophocles, nor to revive an ancient form with pedantic rigor. He was as far as possible from a one-sided worship of the Greeks. His reference to his 'strict form' hardly means more than is implied in simplicity of plot, fewness of characters and observance of the unities. He did not write 'The Bride of Messina' in any doctrinaire spirit,—either to reform the German drama, or to furnish a model for imitation. The play is simply an æsthetic experiment; a tentative excursion into a field confessedly 'strange'. What Schiller wished was to produce upon a modern audience, by an original treatment of a medieval theme, a tragic effect similar to that which, as he supposed, must have been produced upon

an Athenian audience by a play of Sophocles,—more
especially by the ' King Œdipus '.

For the groundwork of his tragedy he resorted to
the well-worn fiction of the hostile brothers, giving it
this form: Two princes grow up in mutual hatred, but
are finally reconciled through the influence of their
mother. Both fall in love, each without the other's
knowledge, with a young woman of whose family they
know nothing, and who is in reality their sister. One
day the younger prince finds the object of his passion
in the arms of his brother, who has just learned the
secret of the girl's birth. Instantly the old hate blazes
up anew, and in a paroxysm of blind rage Don Cesar
kills his brother. Then, when he discovers the whole
truth, he expiates his crime by a voluntary death.—In
this scheme, it will be observed, the salient point is the
fratricide committed in a sudden frenzy of passion:
everything else leads up to this or grows out of it.
From a modern point of view the crime is adequately
accounted for by the character of Don Cesar; but if
the story was to be given a Sophoclean coloring it was
necessary that the horrors appear as the necessary
evolution of ineluctable fate.

In employing the fate-idea for dramatic purposes the
Greek poet had, in the first place, the great advantage
of a definite mythological tradition which was known
to everybody. In the second place, he wrote for
people who still believed in oracles and received them
seriously as credible manifestations of divine foreknowl-
edge. Again, he could count on a living belief in the
hereditary character of guilt: the belief that a good
man, leading his life without evil intent, might be led

to commit horrible and revolting acts because of some ancient taint in his blood; or because the gods, in their inscrutable government of the world, had decreed that he should thus sin and suffer. Just how far the Greek conception of moral responsibility differed in a general way from the modern, is a trite question which need not be gone into here. Suffice it to say that the difference has often been too broadly and too sharply stated. Not all Greek tragedies were tragedies of fate, —indeed it was a saying of Schiller that the 'King Œdipus' constitutes a genus by itself—nor is there any definite unitary conception which can be described as 'modern' for the purpose of a contrast.

After all, that which affects us in tragedy is very much the same as that which affected the Greeks, namely, the sense of life's overruling mystery. And whether we refer the happenings of life to an all-wise Providence, or to a scientific order which is so because it is so, they remain alike incommensurable with our ethical feeling. The bullet of a crazed fanatic, or a lethal germ in a glass of water, may end the noblest career in horrible suffering. In the drama, it is true, we prefer that no use be made of such mad calamities and that what befalls a man shall at least seem to grow out of his character. But then a man's character is the effect of a hundred subtle causes which began their operation in part before he was born; so that there is an element of essential truth in the saying that character is fate. We have become aware that there is a sense in which it is exactly true that the sins of the father are visited upon the children.

In short, modern thought has not tended to clear

up but rather to deepen the mystery of life in its relation to antecedent conditions; of fate in its relation to desert. Our common sense, as embodied in law, treats a man as responsible for the good or evil that he personally intends. This is no doubt an excellent practical rule, without which society could hardly exist at all; but looked at philosophically it does not really touch the heart of the great mystery which is the theme of ' King Œdipus ' and of ' The Bride of Messina '. The young Œdipus, while living at Corinth with his foster-father, Polybus, whom he supposes to be his real father, is told by the oracle that he is destined to kill his father and marry his mother. What should he do ? Commit suicide in order to stultify the oracle, or resolve to kill no man and to marry no woman ? The story imputes to him no blame for doing neither of these things. He acts as a man would act who sees himself confronted by an evitable danger. He leaves Corinth, but the very step that he takes to avoid his fate brings it surely to pass. He meets a stranger in the road. A quarrel arises over the question of passing,—a quarrel as to the merit of which the legend is silent. Œdipus kills his antagonist, and that antagonist is his father. Then he delivers Thebes from the scourge of the Sphinx and receives the hand of Queen Jocasta as his due reward. He has forgotten the oracle, or imagines that he has eluded his foreordained fate by leaving Corinth; but the oracle has fulfilled itself, as the spectator knew from the beginning that it would. The interest of the tragedy turns largely upon the overwhelming remorse of Œdipus and Jocasta when they discover the truth.

To match these conditions Schiller requires us to imagine a medieval prince of Messina reigning at some indefinite time in the Middle Ages. While his two sons are yet children he has a dream in which he sees two laurel-trees growing out of his marriage-bed, and between them a lily which changes to flame and consumes his house. An Arabian astrologer, for whom he has a heathenish partiality, interprets the dream as meaning that a daughter yet to be born will cause the destruction of his dynasty. So when a daughter is born he orders her put to death. But the mother has also had *her* dream,—of a lion and an eagle bringing their bloody prey in sweet concord to a little child playing on the grass. A pious Christian monk explains this dream as meaning that a daughter will unite the quarrelsome sons in passionate love. So the queen saves the life of her new-born child and has her secretly brought up in a convent not far from Messina. As long as the father lives the hostile brothers are restrained from fighting, but when he dies their feud breaks out in open war. Each surrounds himself with retainers, Messina is torn by factional strife, and there is danger from external enemies. Citizens implore the mother to effect a reconciliation, failing which they threaten a revolution. At last she succeeds in arranging a peaceful meeting in her presence.

Such is Schiller's presupposition,—a singular blend of Christianity and paganism, such as at once gives difficulty to the imagination. A prince reigning under a Christian order of things, in a city of churches and convents, yet willing to murder his child on account of a dream interpreted to him by an Arab soothsayer, is not a very plausible invention. And the same may be said of much that follows. In half-a-dozen places the tragedy would come to an untimely end did not one or another of the characters conveniently refrain from doing or saying what a human being would inevitably do or say under the circumstances. Beatrice grows up in the convent without taking vows and is kept in ignorance of her lineage. Though her mother longs for her, she never sees her, and communicates with her only through the old servant, Diego. Such conduct is perhaps intelligible during the life of the king, but with him out of the way one would expect the mother to take her daughter home without a moment's delay. Instead of that she waits two months, merely sending word to Beatrice to prepare for some unnamed change of fortune. She also keeps the secret from her sons during these two months, without any sufficient reason. When questioned on the subject by Don Cesar in the play, she makes the bitter feud of the brothers her excuse:

> How could I place your sister here atwixt
> Your bare and reeking swords? In your fierce rage
> You would not hearken to a mother's voice;
> And could I have brought her, the pledge of peace,
> The anchor of my every dearest hope,
> To be perchance the victim of your strife?

But this is strange logic. One does not see at all how the sister's life would have been imperiled; and if she was to be the pledge of peace,—as the mother's dream seemed to foretell,—then there was the best of reasons for bringing her home at the earliest possible moment.

And then how singularly Don Manuel behaves!

He is the elder son, and as such must be heir to the throne; but of that we hear nothing in the play. He falls in love with Beatrice, sees her often during a period of months, and secures from her a promise of marriage; but he never tells her who he is, nor does he ask her a question about her own lineage. When she tells him of an old man who comes to her occasionally as messenger from her unknown family, and who has at last bidden her prepare for a change of abode, he makes no attempt to see the stranger and find out whither his bride is to be taken. For such conduct *he* can have no possible reason, but Schiller has one; for were Don Manuel once to set eyes on the old family servant, Diego, a clearing-up would of course be inevitable. Instead of doing the one natural thing, Don Manuel abducts his sweetheart during the night, with her consent, and takes her to a garden in Messina. There he leaves her alone to await his coming,—a singular thing for a prince to do with his bride, but necessary to the tragedy.

More dubious still is the remarkable silence of Beatrice when she is exposed to the stormy wooing of Don Cesar in the garden. The fiction is that he has caught a glimpse of her two months before, on the occasion of his father's funeral, and has since been constantly searching for her. Having now found her, through one of his spies, he makes love to her jubilantly through sixty lines of text, but she answers never a syllable and lets him go away in supposed triumph. A bare word from her, such as a woman could not help saying under the circumstances, would end the complication, since it would send Don Cesar away

baffled; and then there would be no occasion for his
returning to the garden a little later.   Maidenly fright
and consternation cannot account rationally for such
behavior; one sees that she holds her tongue because
to set it in motion would be dramaturgically disastrous.

But the climax of unnaturalness is reached in the
scene between the queen and her two sons, when old
Diego reports that Beatrice has been abducted from
the convent—presumbly by Moorish corsairs.   The
distracted mother urges her sons to go at once to the
rescue of their sister.   But here a difficulty presents
itself.   If the brothers are to have the faintest chance
of finding their sister, it is clearly of the first importance
that they know something about her, and particularly
that they know where she has been kept in hiding.
Now this knowledge can be safely imparted to Don
Cesar but not to Don Manuel.   So Don Cesar is
made to rush away hotly, at all adventure, without the
slightest clew of any kind,—the reason being that it
would not do for him to hear that which Diego is about
to tell.   The younger brother thus conveniently out
of the way, Don Manuel, who has begun to suspect the
truth, implores his mother to tell him where the lost
Beatrice has been concealed.   Evidently the only
natural part for the mother is to answer the question.
But that would not do; so she interrupts him and
urges him away with such senseless exclamations as
' Fly to action!'   ' Follow your brother's example!'
' Behold my tears!'   And when at last he succeeds in
bringing out the fateful inquiry, she only answers:

The bowels of earth were not a safer refuge !

Then Don Manuel ceases to press his question and stands quietly by while Diego tells his remorseful story of Beatrice's visit to the church on the day of her father's funeral. Strangely enough this recital suggests to Don Manuel the hopeful suspicion that his sister and his sweetheart may, after all, not be the same person; so he rushes away to question Beatrice, when he must know that his mother is the one person in the world who can best resolve his doubts. Then, when he is gone, Don Cesar comes back, and the mother very calmly proceeds to give him the all-important information which she has just withheld from Don Manuel.

Such is the device, of convenient silence at critical points where speech would be natural but ruinous, by which Schiller leads up to his climax. There is no other play of his, early or late, the entanglement of which is so palpably artificial; so like a child's house of cards, built up with bated breath lest a breath should topple it over. According to Böttiger, Schiller once took note of what some critic had remarked upon this lavish use of silence in 'The Bride of Messina' and expressed surprise that any one could so misconceive him. He went on to say, if we can trust Böttiger, that it is 'precisely in this closing of the mouth at critical moments, when a saving word might rend the iron net of fate, that the unevadable and demonic power of evil-brooding destiny manifests itself most clearly and sends a gruesome shudder of awe through every spectator.' This is certainly a good defense if we assume that the great object of dramatic poetry is to exhibit the working-out of some abstract scheme of mysterious fate. Under that hypothesis one has no right to complain if the characters are treated like puppets,—pulled hither and thither in unnatural directions and made to speak when they should be silent, and to be silent when they should speak. If one finds the scheme impressive, one will think of that, get his thrill of awe and be thankful. But it is somewhat different if one holds that the verities of human nature are more interesting than any scheme, and that the great object of the serious drama should be to exhibit human beings in the stress of life. One who takes that view will wish, while recognizing the great qualities of 'The Bride of Messina', that its author had not gone quite so far in his contempt of realism.

For, after all, the highest law of the drama is the law of psychological truth, which requires that the characters be humanly conceivable and act as human beings would act under the circumstances imagined. This law is not kept in 'The Bride of Messina', with the result that the first three acts fall short of the effect that they are intended to produce. It is different with the fourth act. There everything is in order, and the simple and noble impressiveness of the tragedy leaves nothing to be desired. And it is an interesting fact that this impressiveness depends only in a slight degree upon the fulfillment of the old dreams and prophecies. To be sure they are fulfilled; but we are not required to put faith in the inspiration either of the Arab soothsayer or of the Christian monk. Their vaticinations might be mere fallible guess-work; Don Cesar might live and give them the lie, so far as any external constraint is concerned. But he himself *feels* that the

heavy hand of fate is upon him and that continued life
would be intolerable. The whole pathos of the tragedy
is transferred to the inner being of the surviving
brother, and one feels that his self-destruction proceeds
from the law of his own nature, and not from any
fatalistic necessity that is laid upon him.

The truth would seem to be that the fate-idea, while
of course it must be taken into consideration in any
careful estimate of ' The Bride of Messina ', has been
made a little too prominent by many of the critics.
What the spectator sees, says one writer who is in the
main an admirable expounder of Schiller, is '' gigantic
Fate striding over the stage. He sees a wild, tyrannical race, burdened with ancestral guilt, turning
against its own flesh and blood. . . . He is made to
feel that the self-destruction of this race is nothing
accidental, that it is a divine visitation, a judgment of
eternal justice pronounced against usurpation and lawlessness, that it means the birth of a new spiritual order
out of doom and death.'' [1] But is this what is actually
seen ? Is it not rather true that Schiller makes but
little out of the matter of ancestral guilt ? We hear,
it is true, that the old prince was of an alien stock that
had won the sovereignty of Messina with the sword
and held it by force. But this is no very appalling
crime as the world goes, and especially as the world
went in the Middle Ages. One hardly thinks of
William of Normandy, for example, as a revolting
criminal deserving of the divine wrath. Then we
hear, too, that the old prince had appropriated to him-

[1] Kuno Francke, '' Social Forces in German Literature,'' page 394.

self a wife who was 'his father's choice'. But the whole matter is disposed of in two or three choral lines which leave not even a clear, much less a strong impression. There are no data for an ethical judgment. We are not told wherein the superior right of the father consisted. For aught we know the son may have had the better claim, and the father's curse may have been only the impotent scolding of a disappointed dotard. It is difficult to see anything here which can rationally warrant eternal justice in extirpating the race. And when we pass from the presuppositions to the play itself, we see that none of the characters except Don Cesar does anything seriously blameworthy.

If then it were clearly the central purpose of Schiller to justify the moral government of the world, or to exhibit the workings of an august Fate in itself worthy of reverence, we should have to admit that he has missed the mark; for the fate that he represents is not worthy of reverence at all. But what is the central fact of the play, as seen by the unsophisticated spectator who has never read the Greek poets nor heard of the house of Labdacus? Evidently it is the murder expiated by a voluntary death. A high-minded youth knowingly kills his brother in a moment of blind rage, because he thinks that his brother has deceived him. When he learns the truth, and learns also of the old dreams and prophecies, he feels that he too must die. Here is the real tragedy,—in the resolution of Don Cesar and his steadfast adherence to it in the face of his mother's and his sister's entreaties. The apparatus of dreams and prophecies and fate is meant to work upon the mind of Don Cesar rather than upon that of the spectator. Superstition adds to the burden of his remorse until it becomes unbearable and death appears the only road to peace:

> Dying I bring to naught the ancient curse,
> A free death only breaks the chain of fate.

In a prefatory essay upon 'The Use of the Chorus in Tragedy' Schiller defended his innovation and incidentally set his heel upon the head of the serpent of naturalism. True art, he insisted, must have a higher aim than to produce an illusion of the actual. Its object is not to divert men with a momentary dream of freedom, but to make them truly free by awakening and developing the power of imaginative objectivation. Nature itself being only an idea of the mind, and not something that appears to the senses, art must be ideal in order to represent the reality of nature. To demand upon the stage an illusion of the actual is absurd, since dramatic art rests entirely upon ideal conventions of one kind or another. Therefore, so the argument goes on, it was well when a poetic diction was substituted for the prose of every-day life, and the next great step is to reintroduce the chorus and thereby 'declare war openly and honestly against naturalism in art'. The chorus is likened to a 'living wall which tragedy builds about itself in order completely to shut out the actual world and to preserve for itself its ideal domain, its poetic freedom'.

In consonance with these ideas we have a chorus divided into two parts, one consisting of the elderly retainers of Don Manuel, the other of the younger retainers of Don Cesar. These two semi-choruses take a certain part in the action. On the one hand they are like the materialized shadows of their respective leaders, having no will of their own. When the brothers compose their feud and embrace each other, the semi-choruses do likewise,—which comes perilously near to the ridiculous. On the other hand the semi-choruses have a horizon of their own and perform, to a certain extent, the old function of the ideal spectator. They comment in sonorous strains upon present, past and future, and upon the high matters of life and death and fate.

Schiller's argument on the use of the chorus, while interesting in its way, does not now sound very convincing; perhaps because we have come to have less faith than he had in the possibility of settling such questions by abstract reasoning. Forms of art spring out of local and temporal conditions; they have their exits and their entrances. Now and then a reversion to some earlier form may prove acceptable, but in general it can have only a curious or antiquarian interest. The man of reading, who knows his Greek poets, will be glad to have seen once or twice in his life a genuine Greek play,—preferably in the Greek language, with all the accessories as perfect as possible. Next to that he will enjoy a perfect imitation, like the first portion of Goethe's 'Helena'. But just in proportion as he is permeated by the Greek spirit he will feel the spuriousness of Schiller's so-called chorus. For the effect of the Greek chorus depended not so much upon the meaning of the words as upon the sensuous charm of the music and the dance. To sacrifice these is to sacrifice that which is most vital and leave only the simulacrum of a chorus. Some small effects in the line of the picturesque can be achieved by means of costuming, marching and grouping, but the rest can be nothing but elocution,—a frosty appeal to the ethical sense, offered as a surrogate for the witchery of song and rhythmic motion. One may be pardoned for thinking that a good ballet would have served the purpose better.

The reader of the play, however, is not disturbed by any considerations of this kind. For him the choruses are simply poetry,—admirable poetry, for the most part, in Schiller's very best vein. What a wealth of imagery and what a splendor of varying rhythms! And how cunningly the gorgeous diction twines itself, like ivy about a bare wall, concealing the nakedness of commonplace and giving an effect of noble sententious wisdom! This is and must remain the great value of ' The Bride of Messina ',—to delight the reader with the charm of its style. Schiller's plea for the chorus passed unheeded save by the philologists. His example was not imitated; indeed he himself probably had no serious hope that it would be. On the other hand, there did spring up in the next two decades a most luxuriant crop of so-called fate-tragedies, which, with their horrors, banalities and puerilities, soon brought the species into contempt and made it fair game for the telling satire of Platen. The fashion,— a thoroughly bad fashion in the main,—was undoubtedly set by ' The Bride of Messina '; but we cannot make Schiller answerable for the hair-raising and blood-curdling inventions of Werner, Houwald, Müllner, Grillparzer and Heine.

CHAPTER XX

William Tell

Der alte Urstand der Natur kehrt wieder,
Wo Mensch dem Menschen gegenübersteht ;
Zum letzten Mittel, wenn kein andres mehr
Verfangen will, ist ihm das Schwert gegeben.
                                    'William Tell'.

SCHILLER'S last play, like his first, was inspired by the Goddess of Freedom, but what a difference between the wild-eyed bacchante of the earlier day and the decorous muse of ' William Tell ' ! There the frenzied revolt of a young idealist against chimerical wrongs of the social order; here a handful of farmers, rising sanely in the might of union and appealing to the old order against intolerable oppression. There the tragedy of an individual madman; here the triumph of a laudable patriotism.

' Tell ' is a fresh illustration of its author's versatility, for nothing more different from its immediate predecessors could easily be imagined. It is also the most thoroughly human among his plays, and the only one that does not end upon a tragic note. Finally it is the most popular, though the most loosely articulated,—a fact that shows how little the permanent interest and classical prestige of a dramatic production depend upon its satisfying the ideal demands of critical theory.

It was noted casually in the preceding chapter that rumor began to be occupied with speculations about Schiller's ' Tell ' before he had seriously thought of writing a play on the subject.   In the summer of 1797 Goethe had revisited Switzerland and brought back with him the idea of a narrative poem about William Tell.   He discussed the matter with Schiller, incidentally telling him much about the Forest Cantons.   Possibly he may have suggested, in the presence of a mutual friend, that the theme had dramatic possibilities,—which would account sufficiently for the aforesaid rumor.   Finding his supposed plan the subject of curious gossip, Schiller was led to look more closely into the subject.   He read Tschudi's ' Chronicon ' and found it Homeric and Herodotean in its simple straightforwardness.   The legend fascinated him and he began to see in it the material of a popular drama that should take the theatrical world by storm.   He was eager for such a triumph, and the more so because ' The Bride of Messina ', as staged by Iffland in Berlin, had met only with an equivocal success: many were pleased, but there was a plenty of adverse comment.   Iffland was now the director of the Royal Prussian Theater, and thus in a position to serve the interests of Schiller, whom he devotedly admired.   It was therefore worth while for a man who had chosen to be a dramatic poet, and whose income depended upon his popularity, to forego further experimentation with unfamiliar art-forms and set about supplying that which would interest average human nature.

Work began in the spring of 1803 and proceeded very steadily during the ensuing months. The letters of the period express unbounded confidence in the nascent play. It was to be a ' powerful thing which should shake the theaters of Germany ', and a ' genuine folk-play for the entire public '. Honest Tschudi continued to be the great source, but other writers were read and excerpted. Schiller took infinite pains with his local color, noting down from the books all sorts of minutiæ that might aid his imagination. Take for illustration the following jottings from Fäsi and Schleuchzer, two of his subsidiary authorities:

There are mountains that consist entirely of ice.—*Firnen;* they shine like glass and get their isolated conical shape from the process of melting in the summer.—Clouds form in the mountain-gorges and attach themselves to the rocks ; herefrom prognostication of the weather.—View from on high when one stands above the clouds. The landscape seems to lie before one like a great lake, from which islands stand forth.—In the summer, cascades everywhere in the mountains.—Chamois graze in flocks, the picket (*Vorgeis*) piping in case of danger.—Weather signs : Swallows fly low, aquatic birds dive, sheep graze eagerly, dogs paw up the earth, fish leap from the water. ' The gray governor of the valley (*Thalvogt*) is coming'; when this or that mountain puts on a cap, then drop the scythe and take the rake.—Peculiarity of a certain lake that it draws to itself persons sleeping on its bank.

A large amount of such conscientious note-taking, aided by a marvelous power of visualization, and supplemented also by what Goethe could tell from personal observation, resulted in a remarkably vivid and accurate local color. A letter of Schiller's written in December, 1803, tells of a purpose to go to Switzerland

before he should print his play. The plan was not
carried out, but if it had been there would have been
little to change; for 'William Tell' reads throughout
like the work of one thoroughly familiar with Swiss
character, topography and folk-lore. There is not a
slip of any importance in the entire play. Of course
the conspiring farmers are idealized and their enemies
are diabolized; but all this is so in the saga. Schiller
had to deal with a patriotic myth, and he made no
attempt to go behind the romantic veil of tradition;
his purpose being simply to present the poetic essence
of the saga as handed down by Tschudi. And he
succeeded admirably. So far as the Swiss people are
concerned, he well deserves the memorial they have
placed in his honor upon the Mythenstein, near the
legendary birth-place of their national independence.

Toward the close of the year 1803 came an interruption, Weimar society being thrown into a flutter by
the visit of Madame de Staël, now on her famous tour
of inspection. It was of course fitting that Schiller,
as a local lion, should take his part in entertaining her;
but the voluble lady was an *Erscheinung* new to his
experience, and with his imperfect command of collo-
quial French he was hard put to it to bear up against
the torrent of her conversation. He measured her very
correctly at their first meeting, when they fell into an
argument on the merits of the French drama. 'For
what we call poetry', he wrote to Goethe, 'she has
no sense'; nevertheless he gave her full credit for her
great qualities, in especial for a good sense amounting
to genius. And she in turn was pleased with the
serious German who argued with her in lame French,

not as one caring to hold his own in a conversational fencing-match, but as one wishing to convince her of important truths in which he really believed. It must have been an interesting occasion in a small way, this first rencontre between Schiller and the lady who was afterwards to speak of him so nobly and withal so justly in her celebrated book about Germany. Madame de Staël's sojourn in Weimar lasted some ten weeks, her portentous gift of speech becoming gradually more and more irksome to Schiller and Goethe. The social gayeties occasioned by her presence caused some retardation in the progress of 'William Tell', but on February 18, 1804, it was completed, and two days later the final installment was despatched to the waiting Iffland. How eagerly he was waiting may be inferred from the language used by him after perusal of the first act, which had been sent him a month earlier:

I have read, devoured, bent my knee; and my heart, my tears, my rushing blood, have paid ecstatic homage to your spirit, to your heart. Oh more! Soon, soon, more! Pages, scraps—whatever you can send! I tender hand and heart to your genius. What a work! What wealth, force, poetic beauty and irresistible power! God keep you! Amen.

These high-keyed expectations were not disappointed. The first performances of 'Tell', in the spring of 1804, were received with prodigious enthusiasm, and ever since then it has been a prime favorite of the German stage. It has no characters that can be called great, as Wallenstein is great, no complexity of plot, no thrilling surprises; and as for its psychology, a fairy tale could hardly be more simple. That which has endeared it to the Germans is its picturesqueness and its passionate zeal for freedom.

The theme of ' Tell ' is the successful revolt of the Forest Cantons against their governors. Three actions that have no necessary connection with one another —the conspiracy of the cantons, the private feud of Tell and Gessler, and the love-affair of Rudenz and Bertha—are carried along together in such a way that all find their natural conclusion in the final celebration of victory. This feature of the play has often been criticized as impairing its unity; and certainly, from the conventional point of view the objection has some force. ' Tell ' is a play without a preponderating hero. We may say that it has three heroes, or rather five, since among the conspirators interest is pretty evenly distributed between Stauffacher, Melchthal and Walther Fürst. But in reality the hero is the Swiss people considered as a unit. Stauffacher and the other conspirators interest us as representatives of a suffering population. To portray the suffering and the termination of it through sturdy self-help is the central purpose of the play. This it is which gives it an essential unity, notwithstanding the three separate actions.

The theme is an inspiring one, and the modern world owes Schiller an immense debt for presenting it in austere simplicity, unincumbered with any dubious or disturbing philosophy. One cannot help loving so good a lover of freedom; for the sentiment does honor to human nature, notwithstanding some latter-day indications that it is going out of fashion. It may not be the highest and holiest of enthusiasms for the individual,—we give our best homage rather to self-surrender,—but if any political emotion is worthy of a lasting reverence, it is that one which attaches men to the motherland and leads them to stand together against an alien oppressor. Sometimes it may be well, in God's long providence, that a weak or a backward people should be absorbed or ruled by a stronger power; but the sentiment which leads it to fight against absorption or subjugation is none the less admirable. And when the foreign domination is reckless and inhuman, standing for nothing but vindictive malice and the greed of empire; and when the victims of the misrule are strong in the simple virtues of the poor, we have the case in its most appealing aspect.

This is the case that is presented in ' William Tell ', —the most notable drama in modern literature upon the theme of national resistance to foreign tyranny. Its influence in Germany as a classic of political freedom—during the Napoleonic era and later, when it was a question of setting a limit to domestic absolutism—has been immense. And there is really no danger of its losing its potency; for it appeals to a sentiment which, while it may wax and wane with the movements of the *Zeitgeist*, is now wrought into the heart-fiber of all the occidental nations, and not least of all—contrary to an opinion widely accepted in this country—of the Germans.

The uppermost thought of Schiller, then, was to win sympathy for freedom and the rights of man; yet in ' William Tell ' we have nothing to do with any species of cloud-born idealism. The bearers of the message are not fantastic dreamers, like Posa; they do not call themselves ambassadors of all mankind, or citizens of the centuries to come. They are a plain, practical folk, whose wishes do not fly far afield and who attempt nothing that they cannot carry through. They are not in the least given to fighting for the sake of fighting; on the contrary, the thought of bloodshed is abhorrent to them. All they wish is to be allowed to pursue their peaceful, partriarchal industries, as their fathers did before them, under laws of their own devising. But things have come to such a pass that their lives, their property and the honor of their women are not safe from the malice, cupidity and lust of their rulers. And even under such conditions the thought of a radical revolution does not occur to them: they do not rise against the overlordship of the emperor, but only against the brutal tyranny of the governors who disgrace him. Their final triumph opens no other vista of change than that, in the future, another emperor will send them better governors. Thus the upshot of the whole revolution is simply a provisional demonstration of Stauffacher's proposition that 'tyrannical power has a limit'.

This seems, at first, like a rather lame vindication of the sacred majesty of freedom, especially when we reflect that the whole question at issue is not a question of independence at all, but merely whether the cantons will give up their *Reichsunmittelbarkeit*,—and with it certain old customs to which they are attached,—in order to become vassals of the House of Hapsburg. Were they willing to do that,—so it is said by Rösselmann at the Rütli meeting,—all their troubles would end forthwith; the cruel governors would deal kindly with them, would 'fondle' them. If this is so,—and other passages confirm the saying of the priest Rössel-mann,—then it is patent that the conduct of Gessler is not the aimless brutality of a brute, but a policy deliberately pursued for the purpose of terrorizing the cantons into an acceptance of Hapsburg overlordship. And this in turn throws its own light on the character of Gessler. Only a blockhead would try to gain such an end in such a way. This, however, is only another way of saying what has often been pointed out, that Gessler is simply a fairy-tale tyrant, copied very closely from Tschudi; a sort of typical bad man, whom the saga, after inventing him out of nothing, has made as black as possible in order the more clearly and strongly to justify the revolt. And yet, in the play, Gessler never becomes entirely ridiculous; he does not seem a caricature of humanity,—perhaps because history teems with governors and viceroys who have exercised their little brief authority very much in his spirit, even if they have failed to commit his particular atrocities.

These last considerations are meant to light up the fact that the effect of the play does not, after all, depend mainly upon its vindication of any political doctrine. We are nowhere in the region of abstractions. The sympathy that one feels for the insurgents is in no sort political, but purely human; it is of the same kind that one might feel for a community of Hindu ryots in their efforts to rid themselves of a man-eating tiger. Only in the play this sympathy is very much intensified by the picturesque lovableness of the afflicted population. It is here, in the picture of land and people, that Schiller's mature art, which had brought him to a sovereign mastery of stage effects, may be said to win its greatest triumph. One may describe his method, fairly if somewhat paradoxically, as that of romantic realism. What a masterpiece of exposition we have in the opening scenes! The beautiful lake, at precisely its most fascinating point; the fisher-boy, all careless of the great world, singing his pretty song of the smiling but treacherous water; the herdsman and the hunter, announcing themselves above on the rocks in characteristic songs, and then conversing for a moment about the weather and their employments; the sudden arrival of Baumgarten with his tale of wrong and vengeance; the storm on the lake, and the hurried dialogue between the cautious fisherman and the stout-hearted Tell, who 'does what he cannot help doing'; the building of the hateful Zwing-Uri; the death of the slater and Bertha's curse; the grief and fury of young Melchthal, and, finally, the solemn covenant for life and death of the three leaders, —what variety and animation are here, and what a wealth of realistic detail! And how perfectly convincing it all is,—not a false note anywhere, nor a note that is held too long! Well might Goethe characterize this exposition as 'a complete piece in itself and withal an excellent one'. The first act of 'Tell' is one of the best first acts in all dramatic literature.

It is quite true that the exposition seems to promise somewhat more than is afterwards fulfilled. One who is familiar with Schiller's usual method naturally expects that something will come of the rescue of Baumgarten; but nothing does come of it except to throw a side-light upon the general situation and to bring out the character of Tell. Again, one expects to see more of Dame Gertrud, the 'wise daughter of noble Iberg'. One looks for her to reappear under circumstances that shall give her something important to do and shall put her sagacity and courage to the test. It is not the habit of Schiller to introduce such weighty personages at the beginning of a play and then drop them. To understand him in this instance one has but to remember that his hero is always the Swiss people. The Stauffachers, as a shining example of thrift and virtue; their dignified and influential position in the community; their fine new house that has roused the venomous jealousy of Gessler,—all this is part of the situation, and it is the situation that counts. And how superbly the picture is completed by the meeting at the Rütli! Such an old-fashioned parliament, held of necessity under the stars and in the darkness of night, but with all possible regard to the ancient forms, was not only a novel and a picturesque idea in itself, but it was the best device which could possibly be imagined for bringing sharply into view the whole character of the Swiss, in its winsome, patriarchal simplicity.

Here again, however, we have a radical departure from Schiller's usual method; for what is actually done at this seemingly important meeting is, after all, in itself rather insignificant, and without direct influence upon the subsequent course of events. The conspirators decide to do nothing immediately, but to wait for a favorable opportunity during the Christmas season, some seven or eight weeks ahead. This determination obviously involves a halt in the dramatic action, so far as the conspiracy is concerned. In dealing with this difficulty, Schiller departs from his ordinary method of concentration and allows himself to be guided by the epical character of Tschudi's narrative. The result is that we have, somewhat as in Goethe's 'Götz von Berlichingen ', a succession of dramatic pictures, rather than a drama bound together by a severe logic. In the third and fourth acts we hear no more of the conspirators,—aside from some expressions of regret for the delay,—and attention is concentrated upon Tell, who has hitherto taken no part except to rescue Baumgarten and to refuse his coöperation at the Rütli, on the ground that he is not the man for a confab, and that 'the strong man is mightiest alone '.

The character of Tell, as depicted by Schiller, has been the subject of much criticism, the strictures relating more particularly to his shooting the apple from his son's head, and then to his subsequent assassination of Gessler. There is an oft-quoted opinion of Bismarck, which may be quoted again, since it expresses so well a thought that has no doubt occurred, some time or other, to most readers and spectators of the play. Busch makes Bismarck say, under date of October 25, 1870:

It would have been more natural and more noble, according to my ideas, if, instead of shooting at the boy, whom the best of archers might hit instead of the apple, he had killed the governor on the spot. That would have been righteous wrath at a cruel demand. I do not like his hiding and lurking; that does not befit a hero—not even a bushwhacker.

Undoubtedly such conduct as is here suggested for Tell would be more 'heroic ', in accordance with our conventional ideas of heroism. And the thing would have been dramatically feasible. We can imagine Tell, for example, as making sham preparations to shoot at the apple and then suddenly sending his arrow through the heart of his enemy; and we can also imagine a further management of the scene such that Tell should escape with his boy. Thus everything would be accomplished on the public square at Altorf, in full face of the enemy, which is subsequently accomplished from the secure ambush by the 'hollow way' near Küssnacht. Such conduct would have been 'heroic', but the obvious objection to it is that it would have destroyed the very heart of the saga, which it was not for Schiller to make over but to render dramatically plausible. It may be urged, perhaps, that a poet who had made Joan of Arc die in glory on the battle-field need not have been so punctilious in following the exact line of Tschudi's story. But the cases are not exactly parallel. There the alternative was a scene of unmitigated and revolting horror, which would have destroyed the effect of the tragedy; here it was simply a question of *when* Gessler should be killed with an arrow. To make Tell do just what the saga makes him do, and do it without forfeiting sympathy, was a delicate problem, which may well have fascinated Schiller, who is surely the last man in the world to be accused of holding tame views as to 'heroism'. At any rate he must have felt that a Tell who should not shoot at the apple and hit it would be simply no Tell at all.

One who looks closely at the famous scene will not fail to see that it is very cleverly constructed and that every objection which has been urged against it is really met in the text. In the first place, Tell is not, and was never meant for, a hero of the conventional sort. There is no element of Quixotry about him. He is a plain man, of limited horizon and small gift of speech. Public affairs do not particularly interest him. He is a hardy mountaineer, with a strong trust in his own strength and resourcefulness; a good oarsman and a great shot with the crossbow; but he makes no fuss about these things. Let it be repeated that he is not foolhardy. The dangers of the mountain, which bulk so large in the imagination of his wife, are simply the familiar element of the life that he loves. He treats her timorous apprehensions with the good-natured coolness of a man who knows how to take care of himself. He is affectionate, but not a bit sentimental. All this makes an eminently natural and consistent character.

Now what must such a character do when required, under penalty of death, by a brutal tyrant whose power is absolute, to hit an apple on his son's head? Naturally his first thought is of the child, and he tries to escape by offering his own life. The reply is that he must shoot or die *with* his child. Thus there is no recourse; to refuse to shoot at all is worse than to shoot and miss. If he kill Gessler on the spot,—and we must suppose that the thought occurs to him,—he will expose not only himself but his child and his wife and children at home to the fury of the troopers. The only safety lies in making a successful shot. And after all Tell knows that he *can* make it; it is only a question of nerve, and he has the nerve if he can only find it. And here

comes in an important touch which is not in Tschudi
—the fearless confidence of Walther Tell in his father's
marksmanship. The effect of this is to touch the pride
of the bowman, to clear his eye, and to steady his
hand. It is also a familiar fact that, with strong
natures, a terrible danger, with just one chance of
escape, may produce a moment of perfect self-control
while the chance is taken.

The whole scene, in addition to its effectiveness on
the stage, is psychologically true to life. With all
deference to the great qualities of the first Chancellor
of the German Empire, one must insist that Schiller
was a better playwright than he and found precisely
the best solution to his dramatic problem.

And so of the later scene in the 'hollow way';
there is nothing wrong with it, unless it be the great
length of the soliloquy. The killing of an enemy from
an ambush, without giving him a chance for his life, is
of course somewhat repugnant to our ideas of chivalry.
We think of it instinctively as the deed of a savage,
and not of a man with a pure heart and a good cause.
But it must be remembered that such ideas are themselves conventional, and that we have in 'Tell' a
reversion to primitive conditions in which 'man stands
over against man'. Gessler has forfeited all right to
chivalrous treatment, and Tell is no knight engaged
in fighting out a gentleman's feud. What is he to do?
For himself, perhaps, he might take the chances of a
fugitive in the mountains, but he cannot leave his wife
and children exposed to Gessler's vengeful malice.
There is no law to which he can appeal, the only law
of the land being Gessler's will. In such a situation,

clearly, there is no place for refined and chivalrous compunctions, or for ethical hair-splitting. Tell does what he must do. He is in the position of a man protecting his family from a savage or a dangerous beast, and is not called upon to risk his own life needlessly. Every reader of the old saga instinctively justifies him. His conduct is not noble or heroic, but natural and right.

If this is so, however, there would seem to be no pressing need of his long soliloquy. He being *ex proposito* a man of few words, his sudden volubility is a little surprising, though it should be duly noticed that the soliloquy is not a self-defense. There is no casuistry in it. Tell does not argue the case with himself, like one in doubt about the rightness of his conduct. That is as clear as day to him, and he never wavers for a moment. But he has time to think while waiting, and his soliloquy is only his thinking made audible. Delivered with even a slight excess of declamatory fervor, the lines are ridiculously out of keeping with Tell's character; but they can be spoken so as to seem at least tolerably natural,—as natural, perhaps, as any soliloquy. And this is true, let it be remarked in passing, of many and many a passage in Schiller. To some extent, very certainly, his reputation as a rhetorician is due to the histrionic spouting of lines that do not need to be spouted. To some extent, but not entirely; for even in 'Tell' his old fondness for absurdly extravagant forms of expression sometimes reasserted itself. Thus what can one make of a plain fisherman who talks in this wise about a rainstorm?

Rage on, ye winds !   Flame down, ye lightning-bolts !
Burst open, clouds !   Pour out, ye drenching streams
Of heaven, and drown the land !   Annihilate
I' the very germ the unborn brood of men !
Ye furious elements, assert your lordship !
Ye bears, ye ancient wolves o' the wilderness,
Come back again !   The land belongs to you.
Who cares to live in it bereft of freedom !

The most serious blemish in 'William Tell' is the introduction of Johannes Parricida in the fifth act,—an idea which Goethe attributed to feminine influence of some sort.[1]   The effect of it is to convert the rugged, manly Tell of the preceding acts into a sanctimonious Pharisee with whom one can have little sympathy. No doubt there is a moral difference between his act and that of Parricida, but it is a difference which one does not wish to hear Tell himself dilate upon. Seeing that the murdered emperor was solely responsible for the brutal governors and thus indirectly for all the woes of Switzerland; and seeing, too, that his death is the only guarantee we have at the end that the killing of Gessler will do any good, and not simply have the effect to bring down upon the land, including Tell and his family, the vengeance of some still more fiendish successor,—considering all this, one would rather not hear those horrified ejaculations of Tell about the pollution of the murderer's presence.   They

[1] See Eckermann's "Gespräche", under date of March 16, 1831. What Goethe there says, however, is in flat contradiction of the following passage contained in a letter of Schiller to Iffland, written April 14, 1804: "Auch Goethe ist mit mir überzeugt, dasz ohne jenen Monolog und ohne die persönliche Erscheinung des Parricida der Tell sich gar nicht hätte denken lassen."

may produce a certain stagy effect of contrast, but the effect was not worth producing at the expense of Tell's character.

As for the love-story in 'William Tell', it is hardly of sufficient weight to merit extended discussion. Both Bertha and Rudenz are rather tamely and conventionally drawn, to meet the need of a pair of romantic lovers; they evidently cost their creator no very strenuous communings with the Genius of Art. Their private affair of the heart has nothing to do with the Tell episode and is but loosely related to the popular uprising. Their absence would not be very seriously felt in the drama, save that one would not like to miss Attinghausen as a picturesque representative of the old patriarchal nobility. The two scenes in which he appears are in themselves admirable.

CHAPTER XXI

The End.—Unfinished Plays, Translations and Adaptations

Es stürzt ihn mitten in der Bahn,
Es reiszt ihn fort vom vollen Leben.

'*William Tell*'.

OUR story of Schiller's life draws to a close. After the completion of 'William Tell' his tireless energy of production found its next theme in the story of Dmitri, the reputed son of Ivan the Terrible. Just how and whence the suggestion came to him is unknown, but the connection of things is patent enough in a general way. Far-reaching intrigues in high life had always had a fascination for him, and recent studies undertaken for 'Warbeck' had interested him in the type of the pretender whose kingly bearing seems to betoken kingly blood. In a work upon Russia,—a land which had been brought closer to the Schiller household by the appointment of Wilhelm von Wolzogen as Weimarian envoy to the Czar,—he read anew the history of the 'false Dmitri', and was struck by its dramatic capabilities. In 'Warbeck' he had thought to portray a pretender who knew that his claims were fraudulent; in Dmitri he found one who believed in himself. The psychological problem, and the idea of conquering an entirely new territory for the German drama, attracted him strongly, and he set about the laborious task of self-orientation.

Ere long, however, there came an interruption which, for a while, seemed to promise a momentous change in the tenor of his life. Iffland wished to lure him to Berlin and had intimated that the Prussian government might be disposed to offer inducements. Schiller was not entirely averse to the idea; at least he thought it worth while to reconnoitre. So, toward the end of April, 1804, he set out with wife and children for the Prussian capital, where he was received with the greatest cordiality. The king and queen of Prussia, to whom he was presented, were very gracious, and it was all decidedly pleasant. So at least he thought and so his wife pretended to think,—keeping down for her husband's sake the dismay which a daughter of fair Thuringia could not help feeling at the thought of making a home on the flat banks of the Spree. After a fortnight Schiller returned to Weimar and was presently invited by the Prussian minister, Beyme, to name his terms. Now came the rub; for he did not really wish to leave Weimar. He had taken deep root there and his affections clung to the place for the sake of Goethe and a few other friends. On the other hand, his stipend was but four hundred thalers, and his other sources of income were by no means such as to free him from anxiety about the future of his family. Feeling that it was his duty to better his position if possible, he laid his case before Karl August, who promptly doubled his stipend. After this it was virtually impossible for him to leave Weimar. Unwilling nevertheless to renounce the Berlin prospects altogether, he wrote to Beyme that for a consideration of two thousand thalers annually he would reside a few months of each year in Berlin. To this proposition Beyme made no answer. Possibly he thought the price too high for a fractional poet.

Pending these futile negotiations Schiller worked with great zest upon ' Demetrius ',—reading, excerpting, examining maps and pictures, schematizing, balancing possibilities, and so forth. But again he was interrupted; first by an unusually severe illness, which brought him to death's door and left him for weeks in a condition of helpless languor, and then by the distractions incident to the arrival of the hereditary Prince of Weimar with his Russian bride, Maria Paulovna. Golden reports had preceded this princess, who was expected to reach Weimar in November, and preparations were made to welcome her with distinguished honors. For some reason Goethe, in his capacity of director of the theater, remained inactive amid the general flutter until a few days before the great event, when he besought Schiller to come to the rescue. The result was ' The Homage of the Arts ', called by its author a ' prologue '.

We have a rustic scene in which country-folk plant an orange-tree and invoke the blessing of pagan divinities. The Genius of Art appears, and with him the seven goddesses: Architecture, Sculpture, Painting, Poetry, Music, Dance and Drama. Genius asks for an explanation of the tree-planting, and is told by the rustics that it is an act of homage to their new queen, who has come from high imperial halls to live in their humble valley. They wish to bind her to them by keeping her reminded of home.   On hearing this Genius assures them that the queen will not find all things strange in her new home: old friends are there after all.   Then he leads forward his seven goddesses, who explain themselves and say pretty things about Russia.   ' The Homage of the Arts ' is in no sense a weighty production, but its graceful verse and well-turned compliments had the desired effect.   Maria Paulovna was pleased with it.

The reaction from these Russophile festivities fell heavily upon Schiller and he became gradually weaker. Unequal to creative effort he undertook a translation of Racine's ' Phèdre ' in German pentameters and finished it about the middle of January, 1805.   After this he threw himself with great energy upon ' Demetrius ', but it was the final flicker of a dying flame.   In February came a fresh prostration, and it was then evident that the end was near.   Nevertheless he worked on for a few weeks longer with feverish eagerness.   On the evening of April 29, he went to the theater.   After the play was over, the young Voss,— a son of the poet, who had attached himself warmly to Schiller during these latest years,—came to him to attend him home.   He found him in a violent fever, which soon led to exhaustion and delirium.   This time the strong will of the sufferer and the eager offices of wife and physician proved unavailing.   He lingered on a few days longer, now and then in his delirium reciting disconnected verse or scraps of Latin, until the end came, on the afternoon of the 9th of May.   Three days later, between twelve and one o'clock at night, the body of the dead man was borne by a little group of friends through the silent and deserted streets of

Weimar, and lowered into a vault in the churchyard of St. James. There it remained until 1826, when the remains were exhumed and, after some curious vicissitudes, were placed in an oaken coffin and deposited in the ducal mausoleum, where they now rest near those of Goethe and Karl August.[1]

The death of Schiller made many mourners. Goethe, who had himself been very ill, wrote to a friend in Berlin: 'I thought to lose myself, and now I lose a friend, and with him the half of my existence.' From every hand came tokens of sympathy for the widow. Maria Paulovna asked for the privilege of caring for the children. Queen Luise of Prussia sent a message of heartfelt condolence. Cotta, whose business relations with Schiller had given rise to a warm personal affection, made generous offers of financial aid. As for the nation at large, however, it can hardly be said that much notice was taken of the event. Schiller had led a secluded life, had been but little in the public eye, and his personality was known to but few. What should the passing of a single dreamer signify in the stirring epoch of Austerlitz and Jena? Not many knew that one of the real immortals had ceased to

[1] In the year 1805 it was still usual at Weimar to have the bodies of the dead borne to the grave in the night by hired workmen. On the death of Schiller the burgomaster gave orders in accordance with the custom, and it was with some difficulty that friends of the dead man succeeded in displacing the guild on which the lot had fallen and securing for themselves the privilege of acting as bearers. While lying in the old churchyard the bones of Schiller became commingled with others in the vault, so that the proper reassembling of his mortal framework, in the year 1826, was a matter of some perplexity. For a while the skull was exhibited in the court library, where it called forth Goethe's well-known poem.

breathe,—one whose figure would loom up larger and larger in receding time, like a high mountain in the receding distance.

But leaving this subject, of Schiller's subsequent influence and reputation, for discussion in the concluding chapter, let us now turn to a brief survey of his unfinished plays and of his more important work as translator and adapter.

And first, 'Demetrius', of which one may say, as Schiller said of the Faust-fragment of 1790, that it is the torso of a Hercules. Such extant portions as had reached something like a final form in verse tell of a tragedy that bade fair to rank with 'Wallenstein', perhaps to surpass 'Wallenstein', in dramatic power and psychological interest. The completed portions pertain mainly to the first two acts; for the rest we have an immense mass of schemes, arguments, excerpts and collectanea. To read through this material, particularly the various schemes laboriously written out in numberless revisions, conveys at first an impression of over-solicitude, as if erudition and logical analysis were being relied upon to take the place of slackening inspiration. The moment one turns to the finished scenes, however, one sees that the poetic spring was still flowing in full measure; and one is amazed at the creative power which could still, with death knocking at the door, so swiftly and so surely fashion great poetry out of dull and contradictory books.

The story of the false Demetrius had been familiar to Schiller from his youth, but there is no evidence that he ever thought of dramatizing it until the year 1802, when we hear of an intended drama to be called

'The Massacre at Moscow'. Just as before in the cases of Fiesco and Wallenstein, he found here a notable conspirator whose character and motives were the subject of dispute among the historians. The more usual view was that Demetrius was an escaped monk who gave himself out as the son of Ivan the Terrible, having either himself invented the fraud or else taken upon himself a rôle that was suggested to him by some one else. On the other hand, there were those who regarded him as the genuine son of Ivan and thus entitled to the throne which he conquered from the usurper, Boris Gudunoff, in the year 1605. Fraudulent pretender, or genuine Czar of the blood of Rurik,—this was the great question. With a fine dramatic intuition Schiller conceived a third possibility, namely, that Demetrius, though not in reality Ivan's son, fully believed himself to be such until he had triumphed, and then, though undeceived, went on his calamitous way as a tyrant because he could not turn back.

His first thought was to begin with a scene at Sambor in Galicia, wherein the escaped monk Grischka, tarrying at the house of Mnischek in complete ignorance of his high birth, but given none the less to ambitious dreaming, should be made known as Ivan's son, Demetrius, supposed to have been murdered sixteen years before at the instigation of Boris. Several scenes, interesting in their way but somewhat lacking in horizon, were elaborated in accordance with this idea. Then, however, the plan was modified and it was decided to begin directly with a session of the Polish parliament at Cracow, at which Demetrius should appear and triumphantly assert his claims before King

Sigismund and the assembled nobles. This scene, though left imperfect here and there, is certainly one of the best that ever came from Schiller's pen. As usual we have a bit of world-drama, for the element out of which the action grows is the national antipathy of Poles and Russians. And what an interesting figure is the young Demetrius, confronting all the pomp and power with the easy dignity of one born to kingship, and carrying the parliament with him by dint of his own self-confidence and royal bearing. He is essentially a new creation, unlike any of Schiller's other youthful heroes, though a certain family resemblance is of course discernible. Ambition of power is the great mainspring of his character, and he is as unscrupulous as Napoleon. Nevertheless he has his sentimental and his ethical promptings, and the whole basis of his conduct in this first part of the play is his perfect confidence that he is the son of Ivan.

It is thus ever to be regretted that Schiller did not live to write the later scenes in which Demetrius, on the eve of his triumphant entry into Moscow, should be approached by the *fabricator doli* and told the true story of his vulgar birth. Here, just as in the ' Œdipus Rex ', was a stupendous tragic fate, unconnected with any conscious guilt and growing entirely out of the circumstances. What should Demetrius do ? What he was to *say* we know from a prose sketch which runs as follows :

You [addressed to the *fabricator doli*, who appears in the manuscript as X] have pierced the heart of my life, you have taken from me my faith in myself. Away, Courage and Hope !. Away, joyous self-confidence ! I am caught in a lie. I am at variance with myself. I am an enemy of mankind. I and truth are parted forever! What? Shall I undeceive the people? Unmask myself as a deceiver?—I must go forward. I must stand firm, and yet I can do it no longer in the strength of inward conviction. Murder and blood must maintain me in my position. How shall I meet the Czarina? How shall I enter Moscow amid the plaudits of the people, with this lie in my heart?

One sees from this whither Schiller's idea was tending. From the time that Demetrius is undeceived his character changes. The youth who, with truth on his side, had it in him to become a great and wise ruler, breaks with the moral law and becomes a Macbeth, or a Richard the Third. His course from this time on is flecked with blood and dishonored by treachery and tyranny. As Czar he excites the hatred of the Russians by his impolitic contempt of their customs. His Poles are insolent and trouble begins to brew about him. Finally there is an uprising against him and he falls—the victim of his own ὕβρις.

Had Schiller been permitted by fate to complete 'Demetrius', we should have had, it is safe to say, the most impressive of all his heroes, with the possible exception of Wallenstein. And we should have had also, in all probability, the very best of his historical tragedies; for his plan had provided for an unusually large number of highly promising scenes. The picturesque Polish parliament, with its tumultuous ending; the first meeting of Demetrius with his reputed mother; the scene with the *fabricator doli;* the triumphal entry into Moscow; Demetrius as Czar in the Kremlin; his love intrigues with Axinia and his perfunctory marriage to Marina; the final gathering and bursting of the storm of indignation,—all this would have been wrought into a dramatic masterpiece of the first order.

Like 'Demetrius' in having a royal pretender for a hero, but unlike it in every other respect, is the play which was to have been called 'Warbeck'. To this subject Schiller's attention was drawn in the summer of 1799, while reading English history in Rapin de Thoyras. During the ensuing years he took it up repeatedly, but each time dropped it in favor of some other theme. At the time of his death he left 'Warbeck' material sufficient to make eighty-four pages of octavo print. The most of this material consists of prose schemes, but there are also several hundred verses, some of them complete, others with lacunæ, great or small. By a close study of these data one can make out the general character of the proposed play and the essential lineaments of the more important characters. The play was not to have been a tragedy, and it would have owed to history hardly anything more than its *milieu* and a few names. The plan was something like this:

About the year 1492 there turns up at Brussels, at the court of Margaret, Duchess of Burgundy, a young man calling himself Warbeck. He is ignorant of his own birth, and does not suppose himself to be of royal blood, but he has a strong resemblance to Edward the Fourth of England. Being herself of York blood and wishing to make trouble for the Tudor king, Henry the Seventh, Margaret persuades the stranger to pretend that he is the son of Edward the Fourth,—one of the two boys supposed to have been murdered in the tower by Richard of Gloucester. He consents to the fraud and speedily acquires a following as pretender to the English throne. In reality Margaret despises him and merely wishes to use him as a tool, but it soon appears that Warbeck is a man of character who insists on playing his assumed rôle in a manner worthy of an English sovereign. Preparations are made for an invasion of England to assert his claim. Meanwhile Warbeck falls in love with Adelaide, a princess of Brittany, for whom the imperious Margaret has other designs. Presently a man named Simnel appears, asserting fraudulently that *he* is a son of the fourth Edward. He and Warbeck fight a duel and Simnel is killed. Then the real Edward Plantagenet appears, with a convincing story of his own wonderful escape from the executioner in the Tower. A murderous plot is concocted against the boy's life, but he is saved by Warbeck, who acknowledges him as his rightful king. All this time Warbeck has supposed himself to be acting a part of pure fraud; and as he is really a man of honor, and in love with an amiable princess, the rôle of deceit has become increasingly hateful to him. At last, however, the old Earl of Kildare arrives, and from the depths of his superior knowledge makes it plain that Warbeck is in truth a natural son of Edward the Fourth. Thus all ends romantically and we have no adumbration of that later scene of the year 1499, when Perkin Warbeck was drawn and quartered at Tyburn.

From this plan it is clear that the principal stress was to fall on the character of Warbeck, conceived as a high-minded youth entangled in an odious lie. To quote Schiller's exact words: 'The problem of the piece is to carry him (Warbeck) ever deeper into situations in which his deceit brings him to despair, and to let his natural truthfulness increase as the circumstances force him to deception.' To arouse sympathy for such a character would have been, to say the least, a difficult task; one cannot wonder that Schiller was perplexed by it. The schemes indicate that his main reliance was the love-story, which would have been very prominent. Of the other characters, the most important, probably, was the Duchess Margaret, conceived as a selfish, overbearing, heartless creature, in sharp contrast with the romantic Adelaide. On the whole, judging from such imperfect data as we possess, one must regard ' Warbeck ' as a far less powerful and promising design than ' Demetrius '.

Contemporaneous with ' Warbeck ' and ' Demetrius ', and broadly similar to them in that it was to deal with a political adventurer and to present an elaborate picture of intrigue in high life, is the plan of a play which was at first called ' Count Königsmark '. The subject occupied the thoughts of Schiller for some little time in the summer of 1804, until it was dropped in favor of ' Demetrius '. Count Königsmark was a nobleman who was murdered in the year 1694, at the court of Duke George I., of Hannover, in consequence of a supposed criminal relation with the Duchess Sophia, a princess of the house of Celle. As he mused upon the dramatic possibilities of the story, Schiller became less interested in Königsmark and more in the compromised duchess; so the name of the piece was changed to ' The Princess of Celle '. From his extant notes and sketches one can make out that the heroine was conceived, like Mary Stuart, as a noble sufferer. She is a virtuous lady who is given in marriage for political reasons to an unloved and licentious duke, whose mistresses insult her. In her misery she makes a friend of the chivalrous but inflammable Königsmark. Their relation excites suspicion, Königsmark is murdered and the duchess sent to prison,—disgraced but innocent. In prison she finds peace of soul, just as Mary Stuart finds it in the presence of death.

Much older than any of these plans and entirely different from them, is that of the 'Knights of Malta', which dates back to the year 1788. While pursuing his studies for 'Don Carlos' Schiller had become greatly interested in the story of La Valette's heroic defense of Malta in 1565. It seemed to him to promise well for a tragedy in the Greek style,—with a chorus, a simple plot and few characters. He began work upon it, but was soon diverted by his historical studies. In subsequent years, however, he returned to 'The Knights of Malta' from time to time, and as late as 1803 was strongly minded to attempt the completion of the work. During these fifteen years the plan underwent various changes. Although certain aspects of the subject made it very attractive to Schiller, he felt from the first that it lacked the 'salient point' of a good tragedy. The extant data show him working tentatively with one idea after another, without ever finding exactly what he wanted. This being so, it is hardly worth while to go minutely into the history of his plans and perplexities.

'The Knights of Malta' was to have been a poetic tragedy of heroic devotion, friendship and self-sacri-

fice.   The exposition, as we have it in outline, shows,
—partly by means of a chorus of ' spiritual ' knights,—
the desperate plight of the besieged Christians.   The
crisis requires absolute devotion to the principles of
the order, but the knights have degenerated.   Two of
them are quarreling over a captured Greek girl, and
so forth.   La Valette, the grandmaster, institutes stern
measures of reform to restore the ancient *morale* of
the order, and these provoke intrigue and opposition.
The defenders of Fort St. Elmo ask to be relieved, on
the ground that the place cannot be held.   La Valette
decides that St. Elmo must be defended to the last: it
is a case where a few must be ready to sacrifice themselves for their principles and for the order as a whole.
Among those thus sent to death is La Valette's own
son, who leaves behind a very dear friend.   In the end
the defenders of St. Elmo are killed, but Malta and
the order are saved.   The Turks raise the siege.

Reading this outline one has no great difficulty in
seeing why Schiller's dramatic instinct could never be
satisfied with ' The Knights of Malta '.   It has no
tragic climax, no point upon which the action could
be focused.   As a stage-play it would have had small
chance of favor, on account of its chorus and its entire
lack of female characters.   Romantic love was to be
left out and friendship to take its place.   But could
anything worth while have been done with the heroics
of friendship after ' Don Carlos ' ?   On the whole one
must regard it as a great good fortune for the German
drama that, when Schiller was hesitating in 1796
between ' Wallenstein ' and ' The Knights of Malta ',
the former carried the day.   As for the pseudo-antique

chorus, the best that he could do with that, by way
of an experiment, was done later in 'The Bride of
Messina'.

Besides those already mentioned, there are a number of other plans which deserve a word, were it only
to show the wide range of Schiller's interest and the
eagerness of his quest after variety. Thus we find him
occupied, at one time or another, with two antique
themes, 'Aggripina' and 'The Death of Themisto-
cles'; with an Anglo-Saxon theme of the tenth century, 'Elfride', and with a medieval romantic theme,
'The Countess of Flanders'. Then we find two
subjects that were suggested by the reading of modern
travels, 'The Ship' and 'The Filibuster'. In one the
scene was to be laid on some distant coast or island,
and the plot was to illustrate sea-life and commerce,
with their characteristic types. In the other the whole
action was to take place on shipboard, bringing in a
mutiny, ship's justice, a sea-fight, trade with savages,
and so forth. Finally there are sketches of two other
plays, based on the annals of crime. In one of them,
called 'The Children of the House', the hero was to
be a thorough scoundrel, whom Nemesis would impel
mysteriously to a course of conduct whereby his long
hidden crimes would be discovered. The other,
entitled 'The Police', was to present a story of crime
and its discovery at Paris,—with telling realistic pictures for which Schiller took a mass of interesting
notes.

Verily, a rich collection, which shows that a good
deal of Schiller failed to find expression in the works
he completed. One could wish particularly that we

had those sea-plays, and the Parisian criminal drama. Perhaps in that case the critics who have taxed him with this or that narrowness would have found it more difficult to make headway.

We turn now from these dramatic might-have-beens to glance at the translations and adaptations made for the Weimar theater.[1] And first it should be observed that in all these, without exception, Schiller's point of view was that of a practical playwright, not that of a literary virtuoso. His concern was to enrich the repertory of the theater with good acting plays; plays which, when put upon the boards, would 'go', and go with such actors and such properties as were to be had. In his efforts to do this he was never restrained by any feeling of piety toward his originals from making such changes as commended themselves to his dramaturgic principles or instinct. The first work of this kind undertaken by him at Weimar was a version of Goethe's 'Egmont', made in 1796. Iffland was starring in Weimar and wished to appear as Egmont. Goethe was just then somewhat lukewarm toward the theater, and even if he had not been, it was by no means hidden from him that his own strength lay in the poetic rather than the dramatic sphere. So it was arranged that Schiller, as a man of experience, should operate upon the play that he had reviewed so candidly some years before. His procedure was 'consistent but cruel', as Goethe afterward phrased it. He dropped the rôle of Margaret of Parma entirely, rearranged

[1] For an excellent discussion of Schiller's more important adaptations the reader is referred to A. Köster, "Schiller als Dramaturg", Berlin, 1891.

here and there in order to avoid a too frequent change of scene, and made a multitude of little changes in the interest of stage effect. As to the propriety of these alterations it is futile to argue on general grounds, since so much depends on the point of view, and the point of view has changed. To-day people who go to the theater to see ' Egmont ' prefer to see the play, for better or worse, as Goethe wrote it. Piety toward the author counts more than abstract principles. For a while Schiller's version of ' Egmont ' had a certain vogue in the German theaters, but it soon gave way to an increasing preference for the original. Goethe himself was pleased when this tendency manifested itself.

Similar considerations apply to the version of Lessing's ' Nathan ', which was made in 1801. Strangely enough, as it seems to us now, Lessing's masterpiece had up to that time met with no favor on the German stage. It was not so much that people objected to its philosophic drift as that something seemed to be lacking in its dramatic quality. Very naturally Goethe and Schiller, who were strongly in sympathy with Lessing's tendency, were desirous of domesticating ' Nathan ' on the Weimar boards. So Schiller undertook an adaptation, taking the task very seriously. Years before, while following up the theory of the drama in his strict and strenuous fashion, he had convinced himself that ' Nathan ' was a monstrosity; it was neither tragedy nor comedy nor tragi-comedy, and he was opposed to a mixture of types. In tragedy, so he had reasoned in his essay upon ' Naïve and Sentimental Poetry ', *raisonnement* is out of place; in comedy, pathos. Lessing had yielded to the ' whim ' of mixing the two. If, therefore, it was desired to make an acceptable stage-play out of ' Nathan ' it would be advisable to modify it in the direction of tragedy by reducing its *raisonnement*, or else to make it more like comedy by reducing its pathos. In other words, theory had given Schiller a point of view which is not the modern point of view. To-day no one, unless it were a pedant, would be disposed to criticize Lessing, because, toward the end of his days, out of the fullness of his heart and following the impulse that was in him, he for once threw his own theories to the winds and wrote a dramatic masterpiece of its own peculiar kind. The very fact that it is unique is for us a part of its merit.

But now, as was pointed out in a preceding chapter, the effect of Schiller's occupation with the drama at Weimar was to weaken his reverence for theory and to convince him of the importance of ' keeping the type-idea flexible in one's mind '. So when he came to adapt ' Nathan ' for the stage he proceeded much less radically than one might expect from his previous utterances. The tendency of the play was left intact, but many changes were made in the interest of brevity, simplicity and rapidity of movement. To these no one can seriously object, since Lessing's text is too long for an evening in the theater, as the matter was regarded in those pre-Wagnerian days. Not so readily to be approved are certain other changes which amount to a retouching of some of the portraits with which Schiller was dissatisfied,—notably that of the Sultan Saladin.

Of much greater interest than either of these adaptations is that of ' Macbeth ', which was made in January and February, 1800. This particular tragedy of Shakspere had always been a favorite with Schiller, and its influence is discernible in some of his plays, especially in ' Wallenstein '. It was only natural, therefore, at a time when Goethe and Schiller were reaching out in every direction for the enrichment of their theatrical repertory, that the staging of ' Macbeth ' should appear as a consummation devoutly to be wished. There were already German versions which had been used at various theaters, but they were wretched travesties of Shakspere. In setting out to make a new and better one, Schiller took as the basis of his operations the translations of Wieland and of Eschenburg, following now the one and now the other. When he was half through with his labor he procured the English text and used it thereafter as a corrective. He added, subtracted and rearranged at will, and converted Shakspere's prose into verse. The result is a decidedly Schilleresque ' Macbeth ', the merit of which has been debated to this day. The Romanticists, with A. W. Schlegel at their head, were disgusted with it and did not hide their emotions. Others have defended it through thick and thin. The questions involved are too far-reaching to be discussed here, but it may at least be remarked that there is no ground for a severely unfavorable judgment of Schiller's work. It is in no sense a translation and is not to be judged as a literary performance at all, but as a stage-play. As such it served its purpose very well; it made Shakspere acceptable at Weimar in the only way then possible under the circumstances. And it helped bring Shakspere into favor elsewhere. The Schillerized 'Macbeth' may be regarded as a sort of necessary transition-stage between the gross travesties of an earlier time and the more faithful presentations that were to come.

With respect to 'Turandot' a few words must suffice. This again grew out of the laudable desire of the duumvirs to acclimate in Weimar dramatic productions that had pleased the public in other climes. Gozzi's so-called *fiabe* belonged to this class. They had had a great though short-lived vogue at Venice, and this had led to a German translation in prose by a man named Werthes. What Schiller did was to turn the prose of Werthes into pentameters of the style that he had made peculiarly his own. He seems not to have looked at the Italian text at all, and indeed it could have been of little use to him. As one would expect, he made an attempt to give some poetic weight to the fantastic trifle, but it was a thankless undertaking, albeit good Italian critics have praised his 'Turandot' as far superior to the original. The comic-opera subject, for such it really is, was not adapted to Schiller's vein. His 'Turandot' is distinctly stiff and operose. It had a short run at two or three theaters, where, as at Weimar, it excited a small interest on account of the riddles and the Chinese 'business', and then it was quietly consigned to the limbo of things that were.

The remaining adaptations made by Schiller were from the French, a language which he knew better than any other except his own. The Duke of Weimar, and with him a considerable portion of the Weimar public, had retained from early education a strong predilection for the French drama, both in comedy and in the *haute tragédie*. It was thus a cause of joy in court circles when it became known, in the autumn of 1799, that Goethe had so far overcome his early anti-Gallic prejudices as to have undertaken a translation for the stage of Voltaire's ' Mahomet '. To this enterprise, however, he was moved not so much by any change of heart, or by poetic sympathy, as by a desire to improve the style of the Weimar actors,—to teach them ideality and self-abnegation. With this purpose Schiller was in hearty accord, as can be seen from his verses ' To Goethe ', written in January, 1800, in which he set forth his dramatic confession of faith. The Frenchman, he declared with unction, could by no means serve them as a model; there must be no bringing back of the old fetters. The Germans had advanced to a new era, and demanded now a faithful picture of nature. Nevertheless their histrionic art was in a backward condition, lacking in ideality and distinction. Wherefore the French tragedy was to be welcomed as a ' guide to the better '. It was to come ' like a departed spirit and purify the desecrated stage into a worthy seat of the ancient Melpomene '.

The result of this new *rapprochement* was that Schiller began to take a more lively interest in the French drama, and out of this interest grew presently his translations of two of Picard's comedies, ' Médiocre et Rampant ' and ' Encore des Ménechmes '. In both he took his task very lightly. Picard's alexandrines, in ' Médiocre et Rampant ', were converted into German prose, and the play was christened ' The

Parasite '. In the case of the other, renamed ' The
Nephew as Uncle ', the original was in prose and
Schiller merely made a free translation. These enterprises were little more than hackwork, which had its
suitable reward of brief popularity. Of an entirely
different character is the version of Racine's ' Phèdre ',
which, as we have seen, was finished a few weeks
before Schiller's death. Here we have for the first
time what can properly be called a poetic translation.
To a large extent Schiller's version is a line-for-line
rendering of the French alexandrines into German
pentameters,—a thing by no means easy to do.
' Phedra ' is by far the best specimen we have of
Schiller's powers as a translator.

CHAPTER XXII

The Verdict of Posterity

Alles was der Dichter geben kann ist seine Individualität ; diese musz also wert sein, vor Welt und Nachwelt aufgestellt zu werden.—*Review of Bürger, 1791.*

RATHER more than in other countries it is the fashion in Germany to regard literature under a national aspect, and to judge of writers not so much according to their power of titillating a fastidious literary taste as according to the degree in which they have entered into and affected the intellectual life of the people at large. Looked at from this point of view, Schiller well deserves the name of a national poet; indeed it would be hard to find another modern man who deserves it better. Critics there have always been to find fault with this and that, yet he remains, after a century, the most truly popular of German poets; not the most admired by the literary class, or by the outside world, but the most beloved in his own country. Most Germans have a different feeling for Schiller from that which they cherish for any other of their great writers.

For this his idealized personality is largely responsible. He is habitually thought of as an exceptionally noble and lofty character; as a man more singly and more strenuously devoted than most men to those starry ideals of truth, beauty and freedom, to which in the abstract all acknowledge fealty. His memory was early invested with a sort of halo, as of secular sainthood, for which, when one soberly reviews the facts of his career, there seems at first but little warrant. Many another man has been no less serious in his philosophizing, no less conscientious in his artistic performance. There is nothing heroic in the story of his life, unless it were his battle with disease; and this might have been managed more wisely, if not more bravely. And yet the halo is not altogether factitious. Many who knew him in his later years have borne witness to his spiritualized expression and the fine dignity of his presence. He gave the impression of an eminent personage whose "soul was like a star and dwelt apart". Withal he was a pattern of the homely virtues; an affectionate husband and father and a loyal friend. There was no dissonance between his life and his poetry. On hearing of his death, the sculptor Dannecker wrote:

The godlike man stands continually before my eyes. I will make him life-like. Schiller must live in sculpture as a colossal form. I intend an apotheosis. . . . The king was lately in my studio, and when he saw Schiller so large he said: 'Zounds! But why so large?' I answered: 'Majesty, Schiller must be thus large; the Suabian must make a monument to the Suabian.' Said the king: 'You must have been a good friend of his.' I answered: 'Yes, Majesty, from my youth up. I occupy myself with him daily, working at the colossal bust. It costs trouble, but it gives me joy, because the colossal image will make an indescribable impression.'

But it was not only his friends who were thus affected by his personality. Madame de Staël said of him in her famous book on Germany, which was published in 1813:

Schiller was as admirable for his virtues as for his talents. Conscience was his muse. . . . He loved poetry, the dramatic art, history, literature, for their own sake. Had he been resolved not to publish his works, he would have bestowed the same care upon them. . . . In his youth he had been guilty of some vagaries of fancy, but with the strength of manhood he acquired that exalted purity which springs from great thoughts. He never had anything to do with the vulgar feelings. He lived, spoke and acted as if bad people did not exist; and when he portrayed them in his works, it was with more exaggeration and less depth than if he had known them. The bad presented themselves to his mind as an obstacle, as a physical scourge.

In this characterization, truth to tell, there is a considerable element of pure moonshine, as any one may convince himself who will read through Schiller's letters, more especially those written during the lifetime of the *Horen*. He had in him quite enough of the fighter and of the schemer, and it came out in human ways. Moreover he wrote constantly for immediate publication, under the goad of strong necessity; what he might have done if this necessity had not existed, no man, or woman, can tell. Still, Madame de Staël's portrait is highly interesting, as the first that went out to the world at large, and as evidence of the impression produced by Schiller in his later years even upon those who were under no peculiar temptation to idealize him.

Much more influential in shaping the sentiment of posterity was Goethe's magnificent 'Epilogue', dating from the year 1815. In this poem the essential lineaments of Schiller's character, as seen through the

soothing but not yet obscuring vista of ten years by
the wisest of those who knew him well, were fixed for
all time.   He was here described as one who had
'mounted to the highest heights, closely akin to all
that we esteem'; and posterity was besought to give
him that which life had denied.   Henceforth it was
possible only for purblind partisanship to think otherwise than nobly of a man concerning whom a Goethe
could say such words as these:

> Denn er war unser.   Mag das stolze Wort
> Den lauten Schmerz gewaltig übertönen.
> Er mochte sich bei uns im sichern Port,
> Nach wildem Sturm, zum Dauernden gewöhnen.
> Indessen schritt sein Geist gewaltig fort
> Ins Ewige des Guten, Wahren, Schönen ;
> Und hinter ihm, in wesenlosem Scheine,
> Lag was uns alle bändigt, das Gemeine.[1]

Nevertheless the purblind partisanship was already
beginning its campaign, though less against Schiller's
character than against his art; and this campaign soon
led to a terrific logomachy, which was destined to
convulse the German empire of the air for something
like two generations.   The controversy related to the
comparative merit of Goethe and Schiller as men and

[1] The meaning of the famous verses, divested perforce of much of
their German music, may be expressed thus :

> For he was ours.   So let the note of pride
> Hush into silence all the mourner's ruth ;
> In our safe harbor he was fain to bide
> And build for aye, after the storm of youth.
> We saw his mighty spirit onward stride
> To eternal realms of Beauty and of Truth ;
> While far behind him lay phantasmally
> The vulgar things that fetter you and me.

as poets. In general the Romantic school was hostile to Schiller, partly for private reasons that had very little to do with critical theories. In his famous ' Lectures on Dramatic Art ', originally delivered at Vienna in 1808 and published a few years later, A. W. Schlegel dealt briefly with Schiller at the end of the course. What he said was not unmixed with just appreciation, but the lectures set a bad fashion in German criticism. Modern poetry was identified with Romantic poetry and Shakspere was held up as *the* Romantic poet. Not only his greatness, but his rubbish, his rodomontade, his quips and quibbles and buffoonery, were treated as if they belonged to a sacrosanct canon of dramatic art. From this the natural inference was that to be like Shakspere was to be great, and that no other kind of greatness was possible for the Romantic, or modern, poet. As for Schiller, he was treated by Schlegel with urbane condescension as a gifted playwright who had tried to imitate Shakspere and met with but limited success. The early plays were dismissed with a mere cry of pain, and the later ones were discussed very briefly and perfunctorily with respect to purely formal matters.

As already remarked, the lectures of Schlegel were sufficiently urbane in tone and gave no foretaste of that bitterness with which he subsequently attacked Schiller in some of his poems. What is here important to observe is that Schlegel, and the other Romanticists who took their cue from him, set the vogue of judging Goethe and Schiller according to their imagined resemblance to Shakspere. Certain catchwords and phrases, such as universality, objectivity, irony, and what not, were imported into the literature of discussion, and these concepts were used as absolute criteria by which to write Goethe up and Schiller down. This naturally provoked the many friends of Schiller, and they replied by assailing Goethe. His ' universality ' was decried as a lamentable weakness: it meant lack of character, of principle, of patriotism. His pleasing form was only the seductive veil of immorality and pococurantism. And so the controversy raged, becoming at last, in some cases, mere blind fury. One who would like to get a vivid impression of the state of German criticism at this time, and of the extent to which partisanship could obfuscate the vision of an intelligent and well-meaning man, should read the third volume of Wolfgang Menzel's ' German Literature ', published in 1828. Menzel's treatment of Goethe is one long diatribe of misrepresentation, becoming at times a mere ululation of malignant hatred. Schiller, on the other hand, is exalted to the skies as the peerless representative of all that is noble in human nature and in poetry.

This fierce old battle of pen and ink, which was really a disgrace to German civilization, is still capable of affording, for the passionate fury and wrong-headedness of it, a modicum of amusement to the retrospective scholar of to-day. And it amused Goethe, who as usual found the sane point of view. Said he to Eckermann, one day in the year 1825: ' These twenty years the public has been contending as to which is the greater, Schiller or I ; they ought rather to be glad that they have a brace of such fellows to quarrel about.' In all his talks with Eckermann Goethe remained steadfastly

faithful to the memory of his friend, giving no comfort
to those who were using his own name as a bludgeon
wherewith to batter the prestige of Schiller. 'Schiller',
said he, 'could do nothing that did not turn out greater
than the best work of these moderns. Yes, even when
he cut his finger-nails he was greater than these gentlemen.' He freely criticized this and that in particular
plays, observing that there was 'something violent' in
Schiller's methods; he even committed himself to the
dubious conjecture that certain weak passages might
be due to physical exhaustion or to the unwholesome
stimulation of flagging energies. But the ever recurring
burden of his discourse was—*Er war ein prächtiger
Mensch.*

The death of Goethe, in 1832, brought to an end
conspicuously the epoch of the Weimarian poets.
Indeed it had ended virtually long before, but it was
not until Goethe too had become a memory that its
significance was fully realized. The Germans now
saw, and the rest of the world saw too, that they had
a classical literature which really counted. They
began to speak of 'our classics', and to compare and
contrast them with the newest literary manifestations.
Writers of every kind,—philosophers, literary critics
and historians, poets, novelists, journalists, politicians
and agitators,—had now to adjust themselves mentally
to Goethe and Schiller and what they stood for, or
were supposed to stand for. And so the river of literature, which in our day has become a great Amazon,
commenced flowing in a small, but steady and ever
widening stream. Hoffmeister's monumental biography
of Schiller, in five volumes, appeared between 1833

and 1842, and in the ensuing years there came a procession of less thorough biographers, writing more for the unlearned public. The criticism of him as a poet and a dramatist was still subordinated, in a large degree, to the consideration of him as the prophet of ideas which were to be examined with reference to their ethical and moral value, or to the degree of their applicability to then existing conditions.

The period now under consideration is, roughly speaking, the period from the beginning of acute political agitation, about 1830, to the realization of national unity in 1871. During the first part of this era academic philosophy was still largely under the influence of Hegel, but the reaction had set in and was destined to grow into a widespread distrust of all speculative philosophy. Not to explain and justify the existing world by the arachnean method of spinning a *Weltanschauung* out of one's own interior, but to make the world different,—was the new watchword. It was widely felt that Germans had speculated and theorized and dreamed too much; it was time to assert their strength in practical affairs. Men's minds began to be engaged with questions of political reform and social regeneration. It was no longer the ideal, the good, the beautiful and the true, that pressed for consideration, but constitutional government, the freedom of the press, popular representation and, above all, German unity. But chaos seemed to reign in the intellectual sphere. Young Germany, so called, began a noisy agitation which had no definite goal in view, but was characterized by a fierce hostility to existing forms in church and state,—to princes, aristocrats, priests,

Christian marriage and conventional morality. And there were other agitations, doctrines, theories and tendencies innumerable. Germany had become, to revive a comparison then much in vogue, an irresolute Hamlet, sicklied o'er with the pale cast of thought. Talk, talk, everywhere, and nowhere the strong hand of constructive statesmanship. And so came the abortive revolution of 1848, with its ensuing disgusts, until finally the man of destiny appeared and conducted affairs, by way of Sadowa and Sedan, to the new German Empire.

Now in that era of the doctrinaires, of the philosophical break-up and of seething political passions, it was but natural that those who thought of Schiller at all thought not so much of the dramatic artist as of the prophet whose sentiments could be quoted for present edification or reproof. The men of the middle part of the century judged him generally from the partisan standpoint of their own political, philosophical and religious prejudices. This is true not only of the forgotten criticasters, but of the most famous, the most widely read and the most authoritative literary historians of the time, such as Gervinus and Vilmar. And in the domain of pure dramatic criticism, or what purported to be such, there was quite too much of that captious dogmatism which had come down from the Romanticists and which had its origin, as we have seen, in the habit of regarding Shakspere, not as the great dramatist of a nation and an epoch, but as *the* universal modern poet, whose methods and peculiarities must be canonical for everybody.[1]   Instead of looking

[1] The disparagement of Schiller on account of his unlikeness to Shak-

fairly and squarely at Schiller's plays and endeavoring to understand and interpret them as the expression of the life of a past epoch, and of an artistic individuality which had its own right to be and to grow in its own way, the dogmatic critics treated him, in many cases, *de haut en bas*, as if they knew everything better than he. Men who would have thought it a little absurd to assail Mont Blanc for not being Chimborazo did not scruple to gird at Schiller for not being something else than that which his nature made him. And so it was that the great dramatic poet of the nation, whose plays were daily proving their vitality in scores of theaters and were giving pleasure to millions of readers, was treated oftentimes with incredible severity by pompous Rhadamanthine critics who did not see that they were thereby making themselves and their critical pretensions slightly ridiculous.

Of course this line of remark is not meant to imply that the works of anybody should have been regarded as above criticism because they were popular and had become classical. What is intended is simply to characterize a past critical epoch which, in dealing with imaginative literature, cared a little too much for abstract dogmas and theoretical standpoints; which, instead of trying to enter humanly into the spirit of an author and to judge him according to the nature of his

spere was carried to almost absurd lengths in the "Shakespeare-Studien" of Otto Ludwig. One of Ludwig's critiques, written about 1858, begins thus: "Ich kenne keine poetische, namentlich keine dramatische Gestalt, die in ihrem Entwurfe so zufällig, so krankhaft individuell, in ihrer Ausführung so unwahr wäre, als Schiller's Wallenstein; keine, die mit ihren eignen Voraussetzungen so im Streite läge, keine, die sich molluskenhafter der Willkür des Dichters fügte."

intentions and his success in carrying them out, preferred to lay him on a bed of Procrustes and hack at
him with the axe of philosophy. Literature, like
language, goes on its way with very little tenderness
for theories and dogmas. That which meets the needs
of human nature lives and after a while its 'faults' are
forgotten; or mayhap they come to be regarded as
merits, and the rules are extended to include the new
case. Not to have seen this quite clearly enough was
a weakness of the vigorous and rigorous German critics
of half a century ago. And yet, some of them did see
it dimly now and then. Reference was made a moment
ago to Gervinus,—certainly one of the most learned,
thoughtful and generally meritorious of German literary
historians,—and it was implied that he too was affected
by the bias of his age. It is thus a pleasure to quote
a passage from him which shows him in a different
light. It is from the fifth volume of his 'National-
Litteratur der Deutschen', published in 1842:

If one insists on condemning 'Wallenstein' as a whole because
one must reject the episode (of Max and Thekla), then one blinds
oneself deliberately to great merits on account of small faults.
The historical critic feels clearly here the disadvantage in which
a living or recently deceased writer is placed, in comparison
with an earlier one whose entire individuality has receded into
the distance and is beyond the strife of the passions. Soon after
Shakspere's death there was the same quarrel about him that
we are having now about Schiller. To-day that which was imputed to him as vice is so interblended with his virtues that it is
regarded as trivial to waste a serious word upon it. So it may
be one day with our poets; and then people will look at the
faults in Schiller's compositions from other points of view. We
shall then manage to get along with what was done and accepted
long ago, and content ourselves with explaining it; whereas

now, at the beginning of its course, though we cannot unmake it, we think perhaps to prevent its acceptance and deprive it of immortality by rejecting it unexplained.

Here is certainly a highly interesting modern case of the fulfillment of prophecy.

Another phase of the Schiller-question which was much discussed in the middle portion of the nineteenth century was his æsthetic idealism. While his plays carry one into the rushing currents of life, and while his ballads are poems of action, it was possible to extract from his ' Letters on Æsthetic Education ' and from some of his poems, notably ' The Ideal and Life ', what seemed to be a message of æsthetic quietism; a message which appeared to say that the attainment of inward peace, freedom and harmony was the highest goal of human effort. Naturally enough the individualism and æstheticism of the Weimarian poets were not welcome doctrine to an excited genera- tion that had caught a glimpse of an immense work to be done for the fatherland. The ever increasing pressure of social emotions made it seem a selfish and unmanly thing to be so concerned about one's own spiritual equipoise. This feeling finds frequent expres- sion in the literature of the time; and so much was it harped on, and so feebly were the countervailing con- siderations presented, that many people, both in Germany and outside of it, got into their heads a radically wrong conception of the Weimarian Dioscuri; a conception which quite forgot that both of them, all their lives long, were very strenuous workers, strongly possessed by the social sentiment. And even those who were too wise to be thus completely misled as to the significance and the value of the Weimarian legacy could not help feeling that for the present, at least, it were better regarded as a dead issue. One can understand the sentiment with which Gervinus closed his great history of the national literature: ' The rival contest of the arts is finished. Now we should set before us the other mark, which no archer among us has yet hit, and see if peradventure Apollo will grant us here too the renown that he did not refuse us there.'

But while the critics and doctrinaires were contending thus variously about the merits of Schiller, his name endeared itself more and more to the many who were chafing under the régime of princely absolutism and were longing for a freer Germany. They idealized him as the poet of liberty,—chiefly, it would seem, on account of ' William Tell ', or, among radical and boisterous youth, on account of ' The Robbers '; for the ' freedom ' of his poems is a metaphysical rather than a political concept. In the year 1844 Freiligrath committed himself definitively to the cause of ' the people ', as he understood it, which proved to be the cause of the Red Republicans. In announcing his conversion he wrote a poem called ' Good Morning ', the last stanza of which, done into rough English rime, runs thus:

> Good morning then ! Behold a freeman here,
> Walking henceforward in the people's ways ;
> For with the people is the poet's sphere,—
> 'Tis thus I read my Schiller nowadays.[1]

> [1] Guten Morgen denn ! Frei werd' ich stehen
> Für das Volk und mit ihm in der Zeit ;
> Mit dem Volke soll der Dichter gehen,—
> So les' ich meinen Schiller heut.

But he read him quite wrongly. For a much saner view of this question one should go back to honest Eckermann, who reports Goethe as saying to him in 1824: 'Schiller, who, between ourselves, was much more of an aristocrat than I, has the remarkable fortune to count as a particular friend of the people.' This is exactly right. Neither man had in him much of the stuff that tribunes of the people are made of, but Schiller had less of it than Goethe. His whole temper was that of an aristocrat. Had he lived in the forties of the nineteenth century, we may be very sure that he would have scented a return of the French Terror, and would have spoken, if at all, as an arch-conservative.

And really there is but cold comfort in 'William Tell' for those who, in the revolutionary epoch, were clamoring against princes as such. The play is in no sense anti-monarchical, nor is it either German or un-German, but simply human. As a curious illustration of the unreason that men could once be guilty of through their habit of regarding Schiller as a political poet, it is worth while to quote a passage from Vilmar, whose history of German literature enjoyed great popularity half a century ago. Speaking of 'William Tell', Vilmar has this to say:

For the rest it is remarkable that Schiller's contemporaries and a large part of posterity looked upon 'Tell' as a peculiarly German play, and that too in respect of its subject-matter. They conceived it as a glorification of German deeds and held it up to admiration as a sort of symbol of German sentiment, in opposition to the French policy of subjugation in 1806–1813 ; the fact being that Tell's deed, as it appears in the saga and in Schiller's drama, represents and glorifies the unfortunate and in part criminal detachment of Switzerland from the German Empire.

Napoleon was in those days the only one who saw this and expressed his amazement that Germans could thus praise such a thoroughly anti-German play as a drama glorifying the German fatherland.

It is sufficient to remark, if the matter were of any importance, that the Swiss revolution, as portrayed by Schiller, is not directed against the Empire, but against the brutes sent out by the Hapsburg dynasty in pursuance of a policy of dynastic aggrandizement. In numerous passages it is brought out that the very thing the conspirators are concerned about is to preserve their ancient *Reichsunmittelbarkeit*. All that they wish is to get back and perpetuate the liberties they have until lately enjoyed *under the Empire*. 'Freedom' nowhere means 'independence', and there is no vista of independence at the end of the play.

The year 1859 was marked by a prodigious ebullition of Schiller enthusiasm. While the hundredth birthday of Goethe had passed, ten years before, with but little notice, that of Schiller was made the occasion of a demonstration the like of which the modern world has hardly seen made in honor of any other poet whatsoever. In every part of Germany, and not in Germany only but in Austria, Switzerland, England and the New World, the memory of Schiller was honored in speech and song, in the unveiling of monuments, and in commemorative writings large and small. It was as if the entire German-speaking world, still dreaming the lately baffled dream of national unity, had turned to him as the noblest of the spiritual ties that bind Germans together. In the mass of literature dating from that time of flood-tide in the veneration of

Schiller, one finds a good deal that is interesting in its own way, for one reason or another, but not very much that is highly valuable for illuminative criticism of Schiller. The best of the biographies are those of Palleske and Scherr; of the minor tributes the famous address of Jacob Grimm in the Berlin Academy. The spirit of the time was not favorable to a calm, objective view, but it is in itself a fact of immense significance that a great and critical, doctrine-ridden and passion-distracted people should have united in honoring a poet as Schiller was honored by the Germans in the year 1859.

A new epoch may be dated from about 1871,—the epoch of the historical critics and philologers. With the realization of national unity the vista of the past rapidly cleared up and new points of view were gained. It was as if a height had been won from which it was possible to see over the dust and smoke of the past three decades. The pride of the new-born nation now looked back with quickened interest to the great writers of the eighteenth century, but with the feeling that they had done enough for the glory of the fatherland in simply being great writers. It was time to see them as they were, without writing them up or down, according to their supposed attitude toward questions which were not their questions. It was in 1874 that Herman Grimm remarked, in a lecture at Berlin, that henceforth there was to be a science called Goethe. All the world knows how the prediction has been fulfilled. During the last two decades the science called Goethe has marched bravely on, enlisting a small army of workers, creating a vast jungle of literature,—*selva*

selvaggia ed aspra e forte,—and making friends and
enemies.   And the science called Schiller is like unto
it, only not quite so big.

To attempt any sort of review or conspectus of all
this Alexandrian activity would be, for the purposes of
this book, a futile undertaking; it would lead off into an
interminable and dry bibliography, which in the end
would convey little instruction as to Schiller's real popularity. It would show that he is very extensively studied
and commented on by the academic class, which in Germany constitutes by itself an enormous public. It would
also show that good judges, of apparently equal com-
petence, still think very differently of the general merit
of his art and are very differently affected by particular works.   This is only to reiterate the familiar truth
that literary criticism has not become, does not tend
to become, an exact science. The feeling one has for
poetry, or the effect produced upon one by a particular
artistic individuality, is the result of a hundred subtle
influences that combine to give each one of us his
private form and range of susceptibility; and this susceptibility itself varies with the *Zeitgeist* and with the
age and nerve-state of the individual. The mere
craving for novelty makes itself felt; so that that which
once gave pleasure gives it no longer, or gives it in a
lower degree. There is disputing about tastes, but
there is no settling of the dispute. For A to give
logical reasons why B should admire that which, as a
matter of fact, B does not admire, or vice versa, is
always a tempting, and in the long run a useful,
form of literary exertion; only one must not expect B
to be convinced or to mend his ways immediately.

Beyond a doubt there have been strong influences at work in Germany, during the past two decades, which are unfavorable to Schiller's prestige. Now and then some cocksure champion of some *nova fede* announces that the day of poetic idealism is past. There have always been such voices, and a few years ago they were perhaps a little more numerous and more shrill than usual. Of late, however, they have seemed to grow fainter, and there are already signs of the idealistic reaction that is sure to come. Meanwhile the day of Schiller does not pass and is not likely to pass. The isms come and go, but his plays retain their popularity, because they appeal to sentiments that are deeply rooted in the affections of an immense portion of the German people who care but little for the doctrines of the doctrinaire. And so it will continue to be. To talk of returning to Schiller, or to hold up his style and technique as models for imitation, is foolish. Of such imitation, which could lead to nothing but the ossification of the German drama, there has been quite enough in the past. To imitate his spirit is to ' keep the type-idea flexible in one's mind ' and reach out continually after that which is new, elevating and adapted to the present need. This is the best form of respect to his memory.

Unquestionably Schiller lacked the supreme qualities that go to the making of a great world-poet. With all his cosmopolitanism he was a German of the Germans. For them his work has a meaning and an importance which it cannot have for others, because he is the organ-voice of their ethnic instincts and idealisms. Think of a sentiment that Germans love, and you shall find it, if you search, expressed in sonorous verse in some poem or play of Schiller. The schools and the theaters keep his name steadily before the great public, while the intellectual classes, as Gervinus foresaw, are coming to dwell less on the great qualities that he lacked than on the great qualities that he possessed. As to the present attitude of sober German thought, nothing could possibly be more illuminative than the following words of Otto Brahm:

As a student I was a Schiller-hater. I make this preliminary confession not because I attach personal importance to it, but because, on the contrary, I think I see in my attitude one that is typical for our time. Every one of us, it seems to me, travels this road : After a period of early veneration, which is awakened in us by tradition and by the earliest literary impressions of youth, there comes, as a reaction against an uncritical overestimate, and under the influence of changed ideals of art, a defection from Schiller, which parades itself in a one-sided and unhistorical emphasis of his weak points. Then gradually this negative attitude corrects itself to a positive one, and we recognize the folly of that young-and-verdant bumptiousness which would think of consigning the greatest of German dramatists to the realms of the dead. And now at last, after it has passed through doubt, our enthusiasm is imperishable ; with clear eye we look up to the greatness of the man, and to the splendid model for all intellectual work which is exhibited in that life of passionate striving for the ideal.

THE END

APPENDIX

A Survey of Schiller Literature

THE mass of literature pertaining to Schiller has now grown so great that an exhaustive bibliography would fill a good-sized volume. All that can be attempted here is a selection of the more important works. The fullest bibliography thus far is that contained in the fifth volume of Goedeke's Grundrisz zur Geschichte der deutschen Dichtung, 2nd edition, Dresden, 1893. Annual reviews of Schiller literature appear in the Jahresberichte für neuere deutsche Litteraturgeschichte and in the Berichte des Freien Deutschen Hochstiftes. Valuable especially for its English titles is the bibliography compiled by John P. Anderson for Nevinson's Life of Schiller, London, 1889.

EDITIONS

During the lifetime of Schiller his writings were printed in different forms by different publishers, and owing to the absence of copyright unauthorized reprints were numerous. He himself undertook no complete and final redaction of all his works, though in his later years he revised and arranged a selection of his poems. 'Don Carlos' and some of the prose writings also underwent revision at the hands of their author.

The first edition calling itself complete was that of Körner, which was published in 1812–15, in twelve volumes, by Cotta of Stuttgart. Körner divided the poems into three periods, —a division which has since been extensively copied. Körner's edition became the basis of the later Cotta editions (down to 1868), which were reprinted in various forms and degrees of completeness, but without important changes or additions. With the expiration of Cotta's monopoly and the opening of the philological era, the works of Schiller began to be deemed worthy of the same scrupulous editorial care that had long been bestowed on the Greek and Latin classics. The mid-century researches of Hoffmeister and others, particularly Hoffmeister's Supplemente zu Schillers Werken, 1840–1, had brought to light much new material not usually printed with the works of Schiller, and the received text, even of the more important works, was known to be more or less faulty and uncertain. To meet the new demand a historico-critical edition was undertaken by Goedeke, with the assistance of several sub-editors. The result was Schillers Sämmtliche Schriften, Historisch-kritische Ausgabe, 15 vols., Cotta, Stuttgart, 1868–76. This edition aimed at completeness, arranged the works chronologically and went deeply into the matter of variant readings. It is still indispensable to the scholar, though not free from pedantries.

Contemporaneous with this work of critical scholarship was the cheaper and more popular edition of Boxberger and Malt-zahn, published by Hempel in Berlin—Schillers Werke, nach den vorzüglichsten Quellen revidierte Ausgabe, 16 parts in 6 vols., 1868–74,—which, though unsightly, is valuable for its introductions and notes. In more recent years several good editions have appeared, the most noteworthy being (1) that of Boxberger and Birlinger, published as a part of Kürschner's Deutsche National-Litteratur, 12 vols., Stuttgart, 1882–91; (2) that of L. Bellermann, Kritisch durchgesehene und erläuterte Ausgabe, 14 vols., Leipzig, 1895 ff., and (3) the latest of the critical Cotta editions, completed in 16 vols. in 1894.

The dramatic fragments have been twice edited by Kett-ner, Schillers Dramatischer Nachlasz nach den Handschriften herausgegeben, Weimar, 1895, and Schillers Dramatische Entwürfe und Fragmente aus dem Nachlasz zusammengestellt, Stuttgart, 1899. The Xenia have recently been edited by Schmidt and Suphan, Xenien 1796, nach den Handschriften des Goethe-Schiller Archivs herausgegeben, Weimar, 1893.

As is well known the later plays of Schiller, to a certain extent also some of his prose writings, are familiar school classics wherever German is studied. The school editions, many of them meritorious works of scholarship, are very numerous. They are not mentioned here because a mere list of names and dates would be of no use, while a selection with discriminative or critical comment would be a difficult and invidious task to which the compiler of this survey has no inclination. Any of the scholarly editions published in recent years, in Germany, the United States or England, will usually be found to contain a sufficient bibliography of the particular work under consideration.

LETTERS AND MEMOIRS

It was the opinion of Goethe that Schiller's style was at its best in his letters (see Eckermann's Gespräche, 14. April, 1824). Letters of Schiller, including some forged ones to Karl Moser, began to get into print in the early years of the nineteenth century, and as interest increased the publications became exceedingly numerous (see the extensive bibliography in Goedeke's Grundrisz, V. 98 ff.). So far as the authentic letters of Schiller himself are concerned, these separate publications have now been superseded by the admirable work of F. Jonas, Schillers Briefe, Kritische Gesamtausgabe, 7 vols., Stuttgart, 1892 ff. It only remains, therefore, to make note of the more important publications that contain correspondence, or reminiscences having a biographical value. They are as follows:

Briefwechsel zwischen Schiller und Goethe, mit einer Einleitung von F. Muncker, Stuttgart, 1893. The correspondence is also to be had, edited by Vollmer, in Cotta's Bibliothek der Weltlitteratur. It was first published in 1828–9 in 6 vols.

Briefwechsel zwischen Schiller und Wilhelm von Humboldt, dritte vermehrte Ausgabe mit Anmerkungen von A. Leitzmann, Stuttgart, 1900. First published in 1830, with a Vorerinnerung by Von Humboldt.

Schillers Briefwechsel mit Körner, herausgegeben von K. Goedeke, Leipzig, 1874 ; also a later edition by L. Geiger, Stuttgart, 1893. The correspondence was first published in 1847 and soon after translated into English by Simpson, 3 vols., London, 1849.

Schiller und Lotte, dritte, den ganzen Briefwechsel umfassende Ausgabe, von W. Fielitz, Stuttgart, 1879 ; later edition, also by Fielitz, 1893. First published in 1856.

Karl Augusts erstes Anknüpfen mit Schiller, Stuttgart, 1857, edited by Schiller's daughter, Emilie von Gleichen.

Schillers Beziehungen zu Eltern, Geschwistern und der Familie von Wolzogen, herausgegeben von A. von Wolzogen, Stuttgart, 1859.

Charlotte von Schiller und ihre Freunde, herausgegeben von L. Urlichs, 3 vols., Stuttgart, 1860–5.

Briefwechsel zwischen Schiller und Iffland, herausgegeben von F. Dingelstedt, Stuttgart, 1863.

Briefwechsel zwischen Schiller und seiner Schwester Christophine, herausgegeben von W. von Maltzahn, Leipzig, 1875.

Schillers Briefwechsel mit dem Herzog von Augustenburg, herausgegeben von Max Müller, Berlin, 1875.

Geschäftsbriefe Schillers, gesammelt, erläutert und herausgegeben von K. Goedeke, Leipzig, 1875.

Briefwechsel zwischen Schiller und Cotta, herausgegeben von W. Vollmer, Stuttgart, 1876.

To these may be added—here better than elsewhere :

Charlotte von Kalb und ihre Beziehungen zu Goethe und Schiller, von E. Köpke, Berlin, 1843, and The Diary, Reminiscences and Correspondence of Henry Crabbe Robinson, edited by Th. Sadler, London, 1869.

BIOGRAPHY

The first account of Schiller by a conscientious and competent writer was that by Körner, which accompanied his edition of 1812–15. This, however, was a mere sketch.

In 1825 Carlyle published his Life of Schiller at London, and a few years later the book was translated into German and supplied with an introduction by Goethe. It was based on very imperfect information, but was an inspiring work of genius nevertheless. It is now more valuable as a Carlyle document than as a Schiller-document.

In 1830 Karoline von Wolzogen, Schiller's sister-in-law, published her memoir of the poet, which is now to be had in Cotta's Bibliothek der Weltlitteratur. It contained a large number of authentic letters and was based upon an intimate personal acquaintance dating from the year 1787. For the earlier years data were furnished by friends and relatives. The little book has many excellencies, but the portrait of Schiller, as it came from the hands of the talented but aging Baroness, is a shade too idealistic and sentimental. Of his virile youth one gets hardly an inkling.

The year 1836 brought a valuable contribution to the knowledge of Schiller's youth in Schillers Flucht von Stuttgart, by Andreas Streicher.

From this time on the biographies are numerous. A mediocre one by Doering, first published in 1832, was often reprinted in subsequent years. Between 1838 and 1842 appeared Schillers Leben, Geistesentwickelung und Werke im Zusammenhang, von Karl Hoffmeister. This monumental work of scholarship, in five volumes, has been indispensable to later biographers, however they might differ with Hoffmeister in matters of critical estimate. Hoffmeister's learned work was made the basis of a more popular biography by H. Viehoff, which appeared first in 1846. A new and revised edition was published in 1875. Of the shorter and more popular biographies which appeared down to 1859, it may suffice to mention those by G. Schwab (1840) and J. W. Schäfer (1853). The sketch by Bulwer, which accompanied his translation of Schiller's poems, London, 1844, was based mainly on Hoffmeister and Schwab.

The great Schiller-festival of 1859 called forth a mass of literature of which the titles fill ten octavo pages in Goedeke's Grundrisz. Of the longer biographies dating from this period the most important are that by J. Scherr, Schiller und seine Zeit, Leipzig, 1859 (English translation by Elizabeth Mac-Lellan, Philadelphia, 1881), and that by E. Palleske, Schillers Leben und Werke, Berlin, 1858-9. Palleske's work, of which an English translation by Lady Wallace appeared in London in 1860, soon attained a remarkable popularity, which it still enjoys with some abatement. It is the work of a conscientious Schiller enthusiast, written with greath warmth of feeling and great fulness of biographical detail, but not strong on the critical side. A twelfth edition, somewhat popularized by H. Fischer, appeared in 1886, a fifteenth edition in 1900.

For some twenty years Palleske and Scherr held the field in Germany without serious competition, and then a new crop of biographies began to appear. That of H. Düntzer, Schillers Leben, mit 46 Illustrationen und 5 Beilagen, Leipzig, 1881 (English translation by Pinkerton, London, 1883), retold the familiar story in a style less attractive than that of Palleske, and without adding anything of great importance in the way of critical appreciation. The same may be said of the biography by C. Hepp, Leipzig, 1885.

Of an entirely different character are the contributions of Weltrich, Minor, and Brahm, which are essentially works of historico-critical interpretation. Unfortunately, however, they were begun on a scale of such magnitude, and with such an uncompromising respect for the infinitely little, that there is small prospect of their completion.

Of the work of Weltrich, Friedrich Schiller, Geschichte seines Lebens und Charakteristik seiner Werke, unter kritischem Nachweis der biographischen Quellen, the first installment appeared in 1885, the second in 1891, and the third (completing the first volume) in 1899.

The work of Minor, Schiller, sein Leben und seine Werke, of which two volumes appeared in 1890, ends with a discussion of 'Don Carlos'. More readable, but proportionally less thorough than either of these, is the work of Brahm, of which the second volume, first part, appeared in 1892, bringing the story down through Schiller's Kantian period.

The learnedly philological character of the works just mentioned, together with their incompleteness, left room enough for further attempts at a popular biography of Schiller. This demand has been met in recent years by Wychgram, whose well-written and handsomely illustrated Schiller, Leipzig, 1891, is worthy of high commendation; and also by the little book of Harnack, Berlin, 1898 (one of the 'Geisteshelden' series), which is admirable within the limits set. Of the short biographies in English the best are those of Boyesen, Goethe and Schiller, New York, 1882, and Sime, Schiller, London, 1882. That of Nevinson, London, 1889 (one of the 'Great Writers' series), contains, along with much sound criticism, a good deal that is rather too peremptory and unsympathetic.

CRITICISM

The following notes take no account of criticism contained in the general histories of German literature and philosophy, nor of the multitudinous articles, essays, reviews, programs and dissertations relating to particular works.

Plays.—The best treatise on the plays as a whole is that of Bellermann, Schillers Dramen, 2nd edition, 2 vols., Berlin, 1898–9.

Bellermann's point of view is that of a learned dramatic critic and expounder. He writes as a warm admirer of Schiller and is at his best when defending him against ill-grounded censures. Occasionally his friendly partisanship carries him a little too far.— A good discussion from the dramatic and histrionic point of view is contained in Bulthaupt, Dramaturgie des Schauspiels, 5th edition, Oldenburg, 1891.—The Studien zu Schillers Dramen, by W. Fielitz, Leipzig, 1876, are excellent, but relate only to ' Wallenstein ', ' Maria Stuart' and ' The Maid of Orleans '.—Suggestive and eminently readable is Werder, Vorlesungen über Wallenstein, Berlin, 1889.—Rather more valuable for facts than for criticism are the Schiller volumes of Düntzers Erläuterungen zu den deutschen Klassikern (beginning in 1876).—References to Schiller are numerous in Freytag, Die Technik des Dramas (first edition in 1859), and also in the Shakespeare-Studien of Otto Ludwig (edited by Heyderich, 1872).—On the work of Schiller as translator and adapter consult A. Köster, Schiller als Dramaturg, Berlin, 1891.—An up-to-date French treatise on the early plays is that of Kontz, Les drames de la jeunesse de Schiller, Paris, 1899.

Poems.—Viehoff, Schillers Gedichte erläutert, und auf ihre Veranlassungen, Quellen und Vorbilder zurückgeführt, 7th edition, Stuttgart, 1895.—Hauff, Schillerstudien, Stuttgart, 1880.— Philippi, Schillers Lyrische Gedankendichtung in ihrem ideellen Zusammenhange beleuchtet, Augsburg, 1888.—Helene Lange, Schillers Philosophische Gedichte, sechs Vorträge, Berlin, 1887. —Schiller als Lyrischer Dichter in Düntzers Erläuterungen.— Considerable commentary is contained in The Poems and Ballads of Schiller translated by Sir Edward Bulwer Lytton, 1st edition, London, 1844.—On the Xenia consult, in addition to the edition by Schmidt and Suphan, Boas, Schiller und Goethe im Xenienkampf, Stuttgart, 1851.

Historical Writings.—Tomaschek, Schiller in seinem Verhältnisse zur Wissenschaft ; von der kaiserlichen Akademie der Wissenschaften zu Wien gekrönte Preisschrift, Wien, 1862.—Janssen, Schiller als Historiker, 2nd edition, Freiburg, 1879.—Ueberweg, Schiller als Historiker und Philosoph, Leipzig, 1884 (written, however, in 1859 in competition for the prize of the Vienna Academy, which was won by Tomaschek).

Philosophical Writings.—Harnack, Die klassische Aesthetik der Deutschen, Würdigung der kunsttheoretischen Arbeiten Schillers, Goethes und ihrer Freunde, Leipzig, 1892.—Berger, K. (pseudonym for Adolf Wechssler), Die Entwickelung von Schillers Aesthetik, Weimar, 1894.—Kühnemann, Die Kantischen Studien Schillers und die Komposition des 'Wallenstein', Marburg, 1889.—Gneisse, Schillers Lehre von der aesthetischen Wahrnehmung, Berlin, 1893. Zimmermann, Schiller als Denker, 1859.—The works of Tomaschek and Ueberweg (see above under 'Historical Writings') deal also with Schiller as a philosophic thinker.

Miscellaneous.—Fischer, Schiller-Schriften, Heidelberg, 1891 (revised edition of earlier studies comprising Schillers Jugend- und Wanderjahre in Selbstbekenntnissen, Schiller als Komiker, and Schiller als Philosoph).—Belling, Die Metrik Schillers, Breslau, 1883.—Rudolph, Schiller-Lexikon, Erläuterndes Wörterbuch zu Schillers Dichterwerken, 2 vols., Berlin, 1890. — Rieger, Schillers Verhältnis zur französischen Revolution, Wien, 1885. —Pietsch, Schiller als Kritiker, Königsberg, 1898.—Mauerhof, Schiller und Heinrich von Kleist, Zürich und Leipzig (no date). —Ehrlich, Goethe und Schiller, Berlin, 1897.—Portig, Schiller in seinem Verhältnis zur Freundschaft und Liebe, sowie in seinem inneren Verhältnis zu Goethe, Hamburg, 1894 (long-winded and amorphous, but useful in places).

GENERAL INDEX

A figure in **full-faced type** calls attention to the passage in which a subject is most fully treated; a figure with a superior number to a foot-note.

INDEX OF WRITINGS

PROSE WRITINGS

(a) Æsthetic and Critical

GOETHE : POEMS

Selected, and edited with introduction and notes, by
JULIUS GOEBEL, Lecturer in Harvard University. xix +
239 pp. 16mo. 80 cents.

Gives more than a hundred of Goethe's best short poems,
representing every period of his literary life. The general
introduction discusses Goethe's position as a world-poet, and
especially his position in German literature as a poet of freedom and of high but sane idealism. The minor introductions
to the various periods and the accompanying notes give all the
historical and biographical information necessary to a full
understanding of the poems and the influences under which
they were written.

A. R. Hohlfeld, *Professor in the University of Wisconsin:*—An
excellent piece of work, combining in a delightful manner
critical scholarship with depth and breadth of judgment.

W. T. Hewett, *Professor in Cornell University:*—Professor
Goebel's poetic insight admirably equips him to prepare an
edition of Goethe's poems. His acuteness in tracing the sources
of some of these poems he has already admirably illustrated,
and it is recognized by all scholars.

W. H. Carruth, *Professor in the University of Kansas:*—Its
arrangement actually throws light upon Goethe's career and
his other works. But the best part of the book is the introduction—this without reflecting at all upon the scholarly and
painstaking notes.

SCHILLER : POEMS

Edited by JOHN S. NOLLEN, Professor in Indiana University. xlii + 381 pp. 16mo. 80 cents.

A careful selection of Schiller's best lyrics and ballads, made
with the special purpose of showing the relation between
Schiller's poetry and his life, and to bring out his relation
to Goethe and to the esthetic and philosophic movement
of the classical period in German literature. It is believed
that Schiller's minor poems are very well suited to this purpose,
entirely aside from their intrinsic merit as poetry of a high
order.

HENRY HOLT & CO. 29 West 23d Street, New York
378 Wabash Avenue, Chicago

FRANCKE'S GERMAN LITERATURE

As Determined by Social Forces. Being the fourth and enlarged edition of the author's *Social Forces in German Literature.*

By Prof. KUNO FRANCKE of Harvard.

595 pp. 8vo. $2.50, *net.*

A critical, philosophical, and historical account of German literature that is "destined to be a standard work for both professional and general uses" (*Dial*). Its wide scope is shown by the fact that it begins with the sagas of the fifth century and ends with Sudermann's biblical drama *Johannes* (1898).

"The range of vision is comprehensive, but the details are not obscured. The splendid panorama of German literature is spread out before us from the first outburst of heroic song in the dim days of the migrations, down to the latest disquieting productions of the Berlin school. We owe a debt of gratitude to the author who has led us to a commanding height and pointed out to us the kingdoms of the spirit which the genius of Germany has conquered. The frequent departures from the orthodox estimates are the result of the new view-point. They are often a distinct addition to our knowledge. . . . To the study of German literature in its organic relation to society this book is the best contribution in English that has yet been published."—*The Nation.*

"It is neither a dry summary nor a wearisome attempt to include every possible fact. . . . It puts the reader in centre of the vital movements of the time. . . . One often feels as if the authors treated addressed themselves personally to him; the discourse coming not through bygone dead books, but rather through living men."—*Prof. Friedrich Paulsen of University of Berlin.*

"A noble contribution to the history of civilization, and valuable not only to students of German literature, but to all who are interested in the progress of our race."—*The Hon. Andrew D. White, ex-President of Cornell University.*

"For the first time German literature has been depicted with a spirit that imparts to it organic unity . . . rich in well-weighed, condensed judgments of writers . . . not mere rewordings of the opinions of standard critics. . . . The style is clear, crisp, and unobtrusive; . . . destined to be a standard work for both professional and general uses."—*The Dial.*

HENRY HOLT & CO., 29 W. 23D ST., NEW YORK.

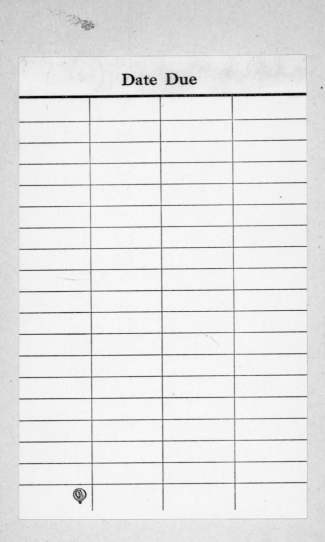

Date Due